Au Te Waate
We Remember It

Hiaki Survival Through a Bitter War

Maria Fernanda Florez Leyva
EDITED BY HEIDI HARLEY

THE UNIVERSITY OF
ARIZONA PRESS
TUCSON

The University of Arizona Press
www.uapress.arizona.edu

We respectfully acknowledge the University of Arizona is on the land and territories of Indigenous peoples. Today, Arizona is home to twenty-two federally recognized tribes, with Tucson being home to the O'odham and the Yaqui. Committed to diversity and inclusion, the University strives to build sustainable relationships with sovereign Native Nations and Indigenous communities through education offerings, partnerships, and community service.

© 2025 by The Arizona Board of Regents
All rights reserved. Published 2025

ISBN-13: 978-0-8165-4355-7 (paper)
ISBN-13: 978-0-8165-4356-4 (cloth)
ISBN-13: 978-0-8165-4538-4 (ebook)

Cover design by Leigh McDonald
Cover art pencils by Johnny Gary
Designed and typeset by Sara Thaxton in 10.5/14 Warnock Pro with Helvetica Neue LT Std and Adobe Caslon Pro

Library of Congress Cataloging-in-Publication Data
Names: Leyva, Maria Fernanda, 1945– author. | Harley, Heidi, editor.
Title: Au te waate = We remember it : Hiaki survival through a bitter war / Maria Fernanda Leyva ; edited by Heidi Harley.
Other titles: We remember it
Description: Tucson : University of Arizona Press, 2025. | Includes bibliographical references and index. | Yaqui and English.
Identifiers: LCCN 2024032660 (print) | LCCN 2024032661 (ebook) | ISBN 9780816543564 (cloth) | ISBN 9780816543557 (paper) | ISBN 9780816545384 (ebook)
Subjects: LCSH: Yaqui Indians—Mexico—History—20th century—Interviews. | Mexico—History—1867–1910—Interviews. | Mexico—History—1910–1946—Interviews. | LCGFT: Interviews. | Oral histories.
Classification: LCC F1221.Y3 L49 2025 (print) | LCC F1221.Y3 (ebook) | DDC 897/.4542—dc23/eng/20250221
LC record available at https://lccn.loc.gov/2024032660
LC ebook record available at https://lccn.loc.gov/2024032661

Printed in the United States of America
♾ This paper meets the requirements of ANSI/NISO Z39.48-1992 (Permanence of Paper).

Kaivu te aa koptane, wame'e itom yo'owam lutu'uria, haisa vem hiokot hoosuwaka'apo, vem attea hinnu'uvaekai. I'an katriam, huevenakai kaa aa ta'a intok kaa aa hikkaila inika lutu'uriata. Vempoim, si'imem lu'uteko, hunak veha koptana wa itom yo'owam lutu'uria.

We shall never forget our elders' truths, how they were treated inhumanely during those years when they fought to defend their land. Today, many of our people do not know about, nor have they heard about, our elders' truths. Sadly, when they are all gone, then our elders' truths will be forgotten.

—MARIA CARLOTA ALVAREZ DE TAPIA

CONTENTS

List of Photographs	xi
Foreword by Heidi Harley	xiii
Preface by Maria Leyva	xvii

Introduction	3
Background Concerning the Porfiriato and the Hiaki Diaspora	3
The Collection of the Interviews	4
Speaker: Doña Luisa (Chata) Buitimea	8
Speaker: Don Andres Sol	12
Speaker: Maria Hesus Rivera de Romero	15
Speaker: Reynaldo Romero	16
Speaker: Jose Juan Buitimea	19
Speaker: Jose Maria Cupis (Chema Tosaria)	19
Overview of Hiaki Guerrilla Strategy (Jose Maria Cupis)	24

PART I. IN SONORA

1. **Survival**	43
Escape from Hermosillo (Luisa)	43
Traveling and Living in the Mountains (Luisa)	50
Shelter (Luisa)	56
Mountain Food (Luisa and Andres)	60
How to Hide a Fire (Luisa and Andres)	74
Making Fire (Luisa)	76
Being a Child in the Mountains (Luisa and Maria Hesus)	84
Childbirth and Medical Care in the Mountains (Luisa)	90
Health and Hygiene in the Mountains (Luisa and Andres)	96

	The Problem of Crying Babies (Luisa and Andres)	100
	Maintaining Ceremonial Life in the Mountains (Luisa)	102
	Supplying the Mountain Ceremonies (Luisa and Andres)	108
	Escape to Nogales (Reyno)	110
	Walking to Tucson (Andres)	116

2. Battle in Sonora — 125

Flight into the Mountains (Luisa)	125
The Death and Mutilation of Dolores at Torreón (Luisa)	128
The Story of Sisto, and the Attack at Desert Spiny Lizard Waters (Luisa)	134
The Killing of Guillermo (Andres)	140
Dealing with the Dead (Luisa and Andres)	146
Caring for Wounded Warriors (Luisa)	150
Arizona Hiakis, Gunrunning to Tucson, and Gathering Munitions (Andres)	154
Southern Indigenous Soldiers in the Mexican Army (Luisa)	160
Papago Fighters Contract with the Mexicans (Chema Tosaria)	164
Slaughter and Capture at Tall Bamboo (Luisa and Andres)	168

3. Life Under Siege, Coercion, and Collaboration — 181

Hiakis Living in the Mountains Before 1910 (Luisa)	181
Hacienda Life Under the Mexicans (Luisa)	186
Violence Between Mountain Hiakis and Hacienda Hiakis (Luisa)	194
Life in the Villages up to and During the Escobar Rebellion (Reyno)	200
Coercing Hiaki Men to Enlist by Holding Families Hostage (Luisa and Andres)	218
On Coerced Hiakis Serving in the Mexican Army (Maria Hesus)	226

4. Capture — 231

The Story of the Shawl (Maria Hesus)	231
The Story of the Cookies (Maria Hesus)	236
Leaving Her Little Dog (Maria Hesus)	240
Children Stolen by the Mexican Soldiers (Maria Hesus and Luisa)	244
The Motherless Children (Reyno)	250
Mom's First Capture and Grandmother's Death, in 1902–1903 (Maria Hesus)	252

Teasing Luisa About Capture (Luisa and Andres)		264
Where the Three Groups of Hiaki Hostages Were Captured (Luisa)		266

PART II. IN THE SOUTH

5. Deportation — 273

Urbalejo, the Execution Order, and Surnames (Maria Hesus) — 273
On the Transport Ship *Progresa* (Maria Hesus and Luisa) — 282
Life in the Holding Center at Paraíso, in Tabasco (Luisa) — 290
Southern Plants That Cause Disease or Death (Luisa, Reyno, and Maria Hesus) — 302

6. Life, Labor, and Death in the South — 309

The Sale of Hiakis as Slave Labor (Maria Hesus) — 309
The Black Beans and the Hiaki Cook (Maria Hesus) — 314
Labor on the Henequen Plantations (Maria Hesus) — 318
Her Mother's Depression in the Yucatán (Maria Hesus) — 322
Luisa's Sister's Life in the South (Luisa) — 330
The Ration Cards (Maria Hesus and Luisa) — 336
Nacha Mayo and the Drunk Women at the Soap Factory (Maria Hesus and Luisa) — 342
Maria Hesus Learns About Lent in Toluca, and Her Sister Dies (Maria Hesus) — 350
Disease, Death, and the Ceremonies in Xochimilco (Maria Hesus and Luisa) — 356
Micaela and the Dolls (Luisa) — 366

7. Military Service — 373

Traveling South to Sign a Peace Accord (Reyno and Luisa) — 373
Hiakis Are Enlisted in Pitaya and Toluca (Luisa and Maria Hesus) — 378
The Hiaki Battalion (Luisa and Andres) — 392
The Hiaki Battalion in Battle During the Escobar Rebellion (Maria Hesus) — 398
Searching for Her Father Among the Wounded (Maria Hesus) — 417
Surviving While the Men Were in Combat (Maria Hesus) — 424
The Suffering of Hiaki Soldiers and Their Families (Luisa and Maria Hesus) — 428
Escaping Mexican Military Service (Maria Hesus) — 432

PART III. CONSEQUENCES

8. **Mexicans, Deportees, and Divisions Among Hiakis** — 453
   - Mexicans Moving into Hiaki Territory (Maria Hesus) — 453
   - On Renting Hiaki Land to Mexicans (Luisa) — 458
   - The Legacy of Madero and Mori (Luisa) — 462
   - Those Who Stayed in the South (Luisa) — 468
   - The Loss of History, the Loss of Land, and Divisions Among Hiakis (Luisa) — 472
   - The Charcoal Contract (Jose Juan Buitimea) — 480
   - The Flies That Came Out of Boxes Thrown from Planes (Jose Juan Buitimea and Chema Tosaria) — 488

9. **The Contemporary Situation** — 497
   - Peo Maachil and the Big Black Snake (Luisa) — 497
   - The Highway, the Railroad, and Broken Promises (Andres) — 500
   - Andres Gets a Pension (Andres) — 504
   - Tata Va'am (Hot Water) and Papalote (Luisa and Andres) — 508
   - Luisa and Andres's Life at Papalote (Luisa) — 516
   - The Dam at Oviachi and Hiak Vatwe Nowadays (Andres) — 533

10. **People of Hiak Vatwe** — 539
    - Kala (Maria Hesus and Luisa) — 539
    - Antonio Tosaria's Wives and Children (Maria Hesus and Luisa) — 544
    - Dolores Maehto and Bartolo Pa'amea (Maria Hesus, Reyno, and Luisa) — 556
    - Birthplaces and Baptismal Locations (Luisa, Reyno, and Maria Hesus) — 558
    - Reynaldo's Family and Their Tucson Connections (Reyno) — 566

Afterword. *Iiyika Te Lutu'uriata Hippue*: **We Have These Truths (Jose Maria Cupis)** — 571

Timeline of Hiaki Military and Political Events in Mexico and Sonora, 1875–1952 — 597
Index — 623

PHOTOGRAPHS

1. Hiaki family in Mexico by their dwelling, ca. 1910 — 42
2. Stagecoach drawn by five horses along the river route, Río Yaqui, ca. 1900 — 51
3. Hiaki women and girls in a temporary shelter, ca. 1911–12 — 58
4. A Hiaki woman with a basket of *torim* in Guaymas in 1908 — 72
5. A Hiaki mother and child in Arizona, 1910 — 94
6. An escaped Hiaki family living in Arizona, ca. 1910 — 117
7. Hiaki men captured in Arizona by U.S. cavalry — 155
8. Ammunition taken from captured Hiakis in Arizona — 161
9. *Plano del Valle del Yaqui* — 180
10. Men threshing grain in a field — 187
11. Men threshing chickpeas — 187
12. A Hiaki family with home and dog — 201
13. A government outpost — 219
14. Conscripted Hiakis at El Jori and annotation on the back of the photo — 228
15. Captured Hiaki women and children — 230
16. Hiaki guards watching over a line of Hiaki women prisoners with bundles on their heads in a town — 240
17. A girl, a baby, and a dog — 241
18. A boy standing outside a house — 253
19. The penitentiary at Guaymas — 272
20. A Mexican warship — 283
21. The harbor at Guaymas — 288
22. A man cutting henequen — 319
23. A family selling food on the street in 1902 — 340

24. Hiaki warriors en route to peace conference 372
25. General Mori 396
26. Men fighting in a foxhole 399
27. Hiaki "Constitucionalistas" 416
28. Hiaki solders on a transport train, ca. 1920 448
29. Track-laying camp in Santa Cruz Canyon 502
30. The Hiaki River 532
31. The dam at Oviachi 536
32. Jose Maria "Chema" Cupis 570

FOREWORD

This unique and irreplaceable book is the realization of many years of work, determination, and dedication by an amazing woman, Mrs. Maria Fernanda Florez Leyva. It is a true honor for me to introduce it in this brief foreword.

 I was introduced to Maria Leyva in 2001 by my late colleague Dr. Eloise Jelinek, who had been working with Mrs. Leyva on the Hiaki language for a number of years. Mrs. Leyva and I began our collaboration on a detailed study of the grammar of the Hiaki language. After a couple of years of working together, she mentioned that she had a number of cassette tapes of interviews she had conducted in the Hiaki language in the 1970s, with elders in Sonora, about their experiences during their early lives between 1900 and 1930, kept in her home in a shoebox. She was concerned because the quality of the tapes was deteriorating over time, and she feared that the information on them would be permanently lost. She could no longer make out the speech on several of them. I was immediately concerned as well, as the historical and linguistic content that she described is irreplaceable. Such a record of this history through the eyes of the people who lived it, in their own language, could never be collected again.

 A few years later, the Confluence Center came into existence, and, in collaboration with Bill Beezley of the History Department at the University of Arizona, we seized the opportunity to apply for funding to digitize and remaster the severely degraded tapes, and to transcribe and translate them. The grant we received enabled audio engineer Jim Blackwood, of KUAZ, to produce reasonably decipherable digital audio recordings from the tapes, and allowed Maria to devote a year to transcription and translation. The resulting 35,000 words of Hiaki and their English translation represent a priceless record of a period in Mexican (and Arizonan) history, presented from the point of view of the people most affected.

This work will stand over time as a record of these events preserved for the Hiaki people themselves, in the language of the people, as its author intends. However, it has great importance for scholarship on the language and the era as well. Linguistically, the material represents a corpus of naturally produced speech in an entirely Hiaki context, a type of data that is essentially impossible for an outsider to collect. It represents an opportunity to study the narrative styles and discourse properties of conversational Hiaki, besides providing illustrations of the use of vocabulary and grammatical constructions in context, rather than in elicited speech. Further, it represents the speech of an older generation, now passed away, and may provide information about how and in what directions the language has changed over time. Finally, it represents a cross section of Hiaki communities, and may therefore help answer questions about dialect differences and dialect shift, and provide insight into the development of the Hiaki language here in Arizona. Hiakis who are studying their own language will be able to turn to this book as a rich resource on the language, as well as the history, of their people.

Historically, the material has the potential to fill an otherwise yawning void in the literature on the dictatorship of Porfirio Díaz in Mexico (1876–1911) and the early years of the revolution. These first-person accounts of the period from the Hiaki perspective offer an insider's view of Porfirian repression of Indigenous peoples. The extant literature tends to focus on providing a comprehensive account of these events and the revolutionary promises to restore Hiakis' lands, water, and dignity using government documentation produced by non-Hiakis. Hu-deHart writes regretfully, in the introduction to her history of Hiaki resistance, that "the Yaquis . . . have left very little written record of their own history. Thus, I have had to rely more on what others have said about the Yaquis than what the Yaquis have been able to say about themselves."[1] There are

---

1. Evelyn Hu-DeHart, *Yaqui Resistance and Survival: The Struggle for Land and Autonomy, 1821–1910* (Madison: University of Wisconsin Press, 1984).

only two publications in which personal histories are documented,[2] and in both cases the histories are one generation removed—the stories are retold by the children or grandchildren of deportees. No other archive or documentation exists that can provide this kind of wholly Indigenous, contemporary perspective on the Porfirian repression of the Hiaki people and the revolutionary response.

—*Heidi Harley*

---

2. Rosalio Moisés, *A Yaqui Life: The Personal Chronicle of a Yaqui Indian* (Lincoln: University of Nebraska Press, 1991); and Raquel Padilla Ramos, *Yucatán, fin del sueño yaqui: El tráfico de los yaquis y el otro triunvirato* (Hermosillo: Gobierno del Estado de Sonora, 1995).

PREFACE

Unfortunately, if things continue as they are for my people in Sonora, they will no longer be a unique tribe, as they will gradually be assimilated into the dominant Mexican society by their own choosing. All the suffering of my ancestors, and the continued difficulties that my people in Sonora now encounter on a daily basis, seem to have no end. Thus, in many ways it would better behoove my people to pass themselves off as "Mexicans," not as "Indios." There is the overall feeling that it does not pay to be an Indio in Mexico. As a consequence, all the things that Creator had given to my people prior to Spanish colonization and the beginnings of Mexico—the river when it was alive, the tall trees lining its banks, the deer and other wild animals, plentiful food by the delta and in the desert, the fish in the coastal waters, and much, much more—will become only a memory in the minds of future Hiaki generations as they read about them in some book. I ask Creator to release me from my earthly obligations before this happens. It will indeed be a very sad day for my people when all their efforts, the ultimate sacrifices, the hellish experiences of our ancestors, and the blood they spilled will be for naught. As a consequence, the richness of our culture, our language, our knowledge, and our spirit will cease to exist.

I dedicate this book to my uncle Anselmo Valencia and to all the people whom I interviewed. My uncle and I had always planned to collaborate on this book. Years after we first discussed it, he would ask me, "So when are we going to write this book, comadre?" (By this time he was my "compadre," as he was now my son's godfather.) I would simply reply, "Whenever you are ready, compadre." This book was a project that both my compadre and I had placed on the back burner for a long time, and time waits for no one. But now, before I join my compadre in the next world, I want to finish our project.

All of them are now gone, and I am looking forward to joining them to share this accomplishment with them. I am sure that they are aware that our dream is about to be realized, and my uncle is probably beside himself waiting for "our project" to be completed. Compadre, I hope that you will not be disappointed with this work.

—Maria Leyva

Au Te Waate / We Remember It

INTRODUCTION

Background Concerning the Porfiriato and the Hiaki Diaspora

My name is Maria Fernanda Florez Leyva, and I am a Hiaki woman from Tucson, Arizona. I collected the interviews that are presented in the following pages. Before I give a few details about the collection of the interviews and the five main individuals whose words appear in this book, I will offer a brief perspective on the circumstances which led to the tumultuous years that doña Luisa and the others spoke about.

Porfirio Díaz's first term as president of Mexico was from 1877 through 1880. Prior to that time Díaz was influenced by his tutor Benito Juárez, who had been a beloved president of Mexico due to his commitment to social justice. Díaz's early allegiance was thus to the ideal of liberalism. Indeed, during his first term as president of Mexico, Díaz had crafted the Plan de Tuxtepec, a plan of governance that rested on the principle of a one-term presidential office with reelection forbidden. However, despite this, he ran for the presidency again and was reelected in 1884, remaining in power until the Mexican Revolution in 1911.

During this second term as president, he became a notorious dictator, and it was during this time that Díaz formulated the deportation and extermination program against the Hiakis. This program was being carried out against the Hiaki people because for a long time they had been a thorn in the side of the Mexican government. Not only that, the Hiakis lived on delta land that was very rich and fertile. Parts of Hiaki land were also on the coast of the Gulf of California, and the waters had bountiful fish, shrimp, and other seafood. The desert provided many different types of cactus fruit and trees that also yielded fruit. Game was also plentiful in the mountains and desert for my people to feast on. No wonder, then, that the Mexican government coveted Hiaki territory; the dictator Porfirio Díaz made it his goal to wrest this valuable real estate from the Hiakis through whatever means he found at his disposal.

When years of warfare against the Hiakis proved to be unsuccessful in removing them from their territory, Díaz begin to carry out the deportation and extermination program against my people. It was during this time that horrific atrocities were imposed on my people. The Hiakis who were captured were sold to plantation owners as slaves. Those who did not appear to be strong enough to work were put to death, primarily infants, very young children, and the elderly. The elderly knew that they were going to be put to death. They would bid farewell to their children and tell them they were going to be given some kind of injection. Although their children would cry and beg the nurses not to kill their elders, saying that they would do the work of the elders, their pleas fell on deaf ears. By the next day the elders were dead. The Hiakis who were not captured and deported to the henequen plantations in southern Mexico sought refuge in the Vakateeve (Tall Bamboo) Mountains[1] and waged guerrilla warfare against the Mexican soldiers (also known as the *pelones* or *peronim*, "bald ones"). Many others came north to Arizona, New Mexico, Texas, and California. It is these events, and the continued persecution of Hiakis even following the revolution, that are described in the interviews presented here.

The Collection of the Interviews

So that you can understand something about myself and my reasons for collecting these interviews documenting the history of the Hiaki people, I would like to share with you some of the story of my family and my life.

My siblings, my father's younger brother, and I grew up in a four-room house in Barrio Libre in South Tucson, Arizona. I had two brothers and three sisters, but one brother died as an infant. My paternal

---

1. These mountains are labeled "Bacatete" on maps of Sonora, a corruption of the Hiaki name Vakateeve.

grandmother Maria Carlota Alvarez de Tapia—my Haaka—raised us in that home that her father Juan Alvarez had built, along with my paternal grandfather Fernando Flores and an uncle, Ramon Alvarez. This was in close proximity to a Hiaki settlement, Bwe'u Hu'upa (Big Mesquite). Bwe'u Hu'upa was located between 22nd and 25th Streets immediately east of where I-10 now runs. This comfortable old home, on 26th Street, was built in or around 1914 when my grandmother was about sixteen years of age and already married to my grandfather, Fernando. At that time, they already had my father, Vicente Flores, who was one year old. Prior to that, my grandmother and her parents had lived in Yuma, Arizona, where she was born in 1898. Her father, my great-grandfather, arrived in Yuma when he was sent there by the railroad company, and eventually settled there.

I write primarily about Haaka, as she is the one who raised us. My grandmother was a very intelligent woman who was well-versed in the Hiaki language and also in Spanish. Her mother, my great-grandmother, Eusebia Valenzuela, was also very fluent in Hiaki and Spanish. Haaka's mother and father arrived in Arizona from Sonora in or about 1877. Prior to coming to Arizona, they had lived in Magdalena, Sonora, Mexico, for a number of years. Eusebia's mother had traveled to Magdalena, along with her daughter and other Hiakis, to escape the ever-escalating turmoil in Hiaki territory farther south. At that time, Hiakis were being captured and deported to the henequen plantations in southern Mexico. Eusebia's mother, my great-great-grandmother, purchased several hectares of land by the riverbank there in Magdalena and kept a small farm. However, when the *peronim* began to arrive in the area looking for Hiakis, my great-great-grandmother sold the farm, and she and her family, including my great-grandmother Eusebia and her husband Juan, made their way to Arizona. According to Haaka, her mother and grandparents were very happy living on their small farm in Magdalena, and it was a sad day when they had to pull up stakes and relocate to Nogales. My great-grandmother Eusebia was about fourteen years of age and already married to Juan when they left Magdalena. They arrived in Nogales, Arizona, and settled there for about three years, during which time Eusebia's mother, my great-great-grandmother, passed away. They then left Nogales as the *peronim* made excursions into Arizona to round up Hiakis. The *peronim* were not concerned that they were entering another country to capture the Hiaki refugees. In fact, they came as far north as Tucson to capture Hiakis and return them to Mexico.

From Nogales, the family joined ranks with other Hiakis and traveled to Tubac. Since there was little work to be had in Tubac, they again pulled up stakes and moved to Tumacacori at the invitation of the missionaries there. Due to the continous raids and pillaging conducted by the Chiricahua Apaches on the church grounds, the missionaries decided that drastic measures had to be taken. The raiders were making off with foodstuffs that the missionaries and the people, including some Hiakis who had taken up residence there, needed. Some Hiakis and others who lived among the missionaries were killed or injured during those raids. The Apaches would make off with not only vegetables but also horses, cattle, goats, etc.—any livestock that the missionaries had. By inviting more Hiakis to come and settle there, the missionaries hoped to protect the settlement. After spending some time in Tumacacori, however, the family decided to move again, to Tucson, in search of a larger Hiaki community where ceremonies and other traditional activities could be carried out. They also wanted to get as far away as possible from the border dividing Arizona and Mexico, to a place where they felt they could live in relative peace.

Many circumstances led to the Hiaki people leaving their homeland in Hiak Vatwe (the Hiaki River), but primary among those circumstances was that my people were seeking a peaceful existence with their family members, far away from the ravages of war and the cultural genocide that was going on all around them in Sonora. So it was that my ancestors' and other Hiakis' arrival in Arizona and other parts of the United States became necessary due to the difficult life that they had in Mexico.

In the evenings, all through my childhood, Haaka would gather us around her and share accounts about the atrocities committed against our people in Mexico. This kept me intrigued. She would weep as she recounted the horrors that our people suffered under the Porfirio Díaz regime and how thousands of our people perished during those tumultuous years and afterward. My heart would grow sad as I listened to her words, and I felt that this sad history of our people had to be shared with others. This history of our people became very important to me, and at this time I resolved to learn more about this sad time in my people's lives. However, as a child, my interest in certain subjects was short-lived, and

I would soon put my Haaka's words somewhere in the deep recesses of my mind.

Many years later, my uncle, Anselmo Valencia, inspired me to actually begin the collection of these histories. When I was a young woman raising a family, he was working toward gaining federal recognition for our tribal members. He worked tirelessly to realize his dream of gaining recognition status for our people. Many Hiakis were against this idea, but many more liked it and joined ranks with my uncle in support of his endeavors. My grandmother was very supportive of my uncle's work because, in those years, my people were among the most impoverished American Indians in the United States. With federal recognition, our people would enjoy some of the benefits that other federally recognized American tribes already enjoyed, especially better health care.

One day, during work on the land that would become our future reservation, my uncle returned to the kitchen area for a coffee break, where my sister and I helped with food preparation for the men clearing the land. I sat down with him and questioned him about his goals in securing recognition for our people. He clearly outlined his goals, and I was thoroughly convinced that my entire family should support him.

One of the things my uncle and I discussed whenever we met was a book that we could co-author. In this book, we would inform our people and the world as to why the Hiakis had to leave the old country and resettle, not only in Arizona, but also in the neighboring states of California, New Mexico, and Texas.

In the years that followed, my uncle and I each made trips to visit the Sonora Hiakis to collect stories about the extermination program and the deportation of our people to the southern Mexican states. We did not travel together; rather, he would go on his own, and I would travel there with my husband, my children, and my father-in-law. Those trips were the source of the interviews in this book.

In the early 1970s, when I went to Sonora to conduct the interviews, I usually traveled with my husband, my children, and my father-in-law. Whenever my husband could not travel with us due to his job, my mother and stepfather would also accompany us. Sometimes my uncle Anselmo Valencia would offer me twenty or thirty dollars for gas money. It was not usually more than that, as we were both operating on a slim budget. At the time, I was also working, so I would save money from my own earnings and my husband's earnings and use those funds for the expenses. Additionally, if my mother and stepfather joined us, they would graciously bear some of the expenses for food, gas, etc. We usually stayed at the home of one of the interviewees, Maria Hesus, since my father-in-law Chema was her uncle. (Chema and Maria Hesus's mother were first cousins.) My father-in-law was drawing a pension and he also helped to defray some of the travel expenses. I was also fortunate that my supervisor was considerate enough to allow me to take a long weekend three or four times a year to travel to Hiaki territory.

My father-in-law and Maria Hesus introduced me to most of the people that I interviewed. Since Chema had also experienced the hardships of living in the mountains as a child refugee and as a guerrilla fighter, he knew many of the people who had survived their ordeal. These people in turn would recommend that I interview another individual who had also survived and would be willing to share their experiences with me. There were many individuals whom I interviewed but was unable to record, since initially, at the onset of this project, I did not have a recorder. When I finally acquired a recorder, it was one of those that operated on batteries alone. When the batteries on my recorder died, I would use up the extra batteries that I had brought with me. Sometimes I would run low on money, and I could not spare the money to purchase any more batteries, or, for that matter, more blank cassettes. I was forced to write down some of the narratives, but over the years I lost most of those notes. I also had to save money for gas to return to the States and to buy food, not only for us, but also for the family that I was visiting. Due to my father-in-law's, my mother's, and my stepfather's generosity, I was able to take care of the expenses that came up during this project.

I interviewed many people during my visits to Sonora, but, as outlined above, only a fraction of the material has survived the intervening years. The stories here are taken from this remaining material. Five main speakers are represented.

Doña Luisa (Chata) Buitimea

Doña Luisa lived in El Papalote (The Windmill), a ranch located in the western part of the Vakateeve Mountains. She was a delightful little lady

INTRODUCTION

who possessed a keen memory of her experiences during the deportation and extermination program.

Doña Luisa was introduced to me by Maria Hesus Rivera de Romero because Maria knew of my interest in learning more about the experiences of the Hiakis during those years of upheaval in Hiak Vatwe. Indeed, doña Luisa was a young girl when she fled with her mother and many other Hiakis to seek refuge in the sacred Vakateeve Mountains, or Itom Toosa (Our Nest). She survived the harsh living conditions in the mountains, the deportations, and the cruel and inhuman treatment for many years as a prisoner of war. She had been captured twice and sent to Mexico City and to other prisoner encampments in southern Mexico.

I spent many hours interviewing doña Luisa at the home of Maria Hesus, and occasionally at the home of Herarda Romero de Cota (Heera), daughter of Reynaldo and stepdaughter of Maria Hesus. Maria Hesus, Reynaldo, and Heera lived in Vikam Swiichi.[2] Maria Hesus and Reynaldo lived on the north side of the railroad tracks, next to the road that heads into the Vakateeve Mountains. It was quieter here and was ideal for conducting the interviews. Heera lived next to Highway 15, the main road that heads southeast to Ciudad Obregón and west to Guaymas. Since it was the principal thoroughfare from Guaymas to Obregón, it carried a lot of traffic, especially semi trucks, which made a lot of noise. She also had many small children who were a noisy bunch, so recording stories was not very ideal at this location.

Doña Luisa was related to Maria Hesus and Herarda through the "comadre/compadre" kinship system. When she and her husband don Andres came to Vikam Swiichi, they would stay at their daughter's home or stay in Swiichi with other relatives. If their daughter was not at home during their visit to Swiichi, doña Luisa and don Andres would stay at Heera's home. I interviewed doña Luisa for the first time at Heera's home. Once I explained to doña Luisa that I was planning to use the information I was gathering to co-author a book with Anselmo Valencia, she became very anxious to share her stories with me. She shared with me the names of many of the places where she had traveled, both in the mountains and

---

2. Vikam Swiichi is the train switching station, so it is called Swiichi, or Vícam Switch, while the town itself is known as Vikam Pueblo / Vícam Pueblo or simply Vikam/Vícam.

in southern Mexico. She was a little fuzzy as to exact dates, but for the most part she was able to recall most of the years when she had been captured and when and where she had been sent as a prisoner of war. She thought she was seventy-seven years of age when I interviewed her, but wasn't quite certain, since she did not know when she had been born. She indicated that she did not have a problem being recorded.

Doña Luisa was very short in stature, probably not even five feet in height. I am 5'2", and I stood about two inches taller than her. That's why she had the nickname "doña Chata" (*chata* is Spanish for "short-statured" or "pug-nosed"). She had a slight build and was somewhat fair-complected. She had beautiful white curly hair and a bright smile. She would braid her hair, but her hair was so thin that by the end of the day it stood about her head like a halo. As she spoke, she would always wring her hands, particularly when she recounted some of the more traumatic things that she had experienced. It was during these times that I would offer her a break from the recording. We would then have a cup of coffee or a soft drink. I would offer her some sweet bread from the local bakery to enjoy with her coffee. Other times I would offer her some fruit or some other tasty item. She usually accepted the coffee, but always took the fruit and bread to her children and grandchildren.

Doña Luisa spoke very little about her parents and she never revealed to me their names. Evidently her father had been killed in the mountains, as she had indicated that during one of our unrecorded conversations. I know that it saddened her to speak of them. She mentioned an older sister Simona, who had survived the plantations in Yucatán and had returned to Vikam. After her older sister returned to Vikam, she shared with doña Luisa some of her experiences on the plantation where she was held, but for the most part she maintained silence about the years she was held prisoner. Occasionally she would speak about the trip to Yucatán from Guaymas, aboard the military boat. Hiakis would be packed into every hold in the boat. Some would be inside the boat, while others would be on the deck. Simona had shared with doña Luisa an account of the disposal of the Hiakis who died during the long boat trip. Evidently she had very unpleasant memories of these events and so did not discuss her experiences at length. After her return, she became a ceremonial person there in Vikam Pueblo.

Doña Luisa spoke about hiding in the mountains with her mother, but it was apparent that it was very difficult for her to speak about her mother and how she suffered. Every so often, she would laugh at herself and giggle about amusing things that she recalled. Her husband, don Andres Sol, would also tease doña Luisa about the number of times that she had been captured and sent away. However, there were not too many of those less-serious moments. How she was able to talk about the horrific things she had witnessed and the traumatic experiences she had suffered through, and in the next breath talk about some funny episodes that made her giggle, was beyond me. It was difficult for me to listen to the recordings and not feel anger and sadness at what I heard. But doña Luisa had within her such courage and strength of heart from growing up in a hostile environment, each day a struggle to survive. Still, sometimes I would see her staring off into the distance, not uttering a word, when don Andres was speaking. She would just listen to him, while wringing her hands.

Doña Luisa was a scared little girl when she first accompanied her mother into the mountains, and almost overnight she had grown into a brave young woman who managed to survive her terrible ordeal and, later, talk about it. I learned a lot from doña Luisa, this little lady who had a tremendous fighting spirit, who kept fighting in spite of the overwhelming odds against her, in order to keep alive those things that she believed in. In spite of having one of her little infants die in her arms while she was held prisoner, and having the other die while they were struggling to survive in the mountains, she maintained this strong spirit. She truly represented our people in Sonora, who were also very tenacious and strong, who would not yield to the Mexican government's military machine, even though it meant suffering and death for so many of them.

Doña Luisa lived at Papalote de Arriba (Windmill Above) with her husband Andres and her four children. She also mentioned Papalote de Abajo (Windmill Below), which was located at the base of the mountain where they lived. In order to arrive at their home atop the mountain, one had to head toward Hiapsi Kawi (Heart Mountain), then northwest toward El Papalote. She and don Andres would come down from the mountain once or twice a month to collect his pension, purchase provisions and other goods, and conduct other business.

Don Andres Sol (Luisa's Husband)

I was introduced to don Andres by his wife, doña Luisa, in 1978. At the time of the interview, around the second week of April, he indicated that he was seventy years of age, going on seventy-one. His pension papers show his birthdate as May 15, 1907. He indicated that he was born in Maytorena, Sonora, Mexico. Evidently he was related to Heera and used to come to her home if he and doña Luisa did not find their own daughter at home. They came down from the mountain each month to collect his pension and to make purchases of food and other goods, or to conduct other business. They lived off his pension and a small salary that he was earning as a part-time cowboy. His sons helped him on the ranch.

Don Andres was a tall, slim, handsome gentleman with a beautiful head of white hair. I believe that he had a white mustache also. He had a very dignified air about him. He spoke Spanish fluently, having learned it when he was forced to serve in the Mexican military. He, like doña Luisa, had a bright smile and was always joking around. Don Andres seemed to be happy about their present-day situation, although he was not totally satisfied with the amount of his pension and his small salary. But he admitted that they were most fortunate to have what they had: a monthly pension, a small salary, a home, and their health and that of their children. They both wished to secure some land for their sons and were working diligently toward that end.

He was also happy that he had survived the deportation and extermination program, but, like doña Luisa, he was sad because he had lost his parents, other family members, and acquaintances during the war. He was also sad because he had not been with doña Luisa when she suffered the deaths of their two infant children. This weighed heavily upon him, and occasionally he would remain quiet while he pondered what these children would have looked like. I would remind him that these unfortunate situations were completely out of his control and he should not accept blame for their deaths. I also told him that these infants were at home with Creator. Had they lived, they would have suffered much from hunger, thirst, heat, or being put to death by the *pelones*. Doña Luisa agreed with me, and together we would console him. I would ask him other questions to steer him away from this sad subject, and he would allow me to do that. I was fortunate that he did not mind my interviewing him. Sometimes he and doña Luisa would get into small disagreements regarding places, dates, and people. However, doña Luisa would eventually "win the war of words," and don Andres would admit that he did not recall some things since he was not quite as focused as doña Luisa was. He would tease doña Luisa and say that it was because she was so focused that she had won a prize such as him. Doña Luisa would scoff at him, then start giggling like a schoolgirl as he continued to work his charms on her. It was delightful to witness this interaction between those two.

I am not sure when and where doña Luisa and don Andres Sol had met and I never asked either one, since it is considered impolite to ask these types of personal questions of elders, or anyone else for that matter. I do know that when I interviewed them, they were much devoted to each other and their love for each other was very evident. I had learned from Heera that they had three sons and a daughter. At this present time, two sons and their families remain in the Vakateeve Mountains on the cattle ranch where their parents used to live. The two sons still work as cowboys, just as their father did, taking care of the cattle that are kept there. I never had the pleasure of visiting don Andres or doña Luisa at their home in the mountains, although they had invited me to go there various times. They were anxious to show me their home and always seemed happy to see me. I was very blessed. Although I would have loved to visit them at their home, I was aware that the road up to it was in bad shape and my small vehicle would never be able to negotiate it.

As a young man don Andres escaped into the mountains with his parents, trying to avoid capture. He indicated that he spent most of his youth there. During this time, his mother, Ramona Sol, his sisters, and other family members were still alive. His mother later died in 1949. When the fighting resumed, the entire family again returned to the mountains, then later went north to Tucson. Don Andres rarely spoke about his father, Casillas Buitimea, but he must have been killed early on when the fighting first erupted and when don Andres was very young. Both of his parents were raised in the mountains. One story he told during the interviews indicated that when he was a young man, he and a friend had been out, away from their camp, looking for rabbits, and had come upon the *pelones*. His friend was shot and killed by the Mexican soldiers, but don Andres had escaped and made his way back to where his mother and the other Hiakis had set up camp. Years later when he was captured by the *pelones*, don Andres was given the option of being deported to the haciendas in southern Mexico to work there as a slave or being conscripted into the Mexican military. Don Andres chose to go into the military and was then sent to other parts of Mexico, where there was a lot of unrest during those turbulent years.

During my latest visit (January 15, 2012) to doña Luisa and don Andres's grandchildren and great-grandchildren, who are living at a place known as Tomase Woho'okuni,[3] which is located between the small settlement of Lencho and Torim, I learned that one of the sons had taken his own life there and their only daughter had already passed on and joined her mother in the next world. I was told that doña Luisa was already gone when her son committed suicide, but don Andres was still alive and witnessed this tragic event. Don Andres was living in the home of his daughter and her children when he passed away. He had been sick and frail for some time, and, according to his granddaughter, he was sitting outside on the outer edge of the ramada, warming himself in the sun. He had a blanket wrapped around him and had fallen asleep, something that he did often in his later years. His granddaughter was going to wake him to offer him a bite to eat. However, don Andres had fallen into a sleep from which he would never awaken. The brave old jokester soldier who made me laugh with his jokes every time I interviewed him had finally completed his mission on this earth. The time had come for him to go and join doña Luisa and their two children in the next world for a much-needed rest. Don Andres and doña Luisa were two wonderful, delightful treasures that I shall not soon forget. After the war was over and they had settled down, they appeared to be somewhat content with their lot in life, and they considered themselves fortunate because they had a place to live and a little money that they could rely on each month, and because they had survived their terrible ordeal. At the same time, they were sad that they had lost their parents, their two infant children, their siblings, and other family members during those horrific years under the Díaz regime. They suffered much in this world, as did so many of my people, during the Díaz dictatorship. But in spite of the atrocities that they had witnessed and the horrors that they had experienced, both don Andres and doña Luisa remained positive and were able to laugh at

---

3. This place was not really a hole. It was a dry river bed that was quite deep. The occupant was a man named Tomas, hence the name.

some of their experiences. I am so fortunate that they gave me the honor of interviewing them because I learned so much from them. I gave them my word that their story would be told, and I must keep my word even if it has taken this long to share their story. Their voices have been silenced forever, but their words shall remain alive in this book. I shall never have the pleasure of hearing their voices again on this earth, but their spirits will remain forever in my heart. I look forward to the day when I may see them in the next world and hear their joking, their teasing, and their laughter once again. This old couple is buried in Torim, and someday I hope to acquire grave markers for them.

Maria Hesus Rivera de Romero, My Father-in-Law's Niece

I met Maria Hesus the first time that I traveled to Hiak Vatwe with my husband, my children, and my father-in-law. We traveled there in my in-laws' vehicle, since they had a fairly new car. I had my two daughters at the time. My oldest daughter was about four and a half years old, and my youngest daughter was a little over two years of age. Maria Hesus, her family, and her father gave us a warm welcome and cleared out one of the rooms so we could settle there while we visited them. She and her daughter Lucia begin to prepare food for us. Since my in-laws had not visited them for quite some time, they had a lot to talk about. I remember that they had a number of dogs, and in the evening as we sat around drinking coffee, trying to keep warm by the coals, the dogs would also lie around the coals trying to keep warm as well.

Maria Hesus had two children with Reynaldo: her daughter Lucia and a son, Jose Juan. Lucia had two children, then later had one additional child. Her husband had passed away, but I was not sure under what circumstances he had died. Be that as it may, Maria Hesus was a harsh disciplinarian and a very strong matriarch in her family. I gathered this from the way she related to her family. She was very respectful of her aging father, who died shortly after I met him. She was a little bit more flexible with her son, as he was the younger of her two children. However, with her daughter she was quite strict. She pretty much ruled the roost, and even Reynaldo bent to her will, except when he was on a drinking binge. He was quite an alcoholic, and we considered ourselves fortunate whenever we found him at home.

Maria Hesus had been a very pretty woman when she was younger, as I saw in some pictures that she shared with me, and she still remained very attractive when she became older. She was very outspoken and verbal, while Reyno was more laid-back and soft-spoken. Maria Hesus was very intelligent and spoke Spanish fluently. This could be attributed to her growing up surrounded by Mexicans. Her Hiaki was also good, but occasionally she would make mistakes while speaking in our language. She would often ask Reyno for clarification of certain Hiaki terms, since he was quite fluent in our language.

People who knew her called her a *surenya* (southerner) because she grew up in the south of Mexico and not in Hiaki country. Maria Hesus told me where she was born, although I do not remember it now. I remember jotting it down in some notebook, long since lost. At the time that the recordings were done, I was very naïve and did not know about interviewing techniques, otherwise all such vital information would have been recorded. Maria Hesus did not appreciate the fact that the local Hiakis referred to her father as a *toroko yoi* ("gray Mexican" or traitor). She said that her father was forced into the Mexican military and spent close to twenty years as a Mexican soldier. Sometimes she would speak out against the Hiaki rebels, but she would also speak against the Mexican military and their treatment of the Hiakis, and even of their own soldiers. She also had a keen memory of their capture (her mother, her sister, and her) and how they were deported from the port of Guaymas. She was probably about eight or nine years of age when she was captured. She had a younger sister who was seven years of age, and this sister died when they were being held captive. According to Maria Hesus, many young children, including her sister, died that year from *sarampión* (measles). Maria Hesus died sometime during the late 1980s and is buried in Swiichi.

Reynaldo ("Reyno" or "Chikul") Romero (Spouse of Maria Hesus)

Reynaldo (Reyno for short) was a small child when his parents and brother escaped into the mountains. Later his parents left for Arizona and lived here for a number of years. The family returned to Hiaki territory when things seemed to settle down.

Reyno, or Chikul, as many people referred to him, was a rather quiet, low-key person. He had a positive attitude and seemed to be satisfied with his current status in life. When he was drinking, he became a little more boisterous. People called him Chikul Pahko'ola (Mouse Pascola) because he was a pascola dancer with a rather small stature. He was probably no more than 5'3" in height with a slight body. He was about sixty years of age and becoming slightly bald when I first met him. He was one of those persons who spoke only when spoken to.

He and Maria Hesus were totally the opposite of each other; she was very talkative and spoke in a loud voice, while he was very quiet and spoke in a soft voice. According to people who knew this couple when they were younger, Reyno met Maria Hesus when he lived in Torim (Wood Rats),[4] although he was born in Tetaviekti (Rolling Stone). They established a residence on the outskirts of Torim, and at some point in their lives they moved to Vikam Swiichi. At this time Reyno was already widowed and he had a daughter, Heera, from his first marriage. Reyno's first wife passed away when Heera was quite young. By the time that Reyno and Maria Hesus became a couple, Heera was already married and had her own children (nine). Heera lived with her husband (Ilario Cota) by Highway 15. We always knew when Heera was coming to Maria Hesus's home because you could hear Ilario's motorbike from a long distance away. They would arrive with one or two of their youngest children on the motorbike, then Heera's oldest daughter would arrive later with her younger siblings in tow. They came every day that we were staying at Maria Hesus and Reynaldo's home. Maria Hesus always seemed annoyed when Heera arrived with her husband and the kids. Perhaps it was because Maria Hesus's grandchildren were very well behaved, while Heera's children were quite naughty and were always underfoot. Indeed, there was no love lost between the two women. I myself would get very annoyed with Ilario since his motorbike was so loud and noisy and his arrival would necessitate the cessation of the recording sessions. He

---

4. I am not sure if this type of rat is indeed a wood rat, but they are vegetarians and build big nests up in the trees. Many people say that these rats provide a rather tasty meal.

knew that we had the recording project going on, but he had to make his appearance every day, each time on his noisy motorbike. Finally Maria Hesus spoke up. She informed Ilario that if he had to come to her house, he should use his bicycle, not his motorbike, as this was very disruptive to the recording session. She also ordered Heera to control her children or to leave them at home with her oldest daughter. I felt a little guilty about Heera having to leave her children at home because I knew she did not have enough food to feed them. Since Ilario did not work, there was never enough food for Heera and her children. This is why she came to Maria Hesus's home when we were there, because as long as we were there, there would be plenty of food to go around. I had known hunger myself as I was growing up, and I knew how desperate my own grandmother felt when there was not food to feed all of us. So I knew how Heera must have felt. I know that Reyno felt uncomfortable whenever Maria Hesus scolded Heera in front of him, but he never spoke up to defend his oldest daughter. These scoldings did not deter Heera from making her daily visits to her father's home. More often than not, I had to witness this sad state of affairs.

As I mentioned above, Reyno and Maria Hesus had two children, Lucia and Jose Juan. Lucia had three children but was widowed very early on in her marriage and never remarried. People always referred to Reyno and his family as Chikulim (mice). Even people who are related to Reyno nowadays will refer to themselves as Chikulim.

Reyno's parents also survived the war-torn years, and, like many other Hiakis, they had traveled to Arizona to escape the ever-increasing turmoil in their homeland. I never learned their names, as Reyno only referred to his father as Achai (Father) and his mother as Maala (Mom). He had an older brother named Damasio who used to come to Tucson as a cultural participant (as a Moro). The family lived in Tucson for a number of years but eventually returned to Vikam Swiichi when it appeared that the fighting had stopped. They still experienced some difficult years in Hiaki land, but the severity of the harsh treatment that had been meted out to the Hiakis during the Porfiriato had ceased. Francisco Madero had become president of Mexico and he had ordered that all Hiakis be returned to their homeland. When Reynaldo's parents returned to Hiaki territory from Arizona, they shared with him their ordeal in the mountains. Since Reynaldo was an infant when his parents were in the mountains and later in Arizona, he did not recall any of the events that his parents had witnessed. By the time things had settled down somewhat, Reynaldo was a little older and could understand what his parents had talked about. During the interviews, he recounted what his parents had shared with him. He was a young lad when his parents, his brother, and he returned to Swiichi, and he recalls the Mexican soldiers who were still stationed in Vikam Swiichi. He also recalled some of the events that took place during that time. Eventually, the Hiaki authorities had the Mexican government remove the soldiers, and the garrisons were torn down.

After Maria Hesus died, Reyno lived in the same place that he had shared with his family and, unfortunately, continued to drink. Lucia, his daughter, also lived in the same home and took care of Reyno when he became ill. I visited him once, along with a medical doctor, and the doctor announced that Reyno's condition was quite serious; at the time, it seemed that his system was already shutting down. He appeared to be in a coma and did not speak or recognize us. He died sometime in the mid-1990s and was buried in Swiichi. Unfortunately, Lucia did not inform us of his death and we did not attend the funeral. However, Reyno's likeness was captured forever in a video that was produced by the U of A. The late Anselmo Valencia and I directed this video.

Jose Juan Buitimea (Also Known as "Capitan" or "Merikano")

I was introduced to Jose Juan by Mr. Jose Maria Cupis during a visit to Vikam Pueblo. He played the violin. We were looking for a violinist as an entertainer and to participate in the death-anniversary ceremony for Reyno's older brother. The reason they called him "Capitan" was because he was a member of the tribal authority in Vikam Pueblo, serving in the role of *capitan*. He was also a cultural leader, a *monaha*—that is, a leader with the matachin group. He was a very decent and respectable man. He had several nicknames besides Capitan, including Merikano ([the] American). His grandson is a *pahko'ola* dancer who frequently comes to Tucson for cultural ceremonies. Jose Juan did not participate in as many interviews as the other speakers, and his accounts, found only in chapter 8, form a smaller part of the volume.

Jose Maria Cupis (Chema Tosaria, My Father-in-Law)

He and one of his brothers became separated from their parents while they were trying to escape to the mountains with their sons. The two brothers believed their parents had died. Mr. Cupis later became a guerrilla fighter.

My late father-in-law did not recall when he was born. His older brother Antonio and he were accompanying their parents in the mountains during one of those tumultuous years, when a group of Mexican soldiers fast approached. Their parents hid the two young boys in some bushes and quickly moved away to lead the soldiers away from their sons. Their parents had advised their sons previously that if the time came when there was the danger of being captured by the soldiers, the boys had to remember and heed their parents' words. Once hidden in the bushes, they were not to emerge from there until it was dark and until they could no longer hear the Mexican soldiers talking. This would give them the opportunity to make their way to the Hiaki hideouts in the mountains.

What their parents did not mention was that in the event that they were captured or killed, the children would never see them again.[5] Children were taught basic life skills at a very young age, in times of peace or of turmoil. Chema believed that Antonio was nine years of age at that time and he was about seven years of age, but of this he was not quite certain. He did know that Antonio was two years older than him, as his parents had stated this to him in the past. They had no documents, no records of their existence. I remember that at some point in time I had written down Chema's parents' names, but he did not know their ages. He thought that he and his brother were born in Vikam Pueblo. There are people buried in Vikam Pueblo with the surname Cupis. Chema indicated that Cupis was not his real surname, however; it was borrowed from another Hiaki family, that of a mountain Hiaki who found the brothers and took them in when they were wandering alone in the wilderness. Many Hiakis who were captured and worked on haciendas owned by Mexican people assumed the surnames of the owners. Consequently, many Hiakis have Spanish given names and surnames. Many Hiakis who came to Arizona

---

5. Although Chema and Antonio were left alone in the wilderness and did not see their parents again as children, their mother Kala Nestor had in fact survived. An account of her last days is given in chapter 10.

used Spanish surnames and never spoke Hiaki for fear of being caught and deported back to Sonora. Many posed as Mexicans, particularly if they spoke Spanish.

Chema entered Arizona as a young man, possibly in his early twenties. He was a tall, angular, very handsome man when I used to see him as he was coming home from work (see figure 32, p. 570). Of course he was older than I and was always friendly and jovial if I ran into him at a ceremony or some other type of gathering. Chema and his family lived right across the street from my grandmother's home in Barrio Libre and were considered to be a family that was generally well-off compared to most Hiakis. Most Hiakis were farmworkers and earned relatively low wages. Chema had a job working for the railroad, and his wife, my mother-in-law, worked in a hospital.

He entered Arizona when he was traveling with a group of Hiakis, men, women, and children, who were making their way to Tucson from Sonora. Other Hiakis kept on going north, and many settled in the farming communities of Eloy, Coolidge, and Casa Grande, while others kept on going to Guadalupe. Chema's brother Antonio did not join the travelers, as he was a guerrilla fighter and the other Hiakis did not feel that they could spare him. Chema recalled that it took about three months to arrive here. They traveled only at night and in the daytime they rested. The Mexican *pelones* were always looking for Hiakis, and anyone who offered assistance to the Hiakis was punished. There were some Mexican farmers who felt pity for the Hiakis and would allow them to fill their water containers from their wells, but there were few of these good-hearted people along the way.

Upon arriving in Tucson, Chema recalls, they arrived at the home of one of the Hiaki families who lived along the banks of the Santa Cruz River. This settlement was known as Ili Hu'upa (Little Mesquite). At the time, the river still had water and there were tall cottonwood trees lining its banks. The travelers would rest for a short while and after bathing would try to wash their clothes in the river. But the hardships involved in the months of travel would result in their clothes being tattered and worn. When a Hiaki lady tried to wash their clothes, the clothes would generally fall apart. The only thing holding the fabric together was the dried sweat and dirt that had accumulated on it. Chema indicated that his clothes were as stiff as cardboard when he removed them to take a bath and to wash them. Fortunately, the local Hiakis always kept extra clothing around for these travelers. My paternal grandmother and her parents were some of the local Hiakis who received Hiaki travelers from Sonora and clothed and fed them upon their arrival. My maternal grandparents also did this.

The travelers would arrive with letters and messages from the Sonora Hiakis. The local Hiakis would gather at my great-grandparents' and grandparents' homes in anticipation of the arrival of the Sonora Hiakis. They knew of their pending arrival because there were generally one or two runners or scouts who traveled ahead of the larger group to inform the local Hiakis of it. These scouts would also check the trail ahead of the larger group to warn them of any Mexican soldiers or other dangers that lay ahead of them. Chema stated that after staying in Tucson for two or three days, or however long it took to gather weapons, ammunition, letters, money, and other vital items, the group would begin their return trip to the Hiaki pueblos in Sonora. Not all the Hiakis would return to Sonora. The men who had their wives and children with them generally stayed behind and settled here, while the rest of the men began the arduous journey back to the Hiaki pueblos. Some of the women who had traveled without their husbands would stay at the homes of relatives.

After two more "walking" trips to Tucson, Chema decided to stay in Tucson. By this time he had met my late mother-in-law. They married, settled down, and had six children. Occasionally Chema would travel back to the pueblos, but since he had a good job as a laborer with the Southern Pacific Railroad, he did not want to risk losing this job by traveling to the Hiaki pueblos on a more frequent basis. Upon retirement, however, he would urge my husband and me to travel to the Hiaki pueblos, and he would bear most of the expenses. It was during the first trip that I made to the Hiaki pueblos that I met Maria Hesus. Maria Hesus was Chema's niece, as Chema and Maria Hesus's mother were first cousins. Maria Hesus's own mother had been orphaned at a very young age, so details about her mother were sketchy and almost nonexistent. In fact, very few details of Maria Hesus's mother were ever revealed to me. If I recall correctly, Chema's mother and Maria Hesus's grandmother were sisters or half sisters. In those years, the Hiaki people adopted many orphaned children and foster children and raised them as their own, so kinship was very difficult to determine.

I would listen to Maria Hesus as she conversed with Chema about the difficult war-torn years. My ongoing interest in learning more about our people during those years sparked my interest in recording the history that they shared. My own maternal grandparents arrived here in a horse-drawn wagon, but their trip had started in Hermosillo, not in the Hiaki pueblos. Once they arrived here, along with my great-aunt, her husband, and some other relatives, they stayed here in Tucson.

Chema knew all the points or boundaries of Hiaki territory in Sonora, as he generally traveled with the Hiaki guerrilla fighters when they made the rounds of the land that they claimed as their own. He spoke of this often whenever we engaged in conversation during the time that he lived with my husband and me. He used to say that he became a man while in the mountains and that his brother and he were raised by a Hiaki man as his own sons. I believe it was this man's surname that Chema and his brother assumed. His name was Tomas Cupis, and he was the captain of the Hiaki guerrilla fighters. He is buried in Vicam Pueblo.

Chema was usually happy, except when he and my mother-in-law were fighting. When he talked about his past, he would become sad, but he would quickly change his mood, dwelling on the positive things in his life. He liked the barrio where we lived and had many friends and acquaintances, not only in our neighborhood, but in the surrounding Hiaki communities as well. He was always willing to discuss his past history with me. He told me frequently that he had attempted to share his stories with his own children but that they were too busy with their own lives to take time to sit down and listen to him. Instead they would tell him that his stories were old and had already "been rained on," and they had other more important things to do.

I learned much from Chema, about the difficulties he faced as a young child, about the hunger and thirst that he faced almost daily while growing up in the mountains, about the loss of his mother, to whom he was very close. He would say that when he had his mother, he always felt very confident and secure and felt that all was well with the world. But in an instant she was gone, and he lamented the fact that he had never thanked her for being the loving, caring mother that she was. But he always thanked Creator that she had been his mother, even if it was for such a short period of time. He looked forward to the day when he would see her again in the next world. By this time, Antonio was also deceased, so Chema had only a few relatives that he visited in Hiak Vatwe.

I respected Chema very much because he was a loving, caring, and supportive person. He watched my own children when both my husband and I worked. He helped us through good times and bad times and he was a very important member of our immediate, little family. He usually stayed with us, because he and my mother-in-law would fight and separate frequently and he felt comfortable in our home. Chema was also a cultural participant and knew the important ceremonial greetings, speeches, and history of our people. Most of our interviews were at his home. Sadly, he left this world too soon. He died in May of 1977 and is buried at San Xavier Cemetery. Incidentally, all the children (five sons and one daughter) that Chema had with my mother-in-law are also gone now, including my children's father. But they are all together once again in the next world.

Overview of Hiaki Guerrilla Strategy (Jose Maria Cupis)

Jose Maria (Chema) Cupis describes the overall picture of Hiaki resistance and the Hiaki-Mexican conflict. He describes the Hiakis' strong motivation to protect their land, which sustained them, and the Mexicans' desire to enrich themselves by taking it. He lists the strategies used against the Hiakis: captivity and deportation, forced labor, military attacks. He describes the strategies the Hiakis used against the Mexicans: hiding vulnerable women and children in the mountain caves, nightly raids on settlements and foraging for food wherever possible. When the Mexican soldiers pursued them in the mountains, the Hiakis would ambush them. Following the battle, they would resupply themselves from the killed soldiers' supplies

---

Chema: Itepo inim aa atteakame, inim ama nah kuaktisaewa
ito aniavetchi'ivo, itom yoremiam itom anianevetchi'ivo.
Hunulen itou hu'unaktewak. Huntuksan te
i'an orapo te aet tekipanoa. Ko'okosi te aet hoowa
intok te kia iyim pocho'okun vicha itom aet yeu veva
uu yoori, veveheeri, itom . . .
inika bwiata itom aa u'avaekai.
Vempo inim aa nu'uvaekai. Vempo emo aa makvaekai.
Inim emo ama aniavaekai. Aa etvae, vempo, uka bwiata,
bweituk inii bwia tua huevena tomi ama aayuk.
Riiko inim aane. Inii bwia chikti si'imeta hippue.
Wa aa au aniame, inim au aniane.

for future attacks. He describes how the Mexican army would place their conscripted Hiaki soldiers in the front lines when attacking, with the result that the mountain Hiakis then had no choice but to kill them. Hiaki supply parties would range widely looking for clothing and supplies, from Sinaloa in the south to Soyopa and up to Magdalena in the north. Mexican soldiers would follow their tracks, so Hiakis would lay tracks on purpose leading to a secure position and wait for the pursuers to arrive, then bayonet them. They would use bullets only if the shot was a sure thing, so as not to waste ammunition. These battles were quickly over. Using these techniques, the Hiakis resisted the Mexican government for seventy years, and the Mexicans thought that Hiakis in the United States must be providing supplies, but in fact it was mainly the Mexican army itself that supplied them (with the equipment the Hiakis were able to salvage after a battle). Many Mexican soldiers were killed in the mountains, since the Hiakis knew the territory and the Mexicans did not. In the cooler months, they would then put on the bloodied clothing of the dead Mexicans since their uniforms were warmer than what the Hiakis wore. Chema emphasizes that the Hiakis alone among the many Native peoples of Sonora were never defeated by the Mexicans, and that the Hiakis used the Mexicans' own equipment to resist. Some Hiakis even became leaders in the Mexican army, like General Amarillas and General Urbalejo. And many Hiakis were left in the south, as far south as Mexico City and beyond.

Chema: Those of us who own it [our Hiaki land], we are to walk upon it
to support ourselves, to support our children.
That is why it was meant for us. That is why we,
at this hour, we are working on it. They hurt us over it
and just chase us out to the wilderness,
the Mexican, the devil, our . . .
because they want to take this land away from us.
They want to take it from us. They want it for themselves.
They want it to support themselves. They want to plant it, the land,
because this land is worth a lot of money.
There is richness here. This land has everything.
The one who can work, can support himself here.

Itepo aa atteakame.
Hunuevetchi'ivo inika tomita inim hu'uneiya.
Wa yoi, veveheeri tua itot tekipanoa,
itom lu'utavae. Itom hakun vivittua, Yukataaneu
vicha itom toivaeka iyiika itou hooa.
Itom bwibwi'ise, poloovem. Hikau itom wiike.
Itom chochoilaka itom nah nunu'ubwa
itom animaalimtukavenasi, ho.
Iyim mampo itom maakoena
muramvenasi itom maakoena, itom nah totoha.
Kia imin tetakariu vichaa itom yeu totoha.
Ta hunum vicha hume kaa nokvaeme
hunum vicha vea vittua, Yukataaneu vicha,
mekka bwiapo vicha. Kaa vem bwiaveemu vicha yeu am totoha.
Bweituk hunulen aa lu'utavae uka Hiakita inimi'i.
Ika bwiatavetchi'ivo. Uka bwiata am u'avae.
Vempo aa atteavae, vempo aemak tawavae.
Hunume huname'e, inim aneme, yoim, ho.
Hunaavetchi'ivo vea im itou kikkimu, vayoneetaka itou kikkimu.
Iiyimin pocho'okun vichaa itom tave.
Tea vesa itepo, komo hunen aa maki, kaa ito su'utoi'ii'aawa,
kaa itepo ameu aa totettenia, bueno te aa tohahapte,
ta te hunaman itom ito hinneuvaevetchi'ivo kawiwi.
Bweituk hunaman te aa ito ania, kaupo,
intok hunaman kaita tua wa ko'okosimachik itou aune,
bweituk te ito suane. Inim intok itepo kaita lugarta hippue
bweituk te waka itom ae ito aniane katte aa hippue.
Kaita te huevenak hippue itom ae aniane'u,
itom ae am kontane'u. Iyiavetchi'ivo te vea yeu toto'ote, ho.
Hunaman te waka itom ayem hippuekai hunaman vepa am esso,
haksa itom aa am essopo am esso.
Essoka vea te pos, hoone. Haksa in wain
kom ili waho'opo chupemta te nunu'eka vea te ae hiapsa.
O chea ili wakasim, hitasa animalta itom aa bwa'e'u
aa tovoktaka ameu yeu aa totohaka familiata, anhelitom,
ae ania. Hunulen vea te tekipanoa.
Ta te kaa aa suutottoha waka itom bwia, aet te cha'aka.

We are the ones who own it.
They know that there is money to be had here.
The Mexican, the devil is really threatening us,
they are going to finish us. They send us far away, to Yucatán,
they want to take us there, so they do this to us.
They capture us, the poor ones. They hang us.
They lasso us and haul us around
as if we were animals, see.
They tie us by the hands and put us in chain gangs,
like mules they put us in chain gangs and move us about.
Just over here, the rock houses, they take us out there.
But over that way, those who do not want to talk,
they are sent over there, to Yucatán,
a faraway land. To a land not their own, they take them.
Because that's how they want to get rid of the Hiakis, right here.
For this land. They want to take that away from them.
They want to own it, they want to stay with it.
Those are the ones, those who are here, Mexicans, see.
That is why, then, they attack us here, with bayonets they attack us.
To the wilderness they send us.
But then, we, since it was given to us, we are not to leave it to them,
we are not to run away from it, well, we do leave it,
but [only] to defend ourselves, [we go] there to the mountains.
Because there in the mountains we can support ourselves,
and over there we experienced nothing very painful,
because we would guard ourselves. And here, we do not have any place
because here we have nothing with which to defend ourselves.
We do not have very much to defend ourselves,
with which we can surround them. This is why we leave here, see.
Over there, we have our mothers there and we hide them up there,
wherever we can find a place to hide them, we will hide them.
After hiding them, well, we will sit there. Somewhere, over here
we take what's growing on a small farm and that will give us life.
Or perhaps a small calf, whatever animal we can eat,
we take it and bring it to them, our wives, little angels,
we support them with that. That is how we work.
But we do not abandon our land, we hang on to it.

Hunaka kauta huni'i.
Atta hihharia intok iyika bwiata te aa hihharia.
Hee. Tukaariat naavuhtia te aet kaa kokkoche,
ito te suuaka toto. Hunulen vea te aet tekipanoa
intok hunulen wa veveheeri itou kikkivake.
Itepo kaa aa hahhase intok itepo te kaita au nooka.
Katte aemak nahsuarokaka au nooka.
Si no kee a'apo hunuka bwiata itom u'avaeka
inim utteapo itom vayoneetai yeu veevak.
Hunaman itom tatavek.
Despues de kee hunaman itom tataveka intok
hunaman intok itou kikkimu. Ho.
Huntuksan te inilen itou am kikkimu,
aman pos te am teak,
te kaa aman vepa kaupo um tetat am voovicha,
itepo ameu kom sasaka.
Pa'akuni, lugarta tu'iku te ameu kom sahaka
hunaman am nannanke. Hunama te vea waka ayukamta
ameu hooa. Woi, vahi ili huiwam hippueka huni te vea
hunaman ameu hoteka vea te hunaman am bwihne, pa'aku,
kaa vem lauti emo hinne'umachiku.
Hunama vea te am bwisek
pos hunama veha te amemak aune. Ho.
Am kova'ane. Intok am kova'anekai,
kaa kia veha am mumuisune.
Hunulen vea wame ama tawakame,
o senu takaa o woi takaa o vahi takaa o chea sientotaka
ama tawane, pos
huname te wikoo puane intok huiwata te puane intok waka atteata,
nu'uta, si'imeta te am uuraane.
Hunai mismo vem huiwai hunai te vea
intuchi vea mavetchasaka chukula kateme.
Kaa senu, kaa wosa um itou kikkimu. Ta vesa hunuen
vempo itom aniak. Hunuatukao te vea pos ito hihha'aria,

Even those mountains.
We defend them and we defend this land.
Yes. Throughout the night we lose sleep over it,
we guard ourselves when we are lying down. That's how we work
and that way the devil attacks us.
We do not chase him and we do not say anything to him.
We do not tell him that we want to fight him.
It is for that reason that he wants to take that land from us
It is with bayonets that chased us out.
Over there is where he chased us to;
Even after he had chased us out, then
they started to attack us there. See.
That is why, when they started to attack us there,
well, we found them there,
we were not in the mountains on top of the rocks waiting for them,
we came down to them.
Out there, in a good position we would go down to them
and meet them there. There, then, whatever they did to us, we
do to them. Even when we have just two or three little bullets,
we would ambush them out there, then we would catch them outside,[6]
where it appeared that they could not defend themselves quickly.
There then when we caught them, well then,
we would do to them what had to be done. See.
We would defeat them, and we would overcome them,
we did not just shoot at them.
So then, those who were killed there,
be it twenty or forty or sixty or perhaps one hundred
who were killed there, well,
we would take their rifles and ammo and also their clothes,
rations, we would take away everything from them.
In the same way, with their ammo, with that,
again we would receive those who come later.
They did not attack us [just] once or twice. But in that way
they helped us. We defended ourselves with that,

---

6. By "outside," Mr. Cupis means that they ambushed the Mexican soldiers away from their (the Hiakis') camp.

asta huevena tiempopo tahti te ito hihha'aria. Ho.
Inilen vea au ania uu Hiaki.
Kakku'uvo parke au wee,
kakku'uvo munision au wee,
kakku'uvo lonchi au wee,
nuu'u hitasa bwa'ame kaa au wee.
Kia te wa huya ania, o huya naawa o hitae hiapsaka
inilen ito ania. Hunulen te hiapsisuk
hunak tiempopo inilevenak weyeo. Ho.
Iiyika, iiyika weetua, a'apo mismo govierno, ya'ura,
itovenasi yoemem itou vivittua. Intok huname
itom wawaimtakasu vat katne
o chea itom yoemiamtakasu vat katne.
Huname itou kimune, ho.
Pos te kaa vaeka huni'i am tapsune.
Ume vat kateme tapsune
o kava'eka o wokimmea katne, si'imem tapsune.
Pos huname vea te . . . Hunama ito armaroa, itepo.
Hunulen au armaroa uu Hiaki.
Hunulen vea au ania.
Waka munisionta, si'imeta nu'e, aa tovokta.
Kulupti yeu sikaapo
maakinam chukti am u'ura.
Mettrayam am u'ura, chikti vem parkemak.
Muuram am tapria huiwata puateme.
Pos hunama veha ili emo tovotovokta ume Hiakim.
Hunaksan kia ili huni kaa am sumei'ya.
Am kateu kia kachin hiaka am nankine, ho.
Intuchi hunain am ya'ane. Kia hunuen hiva am hooa,
hunuen hiva am hooa. Kulupti weepo vea
hikau hahha'amu porque kaa teuwako intok
uka ourata hakun kampanyao,
ili aa hi'ibwa haiwau o tahoo haiwau wait haku'u,

for a long time we defended ourselves. See.
This is how the Hiaki defends himself.
No one sends bullets to them from anywhere,
ammo does not come to him from anywhere,
lunch does not come to him from anywhere,
food, that which is eaten, does not come to him.
Just from the plant world, or plant roots or whatever we could eat,
this is how we support ourselves. That's how we survived
in those days when this was going on. See.
This, this is what they were doing, he, the government, the leaders,
they send our own people[7] to us. And those
who were our relatives, they were the ones in front,
or even our own children, they would be in front.
They were the ones who attacked us, see.
Well, we had no choice but to kill them.
Those who were in front would be killed,
whether on a horse or walking, we would kill all of them.
Well then, those, we . . . There we armed ourselves, us.
That's how the Hiakis armed themselves.
That's how they supported themselves.
The ammunition, all of it was taken, it was gathered.
Sometimes, as it happened,
even the machines were taken away from them.
We took their machine guns from them, along with the ammo.
They would kill the mules, the ones carrying the bullets.
Well, that is when the Hiaki became inspired.
That's when they were not the least bit scared.
When marching, they met them without fear, see.
Again, they would do this to them. That's what they just kept doing,
they just kept doing this to them. Occasionally, then,
they would climb up when they were not found and
when all the men were out there somewhere on campaign,
when they were out looking for food or clothes somewhere,

---

7. By "our own people" Mr. Cupis means the Hiaki traitors who were inducted into the Mexican army and who were forced to turn, or willingly turned, against their own people.

pueplommewi, im vichaa, Tesio vetana vichau vea yeu sasaka,
Soyopa vetana, wait si'imekut vea te nah kaate.
Asta iyim Maarena vetana si'imekut te iniat nah kaate
ta hunueni, tahoota haiwa intok bwa'amta haiwa.
Inien veha kava'im nu'une, muram nu'une.
Huname puaktituaka veha am nuk saka'ane vem familiau vicha.
Hunuen yeu saka'asuk vea aman kimuk vea
hunuen aman hahha'amu.
Ta vea kaa tua vem wustopo sasaka kechia.
Ama aane kechia, tatawa, o'owim.
Toosasakawa, waka familiata suuane.
Huname veha ili ameu huhhasu.
Inilen vea emo ania. Yaiwak vea,
hitasa ama yeu simlatuk
yaiwak vea, hunak vea intuchi emo lihtaroaka yeu saka'ane.
Huchi hakun hita hariune. Ta kaa nahsuavaekai,
kaa yoitamak nahsuavaekai. Ta vesa
vempo hakun vicha uka wokta yeu am ya'ako
tua wokitat hahapte, Hiakitat cha'akai,
aa wok hahane. Kaituna veekika aet cha'aka katne.
Ime intok Hiakim pos hunuka hooa.
Wokta ameu ya'ane, pake am hahane,
ta vempo kaa ameu kimune.
Asta kee yeu am wikne hak am hoka'apo, am hahane.
Hunaman vea ameu yaine.
Hahamna. Ume intok voovitchakane Hiakim,
hak tu'i lugarpo vea hote'ene.
Hunama hotek vea
hunama am voovitne ume vo'o hoame.
Hunama vea pos ameu am yahak, tua ameu am yaituane,
wikoo puntai am soane. Pos hunama
hetochivela kom am tapsune.
Wokimmea kateme huni hunama tapsune.
Pos hunain vea kia kaita am hohootua.
Katchan woi, vahi orapo huni amemak auk
hetochivela am hahhasune, am suaane. Heewi.

at the villages, this way, they from Tesio,[8]
or when they went out from Soyopa, all over there we used to go.
Until here, from Magdalena, all over, we used to walk around
but that way, looking for clothes and looking for food.
This way we would get horses, we would get mules.
We would load them up and take them back to our family.
That way, after going out then, there we would return
and that's how we would climb up there.
But then we also would not feel comfortable leaving.
They were there also, they stayed, the men.
They were left behind to take care of the families.
Those [left behind] would fire then upon them [attackers].
This is how they defended themselves. Upon returning,
whatever had happened there,
upon returning, at that time they would again get ready and go out.
Again, they would go out and look for something. But not to fight,
not to fight with the Mexican. But then
if they made footprints heading out there somewhere, [the Mexicans]
would actually stand in these footprints, following the Hiaki,
they would follow his footprints. Too many of them would follow.
And these Hiakis, well, that's what they did.
They made footprints, so they would be chased,
but they would not attack them.
They would make them come out of their camp and chase them.
Then that's when they would come to them.
They would catch up with them. And the Hiakis would wait for them,
they would sit in a good place.
They would sit there, then,
there they would wait for those who were traveling.
Then there, well, when they arrived, they would let them get really close,
they would stab them with the bayonet. Well, then there
they would kill them and scatter their remains.
They would even kill the soldiers who were walking there.
Well, in this way they did not let them [the Mexicans] do anything.
Not even for two, three hours did they fight with them.
They would chase them, scattering them and killing them. Yes.

---

8. A village in the mountains of Mayo land in the state of Sinaloa, Mexico.

Inien. Inika ala hippue uu Hiaki.
Ta kaa a'apo aa haiwa. Hahawatek intok nankiwak
hunuen au ania. Au ania,
ousi au ania. Heewi.
Hunen u'ute yee sua ume Hiakim.
Kia chuvalaposu si yee susua ala,
por kee inika konsehota maki.
Ya'uchim yeu saka'atek hitasa venak yeu sika'apo
kaa kia waka huiwata wootasaewa. Waka vachiata kaa kia aa
wootasaewa. Kaita vichaatek, kaa puttisaewa.
Tua waka vichaatek, aa vivichak aa mamasaewa.
Kaa kiali. Kaa kia rumbopo putputtisaewa.
Kaita vichaatek, ela'aposu si'ime taewata ta kaa puttine
intok mekkaik kaa au suasaewa.
Kaa mekka, sewurotumachiak hunak aa maasaewa.
Iyika vea konsehota makna. Waka vachiata kaa aa wootavaane,
bweituk itou faltaroane, chea chuvvaatuk. Ho.
Kulupti te kaita nu'une
ama'a intok te kaa inien ane'etek te kaita nu'une,
kia vea putte'eteko. Nesita kee tua am maso mumuhine, tia.
Kaa kia puttivaane, tua aa vivvichaka
aa mumuine, muine. Hunak em kaita ta'arune huiwata.
Huname vachiakame pos hunume'e enchim aa makne uka huiwata.
Hunuka eme'e aa tekipanoane, hunuen eme'e aa weiyane.
Hunak te waka vachiata tovoktane, tia. Ho.
Inilen vea lutu'uria maktune.
Kaa . . . kia poipoiti hiune uu wiko'i,
ta yee suaka hiune, ho.
Kaa kia vea vala siime.
Inilen yee suane uu Hiaki intok hunulen uute hissua.
Pos hunuen au ania, ho. Komo i'ani vempo hunuen hiia.
Haisa anekai setenta wasuktiapo
kaa emo aa kovak tiaka nooka ume yoim. Ho.
"Setenta wasuktiapo nahsuak uu Hiaki," tia intok te,
"kat te kom aa toimachi intok te katte aa lu'utak," tia.
"Lu'utamachi," tia.
"Haisaakai? Havesa am ania?"

This way. This is what he does, the Hiaki.
But he is not looking for it [a fight]. When he is chased and caught,
this is what he does. He defends himself,
staunchly he defends himself. Yes.
That way, very powerfully, the Hiakis kill.
In a short time they will kill,
because they have been given this counsel.
When the leaders are leaving, if anything happens,
they are not to just waste their ammo. The ammo is not to be
wasted. If the target is not seen, they are not to shoot.
When they really see it they are to fire.
Not just for naught. They are not to fire randomly
if they do not see it, even if they do not fire all day,
and if it is far away, they are to leave it alone.
If it is not far and appears to be a sure target then they will fire at it.
This counsel is given to them. They are not to waste the bullets
because we will need them much later on. See.
Sometimes we would not get anything,
and sometimes, if we do not do this, then we would not get anything
if we just fire. It is necessary to shoot as if deer hunting, they said.
You do not just want to shoot, unless you really see it
you will shoot it, shoot it. Then you will not lose any ammo.
Those with ammo, well, they will give it to you-all, the ammo.
That is what you will work for, this is how you will carry it out.
Then we will gather the bullets, they said. See.
Then, these truths will be given to them.
Not . . . just the rapid fire of the weapon,
but by killing someone, it will be making that sound, see.
The bullet is not wasted.
This is how the Hiaki kills, and they kill very quickly.
Well, that is how he defends himself, see. Now, as they say this.
How, doing this, for seventy years
they did not defeat them, they said, the Mexicans. See.
"Seventy years the Hiakis fought," they say, "and we [Mexicans],
we did not bring them down and we did not finish them," they say.
"We could not finish them," they say.
"Why? Who is helping them?"

Pos hunumsan vea hunen hiia,
kee Estau Unidos vetana aniawa tea.
"Ume Hiakim inim wain hokame,
ermaanom vea am ania tea," ti vea hiia. Ho.
Intok hunuu kaa lutu'uria. Kaa lutu'uria hunu'u.
Vempo mismo kaa aa komprendiaroa uu wovierno.
A'apo mismo am ania.
Si'imeku, atteapo, wikoopo, huiwapo.
Informe uu yoi heneral, tu'ik wiko'ek,
vemelata wiko'ek ume Hiakim hunaka amemak atteak.
Kia hunaka usaaroa amemake, porque,
porque vempo aman aa totoha. Ho.
Kaupo ha'amuk chea vea sewuro. Ho.
Intok vempo kaa ama tata'a.
Hiaki intok, pos vempo ama ho'ak.
Ama hu'unea, haksa luula tu'i'ean.
Iyilen vea hiapsak ume Hiakim. Es cierto, aet aa pasaaroak,
huevena hiapsi ama taawak ta kaa vempoim venasia.
Vempoim hiapsi tua huevena, hunuu ili kawi hunum vo'okame,
tua huevena aet sakvae echi, yoim.
Huevena! Kaa illikika aet susuasuwak.
Si'ime kawichi vem hikau sahaka'apo, vem hikau yahaka'apo,
hunuen susuasuwak. Ta im vea kaa au yumak ala.
Katim kom aa tohak . . .
Yoeme kaita, kaita nahsua.
Kaavetamak nahsuavae.
Yoitamak kaa nahsuavaeka huyau wechek
bweituk wam vatwepo kaa aa hiapsitua, kaa aa ettua.
Bwiam am u'ak. Animalrata vem hippue'u,
va'ai naat am hippue'u, si'imeta am u'ak, ho.
Hose Maria Maytorena, hunuu si'ime hunuka Hiakita vea
hunuu ama nahsuak kaupo, ho. Hunuu Luis Torres.
Hunume vea ama Hiakitau kikkimu.
Ta pos haisa aa ya'ane? Kaachini.
Peinau, heneral Peinau. Kaachin aa ya'ak.
Haisa aa ya'ane?
Hiakim kaa vempoimvenasi pueplopo ho'ak

Well, there, then, they said this,
that they [the Hiakis] were receiving aid from the United States.
"The Hiakis who live here,
their brothers are helping them," then, they said. See.
And that is not true. That is not true.
They themselves do not understand, the government.
It itself is helping them.
In everything, clothing, weapons, bullets.
Information said that the Mexican generals had good weapons,
new weapons, and the Hiakis owned those with them.
They just used that with them because,
because they brought it to them. See.
When they climbed the mountains, then it was a sure thing. See.
And they [the Mexicans] do not know them [the mountains].
And the Hiaki, well, he lives there.
He knows the place, wherever it is good.
This is how they lived, the Hiaki. It is true, they did experience it,
many lives were lost there, but not like them [the Mexicans].
Their lives were very many, that little mountain lying there,
many were planted on it like watermelons, the Mexicans.
Very many! Not a few were killed there.
All over the mountain where they went up, where they arrived,
that is how they were killed. But here then, they did not defeat them.
They did not bring them down . . .
The Hiaki, nothing, nothing does he fight for.
He does not fight with anyone.
Not wanting to fight with the Mexican, he went into the wilderness
because over by the river he cannot live, he cannot plant.
They took their land. The animals that they had,
the ones they had near the water, they took everything, see.
José María Maytorena, that one, all the Hiakis, then,
he fought there in the mountains, see. That Luis Torres.
Those, then, attacked the Hiaki.
But, well, what could they do to them? Nothing.
Peinado, General Peinado. He did nothing to them.
What could he do to them?
The Hiakis do not live in the villages like them,

parake am kovaavetchi'ivo intok
kaa kovaa chupia uu Hiaki, kia hakwo huni'i.
Hee. Mientras kee Hiakita, Hiak tahtia
kaachin aa ya'ane. Ho.
Asta i'an tahti Hiakim hiapsa, ta vea kaa,
kaa yoita dominiom.
No son dominios de, ori wikoo puntai,
vayoneetai, kaa hunuen dominaroarim ume Hiakim.
Komo huevena triivum, Maayom, Opatam, Piimam, Heoreevem;
hunume si'ime kova'im.
Son dominios del gobierno. Hunume'e.
Komo im Papawem intok wate nasionim, triivum,
si'ime son dominios de, de los Amerikanos.
Hunuen vea reservaroarim, por kee dominiom,
intok am ania. Ta bien. Ho. Mehiko intok
am kova'i ta kaa, kaa am ania.
Kia vempo vem aawe'epo eecha. Mehiko kaita
hunuka garantiata am maka. Am kova'ala, es cierto
am kova'ala. Iyilen vea tawala ini'i.
Hiaki inien tawala, hasta la fecha
Hiakita kaa kova'ala uu yoi. Intok no por fuerza de,
woviernota utteampo nahsuak.
A'apo aa utteampo nahsuak, Hiaki,
A'apo aa yuma'alaapo nahsuak. Nahsuak.
Tu'i, nahsua.
Asta mismo a'apo woviernota huni nahsuariak,
pusieron la frente,
woviernotavetchi'ivo pechota nenkak ume Hiakim.
Huevenakai! Ho.
Mehiko kapitaleo tahtia.
Huevena heneraalimtuk,
ya'uchimtuk, heneral Amarillas, heneral Urvaleeho.
Hunume si'ime yau . . . bwe ya'uchimtuk intok
si'imeta uka korporasion Hiakita hippuek.

so they can beat them and
the Hiaki is not meant to be conquered, not ever.
Yes. Meanwhile the Hiaki, as long as he is a Hiaki,
they will do nothing to them. See.
Up to now the Hiakis are alive, but then they are not,
not dominated by the Mexican.
They were not dominated at riflepoint,
with the bayonet, the Hiaki were not dominated that way.
Like many tribes, Mayos, Opatas, Pimas, Eudeves;
those were all defeated,
they are dominated by the government. Those
like here the Papagos and other nations, tribes,
all of them are dominated by the, by the Americans.
That way, then, they are on reservations because they are dominated
and they are being aided. That's good. See. And in Mexico
they were defeated, but are not, not being aided.
They just plant however they can. Mexico does not give
them any guarantees. They defeated them, it is true,
they defeated them. In this way then he remained.
The Hiaki has remained this way, up to this time
the Mexican has not defeated the Hiaki. And not on their own,
with the government's own strength, they were forced to fight.
He fought with his own strength, the Hiaki.
He fought any way he could. He fought.
Good, he fought.
Until, even the same government he fought,
he faced them,
the Hiakis gave their lives for the government.
Many of them! See.
Up to the capital of Mexico.
Many became generals,
became leaders, General Amarillas, General Urbalejo.
Those all led . . . became top leaders and
they had all the cooperation of the Hiaki.

PART I

IN SONORA

This part of the book presents several stories excerpted from the interviews with Luisa, Andres, and Maria Hesus, documenting their memories of their experiences as children and young adults in Hiak Vatwe (the Hiaki territory around the Hiaki River, as well as the river itself) and Itom Toosa ("Our Nest," referring to the Vakateeve Mountains to the northwest),[1] in Sonora. They describe life as refugees and warriors in the mountains, providing first-person accounts of conflict, pursuit, and capture.

The stories in this part are organized into four chapters: "Survival," "Battle in Sonora," "Life Under Siege, Coercion, and Collaboration," and "Capture." Each story is summarized in a prose paragraph at the beginning, and then presented in Hiaki with an English translation, exactly as recounted to the author.

---

1. As noted above, on maps of Sonora, the name of these mountains is often spelled "Bacatete."

FIGURE 1 A Hiaki family by their dwelling, ca. 1910. University of Southern California Libraries, California Historical Society, https://doi.org/10.25549/chs-m14571.

CHAPTER 1

SURVIVAL

Escape from Hermosillo (Luisa)

Luisa describes escaping from Hermosillo in 1910 with a large group of Hiaki refugees, fleeing from fighting in the city. They walked for weeks, even months, to reach the mountains, often going without water. Many died. She describes finding a haven by the San Maciel River, a settled place from which people had fled, leaving all their belongings and animals, which provided some much-needed food for the refugee group. Eventually they arrived in the mountains, where they met up with the rebel Hiakis who never had dealings with Mexicans, and who lived by raiding Mexican wagons and vehicles.

Maria: Empo veha hunu . . . mil nueve sientos diestuk
veha Peesiopo emo yeu siika ti hiia?

Luisa: Huh.

Maria: Kawiwi?

Luisa: Kawiu wattek.
Kia hunum yeu sahak hiva witti sahak.
Inim Vakateveu vicha veha te kom yahak.
Si'ime, kaa iliki, huevena.

Maria: Komo haiki taewapo eme kaate?

Luisa: Katchansa te aa mammatte.
Te si vinwa kaate, wokimmea, hente.

Maria: Haiki semaana?

Luisa: Yo'owe i'an aa e'eteho.
Humaku'u, vahi, naiki metpo humak kaate.

Maria: Aa, karay!

Luisa: Heewi. Intok te ket si vatte va'ae kokok.
Hunum, ori, posom hunum hak manek tea.
Hunaman veha hunama ta'ame veha aman hi'irokaka kaate.
Hunaman hi'irokaka kaate, ta aman yahiwa'apo veha
kaita ume poosom, wechia, kaa vaa'ak.
Intok ketuni mekka va'awi, ho.
Asta imin San Masiel vatweu veha kom heeka.

Maria: Hmm.

Luisa: Kaa machiak veha hunumum kom yaaha,
weepulaika, wowoika, vavahikai.
Ume chea ili veha pappeame veha
uchi amau vicha am va'a nankek, va'am nu'ukae.
Huevenaka veha haivu to'otesukan.
Kaa he'e. Mamni ta'apo kaa he'e . . . ka kaate.

Maria: Hmm.

Maria: Then you, there … in 1910,
you left Hermosillo, you said?

Luisa: Huh.

Maria: To the mountains?

Luisa: We went into the mountains.
We just left there and went directly there.
Here, toward Tall Bamboo, we arrived down there.
All of us, not a few, many.

Maria: How many days were you walking?

Luisa: We didn't even notice it.
We walked for such a long time, the people.

Maria: How many weeks?

Luisa: The elders now speak about it.
Maybe three, four months we may have walked.

Maria: Oh my!

Luisa: Yes. And we almost died of thirst.
There, well, they said there was a well there somewhere.
There, those who knew the place said we would drink water there.
There they said we would drink water, but when we arrived there
there was no well, it was sunken in, with no water.
And it was still very far to water, see.
Until finally, down here at San Maciel River, then we finally drank water.

Maria: Hmm.

Luisa: Then at night, we would go down there,
one, two, or three [people].
Then those who still had a little energy
would go there to meet those bringing water and take it.
Many had already collapsed.
They did not drink. For five days we walked without drinking.

Maria: Hmm.

Luisa: ... Ho. Asta hunumun veha kom he'eka San Masielpo.
Hunum veha yahaka veha naiki ta'apo ama hooka.
Hunum intok, ori, rancho ama katek, ilevena,
lakrio kari ama katek. Trasteom, si'ime ama manek, aayuk, hita.
Kia ori, kee saka'awapovenasi ibwan.
Tu'ulisi hita puatom ama aayuk um ropeeropo,
si'ime hita vem atteawa tu'ulisi ama auka, bwan.
Ta pos ume nassua hapteak sahak.

Maria: Sahak.

Luisa: Heewi.

Maria: Hmm.

Luisa: Wakas ... inen ili hardin ama katek.
Sewam ama eechi.
Hunama veha hooka.
Hunama te veha kia hooka, si'ime, uu hente.
Vahi ta'apo ama hokai veha
si wakase bwa'e, vurum bwa'e.

Maria: [*Laughs.*]

Luisa: [*Laughs.*] Intok hunak kaa pattitukan ume vatwem.
Kia tu'ulisi vuiten, silili'itia,
uu va'a kalasalaikai.
Vuurum, kava'im, wakasim intok
kia hu'upam vetuk tappuni.
Kia tutu'ulisi aane.

Maria: Heewi.

Luisa: Pos ume yoeme intok kia kaa am waatiavenasi
kia am suaka am bwa'e.
Haivu ...

Maria: [*Laughs.*]

Luisa: ... ili, ili pappeame.

Luisa: . . . See. Until there, then, we drank at San Maciel.
When we arrived there, we were there for four days.
And there, well, there was a ranch there, like this.
There was a brick house there. A cupboard, everything was there, things.
Just as if, well, as if no one had abandoned it, well.
The dishes were there, very neatly, in the closet,
all their things were neatly placed there, well.
But when the fighting started, the ranch owners left.

Maria: They left.

Luisa: Yes.

Maria: Hmm.

Luisa: Meat . . . there was a little garden like this.[1]
Flowers were planted there.
That's where we were.
Then we were just there, everybody, the people.
We were there, then, for three days,
we were really eating, beef and donkey meat.

Maria: [*Laughs.*]

Luisa: [*Laughs.*] And at that time the river was not dammed.
The water was flowing so nicely, nice water sounds.
The water was so clear.
And the donkeys, horses, cattle
just stood under the mesquite trees.
Everything was going so nicely.

Maria: Yes.

Luisa: Well, and it was like these animals were just not wanted,
so they would just kill them and eat them.
Already . . .

Maria: [*Laughs.*]

Luisa: . . . [those with a] little, little more energy.

---

1. Luisa points to Maria Hesus's garden, where the interview was taking place.

Maria: Abwe tevaure.

Luisa: Heewi. Pos hunama yeu sahaka veha
humak uchi woi ta'apo kateka veha hunumun yahak,
To'okopo Va'ammewi.
Ta hunume veha hivayu ama ho'aka bwan.
Tua kaa yoimmeu yeu yaaha,
intok kia kaa yoimmeu bwa'amta nunu'e huni'i.
Kia hunuen hiva. Karom saltaroaka hiva
hi'ibwaka ama ho'ak.

Maria: Heewi. Hunuen intok ket parketa . . .

Luisa: Heewi.

Maria: . . . veha nau toha.

Luisa: Hm, hmm. Kaita. Kialim hunuen hiva
emo aniaka ama hooka.

Maria: Mismo uu yoi sontao veha hiva hunaka'a . . .

Luisa: Heewi, heewi.

Maria: . . . armam intok parketa am maka.

Luisa: Mismo vempo ibwan.
Parte am suak veha huiwam am u'ura,
wiko'im am u'ura.

Maria: Voocham . . .

Luisa: Hitasa vem weiya'u. Kamionim saltaroane.
Hunuen veha vem familia aniaka ama ho'ak.

Maria: Well, they were hungry.

Luisa: Yes. Well, we left there and walked
maybe two more days, then we arrived there.
We arrived in Gray Waters.
But then, [some Hiakis], they had always lived there, well.
They never appeared to the Mexicans,
and never even purchased their food from the Mexicans.
Just like that. They would just hijack the carts
and eat what they took from them, while they lived there.

Maria: Yes. And they also took ammunition in that way . . .

Luisa: Yes.

Maria: . . . they collected it.

Luisa: Hm, hmm. Nothing. That's the only way that
they provided for themselves while they were there.

Maria: Those same Mexican soldiers, then, always . . .

Luisa: Yes, yes.

Maria: . . . provided weapons and ammunition for them.

Luisa: Well, they themselves [the Mexicans] were doing it.
They [the Hiakis] killed some, then took their ammo,
[and] took their weapons.

Maria: Shoes . . .

Luisa: Whatever they [the Mexicans] had. They [the Hiakis] hijacked the vehicles.
That's how they lived and provided for their families.

FIGURE 2 Stagecoach drawn by five horses along the Río Yaqui river route, in Mexico, driven by two men holding rifles, ca. 1900. USC Digital Library, California Historical Society, https://doi.org/10.25549/chs-m15061.

Luisa: Ket hiva hunumuni To'i Va'amvetana. Hunumun veha taawak.
Hunum veha te si vinwa hooka.
Hunum te veha kia hitasa itom hia . . . ae hiapsau bwa'e.
Huya naawam, hita, vauwo naawam,
huttuko naawam intok hunume mismo taakam.
Intok hunuka ili kava'i wakas, wakiak, poliakamta,
hita puaka aa bwa'e, ho.
Intok kia haksa ili vem ho'asuka'apo,
hewi, ili waka veam haksa wootim.
Uchi aman yeu yahak veha hunaka puaka aa bwa'ane.

Maria: Hmm.

Luisa: Heewi.

Maria: Va'amsu?

Luisa: Va'am intok pos, aman hakun vatne.
Va'am . . . votammea te vava'ata.

Traveling and Living in the Mountains (Luisa)

Luisa describes how they would travel in the mountains, carrying children and water and eating wild food. A woman with two small children would walk carrying a knapsack of supplies, her infant bundled at her chest and her toddler sitting on top of the knapsack. They would keep water bags and canteens full and at the ready, hanging from a nearby tree or bush, in case they had to jump up to flee at any moment. There were Hiakis living in the mountains from 1910 to 1927. She names many of the places where they would camp. She describes leaving a mountain camp before dawn to undertake the long walk down to collect water, and the longer walk back up to the encampment, carrying it.

Luisa: It is also toward Rat Waters. They stayed there.
That's where we were for a long time.
There, with whatever we could . . . eat, we ate.
Plant roots, something, desert shrub roots,
roots of the graythorn and also the fruit from these shrubs.
And also a little horsemeat, dried, with insects,
and we would pick and eat other things, see.
Just wherever they used to live before,
yes, little cowhides, thrown about.
When they returned again, they would pick that up and eat it.

Maria: Hmm.

Luisa: Yes.

Maria: How about water?

Luisa: Well, the water we had to get far away.
The water . . . we got water with the water bags.

> Bweere vootam, inen.
> Wate sesenu vote ama meeliom nunu'e.
> Wate intok sesenu vootem.
> Huname ya'arika am nunupne, um kaupo.
> Hunamea veha vatne.
> Huname veha ili vu'um nu'une.
> Ta ume amforam, veha tennek veha
> kia listopo am tapuniarika
> aman chaya'ine.

Maria: Hm, hmm.

Luisa: Huname veha koksakane ili usim vetchi'ivo,
va'a nu'um.
Mochilota vepa intok ili usita yecha'ika aa pu'atine.
Woim usek intok wepulaik taupo chaya'ine, ilitchik,
senuk intok mochilota vepa yecha'isimne.

Maria: [*Laughs.*]

Luisa: Ili valdempo intok ili puatom,
ili ae hita ae hooneu wiksimne, ho.
Hunuen veha weene. Tukaarit naavuhti,
taewait naavuhti te hunuen vo'o hoone, animaalimvenasia.
Si'imeta te hunuen aman nah katne, ho.
Taewait naavuhti, tukaariat naavuhti.

Maria: Haiki tiempopo veha eme'e hunen ansasaka?

Luisa: Huu, haivu vinwatu.

Maria: Haivu haiki meecha, o wasuktiapo eme'e hunen ama anne?

Luisa: Heewi. I'an huyau wattiwak,
katin veintetuk, veintisietepo yeu yahiwak.
Intuchi um, ta chukula veras . . . hunum veha im vicha,
va'ampo hunum si'ime ume kawim,

           Big water bags, like this.
           With some we collected one and a half bags of water.
           With others, one bag.
           Having those, we carried them around in the mountains.
           We fetched water with them.
           We were able to collect more water with them.
           But the canteens, when we had to escape
           we always had them ready, had them full,
           and they would be hanging [from a shrub or tree].

Maria: Hm, hmm.

Luisa: We would hang them around our necks for the little children,
           the canteens and water bags.
           And on top of the knapsack we would place the child.
           If we had two children, we would hang one, the littlest, in front,
           and the other would be carried on top of the knapsack.[2]

Maria: [*Laughs.*]

Luisa: In the buckets a few plates,
           a few things to cook with, we would carry those, see.
           That's how it was. Through the night,
           throughout the day, we would walk, like animals.
           We were all walking around like that, see.
           Throughout the day, throughout the night.

Maria: How long were you doing this?

Luisa: Uu, for a very long time.

Maria: How many months or years were you going through this?

Luisa: Yes. When we went into the desert,
           remember, in 1920, we returned in 1927.
           Again, but wait, see . . . from there,
           this way, at the water, all the mountains,

---

2. That is, the littlest child would be carried in a bundle on the mother's chest, and the larger child would sit on top of the knapsack the mother would be carrying on her back.

> Vatachim, Totoi Va'ampo,
> intuchi inen Vas Veetiapo, Otam Tohchivei teapo, Voare.
> Hunai si'imekut kampamentota hohhoa ume yoeme.
> Hunum veha te hoho'a.
> Hunait hokaa veha te mekka vavatne,
> kaa hiapsita pappeawi.

Maria: Hmm.

Luisa: Kaa um hak vetuk vatne, siendo kee mekka ko'omi.

Maria: Haisa mekka tua? Komo . . .

Luisa: Kawimmet hikat ko'omi.
Kau kahonimpo kom vava'ata.

Maria: Como de aquí a . . . hunaman pueblou?

Luisa: Heewi.

Maria: Aa, karay!

Luisa: Mekka ko'omi. Mekka kom tevesi weene, ho.
Kom vicha kaa tua lottiachi, hewi,
ta hikau vicha si lottiachi.

Maria: Hikau vichaa, heewi.

Luisa: Hikau ha'amupo. Pos tua, tua ket ve'eu,
komo im totoim ma kuhne, hewi?
Primer vehpo kuse'etek veha
haivu matchune, hewi?

Maria: Hmm.

Luisa: Hunum orapo sik veha naikim machiau
haivu hoarau yevihne.
Kampamentou yevihne haivu.
Kia va'atak hiva sep nottine.

SURVIVAL

> Frog Mountain, Chicken Waters,
> and here at Burnt Grass, the place known as White Bones, Killing Place.
> The Hiakis set up camp all over there.
> That's where we lived.
> While there, we would fetch water from far away,
> where we did not feel like going.

Maria: Hmm.

Luisa: We did not get water somewhere there, but far, far down.

Maria: How far was it? Like . . .

Luisa: From the top of the mountain, down.
We fetched water down in the canyon.

Maria: Like from here to . . . to the pueblo [i.e., to Vikam]?

Luisa: Yes.

Maria: Oh my!

Luisa: It was far down. We had to go very far down, see.
Going down is not too tiring, yes,
but going up is very tiring.

Maria: Going up, yes.

Luisa: To go up. Well, really, really early,
such as when the roosters crow, yes?
The first time they crow,
it is already dawn, yes?

Maria: Hmm.

Luisa: Leaving at that hour, then when the sun is coming out,
we would already be back home.
We would arrive at the encampment already.
As soon as we fetched water, we would return.

Shelter (Luisa)

Luisa describes how they would camp out under grease-coated muslin sheets, sitting on piled-up brush, and how rainwater would just run off the sheets.

Luisa: Hunuen te kia ili koram ya'arika ama hoone,
seveak hunama ili kovi'iku
ili naya'a'ika hunama mocha'ala hoone.
Hunama te hooka veha ili hita,
kia ama sukaune, hewi?
Kaita bwa'amachine
ta kia ili sukaune ama hooka'ari,
intok hunuen yukeo
intok te karpam hohoan, savanam.
Huname vetuk veha te hoone yukeo
como si hak bweerem kakarekame venasi.

Maria: Am komonak veha kia . . .

Luisa: Heewi. Kia hunuen hekau huni hiva hunama hoone.
Huyata ama vetuk wattaine, papahota.
Hunait veha te hoone. Va'a intok itotuk yeu vuitine.

Maria: Hmm.

Luisa: Kia hunue vetchi'ivo choppo
veha aa ya'arika ama hoone.
Hunama veha . . . kaita va'a.
Katte komonne ala. Kaa vavawe ume savanam.

Maria: Oh, kaa komonne?

Luisa: Kaa papasaaroa. Kaa papasaaroa.
Kia vetuk aman vuitine uu va'a.

Luisa: We used to make little fences and sit there,
when it was cold, we would sit there in the corner
huddled around a small fire.
We would sit there and
just keep warm there, yes?
Nothing to eat,
just sit there keeping warm,
and when it rained
we would make tents, from sheets.
We would sit under those when it was raining,
as if we had some big houses.

Maria: When they got wet, then you just . . .

Luisa: Yes. Even when it was windy we would sit here.
We would place some brush under there, *papaho*.[3]
We would sit on top of that. And the water would run under us.

Maria: Hmm.

Luisa: It was just for that reason
that we would make small hills of dirt and sit on them.
Well, no water touched us there.
We did not get wet, though. The sheets did not leak.

Maria: You did not get wet?

Luisa: It [the rain] did not seep through. It did not seep through.
The water just ran under.

---

3. *Papaho* is a type of shrub that grows in the mountains.

Kaa amet papasaaroa ume savanammetchi.
Tapsisiolaika huni'i. Manta kaa hihikia.

Maria: Kaa hihikia, bwe?

Luisa: E'e. Kia hunuen ama vetuk hoone,
bweere karimpo hokaa venasi.

FIGURE 3 Hiaki women and girls in a temporary shelter, ca. 1911–12. Records of the Compañía Constructora Richardson, S.A., 1904–1968 (bulk 1904–1927), MS 113, box 1, folder 4: Photographs. Courtesy of University of Arizona Libraries, Special Collections.

It did not seep through the sheets.
Even though they were thin. The muslin does not leak.

Maria: It doesn't leak, well?

Luisa: No. We would just sit under them like that,
as if we were sitting in a big house.

Mountain Food (Luisa and Andres)

Luisa and Andres describe preparing and eating spiny cedar root, agave, cholla, prickly pear, barrel cactus, deer, rabbit, and other wild foods. They emphasize the lack of salt. When asked about coffee, they burst out laughing. Where would you find coffee in the mountains? Later, they talk about raiding for horses to eat and scavenging old crops from abandoned homesteads. Luisa describes eating wild turnips or old greasy bones, again without salt. They mention one story in which a starving man even resorted to sucking on the bones of deceased Hiakis. They laugh about another in-

---

Maria: Haisa intok eme'e hu'unene hitaa . . .
  qué se puede comer
  y qué no se puede comer?

Luisa: Pos aet hu'unea pos ite . . .

Andres: Pos aa ta'a haivu.

Maria: Porque katin wate hita hunuen
  ori aa . . . es venenoso.

Luisa: Heewi, ta waate.

Andres: Ta i'an kaita.

Maria: Kaita?

Andres: Kaita. Yu. Sep uu wauwo naawa huni bwa'awa.
  Yoim aa pochote ti hiia.
  Intuchi ono'e.
  Hunuka intok aa orek huni ket aa va'a hi'ine
  tua va'ae mukeeteko bwiatuakai ono'eta.
  Bwe huevenak bwa'ala inepo.
  Choa voram chea si kaa kiam huni bwa'ane.

Luisa: Navo veroam.

stance when Reyno toasted and ate a leather sandal. Small animals were eaten also: mice, *kau churéam* or "mountain roadrunners," lizards, iguanas. People would eat anything they could find, though Luisa emphasizes that they always made sure to feed the children first. A mother would go without food to be sure her children had something to eat. Other foods are also mentioned: the roots and fruit of graythorn bushes, insects, old cowhide, American nightshade, mesquite pods, honey. Water was collected and carried in old boots, and canteens of water were always kept at the ready, hanging from a tree, in case they needed to escape suddenly. Finally, Luisa and Andres describe catching, killing and eating *torim*, wood rats or pack rats.

Maria: And how would you know what . . .
 what you could eat
 and what you couldn't eat?

Luisa: Well, you know, well, we . . .

Andres: Well, we knew already.

Maria: Because remember, some people,
 those things, it . . . it's poisonous.

Luisa: Yes, but some.

Andres: But now there is nothing.

Maria: Nothing?

Andres: Nothing. Look. Right away even the spiny cedar root[4] is eaten.
 The Mexicans say it is pochote.
 Also the barrel cactus.
 And you would also even drink it, that one, that thing,
 when very thirsty, putting dirt on it, the barrel cactus.
 Well, I have eaten a lot.
 Cholla fruit, which are really not tasty, I would eat.

Luisa: Prickly pear leaves.

---

4. *Bombacopsis quinata*.

Andres: Navo veroam, heokom.

Maria: Hmm.

Luisa: Seewa, ku'u seewa.
Ku'uta chuktaka veha aa ma'ane.
Tatemaroana hunaa veha.
Hunaa veha ori maiyata tu'iriak hiva ama bwa'abwasewau
veha senu ta'apo hiva aa ma'ane.

Andres: Heewi.

Luisa: Si kaa aa tu'iriak intok woi ta'apo ama ma'atune.
Hunaa veha bwahne.
Hunaa veha bwehina; hunaka veha bwa'ane.
Komo yoi santavenasi aa piinne,
aa chiune. Nomas el huuwo.

Andres: Ta aa machukaroak huni veha aa va'atene;
aa va'atuane hewi? Hunaka veha aa vasuane.
Hunak veha ori choa voram auk
huni'i hunaka ama va'atene.

Luisa: Como pinol de maíz.

Andres: Hee, hunuen.

Maria: Kafeta intok hiva weiyaane?

Andres: E'e. Kafeta haksa aa teune?
Kaupo kaita kafe.

Luisa: Kaita kafe. Kafeta kaa hi'ine.
Ya ves que ona huni kaita.

Andres: Kaita. Ona huni kaita.
Reeve kia kaa onakamta bwa'ane,
parosta o mahta me'ako.

Luisa: Kaita. Kaa onakamta bwa'ane.

Andres: Kaita.

Luisa: Ta pos hi'ibwava'awa'apo, hiapsiva'awa'apo . . .

Andres: Prickly pear leaves, which are slimy.

Maria: Hmm.

Luisa: Flower, the flower of the century plant.
You would cut the plant and bury it.
It is toasted, that one.
The heart is good when it is cooked through,
so for one day you would bury it.

Andres: Yes.

Luisa: If it is not good, then it would be buried for two days.
Then that would cook.
Then that would be dug up, then you would eat that.
You would suck on it like sugarcane,
bite off bits of it. Only the juice.

Andres: But if you mash it then you would add water;
add water, yes? Then you would rinse that.
If there is cholla fruit
then you would add that to the liquid.

Luisa: Like cornmeal.

Andres: Yes, that way.

Maria: And you always had coffee?

Andres: No. Where would we find coffee?
In the mountains there is no coffee.

Luisa: There is no coffee. We would not drink coffee.
You see, there was no salt either.

Andres: Nothing. There was no salt either.
Half of the time we just ate unsalted meat,
rabbit or deer if we killed one.

Luisa: Nothing. We would eat things without salt.

Andres: Nothing.

Luisa: But when one wants to eat, when one wants to live . . .

[. . .]

Maria: Si ori, hunuen kawipo ane'etek
intok kaita ama ayuko, komo huyam
o hitasa, como matitas o árboles así
hunak veha hitaa bwa'ane?

Luisa: Bwe aa hariune.

Andres: Aa hariune.
Masotune oo paro'osim,
hita hariune.
O hunuka in eteho'u, hewi,
choa vooram, hita saawam iibwan.

Luisa: Hu'et hak veha aa hariune,
aukau vicha sasakane.

Andres: Ama tawalame,
wate intok wam hak kava'im nu'une.

Luisa: Hentem intok wate poloovem
hunen hakun Teta Kuusimmewi,
Empalmeu kava'im e'etbwane,
huname veha bwa'ane.

Andres: Hmm. Kava'im e'etbwane.
Huname veha bwa'ane.

Luisa: Tu'isi yeu sahak, kaa am bwa'awak
veha am nu'upane.

Andres: Henteta inien veha au aa nu'upane.
Huname veha puetituana kechia.

Luisa: Kaa tahkaikamta, kaita.
Kia huneelak bwa'ane.

Andres: Heewi. Kaita.

[. . .]

Luisa: Tua kaita. [*whispering*] Ite veha kia veha,
hunuen haksa hokaa veha ili hitasa kaita,

[. . .]

Maria: If when you are in the mountains
and there is nothing there, like bushes
or something, like little plants or trees like that,
then what would you eat?

Luisa: Well, you would look for it.

Andres: You would look for it.
It would be a deer or a rabbit,
you would look for something.
Or that of which I speak, yes,
cholla fruit, something, capers, well.

Luisa: You would look around there for something,
you would go where there is something.

Andres: Those who stayed behind,
some would go and fetch some horses.

Luisa: And some poor people,
in that way from Rock Crosses,
from Empalme they would steal horses,
then they would eat those.

Andres: Hmm. They would steal horses.
Then they would eat those.

Luisa: If things turned out all right and they did not eat them,
then they would bring them back.

Andres: They would bring them to the people.
They would also then be made to butcher them.

Luisa: With no tortillas, nothing.
We would just eat it like that.

Andres: Yes. Nothing.

[. . .]

Luisa: Really nothing. [*whispering*] We just,
like that, wherever we were, when there was nothing,

>   tua kaita hak tetteuwau veha
>   haksa ili sawam bwehine kechia,
>   sawam auka'apo.
>   Tua kaita sawam auka'apo intok kaita.

Maria: Tua kaita?

Luisa: Tua kaita bwa'amachine, tua kaita,
kia ili otam haksa ili ochokom hokame
huname ili puaka,
am vavakeka am bwa'ane uu hente,
ili va'awata hi'ine, chiivu.
Hunaka hiva ili hi'ine,
intok kaa onakamta intok
kia ili hita hak teako huni kaa onakamta bwa'ane.
Kaita oona. Kia hune'elak bwa'ane.

[. . .]

Maria: Senu historiapo ket, ori, i'an ori, uu lu'utekame,
yo'owe, Chema, bwe Tosari tea.

Luisa: Heewi.

Maria: Hunaa ori, ket aman au anekai ori tua
kaita emo bwa'amachi ti hiia.
Kaita, kaita, ti hiia.
Hunama intok ume ili otam hooka tea
ama kokokame, yoeme.
Huname veha emo chunee ti hiia,
pos kaita intok bwa'amachi.

Luisa: Pos kaita, kaita auka'apo,
tua kaita hak auka'apo, pos hu'uneateko,
intok kaa tua mekka hitasa bwa'amachik auk
intok hunam vicha saka'ane.

Maria: Hmm.

when there was really nothing,
we would also dig for wild turnips
wherever we found them.
And where there were no turnips, then nothing.

Maria: Absolutely nothing?

Luisa: When we really had nothing to eat, really nothing,
just a few greasy bones,
we would pick those,
the people would boil them and eat them,
and drink the soup, bitter.
That's all we drank,
and with no salt and
if we found any little thing, we would eat it without salt.
No salt. Just eat it like that.[5]

[. . .]

Maria: In one story also, now, the deceased one,
elder, Chema, well, Light-Skinned he was named.

Luisa: Yes.

Maria: That one, also when he was over there really
had nothing to eat, he said.
Nothing, nothing, he said.
There were some bones there
of some who died there, Hiakis.
Those they would suck, he said,
because there was nothing to eat.

Luisa: Well, nothing, where there is nothing,
really nothing, well, if one knows
and there is something to eat not too far away,
then you go there.

Maria: Hmm.

---

5. Here her voice falls to a whisper, as she remembers the difficulties they faced at that time.

Luisa: Hunueni. Hmm.

Andres: Aa. Kaupo ta si shinga, tua Dios.
Nee veha tua ama suatuk.

Luisa: Ili otam, hita veha hak pu'ane.
Oo hakwo uchi ama hohoatusuka'apo
wootita veha uchi ili aa pu'aka huna veha ili chivuk
huni vavakeka aa bwa'ane,
ili usim aa bwa'atuane.

Andres: O si chea nai, vahim veraa vochak
huni wepulaim ori tostaroaka am bwa'ane.

Luisa: Komo tuka kompae Reynota etehovenasia.
Katin veraa vocham hak trinchem au teaka
si'imem tostaroa ti hiia yepsakai. [*Laughter*.]

Andres: Heewi, hunen eene bwan, ho.
Hunuen te aa pasaroak.

Maria: Hunuen intok ili animalim intok ket,
komo ori haisa teak ume, wiku'im?

Andres: Kuta wiku'im empo etehoka hunuen hiia?
Bwe kia aa maloka weene.
Aa tea'u bwa'ane.

Luisa: Churuim, hita kau churearn,
si'imeta bwa'ane vem teaka'u.

Maria: Hita intok churuim?

Luisa: Kampaanim, misim vevena; ili tettevem bwasiak,
ili wichapupuila yekak.

Andres: Tehonim ti hiia ume yoim.

Luisa: Yoim am tehonim tea.
Ite intok am kau churearn ti hiia.

Luisa: That way. Hmm.

Andres: Ah. But it is real damnation in the mountains, truly God.
I really wised up there.

Luisa: A few bones, you would gather anything.
Or where there were homes before, a long time ago,
we would pick what is thrown there, and even if it is bitter,
we would boil it and we would eat it,
we would feed it to the little children.

Andres: Or if one has four, three leather sandals,
then you take one, toast it, and you would eat it.

Luisa: Yesterday, like compadre Reyno was saying.
Remember, he found a stack of leather sandals in a trench
and he toasted all of them when he arrived. [*Laughter.*]

Andres: Yes, that's how we felt, see.
That's how we experienced it.

Maria: And those little animals also,
like what are they called, the lizards?

Andres: Iguanas, is that what you are talking about?
Well, you just trusted your luck as you went along.
You would eat what you find.

Luisa: Badgers, things, mountain roadrunners,
they would eat everything they found.

Maria: And what are *churuim*?

Luisa: Bells, they look like cats; they have long tails,
little pointed noses.

Andres: Badgers, say the Mexicans.

Luisa: The Mexicans call them badgers.
And we call them mountain roadrunners.[6]

---

6. It seems likely that Luisa and Andres are here referring to coatis.

Maria: Kau churream?

Luisa: Heewi.

Andres: Heewi. Kaupo,
   inen sivapo, hak huni tettene bwan.

Maria: Chikulim ket ama aanen?

Andres: Ili kau chikulim ket ama aayuk.

Luisa: Ama aane si'ime.

Andres: Kau chikulim tea, iiliti.
   Im hak ili velleppani.

Maria: Huname ket am bwabwa'e?

Andres: Bwe, kia aa tea'u pareehopo aa bwa'ane.
   Aa teaka'u bwa'ane.

Luisa: Kaita, kaita perdonaroane.

Andres: Heewi.

Luisa: Ili usek chea kia a'apo kaa aa bwa'ane,
   ili usimsu aa bwa'atuane.

[. . .]

Andres: Im vatwepo te hiva si mamya vakim bwa'e.
   Tomaatem, kolmeenam, torim, hu'upam.

Maria: Torim ket bwabwa'awa?

Andres: Heewi. Katin bweere.
   Kaa am vitla? Kaa am ta'a empo, hewi?

Maria: Kaa am ta'a.

Luisa: Inen huyammet totosak, sankakara.

Andres: Totosate kechia. Bweerek karine.

Maria: Mountain roadrunners?

Luisa: Yes.

Andres: Yes. In the mountains,
this way, in the cliffs, anywhere, they run around.

Maria: Are there mice there also?

Andres: Little mountain mice are also there.

Luisa: Everything is there.

Andres: Mountain mice they are called, they are small.
They are this small.[7]

Maria: You ate those also?

Andres: Well, whatever you found, equally you ate it.
Whatever you found you ate.

Luisa: Nothing, nothing was spared.

Andres: Yes.

Luisa: When you have small children you do not eat it,
you feed the children.

[. . .]

Andres: Here at the river we even ate some boiled American nightshade.[8]
Tomatoes, honey, wood rats, mesquite pods.

Maria: Are wood rats eaten also?

Andres: Yes. Remember, they are big.
You haven't seen them? You don't know them, yes?

Maria: Don't know them.

Luisa: They have their nests in the trees, scraggly ones.

Andres: They have nests also. Big houses.

---

7. He measures about 2.5 inches with forefinger and thumb.
8. *Solanum americanum*.

Luisa: Hunama veha yeu am tosaa vak . . .
mohaktaka veha
hunama yeu am wiikne, am suaakai.

Maria: Kaa yee keke?

Andres: Ana'aka. Yee kek kaa yee suutottoha.
Ya ves kee, alian veha
kia kutanaat tu'isi aa pittane,
kia pusim yeu ruktek
hunak veha aa suutoine.
Ite intok si kolmeenam bwa'en,
tosai navommake.

FIGURE 4 A Hiaki woman with a basket of *torim* in Guaymas in 1908. Arizona Historical Society, PC 078, Mathews Photograph Collection, box 3, album #54473, page 79, #IV.

Luisa: There you poke them . . .
you take it apart, then
take them out of there, after killing them.

Maria: Don't they bite?

Andres: Yes. When they bite you they do not let go.
You see, before, then as they say,
you just squeeze the neck,
then when the eyes bug out,
then you let it go.
We also were eating honey,
with white prickly-pear cactus.

How to Hide a Fire (Luisa and Andres)

Andres and Luisa describe how, when you would set up camp, you had to be very careful building fires. They must not smoke too much. You couldn't build a fire at night because it would be seen from far away; you could only build one in broad daylight, at noon, behind a small stone wall you would construct to shield it from prying eyes.

Luisa: Intok kia hak huni,
hunuen veha hakun bweere kawimmet hikat
kampamentota yechak,
veha hunaman si'ime uchi nau yahine familia.

Andres: Ta intok kia, hewi,
empo si bwichíiatetek huni'i haivu,
"Si bwichíia Maala."
Bwichiata huni kaa tu'ure.
Haivu et chaene.
"Unna bwichíia maala,
ili aa tuucha," ti eu hiuna.

Maria: Kaa machiak hiva naya'ane?

Andres: Kaa machiak chea mekka maachi kawimmet.
Hunaka huni kaa tu'ure.

Luisa: Tua luulakateko.

Andres: Tetam veha ori, tu'ulisi koateine.
Hunama veha kaa mekka machine.
Hunak veha na'arine.
Hunuen te aa pasaaroala.

Luisa: And just anywhere,
that way somewhere up on the big mountains
we would set up camp,
then there all the families would come together again.

Andres: But just, yes,
when you make a lot of smoke already,
"Too much smoke, mother."
They did not like the smoke either.
They would already be yelling at you.
"Too much smoke, mother,
put it out a little," they would say to you.

Maria: You would build fires only at night?

Andres: At night it can be seen farther away on the mountain.
They did not like that either.

Luisa: Right at noon.

Andres: With the rocks, they made a wall.
There it was not visible far away.
Then you would make a fire.
That's how we experienced it.

Making Fire (Luisa)

Luisa describes how to make a fire with a flint and tinder, lighting a wick in a little oil lamp like a shell, and how they could use that to light their cigarettes. She talks about how they would smoke dried chili pepper leaves or queen's wreath leaves and flowers, since there was no tobacco. She also describes how to make a fire using powdered dried cardon cactus buds for tinder and a seep willow stick to light it, rubbing the stick in the tinder to create heat and start the fire. Luisa and the author marvel at the intelligence of the Hiaki people, who figured out all these methods for

Maria: Ori, haisa, haisa intok tahita hooa?

Luisa: Abwe...

Maria: Kaa fohforok humaku'u.

Luisa: Ta ii chea kaa oviachi; islaavom.
Kaa am ta'a?

Maria: Kaa am ta'a.

Luisa: Islavo meechammea.
Katin ili kachimbam kaa memecha,
sasawali, lolo'alae.
A'ayun ta i'an kaita kechia.
I'an kia ume ori senderonimmea hiva vivam tatta.

Maria: Heewi.

Luisa: Hunak intok mecham hippuen im veeppanim.
Huname veha, ori chuktaine,
sisiwokta ili i'a veleeppanik.
Hunai veha inen...
hunaka metta veha kahkopo am tuttaine, hewi.

survival. Luisa talks about how she would discuss this with her children, emphasizing that women as well as men would make fires, and how this contrasts with today's ways, when things are so easy that you can just light a match whenever you want a fire. Her children would dismiss her accounts, saying they were just Hiaki beliefs, but she emphasizes the truth of her words. Fires would always be burning, and this becomes a kind of metaphor for the unconquerable will of the Hiaki people to survive and resist. Even when they were lynched, when their children and mothers were killed, they would never surrender; they would always defend themselves.

Maria: Well, how, how did you make your fire?

Luisa: Well . . .

Maria: You probably did not have any matches.

Luisa: But this was not difficult; flint.
Do you know what they are?

Maria: I don't know them.

Luisa: With the wick of a flint.
Remember the little lamps that had a little wick,
yellow and round.
They used to exist but now they no longer exist.
Now they just light their cigarettes with lighters.

Maria: Yes.

Luisa: Then they used to have a wick about this size.
Those then, well, you would cut
a little metal, this size.[9]
With that, then this way . . .
that wick you would stick in the shell, yes?

---

9. Doña Luisa indicates about an inch with her forefinger and thumb, to show how long the wick was.

| | Hunama veha inen am ore'ene.
| | Hunaa veha sik chihakti orek hunak veha veetine huname chiinim.

Maria: Oo.

Luisa: Hunamea veha vivata tatta.

Maria: Ta vivam ala hiva hippuen?

Luisa: Vivam kia kokoi sawam hunen ya'ane.
Masa'asai sewata, sawata
wawachaka, am yeyena.
Kaita viivam. Hunuka hiva im yena.
Intok hunuen, huname kaa hippuetek intok echom kaa ta'a?

Maria: Nee am hikkaila, echom.

Luisa: Huname ili echo asoola wakiam
yostilatune, ili, ili, ili voa lolovolai, wawakiatune.
Hunamet veha taatne.
Kaa taheko, kaita hippueteko,
kaa islavom hippueteko.
Hunait veha taatne hewi?
Vachomo wakiata.
Hunaka veha ili wohoktaka, hochisi aa oreka.
Hunaka veha inen aa hootaitine.
Taatne. Hunu'u veha taatne tea.
Hunaa veha bwichiataitine.
Inen. Hunaa veha tahitine.
Hunait veha na'ane.

Maria: Heewi. Hunuka nee kaa hu'uneiyan.
Haisa tua aa hohoan ti nee eene. [*Laughter.*]

Luisa: Hunueni.

Maria: Pos si kaita hippue.

> Then you would do this.
> Then when it sparks, well, then the cotton will burn.

Maria: Oh.

Luisa: With those they would light their cigarettes.

Maria: But did they always have cigarettes?

Luisa: For cigarettes they would smoke chili pepper leaves.
> The flower, leaves of the queen's wreath vine,
> dried, they would smoke them.
> No cigarettes. That's all they smoked.
> And when they did not have those, do you know the cardon cactus?

Maria: I have heard of them, the cardon cactus.

Luisa: Those little cardon cactus buds that are dry,
> that have fallen down, the little fuzzy ones, they would be dry.
> With those we would make a tinder nest.
> When we did not have fire, when we have nothing,
> when we did not have the flints.
> On those, then we would start the fire, yes?
> The dry seep willow.
> We made a little hole [notch] in it, after making a fine powder.
> Then with that we would start to rub it [into the dry cardon flower buds].[10]
> *Taatne.* That is called *taatne.*
> Then that will begin to smoke.
> Like this.[11] Then that will start to burn.
> Then on that you will start the fire.

Maria: Yes. I did not know that.
> I always wondered how it was done. [*Laughter.*]

Luisa: That way.

Maria: Well, since they had nothing.

---

10. Doña Luisa makes a motion with her hands as if rubbing a spindle.
11. She rubs her hands together again to illustrate.

Luisa: Hm, hmm. Ta pos si ho . . .
sabe Dios que haksa humak si'imeta suawaula.

Maria: Si intelihentem . . . ume yoeme.

Luisa: Heewi. Si'imeta hunua suawa,
haksa humak ameu yeu machialataka,
veha hunuka veha hooa.
Hunu'u chea kaa oviachi aet taatpo.
Hunaa veha taatne tea.
Hunaka veha tahita ori, ya'ane. Ho.
Hunue veha haivu chuuvatuk
haivu kia seriokamta venasi naya'ine.

Maria: [*Laughs.*]

Luisa: Heewi. Hunuen aa, hunuen im aa hooa
ume hentem, yoeme. Kaita uhyorim.
Kaita haksa am hippue tiaka
hak wam am eiya'ane, heewi?
Ta pos uu yoeme, pos kaa oviachi. Hak huni . . .

Maria: Kovak.

Luisa: Heewi. Pos aa ya'avaetek, kaa oviachi.
Hunuen veha . . . aa ya'ane, lauti.

Maria: I'ansu kia kaachin anmachine . . .

Luisa: Heewi.

Maria: . . . kaa fofforoko.

Luisa: Heewi, i'an intok kia pohporom hiva waata.

Maria: Heewi.

Luisa: Ite hunen hiune.
"Itesu kaa taheka huni bweerem naya'ane," ti nee hiune.
Usim intok,
ume in asoam intok hunen neu hiune.
"Apoko empo ket nan . . . naya'ane?" ti neu hiune.

Luisa: Hm, hmm. Well, see . . .
Creator knows where they gained all this knowledge.

Maria: They are intelligent, the Hiaki people.

Luisa: Yes. They have all that knowledge,
who knows how they learned it, that,
that they then are doing all this.
That is not difficult, to rub a stick to start a fire.
That is called *taatne*.
Then that fire, well, then you will make it. See.
With that then later,
you will already have a fire as if you had matches.

Maria: [*Laughs.*]

Luisa: Yes. That is how, that is how
the people did it, the Hiakis. Nothing pretty.
Just because they say that they have nothing,
one cannot look down on them, yes?
But the Hiaki people, well, it was not difficult. Anywhere . . .

Maria: Very intelligent.

Luisa: Yes. When they want to do something, it is not difficult.
That way, they will do it, quickly.

Maria: And now they don't know what to do . . .

Luisa: Yes.

Maria: . . . when they don't have matches.

Luisa: Yes. And now they only want matches.

Maria: Yes.

Luisa: We say it this way.
"We didn't have matches, but we had big fires," I would say.
And the children,
my children would say to me,
"And you would make a fire?" they would say to me.

"Abwe hee," ti nee au hiune.
"Apoko oviachi?" ti nee hiune.
"Kaa o'owim hiva nanna.
Hunen vetchi'ivosi ite haamuchim huni nanna,"
ti nee ameu hihia. [*Laughs.*]
Hunuen nee ameu hihia, bwan.

Maria: Hak huni hiva ili veetine, heewi, uu tahi?

Luisa: Heewi.

Maria: Kaa tutuke.

Luisa: Hmm. Hunuen veha nee ameu hiune.
"Haisa em, eme'e kaita pasaroala
kialikun em kaa hu'unea," ti ne ameu hiune.
"Hunuen intok eme'e kaa yee sualne," ti nee ameu hihia.
"Pos huyu'u veha kia Hiak kreyensia tea," ti neu hiune.
"Heewi, lutu'uria," ti nee ameu hiune.

Maria: Kaa kreyensia, tua lutu'uria.

Luisa: Hunuen nee ameu hiune. Tua . . .

Maria: Ta komo kaa archivaroari, hewi? Kaita tua . . .

Luisa: Heewi. Kaita.

Maria: Kaita tua . . .
Es que uu yoi pos kaa aa archivaroa,
porque para él es una vergüenza.

Luisa: Heewi. Kialikun veha . . . intok kia . . .

Maria: Kaita hunuka waata.

Luisa: Heewi.

Maria: Kaa . . .

Luisa: Intok ii Hiaki hakwo huni kaa kova'i, hewi?
Kaa au nenenka.

Maria: Kaa au nenenka.

"Well, yes," I would say to them.
"Is it difficult?" I would say.
"Not only the men make fires.
That's why we women also make fires,"
I say to them. [*Laughs.*]
Well, this is what I say to them.

Maria: The fires would always be burning somewhere, yes?

Luisa: Yes.

Maria: They don't go out.

Luisa: Hmm. This is what I will say to them.
"You have, you have not experienced anything,
that is why you do not know," I will say to them.
"And then you do not believe us," I say to them.
"Well, they say that that is just Hiaki beliefs," they say to me.
"Yes, that is true," I will say to them.

Maria: They are not just beliefs, they are the truth.

Luisa: I say that to them. Really . . .

Maria: But since none of this is recorded, yes? Nothing really . . .

Luisa: Nothing.

Maria: Nothing really . . .
It is because the Mexicans did not want to record this,
because for them it is something to be ashamed of.

Luisa: Yes. That is why . . . and just . . .

Maria: They do not want any of that [to be made public].

Luisa: Yes.

Maria: Not . . .

Luisa: And the Hiaki has never been defeated, yes?
They do not surrender.

Maria: They do not surrender themselves.

Luisa: Kaa au nenenka, kia hakwo huni'i.
Es de que hunuen haksa suawa,
hain chu'umvenasi suawa.
Hain hikau wiikwa,
vem usimmak chukti malaka susuawa,
ta kaa emo nenenka.
Hiva emo defendiaroa.

Being a Child in the Mountains (Luisa and Maria Hesus)

Luisa and Maria Hesus discuss what life was like in the mountains. Luisa remembers going many days without food or drink. Maria Hesus was so small when her family was living in the mountains, before she and her mother and siblings were captured, that she only remembers a few things. She remembers refraining from telling her mother how hungry

M.H.: "Karay, si hiokot maachi kaupo,"
ti hiune uu papa.
"Reeve te tua woi ta'apo
huni kaa hi'ibwaka ama hoone," ti hiune.

Luisa: Hitaa, woi ta'apo?
Haiki, mamni ta'apo huni kaa hi'ibwane.

M.H.: Kaa hi'ibwane. Kaita.

Luisa: Ili va'ak intok kia iilikim ili pompomtane,
kaa am hi'isuvaeteko.

M.H.: Heewi.

Luisa: Hamut intok usek intok a'apo kaa he'eka
huni ili uusim am hi'ituane.

M.H.: A'apo am hi'ituane tea bwan.
Hunu'u kaa yo'otuka ama weamsuk, kechia.

Luisa: They never surrendered, never.
They were killed everywhere,
and they were killed like dogs.
And even when they were lynched,
and the children and their mothers were killed,
still they did not surrender.
They always defended themselves.

---

she was, because she knew that her mother had no food for her. She later wondered how they survived in the mountains and avoided being bitten by the poisonous snakes and insects there. She talks about walking through the mountains at night, and how her saint, the icon of St. Francis her mother tied around her neck, would keep her safe from falling. She kept that icon all the way to Mexico City, after she and her family were captured and deported.

M.H.: "Good heavens! It is very deplorable in the mountains,"
my father would say.
"Half of the time we would go for two days
sitting there with nothing to eat," he would say.

Luisa: What, two days?
More, five days even without eating.

M.H.: We did not eat. Nothing.

Luisa: If we had a little water, we would just sip it,
not wanting to finish it.

M.H.: Yes.

Luisa: And a woman with little children would not drink herself,
instead she would save it for the children to drink.

M.H.: They say that she would make them drink, well.
When I was a child I was there too.

Ta uu, uu humak nee vepa chea ili woi wasukte.
Kia si'imeku tokti waate, tokti. Nee intok e'e.
Haksa veha te yeu saka'ane,
humaku'u . . . haz de cuenta que nee kotne.
Hakun veha nee yeu yevihne.
Ili usim veha nee vitchune am yeeweo.
Nee ket amemak yeune ili usimmake.
O si nee tevaure o nee kaa tevaure kaa nee momonte
porque nee hu'unea, mala kaita hippue.
Mala veha humak itot mammattene.
Ili sawata itou bwihne, ili oona.
"Noolia, aa bwa'e," ti hiune.
Sawa. De las que nos dieron anteayer,
hunaka veha itom makne.
Un pedacito, un poquito de sal y un trago de agua, total.
Ho, haksa ili muunim, tahkaim, kaita.

Luisa: Kaita kafe.

M.H.: Kaita!

Luisa: Kaita teune. Itepo huni kaita.

M.H.: Kaita! Bwa'ame kaita.
Hunum veha te hiokot aa pasaroak hunum kaupo.
Ho, katte hu'unea
o si chuvvatuk te hi'ibwaka to'otene, kaita.
I'an veha nee hunuen au hiune,
"Bueno, Reyno," ti nee au hiune,
"hunum kaupo rehtiwau,
haisa kaita machilim?"
"Ana'aka."
"Vakochim?"
"Ana'aka."
"Hunume intok haksa?
Haksa rehteka kaa itom ke'eka?" ti nee au hiune.
"Abwe vem hoarapo," ti hiune Reyno.

Luisa: Abwe, tua e'akai.
Tua kaita vitne.

But I was younger than [Dolores], who was two years older.
He remembered everything, everything. And I didn't.
Sometimes we would go out,
maybe . . . it seems as if I was asleep.
I would arrive somewhere.
I would watch the other little kids playing.
I would start to play with them.
If I was hungry or not hungry, I would not say anything
because I knew that Mom had nothing.
Mom would sometimes notice us.
A little mountain turnip she would hand to us, a little salt.
"Come on and eat it," she would say.
Mountain turnip. The ones we ate day before yesterday,
that is what she would give us.
A little piece, a little bit of salt, and a sip of water, that's all.
See. Where were the beans, tortillas, nothing.

Luisa: No coffee.

M.H.: Nothing!

Luisa: We would find nothing. We also had nothing.

M.H.: Nothing! Food, nothing.
We suffered very much in the mountains.
See, we did not know
if later we would eat before going to sleep, nothing.
Now I say this to him,
"Well, Reyno," I say to him,
"when they were in the mountains,
weren't there any scorpions?"
"Of course."
"Snakes?"
"Of course."
"And where were they?
Where were they that they did not bite us?" I would say to him.
"Well, in their homes," Reyno would say.

Luisa: Well, that is true.
We would really not see anything.

M.H.: Kaita. Mari. Kaita.

Luisa: Kaita vitne bwan.

M.H.: Kulupti intok katin kia tukaapo huni te vo'o hoone.

Luisa: Kaita. Kia puhpo bwihtavenasi katne. Kaita.

M.H.: Nee kia kokkocheka huni weene.
Hunu'u San Paasiskota katin hunum vo'okame,
hunaka nee tekiakan.
"Peronim a'avo kaate."
Mala sep uka Santota nu'uka
nee aa koktuane.
Hunuemak veha nee aamak vo'o hoone.
Intok nee hakwo huni kaa wechek tea Santotamake.
Hun'u Mehikou noitek, hunu'u San Pasisko.

Luisa: [*Laughs.*]

M.H.: Hunuka hiva ne kokaka weamne tea,
bwan, kaupo uka San Pasiskota.
Intok kaa aamak wechek.
Hakwo huni'i. Wechek aa hamtae'an.

Luisa: Hmm.

M.H.: Ta mala intok si taho'orimpo aa vihtaeka nee aa makne, ti hiia,
uka San Pasiskota.
Hunuen, hunuen aa puateka te
im, imin Waymammeu te yeu toiwak tea San Pasiskota.
Hunuen aa puatekae aman yeu yepsak, tea.

M.H.: Nothing, Mari. Nothing.

Luisa: We did not see anything, well.

M.H.: And remember, sometimes we used to walk at night.

Luisa: Nothing. We walked as if we were blindfolded. Nothing.

M.H.: I would walk half asleep.
That San Francisco that is lying there,
he was my patron saint.
"The bald ones are coming."
Mom would get my patron saint right away
and hang him around my neck.
With him, then I would travel.
And they say I never fell with my saint.
That San Francisco also went to Mexico City with me.

Luisa: [*Laughs.*]

M.H.: They say I always wore him around my neck,
well, in the mountains, San Francisco.
But I never fell with him.
Never. If I fell, he would have broken.

Luisa: Hmm.

M.H.: But Mom always wrapped him in a cloth and gave him to me,
she said,
that San Francisco. That way, that way
I carried him and we
were taken to Guaymas with San Francisco.
Carrying him that way we arrived, they say.

Childbirth and Medical Care in the Mountains (Luisa)

Luisa describes how women in the mountains had no time to rest after childbirth, and no safe place in which to give birth. They would give birth

---

Luisa: Kokoe wattek chea haamuchimtaka
huni kia veha kateka a'asoa.
Chuu'um venasi.

Maria: Hmm.

Luisa: Kia veha weyeka veha asoaka ama tu'utewaka,
taho'orimpo aa yecha'ariawaka,
aa koktuawaka
haivu im vicha aa puatine.

Maria: Ay qué va.

Luisa: Heewi. Hunuen, hunuen weye um kaupo kechia.
Kaita. Kaita wana haksa to'owame.

Maria: Kaa yumhuene?

Luisa: E'e. Kia hunuen asoaka hiva taho'opo,
revo'osampo, aa koktuawako
haivu im vicha weene, kaa asoakamtavenasi.

Maria: Haisa huevenaka kokko hunueni?

Luisa: Wate kokko, ta Dios itom ania,
te kaupo rehteka
kaave kokko a'asoako.

Maria: ¡Fíjate!

Luisa: Fíjate. Im intok yanti hoowaka'apo
intok hunuen tu'isi hoowaka'apo
haksa kokoe watteka huni kokko.

Maria: Heewi, hunuen bwan a'ane.

in the open, or in a makeshift shelter, and then bundle up their infant and keep walking. Still, few died, and Luisa says God must have been caring for them. She describes how they would use a pinch of dirt as a salve on a wound, even a cut umbilical cord, to stop bleeding.

Luisa: When childbirth began, the women
would just bear their babies while walking.
Like dogs.

Maria: Hmm.

Luisa: Then, just standing up, she would take the baby and get cleaned up.
The baby would be placed in a cloth
and suspended around the new mother's neck.
Already she would begin to walk with her new baby in her arms.

Maria: Ay, too much!

Luisa: Yes. That's, that's how it was in the mountains.
Nothing. Nothing, there was no lying down.

Maria: They did not rest?

Luisa: No. Just after giving birth, always, in a cloth,
or a shawl, [the baby] would be suspended from the new mom's neck,
and she would walk away as if she had not just given birth to a baby.

Maria: Did many women die while giving birth or after birth?

Luisa: Some died, but God helped us;
while we were in the mountains
no one died while giving birth.

Maria: Imagine!

Luisa: Imagine. And here where we live in peace,
and this way, even in peace,
some get sick and die.

Maria: Yes, that is what is going on.

Luisa: Im vicha intok e'e.
Kaupo intok kaa kokko, intok kia . . .

Maria: Si emo oulen.

Luisa: Heewi. Intok kia hunain yukeo,
huni'i senu veha ili karpam aa ya'ariaka veha
hunama aa yecha'ine
kuta bweerem ama to'aka veha
huyata ae vepa wattakai hunama hikat
aa yecha'aine.
Intok kia si bwe'um naya'ane pa'aku.
Huname intok kaa tukne, tahim.
Yukeo huni'i,
hiva hunain veetine.

Maria: Bwe!

Luisa: Heewi. Haisa humak,
Dios ket itom a'ania.

Maria: Pos hiva tua, heewi.

Luisa: Heewi. Kaa tutuke hunuen ta'apo.
Hunuen veha aa vitne si'imeta.
Hunuen veha te si'imeta aa pasaroa
intok hunuen veha . . .
Kaita karim iibwan.
Kia hunuen veha te hoone. Nah katne hiva.

Maria: Hittoam intok pos kaita hewi?

Luisa: Kaita. Tua kaita.
Kia veha komo animaalimvenasi a'asoa.
Kaita inyeksiionim, kaita wa'a.
Hitasa ili usi haksa sekapo . . .
hitasa yodeeki ta aet ya'ana'ame,
kaita. Kia veha tua ili bwiata chaetaka
ama aa to'oriaka aa suma'ane. Hmm.
Hunuen am uhu'un ume uusim, kaita.
Yo'owe huni kaita hioriaane.
Tea'u bwa'ane
inen asoako bwan.

Luisa: Not over here.
And in the mountains they didn't die, and just . . .

Maria: They were very brave.

Luisa: Yes. And even if it was raining,
even then, one would make a small tent, then
set it up there.
They would lay some large beams,
then place some branches on top of them
and have her sit there.
And they would make a big fire outside.
And those fires did not go out.
Even though it was raining,
they kept burning.

Maria: Well!

Luisa: Yes. I don't know, perhaps,
God was also helping us.

Maria: Perhaps so, yes.

Luisa: Yes. They did not go out in those days.
That's how we saw everything then.
That's how we experienced everything then.
And then, that's how . . .
There were no houses, well.
We just sat there like that. We just walked around [aimlessly].

Maria: Well, and there were no medications, yes?

Luisa: Nothing. Really nothing.
We just bore children like animals.
There were no injections [for pain], nothing like that.
If a little child, somewhere in the armpit . . .
something, a little salve to be applied,
nothing. Then just take a little pinch of dirt,
pour it in [the wound], and tie it on. Hmm.
That's how we cared for the children, with nothing.
The adults would be careful not to eat anything that would harm them.
They would eat anything they found,
but be careful after giving birth, well.

Maria: Siku chuktak huni'i, kia ili bwiata . . .

Luisa: Heewi, kia ili bwiata chaeta ama aa to'oriane.
Hunuen hiva.
Katte am hihitton ume ili uusim.
I'an intok ket ili usimtaka,
huni'i tu'isi hak hoarapo yeu tomteka
tu'isi vitwamtavenaka huni kokko.

Maria: Kokko bwan.

Luisa: Heewi. Ta hunak kaa kokko.

Maria: Tua bwan. Qué extraño.

Luisa: Tua te hunuen . . . hunuen aa vicha bwan hunum kaupo.
Kaita. Kokoeme.

FIGURE 5 Hiaki mother and child in Arizona, ca. 1910. University of Southern California Libraries, California Historical Society, https://doi.org/10.25549/chs-m16696.

Maria: Even when they cut the cord, they just put a little dirt . . .

Luisa: Yes, they just put a little bit of dirt on it.
That's all.
We did not provide any medicine to the little children.
And now the little children also,
even when they are born at home and
even if they are well cared for, they die.

Maria: Well, they die.

Luisa: Yes, but then [in those days], they did not die.

Maria: Well, really. How strange.

Luisa: Truly, then we . . . that's how we saw it, in the mountains.
Nothing. No sickness.

Health and Hygiene in the Mountains (Luisa and Andres)

Andres and Luisa describe how, despite the danger and hardship, people seemed to be healthy in the mountains; they didn't get sick. They laugh about how the men would be plump, with their cheeks and clothes

---

Maria: Hunama intok ume, hak huni toto entonces, ori . . .

Andres: Bwe kia hak huni aa, aa kuptiriawaka'apo huni.
Tua kaita chansata auk,
kia hiva si'ime tukaapo huni weeka matchune.

Luisa: Vo'o hoaka matchune.

Andres: Si'ime tukaata, kaa hi'ine huni'i.
Hu'ubwa nee katin
ino va'ae tompo . . .

Maria: Ume animaalim intok
kaa enchim molestaroan, komo vakochim?

Andres: Kaita hunak tiempopo, kaita.

Luisa: Tua kaita, intok kia kaa koko'okoe,
hunuu hente, kaupo rehtekai.

Andres: Kaa ko'okoene.
Yantela kia veohkom hopene.
Si a'awine.
No ves kee uu kava'i sukane,
uu manteka hiva yee a'awiria.

Maria: Oo.

Andres: Kaa i'anpo hakvenasi ko'okoene.
I'an veha uu ko'okoa si vu'u.
Vatnaatakai intok e'e.
Si a'awine uu yoeme.
Tai machiak kia veohkosi anne.

greasy and shiny, from eating horsemeat and fat. There was no time to wash or do laundry in the mountains, and even if they had had time, there was no soap. Sometimes they would use a kind of fruit, the desert gourd, for soap, but more often there was no time or inclination for washing.

Maria: And there the, they slept anywhere . . .

Andres: Well, just anywhere, wherever night came upon us.
Whenever we really did not have a chance
we just spent all night walking until morning.

Luisa: We spent the night walking.

Andres: All night long we did not drink either.
Just now, remember,
I filled my stomach with water . . .

Maria: And the animals
did not bother you, like the snakes?

Andres: There was really nothing at that time, nothing.

Luisa: Really nothing, and they just did not get sick,
those people, while they were in the mountains.

Andres: They would not get sick.
Instead they would have shiny cheeks.
They would be fat.
That's because horsemeat is warm,
the lard makes one fat.

Maria: Oh.

Andres: Not like today when one is sick.
Today there is a lot of sickness.
And before there was nothing.
The men were very fat.
In the light of the fires, they were just shiny.

Luisa: [*Chuckles.*] Kia veveloohkom hopene.

Andres: Supem huni veohkone,
　　ii puhva huni veohkone. [*Laughter.*]

Luisa: Pos si haisa au a'anaako pos ochoko si'ime . . .

Andres: Pos si haksa savum teaka aa vaksiane? Kaaku.

Luisa: . . . ii manteka, kia velosasalaine uu taho'ori.
　　Kia tuturuivenane hewi?
　　Pos si kaa vavaksiana . . .

Andres: Ili usim kaa vitla,
　　im kaa kia haisa ume chomim kaa tutu'ute, hewi?

Maria: Hmm.

Andres: Kia hunalevenam supine, veohkom.

Luisa: Saaweam. [*Chuckles.*]

Andres: Haksa, haksa tiempota hippueka au hipaksiariane?
　　Saavum huni kaita.

Maria: Oo.

Luisa: Ket ume hitam amuulim[12] teammea,
　　hiva ili hipaksia.

Andres: Hunaa hiva, ta hunaa intok hahhawatek
　　kaita tiempo, bwan.

Maria: Hmm.

Luisa: Katchansan hipaksiavaeka eene,
　　katchan uva'avaeka eene.

Andres: Kaita.

Maria: Hmm.

Andres: Hunuen te aa pasaroak.

---

12. This gourd is also known as *teta'ahau* or *tetahaum*.

Luisa: [*Chuckles.*] They just had shiny cheeks.

Andres: Even their clothes were shiny.
Even this face would be shiny. [*Laughter.*]

Luisa: Well, how could one get dressed, if everything is greasy . . .

Andres: Well, where would one find soap to wash? Nowhere.

Luisa: . . . a little grease, just makes the clothing shiny.
It would just look thick, yes?
Well, it would not get washed . . .

Andres: Have you not seen the little children,
they just wipe their mucus here [pointing to his shirt sleeve], yes?

Maria: Hmm.

Andres: They would just have their clothing like that, shiny.

Luisa: Their pants [or undergarments]. [*Chuckles.*]

Andres: Where, where would they have time to wash for themselves?
There wasn't even any soap.

Maria: Oh.

Luisa: Also with the things, with only the coyote gourd, as it is named,
we did a little washing.

Andres: Only that, but when one is being chased
there is no time, well.

Maria: Hmm.

Luisa: One doesn't even feel like washing,
doesn't even feel like bathing.

Andres: Nothing.

Maria: Hmm.

Andres: That's how we experienced it.

The Problem of Crying Babies (Luisa and Andres)

Luisa and Andres describe the terrible lengths to which people would go to avoid capture, even going so far as to smother babies who couldn't be quieted. Mothers with crying babies would be left alone; no one would want to be with them for fear of discovery and capture.

Maria: Ili usim veha si ama kokok?

Luisa: Heewi.

Andres: Bwe si kokok.
Wate chea vem asoam huni sussua.

Luisa: Haksa tua yoim enemigota kaa mekka aneu,
pos kaa nu'uvaetek veha
pos am sussua, am hiavih sussua.

Maria: Hmm.

Andres: Haiti bwani ti au hiuna.

Luisa: Pos hentem veha am omtane.

Andres: Haamuchim si'ime am omtane.

Luisa: Usim bwanim asoak veha omtana, bwan.

Andres: Heewi.

Luisa: E'eusiana.
Kaave amemak aa wee'ii'aane.

Maria: Oo.

Luisa: Hunuen im yee hooa, kaupo.

Andres: Tootettenine.
Hunuen im yee hoan.

Maria: Then many of the little children died there?

Luisa: Yes.

Andres: Well, so many died.
Some even killed their own children.

Luisa: Where the Mexican enemy was not far away,
if they did not want to get caught, then,
well, they killed them, they smothered them.

Maria: Hmm.

Andres: "It is crying too much," they would say to her.

Luisa: Well, then the people would be angry at them.

Andres: The women, all of them, would be angry at them.

Luisa: If they had crying babies, they would be angry at them, well.

Andres: Yes.

Luisa: They [the mother and child] would hide from them.
No one would want her to be with them.

Maria: Oh.

Luisa: That's what they did to us, in the mountains.

Andres: They would run away from them [the mother and child].
That's what they did to us.

Maintaining Ceremonial Life in the Mountains (Luisa)

Luisa describes how, even when people were on the run in the mountains, they found a way to observe holy days, particularly the Lenten ceremonies that are the center of the Hiaki religion. She describes how exiled groups from each pueblo would come together for the necessary processions, even if they had to move camp between Ash Wednesday and Good Friday. The figures of each pueblo's saints, normally kept in the pueblo's church, were carried into the mountains, kept safe by church

---

Maria: Ori, ume yoeme, inen kawipo ane'eteko,
ori o hunak aman anekai, cuando waehmata hunuen,
hunum tiempopo veha, kia veha aa pasaroane,
hewi, kaa, kaita, hita hoone?

Luisa: Ime i'an ama hokame?

Maria: E'e, hunak, ori nahsuawau . . .

Luisa: Bwe, hunak chea kaa kia aa papasaaroan.

Maria: Aa . . .

Luisa: Si'ime pueplo, kada pueplo nah kateme
vem, vem kampamento yecha'iku im Loloriaten.

Maria: Ah, ket hivayu aa . . .

Luisa: Hivayu, hivayu, katim aa tatta'aru.
Primer Vienehpo aa hoa . . .
Miekolehtuk naposa'uwau, sep im naposa'une.
Hak vem hoka'apo huni'i,
hak vem hoka'apo . . . naposa'une.
Hunama veha intuchi omot hakunsa yoim am hahhasuk,
intuchi omot kampamento.
Hunaman Vieneseo yumak
intuchi hunaman kontine.

Maria: Ama kontine.

assistants, and carried in processions as they should be on holy days. The *kantoram*, the ceremonial singers, would sing as loudly as if they were safe in their home pueblo, as if they were not afraid of being heard and captured at any moment. Maria marvels at the dedication of the people and the beauty of maintaining their religious observance even in such dire circumstances, but Luisa seems to feel that of course that is the way it is and should be, noting that even the Hiakis on "the other side," in the United States, maintain their ceremonies despite having been driven from their pueblos.

Maria: Well, the Hiakis, when they were in the mountains,
well, or when they were there that way during Lent,
in those days then, they just let it go by,
yes? Not, nothing, they did not do anything?

Luisa: Those, that are there now?

Maria: No, when they were fighting . . .

Luisa: Well, then, they did not just let it go by.

Maria: Ah . . .

Luisa: All the people, each person who was there,
there, where they set up camp, they celebrated Holy Saturday.

Maria: Ah, so they also always [celebrated] it . . .

Luisa: Always, always, they never forgot it.
On the first Friday they did . . .
On Ash Wednesday, they got their ashes right away.
Wherever they were,
wherever they were . . . they got their ashes.
Then, again, somewhere else, when the Mexicans chased them,
they would set up camp again somewhere else.
There, when Friday arrived,
they would have their procession there again.

Maria: They would have their procession there.

Luisa: Kia hunuen hak nah hoosasaka veha
aa hoone, bwan.

Maria: Hmm.

Luisa: Heewi. Katim...

Maria: Hiva, kaa aa tatta'aru, hewi uka...?

Luisa: E'e. Hiva im kaa aa suutottoha...

Maria: ...uka relihionta.

Luisa: ...hiva kaa aa suutotoha, hiva wasuktia.
Hunu, katim ili huni aa tatta'aru.

Maria: Fíjate. Nee chea hunuka veha kaa, kaa am hooan ti e'an.

Luisa: Hiva, hiva.

Maria: Porque hiva hahhawa ti nee e'an.
I'an yanti hoteka veha... Waehmata veha ori...

Luisa: Tua wasuktim kaa aa suutotoha.

Maria: ¡Fíjate!

Luisa: Lominko, es igual. Hak vem hooka'apo,
hiva kontina. Lominkochi, misatene.
Ela'aposu kaa... kia hak ili,
ori lauti nau oreewak,
hunama veha haivu kontina.

Maria: Santomsu?

Luisa: Bwe hiva am puanama.
Waalupeta hiva nunu'ubwa,
Itom Ae, Dolorosata.
Kiiyohtei aa nunupne.
Woi kiyohteim Waalupekamta nunupne.
Kaa aa toosasaka.
Huname'e veha hiva aa puanamsisime.

Maria: Pos hunume, santom veha
am nokrian humaku'u. [*Laughs*.]

Luisa: That way, wherever they settled, then
 they would do it, well.

Maria: Hmm.

Luisa: Yes. Remember . . .

Maria: They never lost it, yes, the . . . ?

Luisa: No. They never let it go . . .

Maria: . . . the religion.

Luisa: . . . they never let it go, every year.
 That, they never lost, not even a little.

Maria: Imagine. I always felt that then they did not do it anymore.

Luisa: Always, always.

Maria: Because they were always being chased, I felt.
 Now they have settled down . . . Lent, then, well . . .

Luisa: Every year, they never let it go.

Maria: Imagine!

Luisa: Sundays were the same. Wherever they were,
 they always did their processions. On Sunday they celebrated Mass.
 It mattered, not . . . just anywhere a little,
 well, quickly together they would [set up camp],
 then there they would have their procession.

Maria: What about the saints?

Luisa: Well, they always carried them around.
 They always carried Our Lady of Guadalupe,
 Our Lady of Sorrows.
 The female church assistant would carry them.
 Two church assistants carried Our Lady of Guadalupe.
 They never left her.
 They [the church assistants] always carried her.

Maria: Well, then, perhaps those saints
 were probably advocating for them. [*Laughs.*]

Luisa: Heewi.

Maria: Yoemeta.

Luisa: Hmm. Hunueni hiva. Katim aa kopkopta.

Maria: Aa. Hunuka nee kaa hu'uneiyan.
Hiva nee aa pensaroane, hewi? Haisa tua aa hohoa?

Luisa: [*Chuckles.*] Hiva. Haisa i'an im pueplompo, ho.
Lominkot kontina.

Maria: Heewi.

Luisa: Intuchi misatune intok vihpaatune Santo team yuma'ane.
Kia hak horapo huni hiva vihpaate.
Santa Kuh, hiva vihpaatena.
Kia hak kampamentopo hak hookaa huni'i.
Kaa mahaimevenasi si ousi bwikne, ho.

Maria: [*Laughs.*]

Luisa: Hakun kusiata bwikne.

Maria: Kantooram, maehtom . . .

Luisa: Heewi, tua Dios!

Maria: Hmm.

Luisa: Kaita!

Maria: ¡Qué va! Qué bonito hewi?

Luisa: Heewi, katim aa suutottoha.
Hiva im aa weetua uka vem relihion.
Katim aa suutottoha.

Maria: Hain hoowaka huni'i?

Luisa: Heewi. Tua kaa aa suutottoha.
Hiva venasi weye. Haisa i'an kaa vicha?
Ume veha waitana
tua pueplou hoakame yeu haharim veha
konkonte.

Luisa: Yes.

Maria: For the Hiakis.

Luisa: Hmm. That's the only way. They never forgot it.

Maria: Ah. That I did not know.
I always used to think about it, yes? How did they really do it?

Luisa: [*Chuckles.*] Always. The way they do it in the villages, see.
They do the processions on Sunday.

Maria: Yes.

Luisa: Again they did [Sunday] Mass and Vespers when the saint days arrived.
At whatever hour, they did Vespers.
On Holy Cross day, they would always do Vespers.
At whatever encampment, wherever they were settled.
They would sing with great enthusiasm as if they were not afraid,
 you see.

Maria: [*Laughs.*]

Luisa: They would sing loudly.

Maria: The female cultural singers and the male cultural prayer leaders . . .

Luisa: Yes, truly God!

Maria: Hmm.

Luisa: Nothing!

Maria: Too much! How beautiful, yes?

Luisa: Yes, they never let it go.
They continued to carry it out, their religion.
They never let it go.

Maria: It did not matter what they were doing to them?

Luisa: Yes. They really never left it.
They always continue to carry it out. Do you not see it?
Those on the other side [in the United States],
those who were chased out,
they do their processions.

Supplying the Mountain Ceremonies (Luisa and Andres)

Andres and Luisa discuss further how Lenten ceremonies were maintained when the Hiakis were in the mountains, sometimes even under attack from the Mexicans. If Lent was coming up, some Hiakis would go

---

Maria: Ta empo intok hiva ori, waehmata, ori tekipanoa . . .

Luisa: Hiva, hiva hoowa.

Maria: Hiva hoowa.

Andres: Hunuu intok hiva weye ala.
　　　　　Hiva weye.
　　　　　Amak kia kaa Looriatek kia te
　　　　　ama ito tootennine.

Luisa: Kia Lominko kontiwa huni
　　　　　kia hak huni vem hoka'apo,
　　　　　hiva aa weetua, katim aa suutottoha.

Andres: Katim aeveah kopkopte hunuaveah ala.

Luisa: Waehmata yuma'apo, kia hak horapo huni.

Andres: Yantela si kava'im hakun nu'uka
　　　　　si kava'i vakriane ume chapayekam,
　　　　　kantooram.

Luisa: Heewi.

Maria: Huname veha etbwane ume kava'im?

Andres: Heewi. Am etbwakai hiapsam nu'upakai veha . . .

Maria: Ume yoi sontaom am e'etbwarian?

Andres: Heewi, pareehopo, kaa faltaroa.

at night to Mexican settlements or soldiers' camps and steal horses to supply the ceremonial participants—for example, the *kantoram* or the Fariseos. The animals would be brought back alive and butchered for Holy Saturday.

Maria: But you always carried it out, well, Lent . . .

Luisa: Always, always it was done.

Maria: Always done.

Andres: And that has always been done.
    Always going on.
    Sometimes when we just did not do the Gloria
    we would just chase each other around.

Luisa: Even when the Sunday processions were being done,
    wherever they were,
    they continued to do it, they did not let it go.

Andres: They never forgot about that, then.

Luisa: When Lent started, just at any time.

Andres: Without any concern, they would take some horses,
    butcher them, cook them for the Fariseos[13]
    and the female church singers.

Luisa: Yes.

Maria: They would steal those horses?

Andres: Yes. They would steal the live animals, then . . .

Maria: They stole the horses from the Mexican soldiers?

Andres: Yes, equally, they did not leave anyone out.

---

13. Fariseos: Participants representative of Roman soldiers.

Luisa: Yoi sontaom intok inen hak hoarampo yeu watwatte.
Hoaram saltataroa.

Andres: Heewi, pareehopo, kaa sontaom hiva.
Ma ite im ho'ak hewi?
Im yeu yahak, huni kava'im ama teak
pos am nu'upane, hihiapsame.

Luisa: Etbwana, tukaapo.

Andres: Looriatuvawau veha
am sua'ane. Peutina.

Maria: Yoim hita e'etbwarian o mismo yoemem?

Luisa: Heewi, yoim.

Andres: Yoim e'etbwarian.

Escape to Nogales (Reyno)

Reyno describes how, when he was still only a babe in arms, his family escaped Calles's final round of deportations by walking first to Hermosillo and then to Continental, Arizona, close to Nogales. He describes a picture of him and his siblings that was taken there, on his birthday, which his paternal grandmother had.

Reyno: Hunuen kau vetana yahisuwak, kee gaacho.
Si hiokot aa pasaroak. "Hitavetchi'ivo kun,
hitavetchi'ivo kun, i'an im, ime aman hooka?"
"Ume yo'owe inien aa pasaroaka veha."
"Por qué, maala?" Hunuen hiia intok achaitukao,
Ermosiyou emo ho'akan ti hiia,
uka Izabalta hunum yee varkaroau.
Hmm, Izaabalta.

Luisa: And the Mexican soldiers would enter the homes.
　　　　They assaulted the homes.

Andres: Yes, equally, but not just the soldiers.
　　　　Just as we live here, yes?
　　　　When they arrived here, if they found horses,
　　　　well, they would bring them, alive.

Luisa: They would be stolen, at night.

Andres: When it was going to be Gloria [Holy Saturday]
　　　　they would kill them, butcher them.

Maria: They would steal from the Mexicans or also from the Hiakis?

Luisa: Yes, the Mexicans.

Andres: They stole from the Mexicans.

Reyno: When they returned from the mountains, it was terrible.
　　　　They suffered a lot. "Why is it then,
　　　　why is it then, now they, they are over there?"[14]
　　　　"The elders experienced it this way, then."
　　　　"Why, Mom?" our father used to ask.
　　　　They used to live in Hermosillo, he said,
　　　　when Izábal was deporting us [the Hiakis].
　　　　Hmm. Izábal.

---

14. Meaning, why do some Hiakis live in the United States?

Huntuan ultimopo uka Kaayesta
uchi ultimopo yee varkaroau, ho,
hunak veha Ermosiyou emo sahak ti hiia.

Luisa: Hmm, hmm.

Reyno: Entonces nee veha ilitchika aman nuk kimuwak,
aman waitana. Tosampo iva'anama'awa.
Hunum hak taawak ume yo'owe, Nogalimpo,
wannavo, ori haisa teuwawa,
Kontinental tea.

Luisa: Hmm, hmm.

Reyno: Hunum veha hooka.
Hunum, hunum veha nee wasuktek humaku'u.
Huntuan hunuman nee weaman
chukti inepo Kontinentalpo.
Entonces hunum Kontinentalpo ho'awak intok
Nogalimvewit ili lomanpo.
Hunaman ket yoem hoaratukan, Nogalitom.
Ta'ata yeu weyeepo.
Hunama ori Loloriatun.

Luisa: Hmm.

Maria: Hmm, hmm.

Reyno: Uka haka orita empo kaa ta'ak? Haka Chepatukauta?

Luisa: Ana'aka.

Reyno: Ahh, huna'a. Huna'a ume rettratom hippuen ibwan.
Nee bwan hiva, hiva au am a'aunemcheaka,
huni hiva kaa au am a'awak.

Luisa: Ay.

Reyno: Hunama'a, hunama ori huma itom yeewe'epo,
humak itom rettrataroak humaku'u.

Luisa: Hmm.

So at the end, when Calles
again started the final deportation, see,
that's when they went to Hermosillo, he said.

Luisa: Hmm, hmm.

Reyno: Then, when I was small, I was taken over there [to the United States],
over there on the other side. I was carried around in a blanket.
There, somewhere, the adults stayed, in Nogales,
on the other side, well, what do they call it,
it is named Continental.

Luisa: Hmm, hmm.

Reyno: That's where they were.
There, there, then maybe I had a birthday.
That's why, I was walking around over there,
there in Continental.
So then, they lived there in Continental and
near Nogales in the little hills.
The Hiakis also lived in Little Nogales,
where the sun comes out [i.e., to the east].
Over there they used to celebrate the Gloria [Holy Saturday].

Luisa: Hmm.

Maria: Hmm, hmm.

Reyno: Did you know my paternal grandmother? The late Chepa?

Luisa: Yes.

Reyno: Ah, that one. That one had the pictures, well.
I, well, always, always felt like I wanted to ask her for them,
even so I never asked her for them.

Luisa: Ay.

Reyno: There, there, well, perhaps where we were playing,
maybe she took our picture.

Luisa: Hmm.

Reyno: Huntuan uu saitukau Ramasio veha nee puaweyek.
Nee intok ili [*inaudible*] kovakame nee vuak.

Luisa: [*Laughs.*]

Reyno: Imin intok pochilai intok ili supem suma'ari.
Uu veha inen nee iva'a wek.
Nee intok inen henompo cha'akan bwan . . .

Luisa: Hmm, hmm.

Reyno: Ii hiva ama yeu siimla.
Im vicha veha nee puhvak. Sai Hesustukau intok chunula katek intok wate ili uusim.

Luisa: Hmm, hmm.

M.H.: Katootam yeuwa.

Reyno: Heewi, nau katoota bwan. Katootampo nau yeewe.

Reyno: My older brother Damasio was holding me like so.
And I had on a bonnet with a small [*inaudible*] head cover.

Luisa: [*Laughs.*]

Reyno: And over here it was short and the little dress was tied.
Then that one [Damasio] was holding me.
And I was hanging on to his shoulder, well . . .

Luisa: Hmm, hmm.

Reyno: Only this one [*pointing to himself*] came out.
I was facing this way. And late older brother Hesus
and the other little kids were squatting.

Luisa: Hmm, hmm.

M.H.: Playing marbles.

Reyno: Yes, well, they were playing marbles. They were playing marbles.

Walking to Tucson (Andres)

Andres describes how, when he was young, he and his family walked to Tucson, to Little Mesquite and Big Mesquite by the river. This is a place in Tucson where Hiakis used to live but where now there are only white people, on the southwest corner of Ajo and I-19. Mountain Hiakis would conceal their hide covers there. These were covers made of cowhide which were used to tie supplies onto horses or burros. When Andres was young, his whole family walked there from Hiak Vatwe, including his mom and older sister. There was plenty of water and food along the way, and they took their time. The journey took about four months. At one point when they were in Green Mountain (Siari Kaupo), they were attacked by Mexicans. Andres describes taking a packhorse to a spring called Outside Water Lily (Kapo Va'am Pa'aku), where the family was gathering tubers called *sa'a bwe'ei* to eat. The horse really started to jump when the Mexicans opened fire.

Luisa: Ii chea Tusoneu kateka huni kaa aman ta'a.

Andres: Heewi. Looriau huni nee ket chuvala hipu'uwan.

Maria: Haisa intok empo aman yepsak?

Andres: Wokimmea.

Maria: Ii . . .

Luisa: Chikta aa malawa . . .

Andres: Heewi.

Luisa: . . . akowa, si'ime wokimmea sahak. Familiata, bwan.

Andres: Kialikun nee hunum revvei hiva ili ta'a,

FIGURE 6 An escaped Hiaki family living in Arizona. University of Southern California Libraries, California Historical Society, https://doi.org/10.25549/chs-m16691.

Luisa: Although this one was in Tucson, he is not familiar with it.

Andres: Yes. I was even in Gloria also for a short time.

Maria: And how did you get there?

Andres: By walking.

Maria: This . . .

Luisa: His mother too . . .

Andres: Yes.

Luisa: . . . older sister, they all came walking. The family, well.

Andres: That's why I only remember a little bit of it,

ili Hu'upapo intok Bwe'u Hu'upa teapo.

Maria: Aa. Ili Hu'upapo nim ori, ori naana, tatatukau ama ho'akan . . .

Andres: Heewi.

Maria: . . . hunama Hu'upapo. I'an kia ringo hoara.

Andres: Huna'a?

Maria: Heewi, ama vatwetanaachi.

Andres: Heewi.

Maria: Kia ringo hoara.

Andres: Ori, humaku'u. Ori, hakia intok imin vo'oka um Bwe'u Hu'upapo, hewi?

Maria: Heewi.

Andres: Hunama ori nakapaalim e'eson um se'epo, ume yoeme um kawiu im aman yahakame.

Maria: Hitaa intok huname'e, nakapaalim?

Luisa: Bwe waka veam . . . inen pisaam amea suma'ane.

Andres: Waka veam, siarim im am sekawaasimne. Mochilata ae suma'ine.

Luisa: Mochilota, mochilota ae suma'ane.

Andres: Heewi.

Maria: Oo.

Luisa: Hunaa bweeka, im veekkani, hewi? Imin veha nakane. Imin, imin aa suma'ane.

Andres: Imin veha wikiata ama yeu tuttaine.

Luisa: Hunama veha yeu am tuttaine. Wikiata, korreata. Hunai veha piisam . . .

Big Mesquite and Little Mesquite.

Maria: Ah. In Little Mesquite my, well, well, my grandmother [and] grandfather lived there . . .

Andres: Yes.

Maria: . . . there in Mesquite. Now there are only Anglo homes there.

Andres: There?

Maria: Yes, there by the river.

Andres: Yes.

Maria: Just Anglo homes.

Andres: Well, maybe. Well, there is a small arroyo there at Big Mesquite, yes?

Maria: Yes.

Andres: There, well, they used to hide the *nakapaalim* [tumpline bundles] in the sand, the Hiakis who arrived there from the mountains.

Maria: And what are those, the *nakapaalim*?

Luisa: Well, they are made of cowhide . . .
this is what they used to wrap and tie their blankets.

Andres: Cowhides, fresh, were wound under their arms.
Their tumpline bundles were tied with them.

Luisa: Tumpline bundles, tumpline bundles would be tied with it.

Andres: Yes.

Maria: Oh.

Luisa: That one is wide, this size, yes?
It would have ears here.
Here, here it would be tied.

Andres: Here, then, they would insert a string through it.

Luisa: There, then, they would insert it.
A rope, cord. Then with that the blanket . . .

Andres: Hunaa veha nakapaliisi.

Maria: [*Laughs.*] Haisa eme'e vinwatuk aman sahakai?

Andres: Bwe, ite si . . . humak naiki metpo te vo'o hoaka
aman yahak. Ta te kia hoosaka bwan.

Maria: Heewi, kaa vamsekai.

Andres: E'e. Kia veha tua kaate,
wakase bwa'asaka aman tahti.

Maria: Va'am intok haksa . . .

Andres: Bwe va'a huevena.
Wam vichaa sene'ekam.

Maria: Oo.

Luisa: Kawimpo.

Andres: Kawimpo, hu'echi.
Ta te hunum hiva si mumuisuwak,
Siari Kaupo, sene'ekapo.
Yoim itou yahaka itom mumuisuk. [*Chuckles.*]

Maria: Kaave ama kokok?

Andres: E'e. Te kaa vu'u, haiki humaku'u, te dies hiva.
Haamuchim intok o'owim te aman yahak.

Maria: Hitaa tiempopo eme'e aman sahak?
Sevepo tiempopo o tataiko?

Andres: Tataiko.

Maria: Tataiko. Ii . . .

Andres: Heewi. Maasu ite hunum ori Kapo Va'am Pa'aku, teapo,
kava'ita nee weiyan, hewi.
Huyuu kava'i, hunum veha puaktimak,
sa'a bweiwa'apo
si puaktitamak chepte uu kava'i.

Andres: Then that one is the hide tumpline.

Maria: [*Laughs.*] How long did it take to get there?

Andres: Well, we very . . . we walked for maybe four months,
then arrived over there. But we were just taking our time, well.

Maria: Yes, you were not in a hurry.

Andres: No. Then, we were really just traveling,
eating meat all the way there.

Maria: And where was the water . . .

Andres: Well, there was plenty of water.
Over that way there were springs.

Maria: Oh.

Luisa: In the mountains.

Andres: In the mountains.
But it was only there that we got shot at,
in Green Mountain, at the spring.
Some Mexicans came and started to shoot at us. [*Chuckles.*]

Maria: Nobody was killed there?

Andres: No. We were not many, I don't know how many, we were ten only.
The women and the men arrived there.

Maria: In what season did you go there?
In cold weather or hot?

Andres: When it was hot.

Maria: When it was hot. This . . .

Andres: Yes. That's why, there, at the place known as Outside Water Lily,
I was leading a horse, yes.
That horse, with the bundle [on his back],
where they were digging for tubers,[15]
he really started to jump with the pack.

---

15. *Amoreuxia palmatifida*.

Maria: Hitaa intok sa'a bwe'ei?

Andres: Bwe sawam tea ori, ori huya naawa.

Maria: Oo.

Andres: Bwa'awa, saawam.

Luisa: Sawam bwehine. Quiere decir que estaba escarbando pa sacarlo pa comerlo.

Maria: Oo.

Andres: Heewi.

Luisa: Heewi.

Andres: Bwa'avetchi'ivo hunaa huya.

Luisa: Ha. Como los koochis.
Wate im hak veve'emu kom hooka.
Hunak veha am deskarbaroane.

Andres: Ili lolovolaim tataka.
Saawam tea hunume.

Luisa: Nassaakariam tiamta,
ket kaa au hu'unea, ti hiia.

Andres: Nassaakariam. Pos uu veha nassaakaria
inen ma kuta nassaakariane, hewi.
Hunaa nassaakaria.

Maria: Heewi.

Luisa: Como unos árboles.

Maria: Hm, hmm.

Andres: Um weekame ket nassaakariak.
Pos hunuu veha nassaakaria.

Maria: Hmm.

Luisa: Yoem nokpo.

Maria: And what is *sa'a bwe'ei*?

Andres: Well, *saawam*, as they are known, well, plant roots.

Maria: Oh.

Andres: They are eaten, the tubers.

Luisa: They would dig for tubers. He means that they were digging to take them out to eat them.

Maria: Oh.

Andres: Yes.

Luisa: Yes.

Andres: For eating, that plant.

Luisa: Ha. Like the pigs.
Some are this far down [*indicates the depth with her hands*].
Then they would dig them out.

Andres: They have little round fruit.
They are called tubers.

Luisa: Branches, as they are called,
she [Maria] also does not know what it is, she said.

Andres: Branches. Well, those are branches,
as the stick has branches, yes.
That is the branch.

Maria: Yes.

Luisa: Like some trees.

Maria: Hm, hmm.

Andres: The one standing there also has branches.
Well, then, that is the branch.

Maria: Hmm.

Luisa: In the Hiaki language.

CHAPTER 2

BATTLE IN SONORA

Flight into the Mountains (Luisa)

Luisa describes how Hiakis fleeing Hermosillo were hunted by the Mexican army. People who were sick with influenza, lying in grass huts, died when the Mexicans set fire to the huts above their heads. Luisa describes how they hid from the army and the cavalry, lying flat on some rocks while the hunters passed by. At one point the group was stranded in a canyon for five days without water. She names many canyons, mountains, and landmarks in her descriptions of their travels: Vakateeve (Tall Bamboo), Navo (Prickly Pear), Teta Hiponim (Rock Drums), Teta Chusaraim (Jagged Rocks), Masa'im (Queen's Wreath), Looria Kahon (Gloria Canyon), Hu'upa Rohi Kahon (Twisted Mesquite Canyon), Vehoori Va'am (Lizard Waters), and Vah Veetia (Burnt Grass).

Luisa: Oriu vicha ... Vakateveu, Navou vicha.
Hunum vicha veha huevenaka yeu sahak,
Teta Hiponimmeu vicha.
Kau kahonechi, hunait veha ...
Teta Chusaraim teau hikau sahak uu hente.
Hunum vicha veha emo hinne'uk, si'ime.
Hunum veha hasta oriu, Masa'aimmeu vicha.
Si'ime sahak uu hente, hunum vicha,
Kawiu vicha veha emo hinne'uk,
si'ime uu hentera, vato'ora, ili u'ute tenneme.
Huevenaka intok pos kaa u'ute tenne, yo'otu'lim.
Intok kia vaso karim amet tayak ume yoorim,
ko'okoeme.
Ket inflensia teame weyen.
Hunait veha kia karim amet taya, vaso karim.

Maria: Hmm.

Luisa: Huet kaita.
Kia hunuen im am ya'aka veha
nau am tohaka veha am nuksahak.
Ume wate intok im Teta Chusaraimmeu vicha sahak
intok Masa'aimmeu vicha.
Hunum veha uchi im Looria Kahoneu,
Hu'upa Ro'i Kahonet veha sahak,
si'ime hunum hikau vicha, kawiu vicha veha sahak.
Hunaman veha hooka.
Intok hunaman itom hunuka bwane'u vicha veha
kaate. Kaita intoko.
Hunuen hiokot ansasaka hunum oripo, Vehoori Va'ampo.
Hunait kahonnet, veha,
bweere teta volampo pepetala to'oka,
yoim itot wam kateu,
kavayeriata itot wam kateu.
Hak mamni ta'apo te ama hookan,
hunama'a kau kahonpo.

Maria: Kaa va'akai ...

Luisa: Toward, well . . . Tall Bamboo, toward Prickly Pear.
Toward there, then, many went out that way,
toward Rock Drums.
In the mountain canyon, that way, then . . .
the people went up to the place known as Jagged Rocks.
Over that way, then, they saved themselves, all of them.
Over there, then, until, well, toward Queen's Wreath,
all the people left, over that way.
In the mountains, then, they saved themselves,
all the people, the baptized ones, who could run a little faster.
And many, well, could not run fast, the elders.
And the Mexicans just burned the grass huts on top of them,
on the sick ones.
The influenza was going on.
They just burned the grass huts on top of them.

Maria: Hmm.

Luisa: On that, nothing.
They just did this to them, then,
they gathered them and took them away.
And the rest went toward Jagged Rocks
and toward Queen's Wreath.
Then from there, back to Gloria Canyon,
to Twisted Mesquite Canyon, they went.
Everyone went up that way then, to the mountain.
That's where we were.
And over there, we walked toward where we would find food,
we walked. And there was nothing.
There we were suffering terribly, there, well, at Lizard Waters.
At that canyon, then,
we were lying flat on some big round rocks,
while the Mexicans passed us by,
the cavalry passed us by.
We were there for about five days,
there in the mountain canyon.

Maria: With no water . . .

Luisa: Kaa va'akai, kaa hi'ibwakai.
Kia veha hunuen ama hooka.
Asta yoim sahak veha
uchi yeu sahaka veha
hunum Looria Kahoneu vicha veha sahaka,
um mesau hikau sahaka veha
hunaman vepa hooka.
Hunama chuvala hooka, veha intuchi sahak,
um Vah Veetia tea
kechia uu kawi, bwe'u meesa. Hunama veha hooka.

The Death and Mutilation of Dolores at Torreón (Luisa)

This story picks up where the previous one ends. There was not much to eat at Burnt Grass Mountain (Vah Veetia Kawi), and several children died there. Eventually the group left the area, traveling toward Rat Waters (To'i Va'am). En route, they were ambushed as they approached Torreón. No lookouts were set, and the first one to be killed was Luisa's brother, Dolores. In the attacking group of soldiers were *toroko yoim*, "gray Mexicans," in particular a unit called the Aguilenyom, or "Eagles." These were Hiaki fighters who served with the Mexican army and helped to track and kill the rebels. One of these traitors then mutilated Dolores's body, hanging him upside down and spread-eagled. His penis and testicles were severed. One testicle was placed in his right hand, the other in his mouth; his penis was placed in his left hand. The attacking soldiers then taunted the rest of the group, who were hiding farther up the canyon, daring them to come down and reclaim Dolores's body. The refugee rebels were out-

Luisa: Hunama hooka veha, vetukun vicha veha
ili hita, hi'itom puppua, hua taakam.
Huname veha bwa'e.
Hunaka veha vavakeka aa bwa'e uu hente.

Luisa: With no water, not eating.
We were there just like that.
Until the Mexicans left, then,
then, again we left, we went there
toward Gloria Canyon,
then up the mesa we went, then
we were up on top there.
We were there for a little while, then we left again,
there to a place named Burnt Grass,
also a mountain, a big mesa. Then that's where we were.

---

numbered, however, and had to move on; they went toward Procession Mountain (Kontia Kawi), where there was sufficient water.

> More than one photo exists in the Arizona Historical Society archive of executed Hiakis hung in the head-down position described in this narrative. One such photo can be viewed in their collection PC 180, Norman Wallace Photographs, box 3, f 333 / I: it depicts an executed Hiaki man hanging head-down from a tree, with armed men standing by. Another photo showing an executed Hiaki man who had worked as a mule skinner hanging head-down from a telephone pole can be viewed in the same collection: PC 180, Norman Wallace Photographs, box 3, f 333 / C. Other images of executed Hiakis can be viewed in this collection, as well as in other collections at the AHS: for example, PC 078, Rena Mathews Photograph Collection, B8 / Album N / Pg. 10 27002.

Luisa: While we were there [at Burnt Grass], we would go down, then, and pick a few things, wild spinach,[1] tree fruit.
That's what we ate then.
The people would boil that and eat it.

---

1. *Palo jito* or *palo San Juan, Forchhammeria watsonii.*

Hi'ito seewam, hitasa.
Echo seewam.
Si'imeta hunuka veha puaka, aa bwa'e uu hente,
vato'ora. Poloovem, kaita bwa'amachikai.

Maria: Hmm.

Luisa: Ili ku'umaiko wakiam intok,
vem vat ho'asuka'apo
vem wa . . . hakwo wootim.
Huname ili puakai veha
ili am poponaka veha, ili am komoniaka
ili uusim am va'a hi'ituane.
Hunuen veha ili am anian
ume ili uusim . . . si'imem.

Maria: Ili usim veha huevenaka ama kokok?

Luisa: Heewi, huevenakai. Hunuen veha sahaka,
hunuen te veha kia kawimmet te rehte,
hunuechi Vatachimmeu vicha.
Hunume kawim si'ime nat cha'aka,
hunum vichaa veha te sahak.
Hunumun, hunaman te notteka.
Hunaman hokaa veha ume yoim itou kiimuk.
Hunaman veha . . .
Hunuka To'i Va'ammeu vichaa katwa'apo,
um Torreonpo,
hunama am hote'eriaka veha am suak.
Porque maukaroapo ama yahak, hewi,
ama yeu matchuk um Torreonpo ime,
intok yoeme kaa hu'uneaka, kia witti aman kiimuk.

Maria: Hmm.

Luisa: Heewi. Kia witti aman kimuka veha hunaa veha
Lorestukau veha tua vat ama meewak.
Huname Torreonim amepat hinne'uvaeka,
tennekasu veha
ume yoim haivu am kova'ala.

The flowers of the wild spinach, anything;
the flowers of the cardon cactus.
All of that, then, was picked and eaten by the people,
the baptized ones, the poor, who had nothing else to eat.

Maria: Hmm.

Luisa: Little dried-out agave leaves
strewn about where people had lived,
their . . . discarded a long time ago.
We would pick a few of those,
then smash them, soak them,
and give the broth to the little children to drink.
That's how they sustained them,
the little children . . . all of them.

Maria: Then many of the little children died there?

Luisa: Yes, many. That's how we went,
that's how we just wandered in the mountains,
that way to Frog Mountain.
Those mountains are all in a chain,
then we went that way.
There, over there, we returned.
While we were there the Mexicans attacked us.
There then . . .
There, walking toward Black Rat Mountain,
at Torreón,
that's where they [the Hiakis] were ambushed and killed.
Because they arrived there in the early morning, yes,
these had spent the night there in Torreón,
and the Hiakis did not know this, so they just went in there.

Maria: Hmm.

Luisa: Yes. They just went right in, then that one,
the late Dolores, was the first one to be killed.
They wanted to rescue the ones in Torreón,
so they ran ahead,
but the Mexicans were already there.

> Haivu amepat ama hooka.
> Hunuen veha am, ama aa me'ak, hunaka.
> Ta hunuen aa ya'aka veha
> kia, kia wakastavenasi im, im aa pettaka
> kia kom kovakamta, inen ekala chayaka,
> um puetapo . . .

Maria: Hunaka yoemeta?

Luisa: . . . va'a vepa. Heewi. Intok aa kaponteka
huname intok wepu'ulaim aa machuktatuak.
Uka intok a'apoik hapchita intok
ivo sekka'atana ket aa machuktatuak.
Wepu'ulaim intok tenpo aa yecha'ariak.

Maria: Tsk.

Luisa: Heewi. Ta yoeme, mismo yoeme hunen am ya'ak.

Maria: Hunen am hooa.

Luisa: Agilenyom teame,
um Potampo yu ho'akame.
Huntuen hunen hiia, amet chaeka veha
hunen hiia tea:
"Vina em kateka Looresta a'avo nu'e,
o'owimtuka'ateko," ti ameu hiia tea.

Maria: Hmm.

Luisa: Hmm. Haisa aman aa nu'une,
vemposu kia ama tapuni tea.

Maria: Uu Hiaki ket hunuen, veha
vempo ket am vehe'etuak, hewi?

Luisa: Heewi.

They were already there ahead of them.
That's how they killed him there.
But then after they did this,
they butchered him, just, just like a cow,
They just hung him with his head down, they spread-eagled him,
there at the entrance [to the canyon] . . .

Maria: That man?

Luisa: . . . above the water. Yes. And after they castrated him,
they took one of the testicles and placed it in his hand.
And his penis
they placed in his other hand.
And one testicle they placed in his mouth.

Maria: Tsk.[2]

Luisa: Yes. But it was a Hiaki, a Hiaki who did this to them.

Maria: That's what they did to them.

Luisa: Those known as the Aguilenyom [Eagles],[3]
the ones who have always lived in Potam.
So then they yelled this to them,
this is what they said:
"Come over here and get Dolores,
if you are men," they said to them, it is said.

Maria: Hmm.

Luisa: Hmm. How could they go and get him?
There were so many of them there, it is said.

Maria: The Hiakis also did this to them, then,
they also paid them like that, yes?

Luisa: Yes.

---

2. The author is horrified to hear that it was the same Hiaki traitors who took this barbarous action against their brothers in blood.

3. The Aguilenyom (Aguileños) were Hiakis who were considered traitors by the Hiaki rebels.

Maria: Ket hiva hunueni.

Luisa: Heewi. Ket hiva hunueni, bwan.
Ume yoimmak rehteme
veha hiva hunen am hooa kechia.
Kaa amevenasi yoememvenasi.
Kaa, kaa yoim hiva ama rehte
siendo kee yoem nau kuraika ama rehte hunumu'u,
hunuen hooa.

Maria: Hmm.

Luisa: Hmm.
Hunumun te veha, hunuet te veha si'imet
Kontiakau vicha. Hunu'u huni ket bwe'u va'a kechia.

The Story of Sisto, and the Attack at Desert Spiny Lizard Waters (Luisa)

This story continues immediately on the previous one. Luisa is asked if she has ever heard of the American businessman Robinson, who leased the land around Hiak Vatwe from the Mexican government and used Hiaki labor to farm their own land for profit; he was notorious. Luisa is not sure at first but then recalls hearing of him. She then describes another notoriously cruel man, a General Sartucho. Sartucho captured a Hiaki boy, Sisto, and threatened him by putting a rope around his neck and tying it to a mesquite branch. After interrogating him, Sartucho then

Maria: Uu Robinsonta veha empo ket ta'ak?
Huna'a ket si hikkaiwan,
Robinson tea.
No sé si yoi o merikaano.
Ket ume Hiakim tua susuan tea.

Maria: Also the same way.

Luisa: Yes. Also the same way, well.
The ones who were with the Mexicans,
they always used to do the same to them also.
As if they were not Hiakis like them.
It wasn't only Mexicans who were there,
it happened that there were Hiakis and a diverse crew of others
who were also doing this.

Maria: Hmm.

Luisa: Hmm.
Then we all went through there,
toward Procession Mountain. There is also a lot of water there.

---

kept Sisto with his troops for three months, forcing him to show them where the water holes were in the mountains. They eventually returned Sisto alive to his mother Mikaela, who had assumed he was dead. Sisto remained in Hiaki territory and was still alive at the time of the recording, an old *pahko'ola* in Swiichi.[4] Luisa then goes on to describe how the group she and her family were with continued farther on to Frog Mountain and stayed there for a long time, free of attacks. Eventually they moved on to a place near Pitaya, Desert Spiny Lizard Waters (Vehoori Va'ampo), and were attacked. They had not posted a lookout, and the attackers descended on them from a mountain. Eight Hiakis were killed in that attack.

Maria: Did you also get to know Robinson?
There was a lot of talk about him,
the one named Robinson.
I don't know if he was Mexican or American.
It is said he also killed many Hiakis.

---

4. Note that *pahko'ola* is the same word that is often written as *pascola* in English.

Luisa: Hunuka nee kaa hikkaila.

Maria: Kaa aa hikkaila.

Luisa: E'e. Hunaa . . . Kia nee aa . . .
aa have kompae ket aa etehon.

Maria: Heewi.

Luisa: Huna'a si chu'utukan tea.

Maria: Heewi.

Luisa: Intok Heneral Sartucho tea.
Ket yoi, hunum Vatayonpo weaman.
Hunaa ket tua kaaveta hihiokoe tea.

Maria: Hmm.

Luisa: Ili usim huni chacha.
Ma i'an hunuka Sisto pahko'orata, ilitchiakan,
im hak velletchiakan.
Hunait kia wikiata im yecha'aika,
hu'upat hikau aa hima'arika
aa tetemai, hunuka Sistota.
Im hiapsa huna'a, yoem yo'owe i'an.

Maria: Ketun hiapsa?

Luisa: Heewi, hiapsa.

Maria: Aa.

Luisa: Hunaka ma kia wikiata aet yecha'ika
kia hu'upat hikat aa hima'arika
aa tetemai.
Kaa, kaachin im aa ya'ak, aa suutohak.
Ta nomas kee si vahi metpo
apolaik aet nunu'ubwa, bwan.

Maria: Hmm.

Luisa: Kaupo aa nunu'ubwa.
Va'apo aa ta'a ti hiiakai.

Luisa: I have not heard of him.

Maria: You have not heard about him.

Luisa: No. That one . . . I just . . .
ah, someone, Compadre used to talk about him.

Maria: Yes.

Luisa: He was a real dog, they say.

Maria: Yes.

Luisa: And also General Sartucho, they say.
He was also a Mexican with the battalion.
That one also did not feel compassion for anyone, it is said.

Maria: Hmm.

Luisa: He even hanged little children.
Like now, when that pascola dancer Sisto was very young,
probably about this size [*indicating knee-high*].
They had placed a rope around here [*indicating her neck*]
and threw the rope over a branch of a mesquite tree
while questioning him, that Sisto.
He is still alive here; he is an older man now.

Maria: He is still alive?

Luisa: Yes, still alive.

Maria: Ah.

Luisa: Like that one; he [General Sartucho] just put a rope on him
[on his neck] and just threw it over a mesquite [branch]
and interrogated him.
Not, nothing was done to him and they let him go.
But for about three months
they kept him isolated by himself, well.

Maria: Hmm.

Luisa: They had him with them in the mountains.
They were aware that he knew where there was water.

Ta pos kaachin im aa ya'ak.
Uchi im yeu aa nu'upak.
Aa malawa intok ketun hiapsan, komae Mikeatukau.
Hunaa veha aa meewak ti hiiaka,
hiva bwaana,
kaa yeu aa nu'upawau.

Maria: Ketun hiapsa huna'a?

Luisa: Uu usi ketun hiapsa, uu Sisto.
Hu, aa malawa muksuk, Komae Mikea muksuk.

Maria: Hunaa haksa hoome?

Luisa: Bwe, im ho'ak, Swiichipo.
Hunum hak ho'ak.

Maria: Oo, hunum hak ho'ak.

Luisa: Huna'a. Hunuen aa ya'ak.
Hunuen veha ... hunum veha ...
hunuka hunumum me'enau veha
te hunum Vatachimmeu vicha veha.
Si'ime uu kampamento emo kambibiaroa, hewi.
Hunaman veha hootek.
Hunaman veha humak ili vinwa ama hooka.
Komo woi metpo te ama hooka.
Kaa itou suawa.
Chukula veha aman kiimuk ume yoorim.
Hunak veha hunum huevena hentem suak,
hunum Vehoori Va'ampo, tokti ochom suak.

Maria: Hmm.

Luisa: Ketun, pos, kaa emo vihiaroan.
Heewi, kia veha ama hooka.

Maria: Heewi.

Luisa: Pos kia um kau ...
kaupo vepa ameu kom hapteka am,
ama am bwisek.

But, well, they did not harm him in any way.
They brought him back.
And his mother was still alive, the late comadre Mikaela.
She thought he was killed, she said,
and was always crying,
because he had not returned.

Maria: Is that one still alive?

Luisa: That child is still alive, that Sisto.
That one, his mother died, comadre Mikaela.

Maria: Where is he from?

Luisa: Well, he lives here at [Vikam] Swiichi.
He lives there somewhere.

Maria: Oh, he lives around there somewhere.

Luisa: That one. That's what they did to him.
That way, then . . . there, then . . .
when they were going to kill him there, then
we went toward Frog Mountain.
All the people in the camp changed their location, yes.
That's where we settled.
We were there for a long while.
We were there for about for two months.
No one bothered us.
Then later the Mexicans attacked us.
Then, that's when many people were killed,
at Desert Spiny Lizard Waters they killed a total of eight people.

Maria: Hmm.

Luisa: Still, well, they were not vigilant.
Yes, they were just there.

Maria: Yes.

Luisa: Well, just in the mountain . . .
then on top of the mountain, they came down upon them
and caught them there.

Maria: Haksa emo hinne'une?

Luisa: Kaachini. Hunuu tua Pitayavewitchi.
Ket hiva hunumuni To'i Va'amvetana.
Hunumun veha taawak.
Hunum veha te si vinwa hooka.

The Killing of Guillermo (Andres)

Andres describes an incident that occurred when he was still a boy, while he was with his mother in the mountains. He and a friend, Guillermo, had been cooking some deer meat in a pot when some Mexicans came upon them. Guillermo and Andres escaped, but Andres couldn't carry the pot easily, so he stashed it. The next day he returned with Guillermo to collect it. Andres describes suspecting that Mexicans were about because of some bird calls he heard. Guillermo wanted to stop

Andres: Chuvala hiva te ama hookan
porque itom hahhasuk ume yoim
ketwotana.

Luisa: Kia kaa vochaka huni hahhawa?

Andres: Heewi. Si nee bwe'u orita intok weiyan. Orita voteta hewi?

Luisa: Wakavakta wiksime.

Andres: Masovakta nee weiyan.
Kee san aa bwaseo yoim intok itou yahak.
Hu'upata weekau veha hiia uu wiko'i.
Ili yoeme intok Guillermo Vasolihti tea.
Hunaamak te nau aanen.
Hunama te yeu sahak, hunaman hak huupapo
intok nee kaa intok aa wiksimpea.
Hunama nee kiala manaka kiala toosiika.

Maria: Where could they save themselves?

Luisa: Not in any way. There, really close to Pitaya.
Also, still there toward Rat Waters.
Then, that's where they stayed.
That's where we were for a long time.

---

and rest, and dismissed Andres's fears. It turned out that the Mexicans were indeed there again and fired on them as they ran away, Andres's sandals flapping off his feet as he ran. Guillermo was hit in the stomach. Andres was alone and afraid, and didn't know where his mother was. He saw some Hiakis, but he wasn't sure about them and stayed away from them, thinking they might be Mexicans; later he approached them and met someone he knew, Ili Wok Kottim (Little Broken Leg), or Juan Maria, who took him to his mother. They camped at Tehapo Va'ampo, aka Moso Canyon, afterward.

Andres: We were there for only a little while
because the Mexicans chased us
in the morning.

Luisa: You were not even wearing shoes and were being chased?

Andres: Yes. And I was carrying a large object. Something, a can, yes?

Luisa: He was carrying a container of meat and vegetable soup.

Andres: I was carrying boiled deer meat.
And before it was cooked the Mexicans came to us.
We could hear the sound of gunfire by a mesquite tree there.
There was a young man by the name of Guillermo Vasolihti.
We were there together.
We left there, somewhere there in the mesquite forest.
And I did not feel like carrying it [the soup] anymore.
I just placed it there and left it.

[*Laughter.*]

Andres: O'omtilatukan. Kaita wawaatak.
Uchi yokoriapo te uchi aman rehte.
Hunaksan te si aman mumuisuwak.
Woikai.

Maria: Hmm.

Andres: Hunaa Guillermotukau, Vasolihti.
Hunaka veha ama me'ak.

Maria: Oo.

Andres: Nee intok vuitek.
"Kat nee toovuivuite omme," ti neu hiia.
Ta pos yoim itom nau kontai.
Itom ama nawichim sua'e'an.
Kia nee vera vocha chukchukti
weetchime, kia wiko'ipea.
Hunaa intok nepat wanten.
Tua inim aa muhuk, tompo.
Itom hooteriaka bwan, komo [*inaudible*].

Maria: Hmm.

Andres: Aman te kakava'eka kaaten.

Maria: Oo. Kava'et eme kaaten?

Andres: Heewi. Kava'ita nee kia ama himaak
aman Chiko Harostawi.
Maso wakasta te intok nunu'ubwan.
Im hak veetchi, teesio im veetchi, kavron.
Hunaka intok te haiwaka kaa aa teaka bwan.
Hunaka itom haiwausu uu wikit kia hunuen . . .
"Veras omme, yoim ama hooka."
"Kaita omme," ti hiva tete neewi.
Kia ventahata bwise.
Hunum veha poove ama meewak.
Wosa hiva au puttek.

[*Laughter.*]

Andres: I was upset. I did not want anything anymore.
    The next day, we were there again.
    It was then that they really started to shoot at us.
    The two of us.

Maria: Hmm.

Andres: That one, the late Guillermo Vasolihti.
    That one was killed there.

Maria: Oh.

Andres: And I ran.
    "Don't run away from me, man," he said to me.
    But the Mexicans had us surrounded.
    They would have killed both of us.
    I was just falling as my sandals were unraveling,
    falling, wishing I had a rifle.
    And that one [Guillermo] was running ahead of me.
    They shot him right here, in the stomach.
    They ambushed us, well, like . . . [*inaudible*].

Maria: Hmm.

Andres: We were going over there on horseback.

Maria: Oh. You were on horses?

Andres: Yes. I just left the horse there
    there at Chiko Haros's place.
    And we had been carrying some deer meat.
    It was about this size, a bundle this big [*indicates size*], [obscenity].
    And we were looking for that but did not find it, well.
    While we were looking for it, we heard a bird . . .
    "Look, man, the Mexicans are there" [said Andres].
    "There's no one, man," he kept saying to me.
    He just wanted to take a chance [to rest].
    Then there is where the poor man was killed.
    They only shot at him twice.

Maria: Eme'e intok wiko'eka kaaten?

Andres: Te wiko'ekan o'oven ta ume peronim chea vu'u.
　　　　　Ite intok woi hiva.

Maria: Woi hiva.

Andres: Hmm. Aman nee veha ino ta'arula.
　　　　　Haivu nee kia in malam huni kaa hu'uneiya.
　　　　　Inepola weama.
　　　　　Chukula veha kompae Hoan Maria,
　　　　　uu Wok Kotti teame veha nee [*inaudible*] teak.
　　　　　Kawit hikat katekai
　　　　　neu puttivae.
　　　　　Nee intok kia kaa konfiansak.
　　　　　"Yoim ha'ani," ti kia e'a.
　　　　　Chukula nee iniean . . . au nee yepsak.
　　　　　Hunak veha kompae Hoan Maria ama katek.
　　　　　Hunak veha malam hokau vicha nee nuksiika.
　　　　　Hunama hiva te hooka,
　　　　　"Ili Wok Kottim" teapo.
　　　　　Hunama te hooka.
　　　　　Um oripo Tehapo Va'ampo intok vaa'a.
　　　　　Hunama bwe'u vaa'a, kaa lulu'ute.
　　　　　Hunum te va'a he'eka ama hooka,
　　　　　Moso Kahonpo teawi.
　　　　　Hunama intok mamyan si vu'u.

Maria: Mamyam.

Maria: And you-all had rifles while you were walking?

Andres: We had rifles, but the bald ones[5] were too many.
  And we were only two.

Maria: Only two.

Andres: Hmm. Then I was lost over there.
  I already did not know where my mom was;
  I was by myself.
  Then later compadre Hoan Maria,
  known as Broken Leg, found me [*inaudible*] then.
  He was sitting up on the mountain
  and was going to shoot at me.
  And I just did not trust him.
  "Perhaps they are Mexicans," I thought.
  Later like this . . . I went to them.
  Compadre Hoan Maria was sitting there.
  Then he took me over to where my mom was.
  That's where we always were.
  "Little Broken Leg," he was named.
  There we were.
  At that place, Water in the Cave, there was water.
  There was a lot of water there, it never dried out.
  We drank water there while we were there,
  at the place known as Moso Canyon.
  There was a lot of *mamyam*[6] [American nightshade] there.

Maria: American nightshade.

---

5. The Hiakis referred to the soldiers as *ume peronim*, "the bald ones," because of their shaved hair.

6. This plant is commonly eaten by the Hiakis of Sonora and Mayos of Sinaloa. It is prepared like spinach and is quite tasty. There are several varieties of this plant. It does not grow in Arizona, so it is virtually unknown to the Hiakis of Arizona. Research indicates the presence of glycoalkaloids, and people should be careful in using this plant as medicine and food. The green fruit is particularly poisonous, and eating the unripe berries has caused the death of children. Although the berries are poisonous, some Hiakis have stated that they have eaten them with no ill effects.

Andres: Heewi. Huname te am hihi'uka
am bwa'ekasu sahak, vatweu vicha.
Hunum te aa pasaaroak, vatwepo.

Maria: Hunak uu vatwe hiva va'akan?

Andres: Hiva va'akan hunako.

Dealing with the Dead (Luisa and Andres)

Andres and Luisa describe how the Hiaki war dead would be burned to prevent animals from desecrating the corpses. If a victim had to be left behind, Hiakis would return when it was safe to return.

Maria: Hunuen ori yoemeta ama hak me'ewako,
aa mukuko
kia hunuen aa su'utoine?

Andres: E'e. Si kaa aa tu'iriak,
yeu aa wikeka hakun aa taya'ane.
Taya'ane uka yoemeta.
Emo tattaa.

Luisa: Vempo yoemem chansata hippuetek,
kaa aa woo . . .
kaa ama aa hima'ane,
hiva yeu wikne.

Andres: Hiva yeu aa nuksimne.

Luisa: Wate veha yeu aa nuksaka'ane, hewi?
Wate intok ae . . .

Andres: Wate intok nahsuane.

Luisa: Aet nahsuane.

Andres: Yes. We picked those
and ate them, and we left and went to the river.
That's where we stayed, at the river.

Maria: The river always had water at that time?

Andres: It always had water at that time.

Maria: And that way, if a man was killed there somewhere,
when he died,
did you just leave him there?

Andres: No. If [the body] is decomposing,
they would take it out and burn it somewhere out there.
We would burn the man['s body].
They used to burn them.

Luisa: If those men had a chance,
they would not . . .
they would not leave him there,
they would always take him out [of the camp to burn the body].

Andres: They always took him out.

Luisa: Some would take him out, yes?
Some with him . . .

Andres: And some would fight.

Luisa: They would fight on him.[7]

---

7. That is, they would use him for cover.

Ume veha wate veha yeu aa weiya'ane,
uka ko'okosi aulata.

Andres: Heewi.

Luisa: Pa'akun yeu aa nuksaka'ane.

Andres: Pa'akun yeewi.

Luisa: Si hunaman haisa aa tawaka,
hunama aa lu'utek, hunama veha
aa ma'ane o aa ta'ane.

Andres: Aa taya'ane o aa ma'ane.

Maria: Haisa intok aa taya'ane?

Luisa: Bwe kutam aet wattane.

Andres: Bwe kutam aet wattaka aa taya'ane.

Maria: Oo.

Andres: Empo ma na'avaetek hak kutam nau toine,
hewi, huevenam.
Pos hunuen veha huevena kutam aet wattak veha
aa taya'ane.

Luisa: Taya'ane.

Andres: Hunak veha bwahne.
Ota tossaala bwahne.

Luisa: Napohtune.

>   Then some would take him out,
>   the gravely injured person.[8]

Andres: Yes.

Luisa: They would take him out of there.

Andres: Out of there.

Luisa: If something happened to him,
        if he died there, then there
        they would bury him or burn him.

Andres: Burn or bury him.

Maria: And how do you burn him?

Luisa: Well, you place wood on him.

Andres: Well, place wood on him and burn him.

Maria: Oh.

Andres: Like you, when you are going to make a fire, you gather wood,
        yes, a lot of wood.
        Well, in that way, then, a lot of wood was placed on him
        and he would be burned.

Luisa: Burn him.

Andres: Then he would cook.
        The bones would cook, become very white.

Luisa: They would turn to ashes.

---

8. If the person was gravely injured, the remaining group realized that any attempt to take the injured person to their next destination, particularly when fleeing from a dangerous situation, would seriously hinder their efforts to escape to a safe place. The injured person would urge the group to leave him or her behind, requesting only that a small amount of water be left with them. The injured person would assure the group that when their injuries were healed, he or she would "catch up" with them. However, everyone knew that the injuries were so severe that the injured person would not survive them, and that death would be a better option for the injured person and the rest of the group.

Andres: Kia napohtune.

Luisa: Kaa hitasa animaalim
aa naikimteneevetchi'ivo,
veha hunama ta'ana.

Maria: Kaa tiempota hippueteko intok kiala . . .

Luisa: Ta pos kiala suutoine.

Andres: Kia ama aa toosimne.
Tiempok veha . . .

Luisa: Ta chukula hiva uchi ama aa hariunemme,
kaaveta ama aneu.
Hunak veha ama aa teak huni'i, kia otata teak
huni hiva nau aa tohaka aa ta'ane.

Maria: Heh.

Luisa: Hm. Hunuen emo hoan uu yoeme,
kaupo rehteme, kau homem.

Caring for Wounded Warriors (Luisa)

Luisa describes some of the healing techniques that were used to treat wounded Hiaki fighters in the mountains. The injured man would be

Luisa: Hunuen intok uu yoeme hakun muiwaka
kaa mukuk intok hakun tesou tohina.
Hunaman veha woika huni aemak aman vittuana.
Huname veha aa hi'ibwa hariuriane.
Ili aa hahairiaka veha ili aa bwabwasaka
veha aman au aa totoine, um tehpo aa tekikai, ho.
Aa vavatriane, au aa ine'etepo tahti.

Andres: They just become ashes.

Luisa: So that the animals would not
take it apart,
you burn it.

Maria: And if you do not have time, you just . . .

Luisa: Then you just leave it.

Andres: Just leave it there.
If you have time, then . . .

Luisa: But later they would still go and search for him,
if there was no one around.
Then if you find him, even if only the bones,
you would gather the bones and burn them.

Maria: Heh.

Luisa: Hm. That's what the Hiakis used to do to themselves,
the ones who were in the mountains, the mountain people.

---

taken away from the fighting to a remote location and cared for by others, who would forage for food, collect water, and treat his bullet wounds with brazilwood and cholla ashes.

Luisa: And that way, if a man was shot somewhere else
and did not die, he would be taken to a cave.
There, then, at least two would be sent with him over there.
They would then look for food for him.
They would prepare it, cook it,
then take it to him there in the cave where he was lying, see.
They would fetch water for him until he got well.

Maria: Valata yeu wikne?

Luisa: Heewi. Hunai veha huchahkoe aa vavaksiane,
intok sevii . . . naposa.
Hunaka veha tatta'aka veha ama aa tottoriane.
Huname veha aa hihittone intok
ili aa hi'ibwa hariuriane. Haksa ili huiwam,
maso sussuakai veha
ili aa aniaka ama aemak hoone.
Hunuen aa hi'ibwa aniatuana.

Maria: Ta wate ket ili hittoa ta'an entonces, hewi?

Luisa: Heewi. Hmm. Ta hunue aa vavaksian
porque hunu'u si tu'i tea, huchahko,
intok uu sevii naposa.
Hunuka veha ama aa totto'oriane.

Maria: Hunaman ket ili yervam aayuk, hewi?

Luisa: Heewi. Huevena.

Maria: Aet ta'ame veha aman am pupuane.

Luisa: Huevena. Hunum emo hihitton, kaupo.
Kaita. Kaita imvenasi, yoi medesiinam,
kaita aayuk. Hunuen hiva.
Vempo hiak hittoae emo hihitto si'ime.
Tua kaita [*whispering*].

Maria: They would remove the bullet?

Luisa: Yes. Then they would wash it [the wound] with brazilwood[9]
and with the ashes of the *sevii* [the jumping cholla][10] . . .
They would burn it, then pour the ashes into the wound.
They would treat him and
look for a little food for him. If they had an arrow,
they would kill a deer then
and help him a bit and stay with him.
This is how they would be made to look for food for him.

Maria: But at that time some people knew about medicine, yes?

Luisa: Yes. Hmm. But with that they used to wash it
because they say that it is very good medicine, the brazilwood,
and the ashes of the jumping cholla.
This is what they poured into the wound.

Maria: There were also a few other herbs there, yes?

Luisa: Yes. A lot.

Maria: Those who knew their way around would gather them.

Luisa: A lot. They used to nurse their wounds there, in the mountains.
Nothing. Nothing like here, Mexican medicine
was not available, there was nothing. Only that way.
They all used to treat themselves with Hiaki medicine.
There was really nothing else [*whispering*].

---

9. A type of red wood.
10. *Cylindropuntia fulgida*.

Arizona Hiakis, Gunrunning to Tucson, and Gathering Munitions (Andres)

Andres describes how the Hiakis who would come south from Tucson would often die in the mountains, because they did not know the area well. One house in Tucson, at Big Mesquite, served as a depot for smuggled arms, which were concealed under grass in a loft. The Hiakis who went for the guns would carry them and the ammo on their backs, all the way from Little Nogales. However, there was another source of arms: the very same Mexican soldiers they were fighting. Whenever they won a battle, the Hiakis would be sure to capture all the armaments and other supplies available, down to the clothes the killed soldiers were wearing. In this way the Hiakis acquired cannons, guns, ammunition, and even new pants.

Andres: Hunuen im yee hoan. Kialikun ume waate,
  inimin Tusonvetana im yahakame, pos chukula si'ime kokok.
  Kaa ama ta'akatua kaupo.

Maria: Heewi, kaa ama ta'a.

Andres: Maa hunu'u Lukas kovavichitukau, hewi?
  Hunum yepsak.
  Chukula humak kia vo'ot hichupak,
  porque haivu ora'atukan.
  Hunum Bwe'u Hu'upapo ho'akan.

Maria: Oo.

Andres: Hunum yaahan ume kau homem,
  si'ime, Lukas kovavichituapo.
  Hunum si'ime yaahan.
  Huntuan inien ve'emu kom wohoi, yu.
  Bwehiri, tu'ulisia.
  Ulevenasi ya'ari.

FIGURE 7 Hiaki men captured near Nogales in Arizona by U.S. Cavalry Troop E, January 9, 1918. Arizona Historical Society, PC 1000, Tucson General Photo Collection, Subjects-U.S. Army-10th Cavalry, #26599.

Andres: That's what they did to us. That's why those others,
   who came here from Tucson, well, later they all died.
   Because they did not know their way around the mountains.

Maria: Yes, they did not know their way around.

Andres: Like the late Lucas Bald Head, yes?
   He arrived there.
   Later he was just finished [died] there on the road,
   because he was already quite old.
   There at Big Mesquite.

Maria: Oh.

Andres: That's where all the mountain men used to go,
   all of them, there at Lucas Bald Head's home.
   Everyone went there.
   So it was this far down, look.[11]
   It was dug up nicely.
   It was made like that.[12]

---

11. Andres indicates the depth of the hole with his hands.
12. Andres points to a hole that was dug to place a pole in.

>   Hunama wiko'im e'ehsowan.
>   Saka'avaeteko veha,
>   intuchi yeu am wikne.
>   Ta inien ilevenasi tapestek, hewi?
>   Vaso intok ae vepa watwattan.

Maria: Oo.

Andres: Hm, hmm. Hunuen veha kaave hu'unean.
   Hunuen aa hippuen.

Maria: Inen ume yoemem aman parketa nu'uvaetek
   veha kava'et aman saka'ane?

Andres: E'e, vo'ot, ho'ot aa puatekai nottine.

Maria: Hiva wokimmea? Oo qué va!

Andres: Wokimmea. Hunum Nogalimpo iivotana.
   Nogaliitom teapo, hewi?

Maria: Heewi.

Andres: Hunum revekti etbwa yeu simne kechia. Etbwa.

Maria: Uu, si vinwatune, casi el año, que no?

Andres: Heewi.

Maria: Aman saka'ane hunak intuchi nottine.

Andres: Poovata si'imeta puatine.

Luisa: Intuchi ume bweere wiko'im huni mohaktaika
   am puatekai am nunnu'upa.

Andres: Tahita, poovata, si'imeta weiyane ho'ochi, ho.
   Ta im huni auk o'oven hewi?

> That's where they used to hide the rifles.
> When they were going to leave, then,
> they would take them out again.
> But they had a *tapesti* [cane carrier][13] like this, yes?
> And then they placed grass on top of it.

Maria: Oh.

Andres: Hm, hmm. That way no one knew.
> That's how they had it.

Maria: When the men went over there [to the United States] to get ammo, then they went on horseback over there?

Andres: No, on the road, and they carried it on their backs and returned.

Maria: Still walking? Oh my!

Andres: On foot. There in Nogales on this side.
> At a place known as Little Nogales, yes?

Maria: Yes.

Andres: There, we would sneak out also, half the time. Sneak out.

Maria: Uu, it would take a long time, almost a year, isn't that so?

Andres: Yes.

Maria: You would go over there, then come back.

Andres: We would carry the gunpowder and everything else.

Luisa: Then again, the big rifles would be dismantled and would be carried and brought here.

Andres: The bullets, gunpowder, everything was carried on our backs, see. But that is available here also, yes?

---

13. *Tapesti*: This cane carrier was a mat made out of bamboo to place a deceased person on, during an overnight wake. The godparents would make the carrier, and, during the night while prayers were being offered for the deceased, the deceased would be laid on it. The following day, this same carrier would be used to the transport the deceased to the burial site. A *tapanko* is similar to the *tapesti* but is used as a table, particularly during the ceremony of All Saints' Day and Day of the Dead.

Mismo ume peronim itou aa totoha.
Pos kaavaeka...

Luisa: Ta humane, huname suak
veha am u'uraane.

Andres: Heewi. Huname tutu'im itom wiwikootua.

Luisa: Kanaanam, wiko'im,
parketa, hita am u'uran.

Andres: Huname tutu'im itom wikootuak.

Maria: Aa.

Andres: Mismo ume peronim...

Luisa: Mismo...

Andres: Hunak intok hunama intok
uka taho'ota vem ama kovakau
huni'i ketuni ohvokampo huni
kovatene. Saweampo huni'i.

Luisa: Aa wattakai.
Hunuen am hohoan ume kau homem ume peronim.

It was the very same bald ones who would bring it to us.
Well, without intending to . . .

Luisa: But those, those, when we killed them,
then we would take them [the weapons] away.

Andres: Yes. They gave us some good armaments.

Luisa: Cannons, armaments,
ammunition, we took things from them.

Andres: They gave us good armaments.

Maria: Ah.

Andres: The same bald ones . . .

Luisa: The same . . .

Andres: And then and there
the clothes they [dead Mexican soldiers] had on,
even those that still had blood,
we would put on. Even the pants.

Luisa: They would take them off.
This is what the mountain men did to the bald ones.

Southern Indigenous Soldiers in the Mexican Army (Luisa)

Luisa describes a lopsided battle between the mountain Hiakis and some conscripted southern Indigenous soldiers known as Labwes or *wilom* (the latter meaning "skinny ones") who had been sent to attack them, during the time when her family was in the mountains with the fighters.[14] The southern recruits had not been trained in the use of rifles and did not know the territory, so the Hiakis were easily able to trap and kill them in a narrow canyon.

Luisa: Wilommak kaa nahsuak.
Kaupo ala.

Heera: Kaupo ala?

Luisa: Heewi. Kaupo ala.
Hunume yoim nahsuasu,
vempo nau nahsuasukai
ime kau homemmeu veha.
Ume hita, Wilom teame
kima'awak.

Heera: Aa, ameu kima'awak?

Luisa: Heewi. Hunume veha
ume kaupo yuu ho'akame hahhatuawa,
si'ime. Ite intok hu'ubwa aman yahame veha
haivu amemak ama nah tettene.

---

14. Here Luisa is reporting an account that her older sister Simona told her; occasionally she will conclude a description with *ti hiia*, "[she] would say."

FIGURE 8 Ammunition taken from captured Hiakis by the 10th U.S. Cavalry, January 9, 1918. Arizona Historical Society, PC 1000, Tucson General Photo Collection, Subjects-U.S. Army-10th Cavalry, #2659XX.

Luisa: They did not fight with the skinny ones.
   In the mountains they did.

Heera: In the mountains they did?

Luisa: Yes. In the mountains they did.
   When the Mexicans were done fighting,
   when they were done fighting among themselves,
   then they were sent to the mountain Hiakis.
   Those things, the ones known as the skinny ones,
   were sent to attack [the mountain Hiakis].

Heera: Ah, they were sent to attack them?

Luisa: Yes. They then
   were sent to chase the Hiakis who always lived in the mountains,
   all of them. And we who had just arrived there,
   we were also running with them [the mountain Hiakis].

Kaupo veha rehte haivu
hunume Wilom aman kimu'u.

Heera: Hunume Wilom intok hitamsa?

Luisa: Bwe yoim, ume sureo ho'akame, Laabwem.

Heera: Laabwem?

Luisa: Hmm. Hunum Samawakapo
senu vatayon tehalwak.
Hunume'e ke'esam aman kimukai.

Heera: Hee? Hunume, veha
aa a'avo nahsuatuawa kechia?

Luisa: Heewi. Si'ime ume surenyom.
Hunume hunuen teuwan.
"Hunume Wilom," ti hiia.

Heera: Wilom, ti hiia?

Luisa: Heewi, kaa pantalolonek.
Kia tosaa saweweak.

Heera: Aa.

Luisa: Mantam kamiseetak.
Intok kaa wiko'im maniharoa huni'i.

Heera: Katim am ta'a?

Luisa: Heewi. Kialikun hunuen kia ama suawak.
Poloovem kechia.
Ume yoeme kia kaitaapo am ya'ak.
Kuvahim kia choovikuvikukti am ponsuriak.
Hunum, Avahtaweeka'apo,
kahonnet asta va'au tahtia.
No ves que ilikkani.
Heewi kau kaahon kovi'ikun vicha.
Siari Va'ammeu vicha, kom vo'ota wecheo.
Woho'okun tahtia, ho?
Ime intok kaa ama ta'a poove yoorim.
Kia veha ama suawak.

| | We were already there in the mountains
when the skinny ones were attacking us. |
|---|---|
| **Heera**: | And who are those skinny ones? |
| **Luisa**: | Well, Mexicans, the people who live in the south, the Labwes. |
| **Heera**: | Labwes? |
| **Luisa**: | Hmm. There at Samawaka [a mountain in the Vakateeve Mountains] one whole battalion was finished.
Those who attacked [us] for the first time. |
| **Heera**: | Yes? Then those
were sent to fight over here also? |
| **Luisa**: | Yes. All the southerners.
That's what they called them.
"They are the skinny ones," they said. |
| **Heera**: | The skinny ones, they said? |
| **Luisa**: | Yes. They did not wear trousers.
They only wore underpants. |
| **Heera**: | Ah. |
| **Luisa**: | They wore muslin undershirts.
And they did not use rifles either. |
| **Heera**: | They did not know how to use them? |
| **Luisa**: | Yes. That's why they were just killed there in that way.
The poor ones also.
The Hiakis just finished them off.
The drums were flattened from drumming.
There, at The Place Where the Cottonwood Stands,
in the canyon where the water is.
That's because the canyon is very narrow.
Yes, there toward the interior of the canyon.
Toward Green Waters, where the road goes down.
Toward the bottom, see?
And the poor Mexicans were not familiar with the area.
They were just killed there. |

Heera: Kia veha ama suawak?

Luisa: Heewi.

Heera: Hee?

Luisa: Pos kialikun hunaatau ket waate vempo, hewi?
Yoim kaa ama kikkimu, ti hiiaka, veha.
Aman kikkimuka veha
hunuen ama ya'awak kechia.

Heera: Oo. Kaupo suawak?

Luisa: Heewi. Hunuen im ya'awak.

Heera: Mismo yoemem am suak?

Luisa: Heewi. Mismo yoeme ibwan am suak.
Huevenam.

Papago Fighters Contract with the Mexicans (Chema Tosaria)

Jose Maria Cupis describes how the Mexican army also hired Papagos (i.e., Tohono O'odham) on a ninety-day contract. They planned to

Chema: Vempo hunuka nooka. Ho.
Emo kom aa toine.
Aa kontratola nunu'e, heneraalim.
Ta pos kaita, kaita au ya'ak.
Kaa, kaa wa promeesa vem yechaka'u
kaa ama yeu sisime. Inileni.
Papawem chukti tatakeasuk.
Papawem sontao ya'aka
aman am kiimak.
Vahi metpo, noventa diapo

Heera: They were just killed there?

Luisa: Yes.

Heera: Yes?

Luisa: Well, that's why some people remember it, yes?
The Mexicans do not go in there, they said.
When they did go in,
that's what they [the Hiakis] would do to them also.

Heera: Oh. They were killed in the mountains?

Luisa: Yes. That's what they did to them.

Heera: It was the same Hiakis who killed them?

Luisa: Yes. Well, it was the same Hiakis who killed them.
Many of them.

---

capture the Hiaki warriors with lassos at a place called Kapo Va'ampo, Lily Waters, and then bring them back alive. The plan did not work. The attackers came running with ropes, and the Hiakis just shot them.

Chema: That's what they [the Tohono O'odham] said. See.
They said they would bring them [the Hiakis] down.
The generals made contracts.
But, well, nothing. They did nothing to them.
That promise that they made,
it did not come out their way. Like this.
They even hired the Papagos [Tohono O'odham].
They made soldiers out of the Papagos
and sent them there.
For three months, ninety days,

am kontrato nu'uka hunu senu heneral.
Ho. Noventa diapo au kom am toine tia,
hiapsame, am choilakai ti hiia, ho.
Haksa aa ya'ak? Kia hakwo huni kaa aa ya'ak.
A lo kontrario vempo ama mumui . . .
suawak. Yu'in suawak ume papawem,
hunumun Kapo Va'am pa'aria teapo. Ho.
Kaaveta hachin ya'ak.
Kaaveta im me'ak, vempo, ho.
Ume Hiakim kaa vempoimvenasi . . .
Kia nokta am himaatuak.
Hoone intok kaa hak bwia wohooriam hooa,
kia ili huyam veah hoone hiva.
Huyam veah hiva nahsua.
Haisa am ya'ane? Pos hunuen.
Kontratokame pos a'aposu vea
kaa kumpliaroaka vea
hunumun hakun Caborcavetana hak meewak.
Ho. Porque hunuka nookak uu papawe ya'ut;
am choilavaekai, chotchoilasuvaekai.
Es cierto, pos si kia wiwikiaka ameu tennek tea
hunama Kapo Va'ampo,
kaa am mumuhe.
Ume Hiakim intok chivela tenneka
am mumui haptek.
Hetochivela am mumuisuk.
Hahhasuk intuchi va'a puntau vichaa,
vea kom am hahasek.
Hunuka ameu ya'ak. Kaitatuk.
Wa kontratowa vea a'apoik koovak.
Pos hunulen yeu sika'apo vea
nehpo inika nookak.
Inien nehpo aa teuwak intok
inien nehpo aa hu'uneiyak inika yoemta.

that one general contracted them.
See. They said that in ninety days they would bring them down,
the ones [Hiakis] still alive, lassoing them, they said, see.
Where did they do it? They just never did it.
On the contrary, they were the ones who were shot . . .
killed. Many of the Papagos were killed,
there at the place named Water Lily Waters wilderness. See,
they [the O'odham] did not do anything to anyone.
They killed no one, see.
Like them, the Hiakis did not . . .
Their threats were just talk.
They would just sit and they did not dig any foxholes,
they would just sit behind the bushes.
They only sat behind the bushes and fought.
What could they do to them? Well, it happened that way.
The one who made the contract,
well, he did not keep his word, then
over there somewhere over toward Caborca he was killed.
See. Because the Papago chief made that statement,
that he was going to lasso them, he was going to lasso them.
It is true, well, as they ran toward them with their ropes, they say,
there at Water Lily Waters,
they [the O'odham] did not shoot at them [the Hiakis].
And the Hiakis took off and scattered
and began to shoot at them.
They were shot and scattered widely.
They [the Hiakis] chased them to the boundary of the water,
they chased them down.
That's what they did to them. Nothing else happened.
His own contract had turned against him.
Well, it turned out that way,
then I have told about it.
This is what I have to say, and
this is what I learned about this man.

Slaughter and Capture at Tall Bamboo (Luisa and Andres)

Luisa and Andres discuss the numbers of Hiaki war dead, talking about an attack at Vakateeve (Tall Bamboo), where many Hiakis were killed. Another man, also named Andres, places the date of the attack at 1914. This other Andres used to be called Dreadlocks (Veetam) and wore dresses rather than trousers; he was a matachin. He is younger than Andres Sol. Andres himself was away in Tucson at the time of the attack, so Luisa tells the story. Luisa describes how the able-bodied adult Hiaki men were all away from camp on a food-gathering expedition, under

Maria: Ama kawimpo enchim aneu
komo haiki Hiakim aman kokok?

Andres: Um kaupo?

Maria: Heewi.

Andres: Hunum te kaa hu'unea haikimsa kokoka'u.
Kaa aa hu'uneiya.

Luisa: Kaa naikiari.

Andres: Huevena hivatua.

Maria: Hmm.

Andres: Huevena.

Luisa: Kaa naikiari kaupo chea.

Maria: Pos i'an kaa huevena ume Hiakim, hewi?

Andres: Um, hm.

Maria: Si'ime pueplompo.

Andres: Huevenaka kokoksuk.

Luisa: Hunum, hunum Vakatevepo chea
si humak haikika humak suawak

the leadership of Hesus Raahu, Captain Chema, his brother Candido, and a commandant named Rego. The Mexican soldiers attacked the unguarded camp at Tall Bamboo. Only elders, women, and children were there. The Hiakis fought back with machetes and axes, but to no avail. The Mexicans massacred the elderly and infirm and took the women hostage, eventually taking them to the jail in Hermosillo. Luisa estimates about a thousand Hiakis were killed. The Hiaki warriors, when they returned, could not attack, for then the Mexicans would kill their wives who had been taken hostage.

Maria: In the mountains when you were there, how many Hiakis were killed there?

Andres: In the mountains?

Maria: Yes.

Andres: We do not know how many died there. We do not know it.

Luisa: They were not counted.

Andres: Very many, for sure.

Maria: Hmm.

Andres: Very many.

Luisa: They were not counted, the ones in the mountains.

Maria: Well, now there are not too many Hiakis, yes?

Andres: Um, hm.

Maria: In all the villages.

Andres: Many died.

Luisa: There, there at Tall Bamboo, more, perhaps a number of, perhaps were killed

hunako i'an Orospo yeu yahinau.
Hunak katorsetukan tea ti bwan hiia uu Andres.
Nee . . .

Andres: A'apo chea kaa hu'unea i'an inii,
hunuu Andres hodiido . . .

Luisa: Hunuen ibwan neu hiia.
Hunak katorsetuko ti hiia
porque nee aa ta'a bwan kechia.
Kaa yo'otukan tea . . .

Andres: Kaa yo'otukan.

Luisa: Haveta, i'an komo
ili Taasiota veletchiakan intok hunuu wepulai . . .

Andres: Ia veletchiakan, yu,
matachinitukan, monaha, oritukan.

Luisa: Chea ilitchiakan.
Ili tevem vetakan huntuan.
Kaa Antessimea ta'ewan.

Andres: Vetammea hiva ta'ewan.

Luisa: Veta ti hiva au hihiuwan.
Ini'i bwan si im hak veekkanim vetakan,
imi'ita a repa cha'ane.
Intok ori, tevem hiva supene, kaa pantalonne,
kia tevem supene. [*Laughs.*]

at that time, now, when they were arriving at Oros.
Then, it was said, it was 1914; well, this is what Andres[15] said.
I . . .

Andres: He really did not know, this one,
that damned Andres . . .

Luisa: Well, that's what he said to me.
In 1914, he said,
because I also knew it.
I was not an adult, they said . . .

Andres: She was not yet an adult.

Luisa: Who, now I was like
about little Tasio's size and that one . . .

Andres: She was like this one's size, look,[16]
he [other Andres] was a matachin, a *monaha*,[17] what's it called.

Luisa: He was much smaller.
He had long dreadlocks, that's why.
He was not known by his real name Andres.

Andres: He was only known as Dreadlocks.

Luisa: Dreadlocks is what they always called him.
This one had dreadlocks this long.[18]
They hung like earrings.
And, well, he always wore a long dress, but no trousers,
just a long dress. [*Laughs.*]

---

15. The Andres that Luisa is referring to is *not* her husband Andres. She is referring to another fellow who was also named Andres but was known primarily by his nickname Veetam (Dreadlocks).

16. Andres points at a young boy who is playing close by.

17. A *monaha* (monarch) is the lead dancer in the matachin ceremonial society. Like a monarch, he assumes a leadership role in this society. In order to become a *monaha*, he has to be confirmed in this role. He provides instruction for the new matachin dancers and will eventually himself become the lead matachin dancer.

18. Luisa indicates the length with her hands.

Andres: Ante . . . haisa, haisa aa bwibwikrian aa achaiwa?

Luisa: I'an intok "Si au yo'owele,"
ti nee au hihia kialikun.
Hunum vahewata weeka'apo hohoan,
tua va'a pusipo,
yeu va'am weye'epo ho'ak va'a vepa.

Andres: Chea nee vepa kaa yo'owe o'oven,
ta intok si heveotula.
[*Chuckles.*]
Tuka imin hak vicha weyen,
Tetaviektiu vicha.
Im neu noitek.

Luisa: Hunum Vakatevepo humak kasi miltaka suari.

Maria: Hmm.

Andres: Oo huevenaka kokola, kaa naikiari.

Luisa: Oo, hunako yoim tua itom ama nau kuutako,
tua kaave tennek, pos si
ket hunak ume yoem yo'otu'im ket taewatten.
Kia taewechia bwan hunuen am ya'akan,
hunuen veha . . .

Andres: Aa pos nee hunaka kaa hu'uneiyan.

Luisa: Ite ala enchim Tusoneu aneu.

Andres: Oriu katekan.

Luisa: Ite ala aman yoimmea nu'uwak.

Andres: Ma nee ket vinwa yuku ween.

Andres: Ante . . . how, how did his father sing to him?

Luisa: And now, "He thinks he is all grown up,"
is what I say to him, that's why.
They used to live there where the mist occurs,
exactly where the spring is,
they lived where the water comes out, above the water.

Andres: He is a lot younger than me,
but now he has vitiligo.
[*Chuckles.*]
Yesterday he was walking over there somewhere,
toward Tetaviekti [Rolling Stone].
He came here to visit me.

Luisa: There at Tall Bamboo perhaps almost one thousand were killed.

Maria: Hmm.

Andres: Oh, many have died there, they were not counted.

Luisa: Oh, at that time the Mexicans really had us confused,
well, no one really ran, well, since
also at that time the elderly men had fever.
Just the fever had done this to them [i.e., made them vulnerable],
that way then . . .

Andres: Ah, well, I did not know that.

Luisa: We did, when you all were in Tucson.

Andres: I was there [in Tucson], well.

Luisa: But we were captured by the Mexicans.

Andres: But I was walking in the rain for a long time.[19]

---

19. It is unclear why Andres would make this comment. *Yuku* is rain. *Ween* means "was walking." Andres was in Tucson while the massacre was going on, and perhaps he was in a pensive mood. Several fluent speakers have read Andres's comments and find them difficult to comprehend. Some have suggested that he might have had feelings of guilt for not being at Tall Bamboo to try to defend his people during

Luisa: Hmm. Pos tua kia inen
ama ha'abweka am suan, yu.
Um tehapo ohvo kia
vahkopovenasi vuiten.
Tua si ousi ama suawak hunumu'u
ume yoem yo'owe.

Maria: Sorpresapo am bwisek?

Luisa: Pos si kaa . . .

Andres: Hunak hiva hunuen am suak.

Luisa: . . . kaa hu'unean hewi, porque
ket ini'i Hesus Raahu teame ket
kampanyan imin hakuni hitasa hariwa.
Tahoori kaita teaka
veha hunumun hakun rehte.
Hunum veha Hesus Raahu yevihsusek ti hiuwa.
Ketwo naateka vitwa hu'e
kawichi kom katekai.
Hiva ume wiko'im veohtopatopakti aane.
Ta si'ime taewai vitwa bwan.
Ta pos konfiansa, bwan.
Hunu'u veha a'avo weye ti hiuwa,
supe kwakteme yaivok ti hiuwa.

Maria: Hmm.

Luisa: Pos haksa? Tua ta'amak veha kia ho . . .
ta'amak ibwan, haivu ta'ata aman wecheo.
Ite intok huevenaka ume hefeim.

Luisa: Hmm. Well, they just
stood there killing them, look.
In the well, the blood was just
flowing like from a pool of water.
There were really so many killed there,
the elderly men.

Maria: They caught them by surprise?

Luisa: Well, they [the warrior Hiaki men] did not . . .

Andres: That's the only time they were killed like that.

Luisa: . . . they did not know, yes, because
this one named Hesus Raahu also
was on a campaign somewhere out here looking for something.
Clothing, [but] not finding anything,
when they were out there somewhere walking around.
Then there they were saying Hesus Raahu is coming.
In the morning they were seen over there
coming down from the mountain.
The rifles were gleaming.
But, all day they were seen, well.
But they [the Hiakis] had confidence, well.
That one [Hesus Raahu] is coming, they were saying.
The traitors are coming, others said.

Maria: Hmm.

Luisa: But where? With the sun, then, they just . . .
with the sun, well, when the sun was already setting.
And we were many, with the large knives.[20]

---

the massacre. The term *ma* translates to "how come?" or "why is it?" Thus another thought was that Andres might have felt, "Why is it that I am here walking in the rain while my people are in a bad situation in Sonora?" Perhaps Andres is saying that he was away from the action, away from the war.

20. The term *hefeim* means "large knives." Luisa is probably talking about machetes, a weapon that Hiakis used to fight their battles, to defend their homes, or as a household tool.

Vattuka itom eteho'um.
Tepuak huet hakiachi.
Vakateveu vichaa hakiachi asta aman vetukun,
sivammeu vetukun tahti te aanen.
Ta ume wate veha kee yahan.
Hunamet veha wiko'i hiutaitek.
Itommeu wikoota hiiau veha haivu
hum tua hoara nanasukut ibwan kaaten, ume Yoim.
Haivu henteta nasuk kia nah kaate.
Hunama veha kia ume yoem yo'owe
kia ume haamuchim nasuk kateme sua.
Ousi am suak hunumu'u. Chea . . .

Andres: Hunak hiva humaku'u hewi?

Luisa: Kia hiva.

Andres: Hunak hiva am . . .

Maria: Hunak hiva si huevenam suak?

Luisa: Bwe, i'an chukula vichaa kia wowoim,
vavahim hak susua,
bwan am bwiseko . . .

Andres: Bwe ko'okoime hewi, yoem o'olam,
itovenasi kateme.

Luisa: . . . ta hunum chea ousi am suala.

Maria: Ta hunak vat kia haamuchim
intok yo'owe ama hookan o ket hiva
ume sontaom, Hiak sontaom?

Luisa: Hiakim ibwan ama hookan,
ta ume ili tutu'i si'ime kampanyan, hakun.
Hita haiwan, hi'ibwa haiwan.
Hunuu Hesus Rahutukau am nunu'ubwan.

Maria: Vempoim notteu veha kia . . .

Luisa: Vempoim notteu veha haivu si'ime suari;
hente veha kia ama revataroari.

The ones we were talking about day before yesterday.
The large knives were there throughout the gully.
In the gully at Tall Bamboo toward the bottom,
we were there near the bottom of the cliff.
But the rest had not yet arrived.
Then they [the Mexicans] started to fire on them [the Hiakis].
When they started to fire on us they were already
in the midst of the homes, the Mexicans.
They were already walking among the people.
Then there, the elderly men
who were among the women were just killed.
They killed so many of them. More . . .

Andres: Perhaps that was the only time, yes?

Luisa: Just all the time.

Andres: That was the only time they . . .

Maria: Was that the only time that they killed so many?

Luisa: Well, now, later on they just killed two,
three they killed,
well, if they caught them.

Andres: Well, the sick ones, yes, the elderly men,
the ones that were about our age.

Luisa: . . . but there they killed so many.

Maria: But then at first was it just the women
and the elders who were there, or also
the soldiers, the Hiaki soldiers?

Luisa: Well, the Hiakis were there,
but the able-bodied ones were out campaigning, somewhere.
They were looking for something, looking for food.
That Hesus Raahu was their leader.

Maria: When they returned then just . . .

Luisa: When they returned then everybody had already been killed;
the people were just massacred.

Maria: Ili haikika hiva . . .

Luisa: Intok inime ket ama hookan,
kompae Chema kapitan, intok hunu'u
Kandido, intok aa sairawa,
intuchi huu kompae Rego komandantetuka'u.
Inime intok Teta Kuusimmeu aane.
Aman kava'im nu'uvok,
hu'e familiata hi'ibwatuavaekai.
Pos hunai ketwo am saka'alaktuk,
ume yoim intok ama yahak.
Hunuen, ume haamuchim ama nau veepsuwak.
Veha vempo intok ama yahak. Reyno,
Kompae Chema kapitantaim kava'im si nu'upak.
Huntuen ii intok familia hunum nau veeviakame,
ko'apo tevepo veha te to'e.
Hunum to'e si'ime ume peronim. Si am hahasetek,
veha hunaman si am suae'an, ume peronim.
Ta komo i'a familitavetchi'ivo veha kaa am hahasek.
Pos hunaa intok familiamsu am sua haptene ti hiupo
veha kaa emo am hahasek ti hiia bwan.

Maria: Hm, hmm.

Maria: Only a few . . .

Luisa: And these were there also:
  compadre Captain Chema, and that one
  Candido, and his younger brother.
  Also that one compadre Rego who used to be the commandant.
  And these men were over at Rock Crosses.
  They went there to go get some horses,
  to feed the family.
  Well, that morning when they had gone,
  the Mexicans arrived there.
  That way, the women were rounded up there.
  Then they arrived there. Reyno,
  compadre Captain Chema, bought a lot of horses.
  So then he and the wives who were rounded up there,
  we slept in the long corral.
  The bald ones all slept there. If the Hiakis had been chasing them,
  then they would have killed all of the bald ones.
  But because of the wives, then they did not chase them.
  And, well, that one said they might start to kill the wives,
  so they did not chase them, well.

Maria: Hm, hmm.

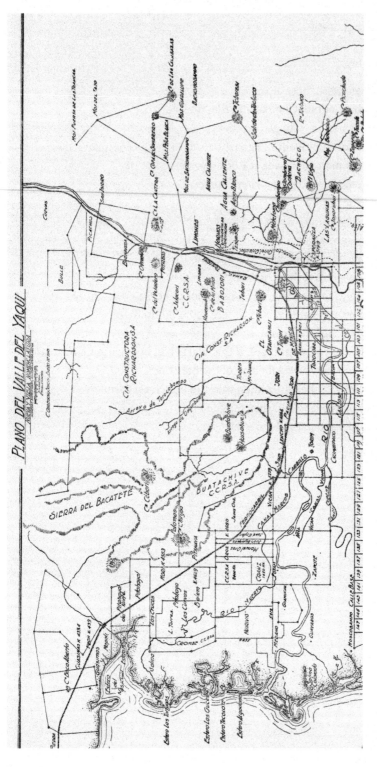

FIGURE 9 Excerpt of *Plano del Valle del Yaqui*, a survey map produced in Ciudad Obregón in January 1943, showing the Bacatete (Vakateeve) Mountains, the Hiaki River, and the Hiaki pueblos, as well as other features of interest: for example, the location of the Mexican fort at El Jori (lit. "The Mexican"), the location of the photograph in fig. 14, pp. 228–29, and the settlement of Agua Caliente (Hot Water), around where Andres and Luisa were living at the time of the interviews. Arizona Historical Society, Tucson Map Collection, Plano del Valle del Yaqui, G4472.Y3.1943.

CHAPTER 3

LIFE UNDER SIEGE, COERCION, AND COLLABORATION

Hiakis Living in the Mountains Before 1910 (Luisa)

Luisa describes a community of Hiakis living in the mountains, at To'okopo Va'ampo (Gray Waters), toward Wo'i Va'am (Coyote Waters). These Hiakis avoided all contact with Mexicans. They kept large herds of livestock (many raided from Mexican ranches) and made cheese, which they sold very cheaply, but only to other Hiakis. They also did not buy anything from Mexicans. When the Mexican campaign against the Hiakis began and fighting broke out in Hermosillo, this was where Luisa and her family and other Hiakis escaped to. The Mexicans did not attack these mountain communities until after they had subdued the Hiaki population in Hermosillo, but at that point they did. Besides Mexican soldiers, the attackers had Hiaki and Mayo conscripts, who knew their way around the mountains and guided the Mexicans to the mountain Hiakis.

Luisa: Ta vu'uriakan, tu'isi vu'uriakan uu hente
itom aman yahau, dieztuko. Hunumu'u . . .

Maria: Hmm.

Luisa: Intok si wakasim vu'uriakan.
I'an uu ama aneme tua kaa au kompararoa.
Hunak intok asta Wo'i Va'ammeu tahti.
Yu, kia toh leste vuurum, kava'im, wakasim.

Maria: Hmm.

Luisa: Keesum, im hak veekkanim im hoa.
Huname kia woi pesotukan.

Maria: Hmm. Fíjate.

Luisa: Ta vempo mismo hiva ama hunuen am nenka.
Kaa yoimmeu pa'akun.
Kaa yeu yaaha bwan. Kaita.
Vempo mismo hiva.

Maria: Hmm.

Luisa: Nau hunuen dilihensia.
Kaita. Kaa hak yoimmeu yeu bwa'amta hinu.
Intok kia huna'a kesu hoowame huni
kaa yoimmeu nenkiwa.
Vempo mismo hiva.

Maria: Vempo am hooa?

Luisa: Heewi. Hunuen weye. Ta pos,
vempo ume wakasim pos huet ranchompo nunu'e.
Intok imin, ori, San Paasiskou vicha,
dispensau vicha,
hunuet veha bweere ranchom hokaa, bwan.
Hunuet veha am nunu'eka,
ama am kiima'i si'imeta, animalta.

Luisa: But there were many, very many people,
   when we arrived there, in 1910. Over there . . .

Maria: Hmm.

Luisa: And there were a lot of cattle.
   Those who live there now really do not compare.
   And then, up to Coyote Waters.
   The donkeys, horses, cattle were just grazing all over.

Maria: Hmm.

Luisa: The cheeses, they made them this big.[1]
   They cost just one peso.

Maria: Hmm. Imagine that.

Luisa: But they themselves only sold them there like that.
   Not out to the Mexicans.
   They never came out [from the mountains], well. Nothing.
   [They kept] only to themselves.

Maria: Hmm.

Luisa: They conducted business among themselves.
   Nothing. They never bought food from the Mexicans.
   And that homemade cheese
   was never sold to the Mexicans.
   Only among themselves.

Maria: They were making them?

Luisa: Yes. That's how it went. But, well,
   they would get the cattle from the ranches.
   And over here, well, toward San Francisco,
   toward the butchering plant,
   then there were some big ranches, well.
   That's where they got them,
   and put the animals in there, all of them.

---

1. Luisa indicates the size with her arms stretched out, showing a twelve-inch diameter.

Maria: Chivam ket hippue?

Luisa: Si'imeta im hippuen; hunume yu
ama ho'akame, itom ama yahau.
Tua im ousi pitti ho'akan, ibwan.
Ta pos . . .

Maria: Hunama veha ume yoim kaa kikkimun?

Luisa: Kaa ama kikkimun, ta chukula veha
ama kiimuk.

Maria: Hmm.

Luisa: Kaa aa hikkaha?
Wilom yee hahhaseu ti kaa e'etehowa.
Ume Wilom, tua hunak veha
itom aman watteu
hunume Wilom veha ama yee hahhase.

Maria: Hmm.

Luisa: Pesiopo nahsuasuwako,
si'imet hunum nahsuasuwak,
veha ameu kiimuk.
Ameu kampanya haptek ume'e govierno.

Maria: Ume Hiak sontaom, bueno,
ume yoimmak cha'akame,
huname pos haivu ama ket hu'unea, hewi?

Luisa: Heewi.

Maria: Huname veha humak aman am toha,
aman am totoha.

Luisa: Heewi, heewi.
Hunume amemak rerehte.

Maria: Hiak traidoorim.

Maria: Did they have goats also?

Luisa: They had everything, those who always
lived there, when we used to visit there.
They lived very close to each other, well.
But then . . .

Maria: The Mexicans did not go in there?

Luisa: They did not go in there, but then later,
they went in there.

Maria: Hmm.

Luisa: Did you not hear about it?
They talked about the skinny ones[2] chasing us.
The skinny ones, right at that time then,
when we arrived there [in the mountains],
those skinny ones were really chasing us.

Maria: Hmm.

Luisa: When the fighting was over in Hermosillo,
when the fighting was over, all throughout there,
then they attacked us.
The government began their campaign.

Maria: The Hiaki soldiers,
those who had joined the Mexicans,
they already knew their way around there, yes?

Luisa: Yes.

Maria: Those maybe are the ones who took them [the Mexicans],
who used to take them there [to the mountains].

Luisa: Yes, yes.
Those were the ones who were with them [Mexican soldiers].

Maria: Hiaki traitors.

---

2. *Wilom*, literally "skinny ones," was one of the terms Hiakis used to refer to the Mexican soldiers.

Luisa: Si'ime hunume ume yoemem.
Haksa im faltaroa ume yoemem?
Hak huni kaa faltaroa. [*Laughs.*]

Maria: Katin i'inia. [*Laughs.*]

Luisa: Hunuen veha
si'ime ume Ko'okoimpo ho'akame, Maayom,
si'ime hunume yee hahhatuawa kaupo.

Hacienda Life Under the Mexicans (Luisa)

Luisa describes how Hiakis worked as field hands on their own land for the large companies that had leased the land in Hiak Vatwe to farm for profit, including the company of the American businessman Robinson.[3] She describes the crops they would plant and harvest, and the "company store" system of credit that kept workers in debt. During government crackdowns, when the men had all either been conscripted into the Mexican army or joined the guerrillas in the mountains, Hiaki women were required to do the physical labor that the men had been doing previously, to pay off the debt accrued by the men. They never were able to. The conscripted men could not visit their wives and families working back on the haciendas.

Maria: Ume asiendampo ho'akame intok . . .
haisa . . . hitasa, ama, vempo ama hita eechi?
O bwe ori ume am atteakame ama eechi?
Hita ama e'echan?

---

3. She probably intended to refer to Richardson, the American investor whose company bought up large chunks of the Hiaki Valley for agriculture and bought mineral rights throughout the area. Many of the illustrative photos in this volume come from the Richardson company archive in the University of Arizona Library Special Collections.

Luisa: All of them were Hiakis.
Where are they not present, the Hiakis?
They are not lacking anywhere. [*Laughs.*]

Maria: Remember that. [*Laughs.*]

Luisa: In this way then
all those who live in Ko'okoim, Mayos,
all of them were made to chase us in the mountains.

FIGURE 10 Men threshing grain in a field. Arizona Historical Society, PC 180, Norman Wallace Photographs, box 42, album #1, page 82, B.

Maria: And those who lived on the haciendas . . .
how . . . what did they plant there?
Or, well, the owners, what did they plant there?
What did they usually plant there?

Luisa: Hakuni? Asiendampo?

Maria: Asiendampo.

Luisa: Abwe, tekowaim, patronim ama ho'ak.

Maria: Heewi. Hita e'echan huname'e?

Luisa: Abwe, muunim, tiikom, kaa, ori kaavansam.
Hunak hunu'u tua e'etwan.

Maria: Hmm.

Luisa: Muunim, tiikom intok kaavansam, kamam. Hunuka e'echan.

Maria: Yoemem veha aman tekipanoan?

Luisa: Yoemem veha ama tekipannoa. Pionimtukan.

Maria: Hmm.

Luisa: Intok kaa, kaa i'anvenasi maakinam aukan.
Kia ume orim, kaviam teame.
Hosommea am chukchukta ume yoeme ume tiikom.

Maria: Hmm.

Luisa: Kaita maakinam ibwan i'anvenasi.
Maakina, chaka karom tea,
bweere lamina kaarom.
Hunama veha nau tohina.
Huname veha kia bwe'usi paava yecha'awak veha.
Kava'immea tavia.

Maria: Hmm.

Luisa: Kava'immea am triyaaroane,
tukaariat naavuhti, taewait naavuhti.

Maria: Ili usim chikti ama tekipanoa?

Luisa: Heewi. Hunak kaita, kaita,
bwan i'anvenasi makinaaria. Kaitatukan.

Maria: Haisa vavanwan ume . . . hunume hitam,
muunim, hitasa ama echime.

Luisa: Where? On the haciendas?

Maria: On the haciendas.

Luisa: Well, the supervisors, the bosses lived there.

Maria: Yes. What did they usually plant?

Luisa: Well, beans, wheat, well, chickpeas.
At that time, that's what they usually planted.

Maria: Hmm.

Luisa: Beans, wheat and chickpeas, squash. That's what they planted.

Maria: The Hiakis worked there then?

Luisa: The Hiakis used to work there then. They were the peons.

Maria: Hmm.

Luisa: And then there were no, no machines, like today.
Just, well, the stalk of the plant.
The Hiakis cut the wheat with a scythe.

Maria: Hmm.

Luisa: There were no vehicles like today.
The vehicles are known as square trailers,
big aluminum wagons.
They gathered the wheat and put it in there.
Then they would make a big stack.
The horses would thresh the wheat.

Maria: Hmm.

Luisa: They would thresh the wheat with the horses,
throughout the night, throughout the day.

Maria: The little children were also working?

Luisa: Yes. Then, there was nothing, nothing,
well, like the machines today. There were none then.

Maria: How did they irrigate the . . . those things,
the beans, the things that were planted there?

Luisa: Bwe kia veha hunuen am vavane. Mesklampo.
Kia, kia inen kuadrausi.
Kaa i'anvenasi kurvam hoowan, hunak huni'i.

Maria: Kaita kanaalim.

Luisa: E'e. I'an intok kurvan, ti hiuna.
Hunak intok kia veha ineni bwan, vavanen.
Ili seekiam bwikola to'one.
Huname veha kia mamayoat ettapowa,
inen wam vicha.

Maria: Haamuchim veha hitaa ama hoone?
Huname veha, ori . . . kosinata weetuane
o si ket ama anne,
ket o'owimmak tekipanoane?

Luisa: Bwe, kaa tekipanoan o'owim ama aneu.

Maria: O.

Luisa: Ta komo o'owim toisuwak, veha komo o'owim . . .
komo i'an maasu pos sosiom, hewi?
Ta valem hipu'une.

Maria: Hmm.

Luisa: Bwa'amta kuentapo yeu wo'otane.
Hunai veha wikiriane, hewi.
Hunuen veha ume yoemem tohisuwak,
o'owim tehalwak veha
ime haamuchim tekipanoatuawan.
Hipesuma'atuawa, si'imeta hitasa, mun hippontuawa.
Hunaka kuentata veha ume haamuchim vehe'etua'ii'aawa.

Maria: Ta hiva huni kaa aa vehe'etuane, hewi, posi hiva . . .

Luisa: Um, um, kaita. Kia veha tekipanoane,
porque kaita ama kova'ane ume haamuchim huni'i.
Mas de kee kia ili munim etbwaka

Luisa: Well, they just used to irrigate them that way. Mixing it up.
Just, just in squares.
They did not make curved rows like today, even then.

Maria: There were no canals.

Luisa: No. And now there are the curved rows, they say.
Back then, well, they just used to irrigate this way.[4]
They would make little ditches alongside the rows.
Then they would just open them on the edge,
from here to there.

Maria: What did the women do there then?
Did they then, well . . . run the kitchen,
or were they also there,
working with the men?

Luisa: Well, they would not work when the men were there.

Maria: Oh.

Luisa: But since they [the Mexicans] took all the men, then like the men . . .
Like now they are members of the society, yes?
But they were given IOUs.

Maria: Hmm.

Luisa: They would get food on credit.
They would owe that bill, yes.
That's how, when they deported all the men,
when all the men were gone,
these women were forced to work.
They were making bamboo mats, all that, threshing beans.
Then the women would be made to pay the account.

Maria: But they would never finish paying it, yes, since always . . .

Luisa: Um, um, nothing. Then they would just work,
even though the women would not earn anything.
They would just steal a few beans,

---

4. Luisa makes a motion of throwing water.

hunuka hiva nuksik hiva aa weiyane
hunaka hiva ili bwa'ane.
Asoa, asoawam veha hunuka ili bwa'atuane.

Maria: Hunuen ori haamuchim hasiendampo hok
haisa ume yoeme am familiakame
ameu yaaha, etbwa ameu yaaha,
o kaa, tua kaa ameu yaaha?

Luisa: Kaa ameu yaaha,
pos si sontaom nuksaka'awak.
Pesio totoiwa,
si'ime sontao hoowa, utteapo.

Maria: Ta kawipo aneme?

Luisa: Kaupo aneme, ala.
Kaupo aneme chea kaa aman yeu yaaha.

FIGURE 11 Men threshing chickpeas in the Hiaki River valley in 1907. Records of the Compañía Constructora Richardson, S.A., 1904–1968 (bulk 1904–1927), MS 113, box 1, folder 4: Photographs. Courtesy of University of Arizona Libraries, Special Collections.

> they would take that and go home,
> and they would eat only that.
> The child, their children were then fed only that.

Maria: When the women were on the haciendas,
did the men who had their wives there
come to visit them, sneak in to visit them,
or not, or really they never came to visit them?

Luisa: They did not come to visit them,
since they were conscripted into the Mexican military.
They used to take them to Hermosillo.
All of them were forced into the military.

Maria: But the men who were in the mountains?

Luisa: The ones who were in the mountains did.
But they hardly came down.

Violence Between Mountain Hiakis and Hacienda Hiakis (Luisa)

Luisa describes how the hacienda Hiakis were caught in the middle. The guerrilla Hiakis in the mountains would attack them, steal from them, and even kill them when they came down for supplies or for other reasons, justifying their actions with the view that the hacienda Hiakis were

---

Luisa: Yu, ume kaupo yu ho'akame
chea kia ume yoemem huni susuan yoimpo ho'akame.
Yoimpo ho'akame huni susuan.
Yu, intok inen taho'ota huni yee u'ura.
Revoosam, su . . . taho'opo pattaka aa nuksimne.
O'owta huni'i. Saaweam, si'imek
aa wattariane, u'ane.

Maria: Hmm.

Luisa: Hunuen yee hoan ume yu kaupo ho'akame.

Maria: Tua ume kau homem?

Luisa: Heewi. Tua hunain yee hooa.
Hunuen hak hoarampo kimuk, ama yahak
kia tepuam kahonim, kaham hamhamti veepne.

Maria: Hmm.

Luisa: Heewi. Hunume kia kau homem huni
hunuen am hooan ume asiendampo ho'akame,
yoemem.

Maria: Haiseaka hunuen am hooa?
Kaa am yoem eiyan o si . . .

Luisa: Abwe vempo kaupo ho'ak.
Kaa yoimmeu yeu yaaha.

"collaborators" working for and supporting the Mexicans and foreigners who had taken Hiaki land. On the other hand, the hacienda bosses and plantation owners suspected the hacienda Hiakis of collaborating with the rebels in the mountains, providing them with supplies, ammunition, and tactical support. When the hacienda Hiakis would go off the plantation to gather firewood, they would be arrested on suspicion of meeting the rebels and providing support.

Luisa: Look, the ones who lived in the mountains
even killed the Hiakis who lived among the Mexicans.
They even killed those[5] that lived among the Mexicans.
And look, they even took the clothing away from us.
The shawls, dresses . . . they wrapped the clothes and took them.
The men also. Their pants, everything
would be removed and taken.

Maria: Hmm.

Luisa: That's what those who lived in the mountains used to do to us.

Maria: The true mountain men?

Luisa: Yes. That's what they really did to us.
When they entered a home, when they arrived there,
they chop the boxes apart, tear apart the cartons with axes.

Maria: Hmm.

Luisa: Yes. Those mountain men
would do that to the ones who lived on the haciendas,
the Hiakis.

Maria: Why did they do this to them?
They did not trust them or . . .

Luisa: Well, they lived in the mountains.
They never came down to the Mexicans.

---

5. Luisa here is referring to other Mexicans, Mayos, and other non-Hiakis who lived in the virtually abandoned Hiaki villages.

Kak taho'ota nu'e.
Kia hunuen, hiva reveldemvenasi kaupo rehteka veha
ume mansom yanti ho'akame veha taho'o watwattaka
am u'ura, amet aa vansaroa.
Hunuen am hooa. Kaita.
Hunuen am u'ura uka taho'ota.
Intok hunuen veha ama yee susua.
Yoim ama ho'akame susua,
porque hunum asiendampo wam vicha,
kaave peronim hohoye.
Kaave peronim ama hohoye.
Kia yoeme, kia hente hiva ama aane.

Maria: Heewi.

Luisa: Kialikun hunumun kom yaaha.
Kaita etetbwa. Ta pos hunuen ket ume yoeme,
amevenasi yoemem huni sussua.

Maria: Ume yoemem, intok pos, ume,
hunume kau homemmak ori, am aniame,
huname veha ket, ori kastigaroana?

Luisa: Katin ume yoim, yoimpo ori, ho'akame,
katin ume yoim, bwe uu govierno, hewi?
Hunu'u veha hunen hiia tea,
katin parketa ameu am totoha ti hiia tea,
ume kawiu ho'akammewi.
Ume yoimpo ho'akame veha,
hunuen parketa ameu totoha ti hiia tea,
bwa'amta ameu am totoha ti hiiaka veha
senu veha hunuen yoimpo ho'akame
veha hakun kau nau ke'ewekame yepsak,
kaa aman hahhasuwaka yepsak
kia veha kia aa ho'awapo yepsak veha
bwihwaka nuksaka'ana.

Maria: Hmm. Kaa, kaita hoaka huni'i?

Luisa: Heewi. Kaita hoaka huni'i.

They had no place to buy clothes.
They were just like that, like rebels always in the mountains then,
they would take clothes from the ones who always lived in peace,
take them from them, taking advantage of them.
That's what they did to them. Nothing.
That's how they took their clothes.
And then that's how they killed them also.
They killed the Mexicans who lived there,
because on the haciendas down that way,
there were no bald ones there.
There were no Mexican soldiers there.
Only Hiakis, only people were there.

Maria: Yes.

Luisa: That's why they used to go down there.
They did not steal anything. But, well, the Hiakis also,
they would even kill the Hiakis like them.

Maria: The Hiakis, and, well, the,
those who helped the men in the mountains,
did they punish them also?

Luisa: Remember, the Mexicans, the ones living among the Mexicans,
remember, the Mexicans, well, the government, yes?
It was said that they said this,
remember, that they took ammunition to them,
to the Hiakis who lived in the mountains.
The [Hiakis] who lived among the Mexicans then
took ammunition to [the mountain Hiakis], they said,
they provided food to them, they [the government] said,
so then anyone who lived among the Mexicans
might be out near the mountains to gather wood, then return
if they were not chased [by the mountain Hiakis], and arrived home,
then just as soon as they got home
they would be caught [by Mexican soldiers] and taken away.

Maria: Hmm. Even if they had done nothing?

Luisa: Yes. Even if they were not doing anything.

>   Hunuen, hunuen hoowan
>   hunum asiendampo hokaari.
>   Porque amemak veha lutu'uriak teana
>   ume kaupo ho'akammake.

Maria: Hmm.

Luisa: Hunuen veha, parketa, hitasa lonchita,
chukti ameu totoha teaka veha
hunuen hoowa ume yoimpo ho'akame.
Hu yoi veha, govierno veha kam tu'ure, hewi.
Hunum veha am bwiseka veha am nuksasaka.
Huntuen hakun ke'eweka yepsak, kaita.
Kia wam am himaak
hiva haivu im vicha weiyaana.

Maria: Hmm.

Luisa: Hm.

Maria: Ume kau homem aman aneme humane veha vem familiam aman hippuen?

Luisa: Huname im am hippuen. I'an in etehoopo, To'okopo Va'ampo, Vakatevepo.

Maria: Heewi.

Luisa: Hunum ho'aka veha aman kom yaaha . . .

Maria: Hm, hmm.

Luisa: . . . ka hunuen veha ume, ori asiendampo ho'akame hooa. Hunuen itom hooan, hunume'e si'ime hunum vicha. Kaa, kaita. Hunuen am susuasuk si'ime hentem.

That's how, that's how they were treated,
the ones who lived on the haciendas.
Because they were said to have a relationship with them,
the ones who lived in the mountains.

Maria: Hmm.

Luisa: This way, then, ammunition, even food
was said to be carried to them [the mountain Hiakis], then
that's what they did to the Hiakis living among the Mexicans.
The Mexicans, then, the government did not like the Hiakis, yes.
That's how they would capture them, then take them away.
So when one went to gather wood and returned, nothing.
They would just throw the wood aside,
they would already be taken this way.

Maria: Hmm.

Luisa: Hm.

Maria: The mountain men who were there,
did they have their wives with them?

Luisa: They had them here. Now, here, the places I am talking about,
Gray Waters, Tall Bamboo.

Maria: Yes.

Luisa: While they lived there, they would then go down there . . .

Maria: Hm, hmm.

Luisa: . . . doing that to those who lived on the haciendas.
That's what they did to us, all of those, over that way.
Not, nothing. That's how they killed all the people.

Life in the Villages up to and During the Escobar Rebellion (Reyno)

Reyno describes how the Hiakis were gathered together and enrolled in a rationing scheme, whereby each person would be placed on a list and receive some payment. The remaining people in the eight villages came together and began to celebrate Lent again, although with great caution; the pascolas and Fariseos would keep their weapons with them even during the ceremonies due to distrust of the Mexicans. Reyno recounts how a man named Teófilo Muñoz, who used to drive into Ko'okoim to get cigarettes and coffee, was killed and buried by the side of the road. Everyone was cautioned not to go anywhere without a bodyguard or other protection. Eventually the men were taken south to sign a peace agreement. They came to where the women and children who had been captured, like Luisa, were being held. Later he describes how there was a guardhouse full of supplies, which he and other children would visit. This was during the Escobar Rebellion. He wasn't sure whether the soldiers were with the government forces or the rebels. It was a frightening time. He recounts how a plane flew overhead releasing leaflets, perhaps concerning president-elect Lázaro Cárdenas, and the men panicked and

Reyno: Pos hunum veha, hunum veha te, te yahak.
    Uchi a'avo kom yahiwak veha te ori, te
    haisa humak, haiki . . .
    nee kaa tua au waate.
    No sé si mamni metpo te ama hookan,
    haisa humaku'u,
    ta hunum intok ume yoeme sosotane teaka,
    intok ori, listapo kima'awak, ume uusim . . .
    hunume kima'awak.
    Hunama veha te sosota haptek.
    Hunum veha te, hunak veha
    Torim, Ko'okoim, Vahkom,
    si'ime pueplo aman kom yahak,
    waate; wate intok im wainni.

ran or threw themselves on the ground, throwing their rifles up in the air, fearing the plane was dropping bombs. The Hiakis were all there together because of their defeat at White Mountain, he reports. During this time, Luisa was captive, down in Mexico City.

FIGURE 12   A Hiaki family, ca. 1910. Arizona Historical Society, PC 078, Mathews Photograph Collection, box 3, album #54473, page 9, #X.

Reyno: Well, there, then, there then, we, we arrived.
        When they came down again, then we, well, we,
        I don't know how, or how many . . .
        I don't really remember.
        I don't know if we were there for five months,
        I don't know how,
        but there, they said, the men would get paid,
        and, well, they were placed on a list, the children . . .
        they were placed on a list.
        That's when we started to get paid.
        That's when we, that's when
        Torim, Ko'okoim, Vahkom,
        all the pueblos began to come down there,
        some; and some over here.

Luisa: Hm, hmm.

Reyno: Hunum veha, hunum veha uu tren
intok hiva bwan im nah weyen.
Tankimpo veha te ha'amuka veha te
ama eta'awak.
Hunak veha te a'avo toiwak.

Luisa: Aa.

Reyno: Hunak veha ori, hunak
veha komo wasuktiapo humak im hoowak.
Hunak veha si'ime pueplo im hookan.

Luisa: Hm, hmm.

Reyno: Imi'i. Si'ime ocho pueplom.
Hmm. Hunum veha
wawaehmate haptek . . .

Luisa: Hm, hmm.

Reyno: . . . ta hunum, hunum ketun ama mamachi.
Inika nee teteswa . . .
uka sementeriata kateka'apo, wanna, hunum ori . . .
ori katekan, ori To-, Torreon . . .

Luisa: Hm, hmm.

Reyno: . . . hunum, hunum hookan ume treinta oochom.

Luisa: Hm, hmm.

Reyno: Hunama kia ori, kia im vina vicha,
kia ori, mettrayadooram
kia a'avo vicha yeu hoarine.

Luisa: Hmm.

Reyno: Waehma hoaka huni,
kia wiko'im ameu ha'abwaine.

Luisa: Hmm.

Luisa: Hm, hmm.

Reyno: There, then, there, then the train
was always moving, well, around here.
Then we climbed into the tanks, then we
were locked in them.
Then we were taken here.

Luisa: Ah.

Reyno: Then, well, well, then,
then like a year, maybe, we were there.
Then, then, all the pueblos were here.

Luisa: Hm, hmm.

Reyno: Here. All the eight villages.
Hmm. There, then
they started to carry out the Lenten ceremonies . . .

Luisa: Hm, hmm.

Reyno: . . . but there, there, it is still visible.
I tell this one [referring to M.H., his wife]
. . . where the cemetery is, over there, there, well . . .
well, it was there, well, To-, Torreón . . .

Luisa: Hm, hmm.

Reyno: . . . there, there were the 38s [probably a military unit].

Luisa: Hm, hmm.

Reyno: There, just, well, just toward this way,
just, well, the machine guns
were just sitting there pointing this way.

Luisa: Hmm.

Reyno: Even during Lent,
they just had their rifles pointed this way.

Luisa: Hmm.

Reyno: Pahko'um, chapayekam.
Pos hiva kaa yoem e'a, bwan.

Luisa: Um, hmm.

Reyno: Vaa, si huneraikan.
Hitavetchi'ivo inii i'an uka poove,
im, im kaa vo'oka, kaa aa vicha?

Luisa: Um, um.

M.H.: Tiofiro Muñoz.

Reyno: Tiofiro Muñoz. Hunaa ma inim me'ewak.
Ta komo u'u ta'ewa, hewi?

Luisa: Heewi.

Reyno: Karopo rehtiwau,
katin Ko'okoimmeu kom yeepsan.

Luisa: Hm, hmm.

Reyno: Hita, kafeta,
hita aman nunu'en, viivam.

Luisa: Heewi, nee aa eteho hikkaila.

Reyno: Hunume humak aa ta'a,
aet nesawek.

Luisa: Hm.

Reyno: Hunum veha me'ewak.
Intok ketun sikim reliikiakan kechia.
Hm, hm. Hunum palasio i'ani.

Luisa: Tsk.

Reyno: The *pahko'olam*, the Fariseos.
Well, they just did not trust them, well.

Luisa: Um, hmm.

Reyno: Yes, it was very ugly.
Why is it then that, that poor deceased one,
here, here he lies [*pointing*], don't you see him?[6]

Luisa: Um, um.

M.H.: Teófilo Muñoz.

Reyno: Teófilo Muñoz. That one, you see, was killed here.
But since he was known, yes?

Luisa: Yes.

Reyno: When they were traveling by car,
remember he used to go down to Ko'okoim?

Luisa: Hm, hmm.

Reyno: Something, coffee,
he used to go for some things, cigarettes.

Luisa: Yes, I have heard him spoken of.

Reyno: They probably knew him,
and ordered it [Teófilo's killing].

Luisa: Hm.

Reyno: Then that's where he was killed.
And he still had on his red protection relic too.
Hm, hm. Now there is a grave there.

Luisa: Tsk.

---

6. A Mexican man named Teófilo Muñoz was killed by the Mexican soldiers and buried by the Hiakis where he fell. A burial site is referred to as a *palacio*, and this is what Reyno is pointing to. The burial site is across the road from Reyno and Maria Hesus's home. During the fighting, people were buried where they fell or just covered with large rocks, as there was no time to bury them.

Reyno: Yo'owe ori . . . hunu'u anima
Hose Muñoz aa saekan.

Luisa: Hm, hmm.

Reyno: Ili Hosetukau.
Hunua sae Tiofilo tea.
Pos hunuen yeu sikaapo . . .
Hunuen veha te, ori . . .
. . . kia hak vem aa tutu'ureka'apo yee sootarian.
Ta huname intok
haivu, haivu kia eskortam ama anne.

Luisa: Hmm.

Reyno: Kia "Emo em listaroaka aman kikkimu.
Katem kia aman kikkimu," ti hiuwan.

Luisa: Hmm.

Reyno: Nee intok ketun uusi bwan . . . kaita.
Hunum veha hunuen a'anen . . .
tea ume ya'uchim.
Hunuen yeu sika'apo veha haksa weeka'apo,
veha uu vehak enchim eteho'u . . .

Luisa: Hmm.

Reyno: . . . ume yoeme veha
inika paasta firmaroane'e teakai ti,
nuksaka'awak. Woosa.

Luisa: Hmm.

Reyno: Ume, ume, ume, ori,
primerpo am vicha sahakame huni huevena . . .

Luisa: Huevena.
Hm, hunueni bwan.

Reyno: Ta huname veha si'ime sahak.
Chukula intuchi ume waate.

Reyno: The elders, well . . . that deceased one,
    José Muñoz was his younger brother.

Luisa: Hm, hmm.

Reyno: The late Little José.
    His older brother was known as Teófilo.
    Well, since it came out that way.
    Well, then, that way we, well . . .
    . . . just wherever they liked it, that's where they ambushed us.
    But they
    already, already had escorts there.

Luisa: Hmm.

Reyno: Just, "Prepare yourselves before going in.
    Don't just go in," they said.

Luisa: Hmm.

Reyno: And I was still a child, well . . . nothing.
    That's where they did this . . .
    the leaders said.
    When that happened then, one day,
    then the one you were talking about . . .

Luisa: Hmm.

Reyno: . . . the Hiakis then,
    who were going to sign this peace treaty, it is said,
    were taken away. Twice.

Luisa: Hmm.

Reyno: The, the, the, well,
    the first to go over there were also many . . .

Luisa: There were many.
    Hm, well, that's the way it was.

Reyno: But then all of them left.
    Again later, some more.

Luisa: Hmm.

Reyno: Ta hunum hakunsu veha ameu yahak,
um aman tohirimmewi.

Luisa: Hmm. Haivu hunaman.
Sochimilkopo itom hok aman yahak.

Reyno: Hee?

Luisa: Hunum te hookan.
Chukula hunume aman yahak.

Reyno: Hmm.

Luisa: Katin uu kompae Antonio Ania
aman yepsak, chukula.

Reyno: Oo...

Luisa: Norita mooneka'u.

Reyno: Hee?

Luisa: Wate hentemmake intok
aa familiawa intok wate familiam
huevenaka aman kia amemak yahak...

Reyno: Hee?

Luisa: ... Pitaayat ho'akame, hunume
Antesta maalam,[7] akowam intok hunu
komae Lus weeratukautaim...
hunume si'ime kia aman yahak.
I'an chukula ultimopo aman yahau.

Reyno: Heewi.

M.H.: Aa, kia vempo voluntariom?

---

7. "Antes" is how Hiaki people refer to men named Andres, or Andrew in English. So doña Luisa's in-laws voluntarily left to witness the signing of the peace accord; however, they were also captured and imprisoned.

Luisa: Hmm.

Reyno: But then they came to them, over there somewhere,
   to those who were already there.

Luisa: Hmm. They were already there.
   When we were already there in Xochimilco, they arrived.

Reyno: Oh?

Luisa: That's where we were.
   Later they arrived over there.

Reyno: Hmm.

Luisa: Remember compadre Antonio World
   arrived there, later.

Reyno: Oh . . .

Luisa: Nori's late son-in-law.

Reyno: Oh?

Luisa: With some people and
   his wife and other families,
   many just arrived with them, there . . .

Reyno: Oh?

Luisa: The ones who lived in Pitaya,
   Andres's mom, his older sisters, and that one,
   comadre Luz, the fair-skinned one and others . . .
   all of them just arrived there.
   Now later, at the end, when they were arriving there.

Reyno: Yes.

M.H.: Ah, they were just volunteers?

Luisa: Kia vempo voluntaa porque
ume yoememmak kaave amemak sahak, o yahak.

M.H.: Kaa mampo . . . kaa, kaa bwihri?

Luisa: E'e.

Reyno: Kia voluntaa.
Katin, kia ori veinte dia . . .
Aa, aa pos hunaa uka ori . . .

M.H.: Escobar.

Reyno: . . . renovasionta weyeo.

M.H.: La renovación de Escobar.[8]

Reyno: Ta hunak vempo mismo nau nahsuan ume . . .

M.H.: Peronim . . .

Reyno: Ume, ume, ume,
ume goviernom toohaptekame,
ume ya'uchim, ume peronimmake . . .
ume hentem . . .

Luisa: Hm, hmm.

Reyno: . . . huname veha, veha goviernou kontrapo haptek.
Hunaksan veha inim ket si mahaiwachiakan hunako . . .

Luisa: Hmm.

Reyno: . . . hunaksan te hunum bombapo wannavo,
i'an ketun ama week uu bwe'u ehea?

Luisa: Hm.

Reyno: Hunama waariatukan.

Luisa: Aa?

---

8. *La renovación de Escobar*: Apparently the residents had to renew their identification cards.

Luisa: They were just volunteers because no one went or arrived with them.

M.H.: They were not . . . not captured?

Luisa: No.

Reyno: Just voluntary.
Remember, just, well, twenty days . . .
Ah, ah, well, that one, that, well . . .

M.H.: Escobar.

Reyno: . . . when the renewals were going on.

M.H.: The renewals of Escobar.

Reyno: But at that time they were fighting among themselves, the . . .

M.H.: The bald ones.

Reyno: The, the, the,
the ones who deserted the Mexican government military,
the leaders, the ones with the Mexican soldiers . . .
the people . . .

Luisa: Hm, hmm.

Reyno: . . . then those, then they started to revolt against the government. It was then that here it also became very scary at that time . . .

Luisa: Hmm.

Reyno: . . . it was then that on the other side of the pump we, now it is still standing, the big ironwood?

Luisa: Hm.

Reyno: The guardhouse was there.

Luisa: Ah?

Reyno: Heewi. Ori, ainam kia haisa tinchea kikne,
provision, paarke, wiko'im.
Hunum veha ume yoeme,
ori wiko'immaktukan.

Luisa: Hee?

Reyno: Porque ume veha hahawame veha,
no sé si hunume vetana o
tua govierno vetana.

Luisa: Hmm.

Reyno: Ta nee hunuen aa vichakan.
Ta kaa hunuka hiva. Sardiinam,
salmoonim, saavum, bueno,
si'imeta makwan.

Luisa: Hmm.

Reyno: Ketun hunait veha senya,
i'an tahtia yoemem hoosuka'apo.

Luisa: Hmm.

Reyno: Ta nee hunuen . . .
chuvala hunum veha wattiwakan . . .
hunum, vaa, hunum.
Hunaman te hooka veha
im yaahan, im waariawi.

Luisa: Hmm.

Reyno: Huntuan hunak intok uu ori,
hikkaiwan . . . Lasaro Kardenas.

Reyno: Yes. Well, the flour was just stacked up,
>	the provisions, ammo, arms.
>	That's where the Hiakis,
>	well, had been given the rifles.

Luisa: Oh?

Reyno: Because then the ones who were being chased, then,
>	I don't know if they were on their [the Hiakis'] side or
>	with the government.

Luisa: Hmm.

Reyno: But I saw it that way.
>	But not just that. Sardines,
>	salmon, soap, well,
>	they were given everything.

Luisa: Hmm.

Reyno: There are still some signs
>	even now, there, where the Hiakis used to be.

Luisa: Hmm.

Reyno: But that way I . . .
>	for a while they stayed there then . . .
>	there, yes, there.
>	While we were there,
>	we used to come here, to the guardhouse.

Luisa: Hmm.

Reyno: And so in those days the, well,
>	it was heard about . . . Lázaro Cárdenas.[9]

---

9. Lázaro Cárdenas del Río was the fifty-first president of Mexico, from 1934 to 1940. It was during these years that the Hiakis fought valiantly to try to keep their territory. Cárdenas believed in land reform, so he revived agrarian reform in Mexico, expropriating large landed estates and distributing land to small landholders in collective holdings. However, he made some promises to the Hiakis, including a very important one that he failed to keep. He promised that the Hiakis would be entitled to 50 percent

Luisa: Hm, hmm.

Reyno: Ume si motchai ibwan uu hente.
Ta hunak si'ime hente im hookan,
ocho pueplom.

Luisa: Ta hunak tu'ulisi nau uniontukan, heewi?

Reyno: Heewi.

M.H.: Ta pos hu'ubwa nau vem mucha'imtaka
hunum nau rehte.

Reyno: Hu'ubwa nau vepsu'im.

Luisa: Heewi.

M.H.: Heewi.

Reyno: Hunak im veha . . .

M.H.: Hu'ubwa yaha.

Reyno: . . . uu avion veha im cha'asime, hewi?
Imin weekai veha,
ori ume hiosiam, hita kom wootak.
Ume yoeme, kia, kia toktokti nat tenne.

Luisa, Maria, & M.H.: [*All laugh.*]

Reyno: [*laughing*] E'e . . .

M.H.: Mahai. Bombam.

Reyno: . . . bombam ti e'akai veha kia chivela,
nat tenneka bwan.

Luisa: Hm, hmm.

Reyno: There were so many people gathered there.
But then all the people were here,
the eight villages.

Luisa: But then they were united very nicely, yes?

Reyno: Yes.

M.H.: But then they had just been defeated
so they were there together.

Reyno: They had just been defeated.

Luisa: Yes.

M.H.: Yes.

Reyno: At that time, here, then . . .

M.H.: They were just arriving.

Reyno: . . . the plane was gliding here, overhead, yes?
When it was flying overhead, then,
well, the papers, some things were thrown down.
The Hiakis just, just ran all over each other trying to get away.

Luisa, Maria, & M.H.: [*All laugh.*]

Reyno: [*laughing*] No . . .

M.H.: They were afraid. Bombs.

Reyno: . . . bombs, they felt, so they scattered,
falling all over each other, well.

---

of the water flowing in the Hiaki River. That was an empty promise that to this day has never been kept by the Mexican government. Instead, two big dams have been built upstream of the Hiaki River, and the once-overflowing river is now totally dry. The water that should have been delivered to the Hiakis for their farms has been diverted to rich Mexican farmers. Not only are the Mexican farmers in and around Ciudad Obregón taking all the water, but now the water is also flowing in huge aqueducts to Hermosillo, the capital of the state of Sonora, Mexico, since its reservoirs are completely dry.

>   Wate kia ama tooka haivu,
>   bwan, um, um bwiapo.

Luisa: A'e! [*laughing*]

Reyno: Tua Santos.
           Nee intok ket kaa hak faltaroa . . .

Luisa: Tuasu ousi womtek?

Reyno: "Ringo bombam emowi!" ti kia hiia.
           Tenneka'a bwan.

Luisa: Bombam chea kia kom su'utohiwak
           kia bwe'usi cha'asimne . . .

M.H.: Hmm.

Luisa: . . . o masak.

M.H.: Heewi.

Reyno: Heewi, masak.

Luisa: O argooyak.

Reyno: No ves kee veha vette.

Luisa: Hmm.

Reyno: Pos hunuen, hunuen veha
           haisa humak auka'apo veha uchi veha . . .
           ta si kia yu, vaiseevolimvenasia katee
           tea ume sontaom, hm, wiko'immea.
           Um hak am wootak.
           Wate intok yoeme am nu'uka.

Luisa: Tsk.

Reyno: Hmm. Imin hakunsa vansaroawakan, tea
           ume yoeme, imin Tosal Kawiu vetana.

Luisa: Hee?

Reyno: Heewi. Ta hunak
           imin enchim hooko, Mehikou.

	Others were just lying there, well, um, um, on the ground.
Luisa:	Oh my goodness! [*laughing*]
Reyno:	Truly in the saints' names. And me, well, I was always around ...
Luisa:	You really got scared?
Reyno:	"The gringo bombs are coming down on you!" they yelled. Well, they ran.
Luisa:	The bombs were just released to come down, they were so huge and just glided down ...
M.H.:	Hmm.
Luisa:	... or they had wings.
M.H.:	Yes.
Reyno:	Yes, they had wings.
Luisa:	Or they had a ring about them.
Reyno:	That's because they are heavy, then.
Luisa:	Hmm.
Reyno:	Well, that way, that way, then, I don't know how it happened, then, again, but just like butterflies they were going, they said, the soldiers, hm, with their rifles. They threw them somewhere there. And some of the Hiakis collected them.
Luisa:	Tsk.
Reyno:	Hmm. Out here somewhere they were defeated, they say, the Hiakis, here toward White Mountain.
Luisa:	Really?
Reyno:	Yes. But that's when you were over here in Mexico City.

Coercing Hiaki Men to Enlist by Holding Families Hostage (Luisa and Andres)

Luisa and Andres describe how Hiaki men were impressed into the Mexican army. There were several ways in which the Mexican authorities forced Hiakis to enter the military. Hiaki women were held as hostages by the Mexican government, having been captured in raids by the Mexican army. The Mexican official Yucupicio entered into an agreement with the Hiaki men whose wives had been captured: the Hiakis would travel to Mexico City to participate in talks and sign a peace treaty, and their wives would be released and returned to them. Andres was among this group, negotiating for the return of Luisa. He and the other Hiaki men went south as agreed, but they were moved from town to town a lot, to Perote and other places, and then the Mexican general Aguirre rebelled against the Mexican government. The Hiakis were made auxiliaries in the army, formed into a battalion of three or four hundred, and sent off to engage Aguirre's forces. They were paid 140 pesos per month. Luisa describes how the Hiaki women were shipped around with the Hiaki battalion, in boxcars, wherever in the wilderness the battalion was sent. There were Hiakis from all the pueblos in the battalion, and many died; one named Lazaro Bule is mentioned. Generals Mori and Wicha were

---

Luisa: Pos si kia
    utteapo sontao ya'awakamme...

Maria: Utteapo?

Luisa: Heewi, utteapo porque im komo kia traicionaroawaka aman vittuawak...

Andres: Aman vittuawak...

Luisa: Ta hunuen...

Andres: Porque hunuu Yukupisio hunuen itou hiia.
    Kinse diapo tahti hiva aman anne, ti hiia.
    Huchi em nottine, ti hiia.

FIGURE 13 A government outpost in the Hiaki zone, 1920. Arizona Historical Society, PC 078, box 3, BH 341.

there. Eventually, by 1946, the Hiakis were sent back to Sonora and put to work repairing the highway. The Mexican government promised to build houses for the enlisted, but only seven houses were constructed. In the end Andres served in the Mexican military for thirty years.

Luisa: Well, they were just
forced to become soldiers [in the Mexican military] ...

Maria: Forced?

Luisa: Yes, forced, because they like just betrayed them
and sent them over there ...

Andres: They were sent over there ...

Luisa: But that way ...

Andres: Because that Yucupicio said this to us.
You will only be there for fifteen days, he said.
You will return again, he said.

Hunaman enchim familiam aman nu'une, ti hiia.
Hunak veha, ori, pasta intok ama firmaroane, tea ti hiia. Hmm.
Hunak te veha vinwa kia wait hoosasaka,
imin Tolukau, Sochimilkopo te hokaa
veha te Peroteu tohiwak,
Perotepo hokaa,
veha te Aguirres intok kwaktek, hewi.
Nau nahsuahaptek um Veracruspo.
Hunak intok te hunaman vicha itou chachaewak.
Si'ime, hente, familia si'ime.
Hunum te veha, ori, Aguirrestamak intok
chaketiaroaka veha sontao ya'awak.
Hunum te sontao ya'awaka veha, intok te sep
ori serviosou veeviak;
eskoltiaroa haptek treenimpo, wawa'ariamtu haptek.
Piisam intok kia roakataine,
ori koyaarim venasi am roaktaika am koksimne.

Maria: Hm, hmm.

Andres: Ii sako rasionta intok koksimne,
hunama intok loncheka weene.
Hunuen te auka veha sontao ya'awak.
Huntuan i'an, i'an im yepsakai veha treinta
wasuktiam kumpliaroak goviernota serviaroakai.

Maria: Hm, hmm.

Andres: Hunak te veha ori, hunum hokaa ori, tua Veracruspo
hokaa veha te Mehikou tohiwak.
Hunak te veha, ori, hunum yahaka veha ori kuarentai sinkopo te
veha im yahak, Mehikopo.
Kuarentai seispo intok vinavicha te sahak.
Im te veha hichupak.
I'an tahti im hooka.

Maria: Ori, Perotepo eme'e haisa vinwa ama hookan?

Luisa: Ausiliarimtukan.

LIFE UNDER SIEGE, COERCION, AND COLLABORATION 221

> You will get your wives over there, he said.
> Then you, well, you will sign the peace treaty, he said. Hmm.
> Then we were just sitting around for a long time,
> here in Toluca, in Xochimilco,
> then we were taken to Perote,
> [and] when we were in Perote,
> then Aguirre became a turncoat, yes.
> They began to fight among themselves in Veracruz.
> And then they called on us to go over there.
> Everyone, the people, wives, everyone.
> And then, there we, well, with Aguirre
> we became turncoats and we joined their ranks.
> We were made soldiers there and then right away we,
> well, we were sent into service;
> we began to escort the trains, we began guard duty.
> We would just roll up the blankets,
> well, we hung the blanket rolls from our necks like necklaces.

Maria: Hm, hmm.

Andres: And we would hang the sack of rations from our necks,
and we would carry our lunches in those.
When we did that they made us soldiers [in the Mexican military].
So then now, now since I have been here I completed thirty
years providing government service.

Maria: Hm, hmm.

Andres: At that time, then, when we were there, well, in Veracruz,
then we were taken to Mexico City.
At that time, then, well, when we arrived there, then in '45 we
arrived here in Mexico City.
And in '46 we arrived here.
Here we completed our service [to the Mexican government].
Ever since then we have been here.

Maria: Well, how long were you in Perote?

Luisa: They were auxiliaries.

Andres: Ausiliarimtukan.

Luisa: Kaa sontaomtukan.

Andres: Si'ime huniat itom nahsahaka'apo, papaloorimtukan vachia.
Uno kuarentata koovan, si'ime hunako.
Sontaom si'ime aa koovan.
Uno kuarentata hunak tiempopo.

Luisa: Kaakun intok aa koovan.

Andres: Hunak kaa vehe'en,
si'ime kaa vehe'en, taho'ori, bwa'ame.

Maria: Heewi.

Andres: Sentavoe veha im huevenak hinune Mehikopo,
huet in weamapo.

Maria: Aa, ha.

Andres: Kaa . . . varaato bwan taho'ori.
Si'ime varaato sapa'atom.
Kaa i'an venaikan.

Maria: Heewi. I'an si'ime vehe'e.

Andres: I'an si vehe'e si'ime.
Hunuen auka Mehikou nee tata'ak kechia.
Vinwa aman nah kuaktek.

Luisa: Hunum sontao ya'awak . . .

Andres: Heewi.

Luisa: . . . intok hunum Aguirrestamak chaketiaroaka
hunaman hak aniapo,
pocho'okun nunupsuwak, kaa itom ta'aku.

Andres: Heewi.

Andres: Auxiliaries.

Luisa: They were not soldiers.

Andres: There, everywhere we went, we were *papalores*[10] first.
140 [pesos] is what we were paid, all of us, at that time.
All the soldiers earned that.
140 [pesos] at that time.

Luisa: They were earning no more than that.

Andres: At that time things were not expensive,
Everything was inexpensive, clothing, food.

Maria: Yes.

Andres: With the money one could buy many things in Mexico City,
around there where I was.

Maria: Ah, ha.

Andres: Not . . . well, it was cheap, clothes.
Everything was cheap, shoes.
It was not like now.

Maria: Yes. Now everything is expensive.

Andres: Now everything is so expensive.
When I did that, I also got to know Mexico.
I was there for a long time.

Luisa: That's where they made him a soldier . . .

Andres: Yes.

Luisa: . . . and there when they fought with Aguirre,
somewhere in that world,
they took us to wander in the wilderness, a place we did not know.

Andres: Yes.

---

10. Like *peronim* and *toroko yoim* (meaning "gray Mexicans"), this is another term for those enlisted in the Mexican military.

Luisa: Konila a'avo tohina tiupo
hunu'u veha Aguirres hunuen am vaita'aka
veha hunaman hak am nunu'ubwa.
Si'ime henteta, uka . . .

Andres: Si'imem.

Maria: Hm, hmm.

Luisa: . . . familiata vagonnimpo kima'itaka
nunu'ubwia hunait pocho'okun
kaa . . . kaa ho'aka . . .

Andres: Ite ori vahi siento o'ow Hiak,
vahi siento porque te sontao [*inaudible*]
mamni, naiki siento, vahi sientota
ori kompletaroak vatayon entero.
Tua Hiak emo [*inaudible*].

Maria: Ii . . .

Luisa: Si vu'uriakan,
im aman yahakame . . .

Andres: Kada pueplompo yeu saka'awak,
yeu wikwaka'a bwan.

Maria: Hm, hmm.

Andres: Heneralim intok hunu heneral Mori
intok uu Wicha; hunume woika
aman vittuawak.

Luisa: Kompae Lasaro Vuuli.

Andres: Huname intok aman kokok.
Pues hunuen, hunuen te aayuk itepo.
Hunuen veha te a'avo yahak.
Im yepsaka te veha im, im hiva hooka.

Luisa: That we would circle around [and return] here, is what they said.
That Aguirre lied to them that way, then,
then he took them over there somewhere.
All the people, the ...

Andres: Everyone.

Maria: Hm, hmm.

Luisa: ... the wives were in boxcars
and were taken around in the wilderness,
not ... not having a home ...

Andres: We were three hundred Hiaki men,
three hundred because we soldiers [*inaudible*],
five, four hundred, three hundred,
were in the complete battalion.
Only Hiakis themselves [*inaudible*] ...

Maria: This ...

Luisa: There were so many
from here that arrived there ...

Andres: They came from each pueblo,
they were taken, well.

Maria: Hm, hmm.

Andres: And the generals, that General Mori
and Wicha [Thorn]; those two
were sent over there.

Luisa: Compadre Lazaro Bule.[11]

Andres: And they died over there.
Well that's, that's what we did.
That's how we came over here.
Having arrived here, we just stayed here.

---

11. This reflects a modern pronunciation that this surname has taken on; Luisa pronounced it the older way, *Buuli*.

Ika intok im kareteerata vo'okamta
hunuka intok te si'imeta tu'utetuawak.
Veha karim ama ya'ariava'awa tea.
Ta hita huni kaita te ya'ariawak.
Aman hakun hiva siete karim,
hunum lu'utek, lu'utek.

On Coerced Hiakis Serving in the Mexican Army (Maria Hesus)

Maria Hesus emphasizes that the Hiakis who enlisted did so because they were tricked; they were told to travel south to get their wives, who were

M.H.: Por eso nee inen hiune.
Inime vato'oim inim
Hiak vatwepo hooka, hewi?
Vempo aa pasaaroak.
Itepo huni aa pasaaroak.
Mekka te aa pasaaroak, kechia.
Kaa haksa itepo sentaditos esperando, no.

Luisa: Pos uu sontau familia
chea im huni doblepo aa pasaaroak.

Reyno: Hmm.

M.H.: Hunueni bwan. Ime'e intok . . .
"Aa, kee peronim ineni . . ."
Pero no saben hitaa vetchi'ivo
hunaman tohiwakamme.
Unos por traición y
otros por voluntad, ho.
Eso es lo que debemos pensar.

Luisa: Hmm.

> And this road that lies here,
> that one, we were made to repair it, all of us.
> Then they said they were going to make us houses.
> But nothing was ever made for us.
> Only seven houses were made over there somewhere,
> and that's where it ended, it ended.

being held by the government, and then they were coerced into enlisting. She objects to those Hiaki soldiers, who enlisted because they had to, being called pets of the Mexicans.

M.H.: That's why I will say this.
These baptized ones
here in the Hiaki River [territory], yes?
They experienced it.
We also experienced it.
We experienced it far away, also.
We were not sitting around waiting, no.

Luisa: Well, the wives of the soldiers
really experienced it twice.

Reyno: Hmm.

M.H.: Well, that's the way it was. And these . . .
"Ah, these bald ones were this way . . ."
But they do not know why
they were taken away.
Some were because they were betrayed and
others because they volunteered, see.
That is what we should think about.

Luisa: Hmm.

M.H.: "Kia peron bokin,[12]
intok inwaami, inen."
No. Lo hicieron por necesidad,
por traición.
"Lauti aman uka familiata nu'use."
Pos wame veha sahak. A ver si el
voluntad el trae a la gente. Hakwoosa?
Pos si wame peesomtaka ama hooka,
ume haamuchim.
Kaivu aa su'utoine uu govierno, ho.

12. She pronounces the word *bokin*; it should be *vukim*, which means "pets." Maria Hesus's father was tricked into enlisting in the Mexican military. He was informed that his wife had been captured and held prisoner and the only way to gain her release was to enlist. He was considered a "traitor" and a pet of the Mexicans by the Hiakis who refused induction into the Mexican military. Maria Hesus was born and raised away from the Hiaki territory, thus did not speak Hiaki fluently.

LIFE UNDER SIEGE, COERCION, AND COLLABORATION

M.H.: "They are just the pets of the bald ones
and this and that, this way."
No. They did it because it was necessary,
because they were betrayed.
"Hurry and go there to get your wives."
Well, they went. Perhaps the
volunteer will bring the people. When?
Well, they were prisoners there,
the women.
The government would never release them, see.

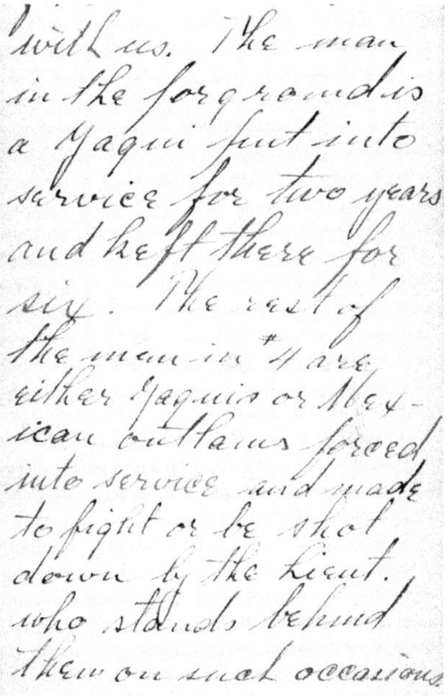

FIGURE 14 (a) A photograph taken on the hill behind the El Jori garrison, in the foothills of the Vakateeve Mountains. (b) On the back of this photo, taken for the Richardson company, the photographer has written in English, "The man in the foreground is a Yaqui put into service for two years and left there for six. The rest of the men are either Yaqui or Mexican outlaws forced into service and made to fight or be shot down by the Lieut., who stands behind them on such occasions." Records of the Compañía Constructora Richardson, S.A., 1904–1968 (bulk 1904–1927), MS 113, box 1, folder 4: Photographs. Courtesy of University of Arizona Libraries, Special Collections.

FIGURE 15 More than thirty captured Hiaki women and children in Guaymas around 1910. Records of the Compañía Constructora Richardson, S.A., 1904–1968 (bulk 1904–1927), MS 113, box 1, folder 4: Photographs. Courtesy of University of Arizona Libraries, Special Collections.

CHAPTER 4

CAPTURE

The Story of the Shawl (Maria Hesus)

Maria Hesus tells how she and her mother and siblings were captured at Samawaka and brought to Guaymas when she was a small child. She had her icon of San Francisco with her. Her mother tried to save a valuable scarf, earrings, and ring by tying them under Maria Hesus's blouse. Maria Hesus, too little to walk, was carried on a soldier's horse, holding his waist. The soldier lifted up her blouse, found the shawl and rings, and stole them from her. He then dropped her in the middle of the group, away from her family. A friend, Pooli, got a supervisor to look for her, and eventually the crying girl was reunited with her mother and told her of the loss of the scarf and jewelry. Her mother realized that the soldier had not returned her daughter directly to her because she would have immediately discovered the theft.

M.H.: Ta mala intok si taho'orimpo aa vihtaeka nee aa makne, ti hiia,
uka San Pasiskota. Hunuen, hunuen
aa puateka te im, imin Waymammeu te yeu toiwak tea
San Pasiskota.
Hunuen aa puatekae aman yeu yepsak, tea.
Huntuen, hunum, hunum Samawakapo bwihwakai.
Inim haksa lugar humaku'u peronim veha
para avanzar pos de nosotros,
aver hitasa te weiya,
a ver si hay algo,
"A ver, hunuka ili usita a'avo yecha," ti hiune tea
uu peron. Pos mala intok pos,
hachin huni'i bwan kaita aa hinnne'u bwan.
Ika aniliota au weiya ti hiia mampo,
komaeta hiulapo, "Cosas así pues, no se puede..."
nee intok repam yecha'ariak, ti hiia.
Huname repam intok pos ume revoosam,
hakunsu humak am nu'uka, Yukatanvetana.
Aniliopo kikkivaken tea huname revoosam.
Seeda lehitima. Pues hunama tu'ulisi nee wikohtek,
supem vetuku hunaman intok repam sumakan.
Nee aa ine'a uka peromta, kavait nee yehsime.
Peron veha im nee mamteriak,
im nee aa bwihtuak, inen.
Bwe nee aa mahaika
huni aa bwihsime uka peronta.
Pos si teeve uu voo'o,
hakunsa humak itom kom hoak. Pos nee weye.
Pues nee, nee ama katek,
ili, ili vepa supem inien nee ya'ariak hikau vicha.
Pos tu'isi aa woitak. Uka'a suma'ita woitak.
Ume revoosam nee uurak.

Luisa: Ay.

M.H.: Malata revoosam nee u'urak, suavem.
Nee am uurak. Voosapo am tuttak.

M.H.: But Mom would wrap him in cloth and give him to me, she said,
that San Francisco. That way, that way
I carried him and here, here to Guaymas we were taken, they said,
with San Francisco.
Carrying him that way we arrived, they said.
So, there, there we were captured at Samawaka.
Here in some place, the bald ones, then,
in order to take advantage of us,
to see whatever we carried,
to see if there is something,
"Let me see. Bring that little child over here," he said,
the bald one. Well, and Mom, well,
it seems like, well, she could keep nothing valuable, well.
This ring, she carried it on her hand, she said,
as Comadre said, "Things like that, well, you can't . . ."
and she took off my earrings, she said.
And those earrings, well, the shawl,
I don't know where she got them, from Yucatán.
You could insert the shawl in the ring, they say.
A legitimate silk shawl. So very nicely she tied the shawl on me
around my waist, under my blouse, she tied the shawl there.
I felt the bald one when I was sitting on the horse.
The bald one had me place my hand here,
he had me hold him here.[1]
Since I was very afraid
in this way I held on to the bald one.
Well, the road was very long,
and I don't know where we arrived. Well, I walked.
Well, I, I was sitting there,
and he moved my blouse a little upward this way.
Well, then he untied it. He untied the shawl.
He took the shawl off me.

Luisa: Ay.

M.H.: He took my mother's shawl, a very nice one.
He took it from me. He stuck it in his pocket.

---

1. She gestures to her waist.

Aniliota intok ume repam. Am vichaka
voosampo am tuttak uu pelon.
Nee am u'urak.
Pa cavalar hunaman hakun haamuchim
hapteka'apo intok kaa nattemaik,
"A ver, ¿de quién es esta chamaca?" ti huni kaa hiia.
Kia hunama hak nee kom yechak tea, ho?
Pos gente intok si vu'u, haksa nee malata teune?
Pos hunama hak weeka nee bwana tea, ho.
Gente intok kaa nee ta'a,
nee huni kaa am ta'a uka genteta.
Nau kontim. Peronim intok
kia konila ha'abweka yee suane,
chivamvenasi ibwan.

Luisa: Nasuk hapne.

M.H.: Nau am kontane.
Hunaa veha haksa ini'i komae Pooli . . .
Mala intok kaa nee tetteaka humak bwansisime
senuk hiva wikwiksisime.
Ho, nee intok hunaman haamuchim nasuk weeka
bwaana tea. Hunaa Komae Pooli intok
yoi ya'uttau kivakeka.
"A esta señora le perdió una niña. La traía un soldado."
Hunaa yoi ya'ut veha aa hariwa uka peronta.
"Havesa nee nuksiika?" Hunak veha haamuchim,
"Hunaa uusi chea aman weeka bwaana."
Pos hunak veha aman vicha siika tea uu komae Pooli.
Pos hunaman nee weeka bwaana tea, ho?
Pos uka inim wikosapo yecha'i, hitaa nee weiya?
Hunak veha maala pos
"Ume peronim ume revoosam nee yecha'ariak."
"Hitaa empo ama weiya?"
"Pos reepam intok anilio.
Nee supem hikau wikriaka nee am yecha'ariak ume revoosam."
"Demonio, ala'akun, kia kaa nee, neu enchi entregaroak."
Pos mala hiva nee vite'an.
Kaita nee weiya.

The ring and the shawl. When he spotted them,
he stuck them in his pocket, that bald one.
He took them from me.
On top of that, there the women
were standing, and he did not ask,
"Let's see, who does this child belong to?" He did not even say this.
He just put me down there somewhere, they said, see?
And there were so many people, where could I find Mom?
Well, I was standing there crying, they said, see.
The people did not know me
and I did not know the people.
They were all around me. And the soldiers
were standing all around us watching us,
as if we were goats.

Luisa: Stood in the middle.

M.H.: They would encircle us.
That one, then, this comadre Pooli . . .
And Mom, who could not find me, was also crying
and she was holding on to another child.
See, and I stood there among the women
crying, they said. And that comadre Pooli
went to the Mexican higher-ranking official.
"This woman lost her child. A soldier had her."
The Mexican higher-ranking official then looked for the soldier.
"Who took her?" Then the women [said],
"That child is standing over there crying."
Well, then, she went there, that comadre Pooli.
Well, over there, I was standing crying, they said, see?
Well, what did I have on my waist, what did I have?
Then Mom, well,
"The bald ones [soldiers] took the shawl off me."
"What were you carrying?"
"Well, earrings and a ring.
He lifted up my dress and took the shawl from me."
"That devil, that's why he just did not bring you to me."
Well, Mom would have seen me.
I was not carrying anything.

The Story of the Cookies (Maria Hesus)

Maria Hesus describes an earlier incident, after capture, when a soldier was harassing her mother trying to get her ring away from her. Another soldier, a Hiaki or Mayo, intervened to protect the women, telling the aggressive soldier to leave them alone. Eventually he threatened the aggressive one

---

M.H.: Hunaman, haksa, im kaupo haksa lugarpo,
ika au waataka bwe aemak hiia tea, uu peron.
Aa uuravae tea uka aniliota.
Hunak chea tu'iriakan.
"Nee kaa inika aniliota aa enchi maka," ti hiia a'apo intoko.
"Ela'aposu nee mam chuktine, ta kaivu enchi aa makne."
Peron veha tetat katek,
mala intok itommak au katek, ti hiia.
Hunak intok, hunak intok hunaa peron . . .
uu humak kaa, kaa ibwan, haisa nee hiune,
kaa yoi ausuulim, hivatua ket Hiakim, Mayom.
"Haisa eu hiia hunu'u sontau, maala?" ti au hiia tea
uu yoi, o si Hiaki, hitasa humaku'u.
"Pos inika aniliota nee u'uravaekai nemak peleita."
"Inim empo kaa inime haamuchimmeu ee suati anne.
Hu'ubwa uu ili hamut ket nee etehoriak.
Eme'e ili usim puaktakame
haisaikai eme'e amet vansaroa?" ti au hiia tea.
Nee intok kee hita u'urawa,
kee peron nee tovokta.
Haksa humak nee tovoktak uu peron,
hakun mekka humaku'u. Hunak intoko, "Si chuvvaatuk
empo haveta inim molestaroatene, kanne monteka;
enchi ne me'ene," ti au hiia tea.
"Inime haivu preesomtaka kaate.
Haisaaka empo am molestaroa?" ti au hiia tea.
Hunak veha yeu siika tea hunaa peron.
Am vicha veha yeu sikaa tea.

with death, and the aggressor left. The protective soldier then spoke Hiaki to the captured women. He had a ration bag full of cookie crumbs, and he asked Maria Hesus's mother for a cup to put some of the crumbs in so that the children could eat them. She was suspicious that he was trying to poison them by giving them gunpowder to eat, but he ate some to prove it was not gunpowder, and the children got to eat the crumbs.

M.H.: Over there, somewhere, in some place in the mountains,
he wanted this from her so he was bothering her, that bald one.
He wanted to take it away from her, the ring.
It was in better shape.
And, "I will not give you this ring," she said then.
"Even if you cut off my finger, I will never give it to you."
[Another] bald one, then, was sitting on a rock,
and Mom was sitting with us, she said.
And then, and then that bald one . . .
that one, maybe, not, not, well, how shall I say it,
they were not Mexicans only, surely there were Hiakis, Mayos.
"What did that soldier say to you, mother?" he said to her,
maybe he was a Mexican or a Hiaki, I don't know what he was.
"Well, he was trying to take this ring away from me, fighting me."
"Here you will not bother these women.
A while ago another little girl also told me something.
You all who picked up the little children,
why are you taking advantage of them?" he said, they said.
And I had not yet had anything taken from me,
the soldier had not yet picked me up.
I do not know where the soldier picked me up,
probably somewhere far away. And then, "If later
you bother anyone here, I will not comment;
I will kill you," he said to him, it is said.
"These are already prisoners.
Why are you bothering them?" he said to him.
Then he left, that bald one.
Then he went out there, they said.

Hunaa, hunaa malata nokriakame
veha ama veha tawak tea.
Katin bweere, ume bweere,
haisa teak? Morral de ración.

Luisa: Saco rasionim.

M.H.: Ándale, hunu'u.
Hunaka'a veha si tapuni ume gayetam nunu'ubwa,
tea, bwan. Kia polvo.
Hunak veha, "Tasata neu bwiise empo maala."
"Haisaakai?"
"Bwe gayetam nee enchi mikvae."
"Haiseakai?"
"Ili usim am bwa'ane."
"Hunaksu ho."
"Haisa, haisa nehpo nee am bwa'ane?
Haisa nee poovata bwa'ane?" ti hiia tea
huna'a yoeme, yoem peron.
"Kaa hoyok, nehpo nee am bwa'e."
Hunak veha, a'apo veha am bwa'e, tea, uu peron.
Hunak veha tasata au bwisek.
Senu tasam aa mikak tea.
Pos am bwa'aka tea huname.
"Ta am kokok enchi ne naatehone."
"Kaivu kokonemme.
Tevaa ala am sua'ane. Ta ini'i bwa'ame
kaivu am, enchim sua'ane," ti hiia tea hunaa peron.
Ta Hiaki o Mayo, hitasa humaku'u porque
yoem noka ti hiia.

The other one, the one who was speaking for Mom,
then, there he stayed, they said.
Remember big, the big,
what are they called? Ration bag.

Luisa: Bag of rations.

M.H.: That's it, that one.
That bag, then, was carried, [it] was really full of cookies,
they said, well. Just powder [i.e., the cookies were all crumbled up].
Then, well, "Hand me a cup, you, mother."
"Why?"
"Well, I am going to give you some cookies."
"Why?"
"The little children will eat them."
"And then [they'll be poisoned by the gunpowder]?"
"How, how could I be eating it?
Would I eat gunpowder?" he said, they said,
that Hiaki, that Hiaki bald one.
"It is not gunpowder, since I am eating it."
Well, then, he was eating it, they said, that bald one.
Then she handed the cup to him.
He gave her one cup [of cookie crumbs].
Well, they [the children] ate them, they said, those.
"But if they die, I will expose you."
"They will not die.
Hunger will kill them, yes. But this food
will never kill them, you," he said, they said, the bald one.
Whether he was Hiaki or Mayo is unknown since he was
speaking Hiaki, they said.

FIGURE 16 Armed guards identified as Hiakis patrolling a line of female prisoners carrying bundles on their heads, walking down a road in a town in Mexico, between 1910 and 1929. Arizona, Southwestern and Borderlands Photograph Collection, item Yaqui Indians-Mexico-g. Courtesy of University of Arizona Libraries, Special Collections.

Leaving Her Little Dog (Maria Hesus)

Maria Hesus tells about a little bushy-haired dog that the family had with them in the mountains before they were captured. The children considered it their own dog, and her mother agreed that it was the chil-

M.H.: Waimammeu vichaa ti hiia uu maala.

Luisa: Hunum vichaa nuksaka'awak?
Wate, huevenaka aman nu'uwakame
Tata Va'ammeu yeu toiwak.

M.H.: Pos nee kaa hu'unea bwan.

Luisa: Hunumun yeu toiwaka veha
vu'uka imin Waimammeu vicha nuk saka'awak.

FIGURE 17 A girl standing beside a structure out of which a toddler is peering. A dog plays on the right side. Arizona Historical Society, PC 180, Norman Wallace Photographs, box 43, album #2, #198.

dren's dog. It came with them when they were brought to Guaymas to be deported, and a Mexican soldier started feeding it. He asked to keep the dog, and although Maria Hesus's mother demurred at first, the soldier said that the dog would be killed if they brought it with them on the boat. When they were taken away, the little dog stayed there in Guaymas with the soldier. It had been a remarkable dog, remaining quiet the whole time in the mountains, never barking. It stayed with them in the mountains even when it was hungry or thirsty, following them everywhere.

M.H.: Over toward Guaymas, my mother said.

Luisa: That is where they took them?
Some, many who were captured there,
were taken to Hot Waters.

M.H.: Well, I do not know, well.

Luisa: When they were brought out,
many were taken here to Guaymas.

M.H.: Pos mala hunumun toiwak.

Luisa: Wate intok Peesiou hookan.
Ta im Waimampo veha
vaporeu kima'ava'aka veha
si'imeka nau toiwak.

M.H.: Hunum te hookan. Hunum veha te, ili chuu'u,
ili chuu'u sambota intok te nunu'ubwan. Itepo aa chu'ukan tea.
Hunaa intok, hunaka ili chuu'u,
intok pos itommak humak weama hewi?
Uu peron intok itom suame
humak uka ili chuu'uta waata.
Hiva aa hi'ibwatua tea.

Luisa: Hmm.

M.H.: Itommak aa weamau huni
hiva, hiva aa hi'ibwatua tea hunaa peron.
Hunen au hiia tea peron:
"Oiga," ti au hiia tea.
"Regálame ese perrito," ti au hiia tea.
"Haisa, haisa empo aa hoovae?" ti hiia tea.
"Haksa empo aa nuksik,
huni'i hunum haksa uka kapitanta aa teak,
huni'i va'au enchi kom aa hima'ariane.
Nee aa maka," ti hiia tea hunuu peron.
"Haisa nehpo enchi aa makne? Ili usim aa chuu'uk."
"Ela'apo," ti au hiia tea.
"Ela'apo, neu, neu hoiwane," ti hiia tea.
"Nee chea aa hi'ibwatua." Aa hi'ibwatua tea bwan uu peron.
Pos itom yeu nuksahak,
uu peron veha uka chu'uta nu'uka tea.

Luisa: Aa. [*Kids talking in background.*]

M.H.: Aa nu'uka. Aman taawak, Waimampo. Ili chuu'u sambotukan.
Hunaa bwan hunum kaupo rehtiwau
tua hakwo huni kaa chachaek tea bwan.

Luisa: Aa.

M.H.: Well, Mom was taken there.

Luisa: And some were in Hermosillo.
But here in Guaymas then
they were going to be put in the steamboats
so they were all gathered together.

M.H.: That is where we were. Then there, we, a little dog,
a little bushy dog we had. It was our dog, they said.
And that one, that little dog,
and, well, he was probably with us, yes?
And the bald one who was guarding us,
maybe he wanted the little dog.
He kept feeding it, they said.

Luisa: Hmm.

M.H.: Even though it was with us,
that bald one always, always fed it, they said.
He spoke in this way to her, they said, that bald one:
"Listen," he said to her, she said.
"Give me that little dog," he said to her, she said.
"What, what are you going to do with it?" he said, she said.
"No matter where you take it,
when the captain finds it somewhere there,
he will even throw it down into the water [to drown it] on you.
Give it to me," said the bald one, she said.
"How can I give it to you? He is the little children's dog."
"It does not matter," he said to her, she said.
"It does not matter, it will get used to me," he said, she said.
"I am feeding it." He was feeding it, she said, well, the bald one.
Well, when we were taken away,
the bald one then took the dog, she said.

Luisa: Ah. [*Kids talking in background.*]

M.H.: He took it. It stayed there in Guaymas. A little bushy dog.
Well, when we were in the mountains,
that one never barked, they said, well.

Luisa: Ah.

M.H.: Kia kamula teneka weamne tea.

Luisa: Hmm.

M.H.: O si hi'ibwapea, va'a hi'ipea,
ta itot cha'aka hiva weamne, tea hunuu ili chuu'u.
Haivu yo'owe, ta ili ko'omela, ti hiia uu maala.

Luisa: Hmm.

M.H.: Hunum veha taawak hunaa ili chuu'u, Waimampo.
Hunuen hiia uu maala.
Waimam veha, Waimampo veha te embarkaroak, tea.
Ay, no sé si, si Mansaniau kom tohiwak
o Masaklanpo hakun. Aa, hunum veha nee tua kaa hu'unea.

Children Stolen by the Mexican Soldiers (Maria Hesus and Luisa)

Luisa and Maria Hesus discuss how the Mexican soldiers used to take children away and not return them during the marches. After the incident with the shawl, when Maria Hesus was nearly lost, her mother was very insistent that they stay together at all times, for fear of losing her. Luisa tells how her older sister was taken, and how they never found out

M.H.: Chukula veha kaa, kaa, kaave,
kaavetau intok nee lisensiak uu maala.
"Ela'apo nemak wokimmea weene,
ta hiovek huni kaita aet teak
huni nee pocho'okun hakun nee aa hima'ariana,"
ti hiia uu maala.
"Kaavetau intok nee suutohak," ti hiia uu maala.
Hunen hunum Waymammeu yahak tea.
Wokkimmea . . . katekai.
Hunuen yee hooan ume peronim.

M.H.: He just walked around with his mouth shut, they said.

Luisa: Hmm.

M.H.: Whether he was really hungry, thirsty,
it always followed us around, they said, that little dog.
It was already mature, but very short, Mom said.

Luisa: Hmm.

M.H.: Then that is where it stayed, that little dog, in Guaymas.
That is what Mom said.
Then Guaymas, in Guaymas, then, we were deported, they said.
I don't know if, if we were taken down to Manzanillo
or to Mazatlán somewhere. Ah, that, then, I really do not know.

---

what happened to her. Thinking of her makes Luisa sad, and she mentions that she often feels like her sister must be out there somewhere. Luisa feels, though, that if they were to meet in the street, she probably would not recognize her sister so many years later. She also mentions a friend, Juana, who lost two children and has never seen them since. It would often happen that a crying child, too tired to walk, would be picked up by a soldier and never seen again.

M.H.: Later then, with no one, no one,
with no one my mother allowed me to stay.
"It doesn't matter if you are walking with me,
but if they find us,
you might get abandoned somewhere in the wilderness,"
said Mom.
"And I never left you with anyone," said Mom.
That way, there, in Guaymas we arrived, they said.
On foot . . . walking . . .
This is the way the bald ones treated us.

Luisa: Intok ili uusim katin vu'um u'urak.
Kaa yeu machiala i'an tahtia.

M.H.: Ay Dios!

Luisa: In ako, katin, ket hunae asoa ket u'awakan uu in mala yo'otu'i,
hunum Tata Va'ampo . . .

M.H.: Heewi, am u'uran!

Luisa: . . . hunum Samawakapo nu'uwak.

M.H.: U'uran, u'uran ume ili uusim!

Luisa: I'an tahti kaave.
Kaa am hu'uneiya.

M.H.: Kaita!

Luisa: Intok huevenaka watem ta'arula bwan.
I'an tahti kaa am hu'uneiya.

Voice in background: Hmm, hmm.

M.H.: Hmm, hmm. Hunuen nee ya'aka bwan.

Luisa: Wate intok . . .
huevenaka intok am teak . . .
huevenaka intok kaa am teak.

Maria: Ili uusim?

Luisa: Heewi. Katwa'apo,
wokkimmea am weiya'ane. Familiataim.
Ili usim bwanau intok am puaktak
intok hunuen am hooa.
Kaa am yumakai. Huna'a ma kaave.
Hakunsa . . . hiva kaa aa teak.
Huna'a aa asoak.
Ke'esamtukan.
Haivu i'avetchiakan.

Luisa: And the children, remember, they took many of them away.
They have never returned to this day.

M.H.: Ay, my God!

Luisa: My older sister, remember, my grandmother's child, was taken there at Hot Waters.

M.H.: Yes, they took them away!

Luisa: ... there at Samawaka she was taken.

M.H.: Taken away, taken away, the little children!

Luisa: To this day, they are gone.
We do not know about them.

M.H.: Nothing!

Luisa: And many have lost them, well.
To this day, they do not know where they are.

Voice in background: Hmm, hmm.

M.H.: Hmm, hmm. That is what they did to me.

Luisa: And some ...
many did find them ...
many did not find them.

Maria: The little kids?

Luisa: Yes. When they were walking,
they were walking with them. The wives.
And when the little children were crying they picked them up
and did that to them.
They could not lift them. That one is gone.
Where ... we never found her.[2]
She was her child.
She was the firstborn.
She was already this size.[3]

---

2. Here Luisa speaks in a very sad, subdued voice.
3. Here Luisa gestures with her hand to show how big she was.

Intok si weratukan uu ili hamut.
Hiva kaa aa teak.
I'an tahtia kaa aa hu'uneiya.
Amak kia hak weamatek,
hak aa weamavenasi e'ea.
Ta como yo'otuk, hewi,
kaa aa ta'ane.

Maria: Kaa aa ta'ane.

Luisa: Mmm, mm.

Maria: Vempo humak ori kaa kokok,
humak ket hiva emou waatine.

Luisa: Heewi.

Maria: Hiva tua ket hak anemme.

Luisa: Heewi.

Maria: Ta kaa am ta'ane.

Luisa: Hm, hm. U'awak hiva kaa aa teak.
Intuchi wa'a komae Huana,
huni ket hiva woim u'awakan.
Hunaa ket i'an tahti kaa am teula.
Wepulaik huni kaa teak.

Maria: Hmm, hmm. Hakun am u'awak?

Luisa: Abwe, hunum Samawakapo nu'uwak
intok hunum vicha wokimmea weiyawakan.
Ume ili usim intok humak lotteka
bwaana, tukaapo,
chuvakteka weiyawaka haku'u.
Wokkimmea weiyawakai.
Pos ime intok am puaktatevok
intok hunuen amemak taawak.
Kaa ameu am entregaroak ume am asoakammeu.

And she was very light-complected, that little girl.
She was never found.
To this day no one knows about her.
Sometimes when I am just walking around somewhere,
I feel as if she is walking around somewhere.
But she is probably grown up,
[I] would not know her.

Maria: Would not know her.

Luisa: Mmm, mmm.

Maria: If they did not die,
they would also remember you.

Luisa: Yes.

Maria: They must be somewhere.

Luisa: Yes.

Maria: But you would not know them.

Luisa: Hm, hm. She was taken away, [we] never found her.
Also that comadre Juana,
she also had two [children] taken.
That one, to this day, she has not found them.
Not even one has she found.

Maria: Hmm, hmm. Where were they taken?

Luisa: Well, they were taken there at Samawaka,
and they were taken that way walking.
And the little children were probably tired,
crying, at night,
they were cold as they were being taken somewhere.
They were on foot when they were taken.
So these [soldiers] were made to pick them up
and they kept them [the children].
They did not return them to their mothers.

The Motherless Children (Reyno)

Reynaldo describes how, after his family returned to Sonora, while he was still a child, there were many children whose mothers had been deported to the south. These children lived in a long house, behind a fence, being taken care of by older siblings and elder women who hadn't been

---

Reyno: Entonces hunaksu veha hunuka veha neu eteho uu maala,
  ta haivu im,
  haivu bwan im te aa pasaroak kaupo.
  Hunak amevetchi'ivo tua suatie'an tea uu anima persona.
  Ume ili uusim, ma ime ili uusim hewi,
  hunua vellechim veha ume vem malawam huname'e veha
  varkaroak, Mehikou, hakun taawak.
  Ume ili usim intok ama tawaawak.

Maria: Imin kom vicha . . .

Reyno: Teve, ori, teve kari, katin hunaa aula,
  alamvre soolai hunaka korakan.
  Ume hamut yo'owem,
  huname intok ameu toosaka'awak.
  Huname am uhuu'un.
  Huname veha ori, huname veha ha'ani,
  am waikame huname veha ameu ha'abweka
  am yo'owa makak. Heewi.
  I'an ume ili aa nokame, i'an ibwan
  ime ili usim venasi kateme malatukau intok
  tahkaim nenenkan kia etbwa bwan nah kaate.
  Tahkaireom aman kateo,
  ama yeu vitchune tea,
  "Si malata venaka wanna'avo weye,"
  ti hiune ume ili uusim.
  "Ke vaa. Kia nee hatchina si eene.
  Eme'e huni ket hunen ya'a'eewan,
  kaa enchim itom,

deported. Reynaldo's mother would sell tortillas close to the holding area, and the children would call out to her, thinking she looked like their mother; she would feel terrible. She told Reynaldo that if they hadn't escaped to Arizona, he might well have ended up like those children. He mentions a couple of names of such children who grew up in those circumstances.

Reyno: Then, then, that, then Mom spoke to me about that,
    but already here,
    already, well, we experienced it here in the mountains.
    Then, she, the deceased, was very concerned about them.
    The little children, how then these little children, yes,
    when they were that size, their mothers were, then,
    deported. They stayed in Mexico, somewhere.
    And the little children stayed behind.

Maria: Here, down here . . .

Reyno: A long, well, long house, remember, that cage,
    the fence was a thin screen.
    The older women,
    and they were left behind there.
    They were taking care of them [the little children].
    Those, then, well, those, then supposedly,
    the older siblings, they were then in charge of them,
    they became their parents. Yes.
    Now, the kids who could speak, well, the same age as
    these little kids, and my late mother
    used to sell tortillas, well, just secretly go around selling.
    When the tortilla makers were approaching them,
    the kids would look out and see them [the tortilla makers].
    "That looks like Mom walking over there,"
    is what the little children would say.
    "My gosh. I used to feel so bad.
    And you would also have been locked up like that,
    if you, us,

bwe kaa inim ika itom hinne'uko," tiia.
"Hunuen humak tawa'e'an.
Kia humak yo'otu'e'an," tiia.
Heewi. Maa inien inime uusim, hewi,
Akusti Kahtiotukau, hiva tua ee aa ta'ak.
Huntuen ini'i Antonio Tosaria . . .

Mom's First Capture and Grandmother's Death, in 1902–1903 (Maria Hesus)

Maria Hesus tells the story of her mother's first capture, as it was told to her by her mother. Her mother's mother, Maria Hesus's grandmother, was also captured. At that time, rather than being shipped via train, captured Hiakis were forced to walk a long distance—it might be as far as Mazatlán or Colima—under circumstances of extreme deprivation: thirsty, tied up, injured, and sometimes sick. In this case they were gathered in Durango, and from there they were sent farther south to Yucatán. Three elderly women, and another younger one who became sick, were left behind in a hospital in Tepic, Nayarit, Maria Hesus's grandmother among them. Although her grandmother was not sick, she had a crippled hand, and a soldier noticed this and left her in the hospital. The younger woman recovered and later was able to tell Maria Hesus's mother what had happened. The nurses were said to have injected Maria Hesus's grandmother and the two other elderly women with poison, saying that they didn't know what to do with them. Their bodies were wrapped in blankets and thrown in a hole. Maria Hesus's grandmother, as she was dying, told the younger woman what had happened and asked her to tell her daughter,

M.H.: A veces nee hunen hiune.
Nee hunuen [*pause*] nee hunuen hihia bwan.
Ini'i Hiaki, uuu, mil nove . . .
mil ochocientos noventatuk naateka hunak
hunumun tohitaitewak, Yukataneu.

well, if we had not saved you," she [Reynaldo's mother] said.
"You probably would have been like that.
You probably would have just grown up," she said.
Yes. And now, like these children, yes,
the late Agustín Castillo, perhaps you knew him.
Then this Antonio Light Skin . . .

FIGURE 18 A boy standing alone outside, holding a stick at port arms. Arizona Historical Society, PC 180, Norman Wallace Photographs, box 43, album #2, #209.

Maria Hesus's mother, that she would not be returning. Later the younger woman was brought to Guadalajara, where the Hiakis were being held. She found Maria Hesus's mother and let her know that her mother, Maria Hesus's grandmother, was dead.

M.H.: Sometimes I say this.
I, this [*pause*] I say this, well.
This Hiaki, 1900 . . .
since 1890, then
they started to be taken there, to Yucatán.

Mala mil novecientos dos o trestuk
hunumun vichaa nuksaka'awak.

Luisa: Tsk. Hmm.

M.H.: Hmm. Duran . . .
Durasneopo nau tohiwakan.
Hmm. Maala intok
aa akoowa intok papa intok
tio Hoan, tia Hoana;
si'ime hunume nuksaka'awak.
O'owim suma'itaka
nuksaka'awak Yukataneu vicha.

Luisa: Hmm.

M.H.: Huname chea, chea huni hiokot ya'awak, ho.
Hunume ket emvarkaroawak imi'i . . .
. . . [*big sigh*] Waimampo, hmm,
Masaklaneo o Koleou
o hunum hak emo yeu tohiwak ti hiia.
Ta wame kaa trenpo nuksaka'awak.
Wokimmea.

Luisa: Hm, hmm.

M.H.: Wokkimmea.

Luisa: Intok hunuen kia
kaa am sisii'aane tea.
Síseme huni sussuawan tea.

M.H.: Ume o'owim, ya'uchim hunama katne,
tea, ho. Ho, haivu . . .
[. . .]

>   Mom, in 1902 or 1903,
>   she was taken over there.
>
> **Luisa:** Tsk. Hmm.
>
> **M.H.:** Hmm. Duran...
>   in Durasneo[4] they were gathered.
>   Hmm. And Mom
>   and her older sister and father,
>   uncle Juan, aunt Juana;
>   they were all taken over there.
>   The men were tied up
>   and taken to Yucatán.
>
> **Luisa:** Hmm.
>
> **M.H.:** Those were more, even more mistreated, see.
>   They were also deported here...
>   ... [*big sigh*] in Guaymas, hmm,
>   to Mazatlán or Koleo[5]
>   or wherever they were taken to, she said.
>   But they were not taken by train.
>   [They went] on foot.
>
> **Luisa:** Hm, hmm.
>
> **M.H.:** On foot.
>
> **Luisa:** And in this way they just
>   would not want them to stop to pee, they said.
>   Those who stopped to pee were killed, they said.
>
> **M.H.:** The elders, leaders were also walking there,
>   they said, see. See, already...
>   [...]

---

4. Maria Hesus probably means Durango. This Mexican state is in close proximity to Chihuahua, Sinaloa, and southern Sonora. Durango is part of the historical and geographical unit of northern Mexico.

5. Koleo: This is probably a mispronunciation. Maria Hesus probably means Colima, which is a state on the Pacific coast in southern Mexico. The port of Manzanillo is located in Colima.

Weye, ho. Ermosiopo hak . . .
. . . intok hi'ipea, bwan intok
pos haivu bwan muki'ise uu yoeme.
Naa veha senu veha aa tovoktak,
aa yechaka aa hi'itua tea.
Hunak veha hiavihtek hunaa yoeme.

Luisa: Aa.

M.H.: Va'ae muken tea bwan.
Hunuen, hunama . . . kia bwan chu'umvenasia,
haz de cuenta que animaalim . . .
que aman pasaroaka te aa hi'ine,
hi'ine o aa he'eka . . . o . . .
pos ume hahawaa bwan.
Kaa haksa chuvala um yeesa
o hunum yumhuene . . .

Luisa: "O chea em gustopo am hi'ine," ti kaa hiune.

M.H.: Kia bwan pasaadapo hi'isaka tea
ume au yumame. Hunuen
emo Wadalahaaruau yahak ti hiia,
katekae uu maala.
In maala, malata maala, hunaa
intok lo'i tea.
Haisa maachi uu Loola.
Hunaa intok pos ume mamman inen ya'ala,
ti hiia hikau vicha.
Turyida . . . Aa weye.
Kecha'awak weene tea,
bwan ta kaita movimiento kaa hippue.
Turyida. Pos haisa?
Kee barbaro ti kia nee e'ene.
Hunumun Tepik katwa'apo,
hunama veha tawak, tea,
naiki haamuchim.

          Walking, see. Somewhere in Hermosillo . . .
          . . . and felt thirsty, well, and,
          well, he was already dying, the man.
          Then, then someone then picked him up,
          sat him up, gave him a drink.
          Then that man took a breath.

Luisa: Ah.

M.H.: He was dying of thirst, well.
          That way, there . . . just, well, like dogs,
          as if they were animals . . .
          we would go in there and drink it,
          drink or drank it . . . or . . .
          they were chasing them, well.
          It wasn't like, sit here for a while
          or sit there . . .

Luisa: "Or drink it comfortably," they would not say.

M.H.: Whenever they had a chance, they drank,
          those who could. In that way
          they arrived in Guadalajara, she said,
          walking, Mom.
          My mom, Mom's mother, that one,
          and she was crippled.
          This was how Loola looked.
          And that one, well, her hand was like this,[6]
          she said, pointing up.
          Frozen . . . She could walk.
          When she was helped up, she would walk, they said,
          well, but she could not move by herself.
          Frozen. Well, how?
          How barbarous, I would feel.
          There going to Tepic,
          then that's where she stayed, they said,
          four women.

---

6. Maria Hesus demonstrates a hand frozen in an upward position.

Luisa: Hmm.

M.H.: Haamuchim, o'owim su'utohiwak tea
porque kaa aa katee tea.
Malata mala intok pos vo'o hoa.
Ta uu yoi bwan hunuen
kaa tu'im aa mamak ti hiiaka,
aa ko'okoe ti hiiaka hunum veha aa su'utohak
en el hospital de Nayarit . . .
Tepik, Nayarit.
Intuchi woi haamut[7] yo'owe
hunume huni kaa ko'okoe tea ibwan . . .

Luisa: Hmm.

M.H.: . . . pos yo'otulimtaka huni kaate.
Wepu'ulaika intok ili veeme he'elai,
hunaa ala taewecheka
ama su'utohiwak hunaa hamut, ho?

Luisa: Hmm.

M.H.: Hunume yoim veha nau nokaa tea.
"Ite intok haisa am hoone?"
ti hiia tea ume enfermeeram.

Luisa: Ay . . .

M.H.: "Vaa am yumhuetua.
Ela'apo yumhue'ene," ti hiia tea.
"I'isu? Pos ii intok kia taeweche . . .
inyeksionta aa maka.
Yoko haivu kaa, kaa, kaa hak wantine.
Vanseka haksa vurupo

---

7. Maria Hesus probably meant to say "*haamuchim*" (women), which is the plural form of *hamut* (woman).

Luisa: Hmm.

M.H.: Women, men were released, they said,
because they could not walk, they said.
Mom's mother, well, was walking.
But that Mexican, well, this,
she did not have a good hand, he said,
he said that she was sick, then he left her there
at the hospital in Nayarit . . .
In Tepic, Nayarit.
Also two other elderly women,
they were also not sick, they said, well . . .

Luisa: Hmm.

M.H.: . . . well, they were very old yet they walked.
And one was much younger,
she was running a fever,
they left her there, that woman, see?

Luisa: Hmm.

M.H.: Those Mexicans, then, were talking to each other, they said.
"And what are we going to do with them?"
is what the nurses said.

Luisa: Ay . . .

M.H.: "Go ahead and let them rest.[8]
It does not matter if they rest," they said, they said.
"And this one? Well, and this one has a fever . . .
give her an injection.
Tomorrow she will already not, not, not feel any pain.
Go ahead and place her on the donkey

---

8. *Yumhuene* means "will rest." This meant that they should be killed. Old people, sick people, and the gravely wounded were typically given an injection of some kind of toxic solution, which was very fast acting so that they would die very quickly after being injected. Maria Hesus referred to it as "*poova*," which is gunpowder, but this interviewer is not sure if, in fact, that is what was being injected into the individuals.

aa yechaka huni aa hahatuane
aver haksa kaate ume indio alsaum,"
ti hiia tea ume enfermeeram.

Reyno: Hmm.

Luisa: Ay!

M.H.: Ume vahi yo'otulim veha suak.
In mala grandeta intok ume woi hamut yo'owe.
Inyektaroawak tea kechia mala Lusia
intok ume woi kaa tua o'oola.
Pos chea chuvvatuk humak kaa tua tu'isi
emo eiya'ataitek pos poova amet kiimu.
Hunak veha hunuen au hiia tea
hunaa hamut taewechemtawi,
"Nana," ti au hiia tea.
"Empo yooko, matchuko," ti au hiia tea.
"Ume itommak werim hahamne . . ." ti au hiia tea.
"In asoata tehwane . . . inim nee taawak." [*inaudible*]

Luisa: Aa.

M.H.: "Kattee, kan nee ko'okoe . . ." ti hiia tea.
". . . ta nee inyektaroak uu yoi," ti hiia tea.
"I'an intok in takaa muuke," ti hiia tea.
Hunuen hiiakasu ropti hinteka
haivusu kaave tea.

Luisa: Aa.

M.H.: Ume vahika hunen auk.
Chuvvatuk hita, hippetampo roaktawaka
woho'oriapo kom wootawak, tea,
ume Hiak haamuchim.
"Haisa itepo am hoone,
esos indios alzados,"
ti hiia tea, uu enfermeera.
Hunaa hamut hunuen hiia,

and make her follow
to see where the hiding Indians[9] go,"
said the nurse, they said.

Reyno: Hmm.

Luisa: Ay!

M.H.: The three elders were killed.
My grandmother and the other two elderly women.
They were injected also, they say, Mother Lucia
and the other two [who were] not really old.
Well, later they did not feel well
since the poison, well, was beginning to take effect.
Then she [Grandmother] said to her,
to the woman who had fever,
"Young girl," she said to her.
"Tomorrow or the next day, you," she said to her, they said,
"you will catch up to our relatives . . ." she said to her.
"Tell my daughter . . . that I stayed here . . ." [*inaudible*]

Luisa: Ah.

M.H.: "We are not, I am not sick . . ." she said, they said.
". . . but the Mexican injected me," she said, they said.
"And now my body is dying," she said, they said.
Having said that, she covered herself with her shawl
and soon she was gone, they said.

Luisa: Ah.

M.H.: They did that to all three.
Later, they were wrapped in a blanket
and tossed down into a hole, they said,
those Hiaki women.
"What will we do with them,
those Indians taking up arms?"
said that nurse, they said.
That woman [the one who had had fever] said

---

9. Referring to Hiakis who were hiding from the soldiers.

>   ave Wadalahaarao yahiwau veha
>   aman ameu tohiwak, tea,
>   peronim aa eskorta tea uka hamutta.
>   Kaa, haivu kaa taeweche tea.
>   Hunum veha aa hu'uneiyaak tea uu mala.
>   Ta haisa aa ya'ane?
>   Pos hunume veha animaalimvenasia namawa,
>   wiko'immea weiya'awa.

Luisa: Hmm.

M.H.: Hunum veha Wadalahaaroau yahak tea uu maala.
Wate, pos ya ves, wate pos
kate'etek pues wok vahiane.

Luisa: Hee.

M.H.: Pos hunuen veha wate veha
kaa, kaa nappat aa katee tea.
Wok kotte.
. . . Hunum trenpo veha
emo nuksaka'awak ti hiia
asta Veracruz, trenpo.

Luisa: Hm, hmm.

M.H.: Ta hiva hunuen suma'itaka
katee tea ume yoeme.
Hunaman tohiwaka veha varkopo veha
nuksaka'awak tea, asta Yukatan.

> when they were almost in Guadalajara,
> she was taken to them, she said,
> the bald ones were escorting her, they said, the woman.
> Not, she was already not feverish, they said.
> That's when Mom found out about her [her mother], they said.
> But what could she do?
> Well, they were guarding them like animals,
> with rifles, carrying them.

Luisa: Hmm.

M.H.: There, then, she arrived in Guadalajara, they said, Mom.
Some, well, you see, some, well,
when they are walking, well, their feet will swell.

Luisa: Yes.

M.H.: Well, that way, then some
could not, could no longer walk, they say.
Their legs were broken.
. . . There on a train, then,
they were taken, she said,
to Veracruz, on the train.

Luisa: Hm, hmm.

M.H.: But they were still tied up
and walking, the Hiakis.
Over there they were brought, then, in a boat,
they were taken, they said, to Yucatán.

Teasing Luisa About Capture (Luisa and Andres)

Andres teases Luisa about how often she was captured, saying that every time there was a skirmish, every time the people went into the mountains, she was captured. Luisa laughs along, agreeing. She says her older sister was never captured. She jokes that it was because

---

Luisa: Pos si si vu'u familiata ama nu'uka hunum Vaka Tevepo.
Ta hunak kaa hunumun te tohiwak,
Peesio tohiwak, teta kariwi, karseleu.

Maria: Hunak empo ama nu'uwak?

Luisa: Heewi. Si'ime, maala . . .

Maria: Aa.

Andres: Ii chea kada ori, tahtiwak
hiva yoim aa bwi'ibwise. Hoiwasuk ii'i.

[*Laughter in background.*]

Luisa: Tua Lios.

Andres: Hiva aa bwi'ibwise iibwan.

Luisa: In ako intok sehtul huni kaa yoi nu'uwaka bwan.

Andres: Ii, intok kada kawiu wattiwak haivu hunumun,
haivu bwihritune.

Luisa: Aa bwe possi si'imek ta'avaekatua.
Kia im hiva nah weetek intok hausa ta'ane?
I'an intok maa nee si'imekut ta'a Mehikou.
Kia aman etehowau
kia aman vichamche'ene.

[*Laughter in background.*]

Andres: Aa, kada kawiu . . .
inii intok haivu hakun tohiritune.

she wanted to see the world. She then reveals the real reason, which was that because she was the youngest child, she was always with her mother, in the main group, while her older sister was more independent. She was captured at least three times, once when the conscripted *wilom* were chasing the Hiakis, once at Oros, and once at Tiko Kawi (Wheat Mountain).

Luisa: Well, they captured a lot, a lot of wives there at Tall Bamboo.
But then we were not taken there,
we were taken to Hermosillo, to the rock house, to the jail.

Maria: Then you were captured there?

Luisa: Yes. Everyone, Mom . . .

Maria: Ah.

Andres: This one, every time there was a skirmish,
the Mexicans would capture her. She is already used to it, this one.

[*Laughter in background.*]

Luisa: Truly God.

Andres: They always captured her, well.

Luisa: My older sister was not caught by Mexicans even once.

Andres: And this one, every time they went into the mountains,
she would be captured.

Luisa: Ah, well, well, that's because I wanted to know every place.
If I am just walking around here, how will I learn about places?
And now I know other places, Mexico City.
When they are talking about it
I just feel like I can see it.

[*Laughter in background.*]

Andres: Ah. Every time to the mountains . . .
and this one will already be taken somewhere.

Luisa: [*Laughs.*] Pos hunak hunume nu'uwaka,
　　　　bwan si vu'ukai.
　　　　Huevenaka yeu sahak hewi?

Maria: Heewi.

Luisa: Ta pos in ako intok kaa nunu'uwan,
　　　　ibwan, yo'owe. [*Laughs.*]
　　　　Nee intok hiva hue malatamak weweamaka veha
　　　　hiva yoi nunu'uwa.
　　　　Wilom yee hahhaseu huni nu'uwakan.
　　　　Intuchi hunum Orospo huni'i. I'an intuchia. [*Laughs.*]

Andres: Hunum Tiiko Kawiu hakun veha
　　　　aa bwisek, ma hunuen hiia.

Luisa: I'an kaa te hunaman si mekka rehten,
　　　　iibwan Tiiko Kawiu rehteka intok . . .

Andres: Ite kaita pasaaroak.

Luisa: Ite ala.

Where the Three Groups of Hiaki Hostages Were Captured (Luisa)

Luisa explains that three groups of women and children were deported. The first ones were captured at Samawaka, the second group consisted

M.H.: Waimam veha, Waimampo veha te embarkaroak, tea.
　　　　Ay, no sé si, si Mansaniau kom tohiwak
　　　　o Masaklanpo hakun. Aa, hunum veha nee tua kaa hu'unea.

Luisa: Si'ime Mansaniau yeu toiwak.

M.H.: Um.

Luisa: [*Laughs.*] Well, when those were captured,
well, there were so many.
Many left, yes?

Maria: Yes.

Luisa: But my older sister was never captured,
well, she was older. [*Laughs.*]
And I was always with Mom then,
I was always captured by the Mexicans.
Even when the skinny ones chased us, I was captured.
Again there at Oros. Now again. [*Laughs.*]

Andres: There at Wheat Mountain somewhere then
she was captured, that is what she says.

Luisa: Now we were over there far away,
well, [we] were at Wheat Mountain, and . . .

Andres: We did not experience anything.

Luisa: We did.

---

of people who had been captured in various places, and the third group had been captured at Gloria Canyon. Luisa says everyone was taken to Manzanillo.

M.H.: Then Guaymas, in Guaymas we were deported, they said.
I don't know if we were taken down to Manzanillo
or to Mazatlán somewhere. Ah, that I really do not know.

Luisa: Everyone was taken to Manzanillo.

M.H.: Um.

Luisa: Si'ime. Ume tua vat nuksaka'awakame.
Pos si primeeram intok ter . . .
segundam intok terseum.

M.H.: Hunuen iibwan hiia uu maala.

Luisa: Hunume Samawakapo si'ime nu'uwakame,
si'ime primeeramtukan.

M.H.: Hmm.

Luisa: Chukula intok ume huet si'ime nau toiwakame,
hunume veha segundamtuk.
Intuchi ultimopo hunum veha
kahonpo Gloriapo nau toiwakame
hunume veha terseamtuk.

M.H.: Aa. Porque nee kaa, nee,
i'an mala hiva hunuen etehone, hewi?

Luisa: Hm.

Luisa: Everyone. The ones who were taken first.
Well, the first ones and thir- . . .
second and the third.

M.H.: That is what, well, Mom said.

Luisa: Those that were captured at Samawaka,
all were the first ones.

M.H.: Hmm.

Luisa: Later the ones who were captured everywhere else,
those were the second [group].
And the last ones captured,
then, were at Gloria Canyon,
those were the third [group].

M.H.: Ah. Because I did not, I,
now Mom would always speak like that, yes?

Luisa: Hm.

PART II

IN THE SOUTH

This part of the book presents accounts excerpted from the interviews with Luisa, Andres, and Maria Hesus, documenting their memories of their experiences as children and young adults in the south. They describe deportation, forced labor on henequen plantations and in a soap factory, the death of children and older people from southern diseases, the arrival of the men to sign a treaty to free their captured wives and children, the conscription of the men into the Mexican military, life as a military dependent, battle during the Escobar Rebellion, and the process of returning to Hiak Vatwe and leaving military service.

The stories in this part are organized into three chapters: "Deportation," "Life, Labor, and Death in the South," and "Military Service." Each story is summarized in a prose paragraph at the beginning and then presented in Hiaki with an English translation, exactly as recounted to the author.

FIGURE 19 The penitentiary at Guaymas, ca. 1910. Arizona Historical Society, PC 078, Mathews Photograph Collection, box 8, album #J, page 13, #26944.

CHAPTER 5

DEPORTATION

Urbalejo, the Execution Order, and Surnames (Maria Hesus)

Maria Hesus describes how, after being captured at Samawaka, she and her mother were held in the jail (the "rock house") in Guaymas while waiting to be deported. While there, a military supervisor named Urbalejo, who was himself a Hiaki, told them that there had been an order to put them all on a boat and sink it, but that he would ensure that that would not happen. He advised them to get into groups of ten or twenty, even if they were unrelated, and tell the record-keepers that they all had a single surname—each group should pretend to be a family. That way, he would make the case that they should all be sent together as a group. Maria Hesus's mother, Paula Buitimea Alvarez, took the surname Flores with the members of the group she was with, and was no longer called Buitimea. Luisa says that the boats went from Guaymas to Manzanillo, and then they were taken to Toluca by train.

M.H.: Inimi'i yu, i'an Waimmampo
hak tetakari ti hiune uu maala.
Haksa humak uu tetakari.

Luisa: Pesiopo.

M.H.: Imi'i, Waimampo.

Luisa: Aa.

M.H.: Kaa uu bwe'u palacio i'ani?

Reyno: Hiva tua huna'a humaku'u.
Si ousi maachi, kati'inia.

Luisa: Hmm.

M.H.: Hunama veha te eta'itukan, itepo.
Pos hunum veha yeu nuksaka'ava'awa ume inime haamuchim,
hunum bwihkame Samawakapo.
Hunum veha hunen au hiia tea Urvaleeho.
Havesa humaku'u uu Urvaleeho.

Luisa: Yoeme. Ta muksuk kechia.

Reyno: Hmm.

M.H.: Hunaa hunuen hiia tea uu Urvaleeho,
porque ini'i Porfiristam ketuni hiapsan.

Luisa: Hmm.

M.H.: "Yeu am nuksiime," ti hiia tea
hunu'u Porfirio[1] Mehiko vetana.
"Hunum yeu am nuksikaa vawe nasuk
huni uka varkota pehtane.
Elapo ama koko ume Hiakim," ti hiia tea.

---

1. Porfirio Díaz, Mexican president from 1877 to 1880, then again from 1884 to 1911. As dictator, he ordered the deportation of the Hiaki people from their homeland to the henequen plantations in southern Mexico: specifically, Yucatán, Quintana Roo, Veracruz, Oaxaca, and several other places. When Francisco Madero became president, he ordered that the Hiakis be returned to their lands. Díaz was exiled to France, where he died and was buried in 1915.

M.H.: Here, see, now in Guaymas
Mom said there was a rock house somewhere.
I don't know where the rock house is.

Luisa: In Hermosillo.

M.H.: Here, in Guaymas.

Luisa: Ah.

M.H.: Isn't it the big municipal building now?

Reyno: It probably is that one.
It is very well built, remember.

Luisa: Hmm.

M.H.: We were locked up there.
Well, that is where these women were going to be deported from,
those who were captured there at Samawaka.
That is where Urbalejo[2] said this to them, they said.
I don't know who this Urbalejo is.

Luisa: A Hiaki. But he also died.

Reyno: Hmm.

M. H.: That one spoke in this way, they say, Urbalejo,
because the Porfiristas were still alive.

Luisa: Hmm.

M.H.: "Take them out," he is supposed to have said,
that Porfirio from Mexico.
"Take them out to the middle of the ocean,
then blow up the ship.
Let the Hiakis die there," is what he reportedly said.

---

2. Evidently Urbalejo was a Hiaki who served in the Mexican military. Many Hiakis were captured and forced into the Mexican military. Although he was a Mexican soldier, Urbalejo still felt compassion for his people and would not tolerate ill-treatment of the Hiaki women who had been captured.

Reyno: Hmm.

Luisa: Hm.

M.H.: I'i intok aa hu'uneiya'ak uu Urvaleeho.
"Tu'i," ti hiia tea.
"Hunum aane," ti au hiia tea.
"Am vicha; ili uusim.
Hitasa kulpaka, inime haamuchim,
ili yo'otulim, inime veha tohiri.
Hitasa ya'arika veha
inim animaalimvenasi eta'i?
Am sua," ti au hiia tea. "Am sua."
"Ta nee ket amevetchi'ivo hu'unea," ti au hiia tea.

Luisa: Hmm.

M.H.: "Nee kaivu nee . . . hunu familia . . .
nee ket emou kwaktine," ti au hiia
tea . . .

Luisa: Hm, hmm.

M.H.: . . . hunu'u Urvaleeho.

Luisa: Yoemem. Isikio Chaavez
intok Hose Amarillas
intok Antonio Amarillas.

M.H.: Hunum veha, hunum veha
ameu, ameu nokaa tea hunuu Urvaleeho.
"Maalam," ti au hiia tea.
"Si chea wam heela, haksa aniapo,
vawepo eme'e kate'eteeteko,
hitasa huni pasaroane
haksa aniapo huni'i,
varko emomak viektine.
Kaa nee hu'unea,
porque uu govierno hunuen hiia," ti hiia tea.
"Ta Dios huna'a," ti hiia tea.
"Kaita em pasaroane.

Reyno: Hmm.

Luisa: Hm.

M.H.: And this Urbalejo had learned about it.
"Okay," is what he said.
"There they are," he reportedly said to him.
"Look at them; the little children.
What have they done wrong, these women,
little old people, that they have been brought here?
What have they done, then,
that they are locked up like animals?"
"Kill them," he [Díaz] said to him, they said. "Kill them."
"But I know what I will do for them," he [Urbalejo] said, it is said.

Luisa: Hmm.

M.H.: "I will never ... that family ...
I shall also turn to you," he said to him,
they said ...

Luisa: Hm, hmm.

M.H.: ... that Urbalejo.

Luisa: They were Hiakis, like Ezekiel Chavez
and Jose Amarillas
and Antonio Amarillas.

M.H.: Then there, then there
that Urbalejo spoke to them, to them.
"Mothers," he said to them, they said.
"If, farther on, somewhere in this world,
when you-all are on the ocean,
something may happen to you,
somewhere out there,
the ship may sink with you,
I don't know,
because that's what the government says," he said, they said.
"But God is the one," he said, it is said.
"Nothing will happen to you.

> Si hunuen enchim ya'awak,
> nee ket si'ime henteta [*inaudible*].
> Kaa kia hunuen tawane," ti hiia tea.
> "I'an intok eme'e," ti au hiia tea.
> Porque maala Vuitime'a.

Luisa: Hmm.

M.H.: Alvarez. Hunak hunen au teak . . .
> "Ta kaa, kaa wepu'ulaim teane.
> Dies o quinsetaka
> wepu'ulai uhteam nau hippu'une," ti au hiia tea.
> "Wepul uhteam."
> Pos ume veha emo ta'aka veha—
> havesa humak Flores. Hunume veha veintetaka
> emo nau tohak tea.
> Pos veha emo priimak, emo maalak,
> emo akok. "A ver si'ime Flores, Flores, Flores."

Reyno: Hmm.

M.H.: Pues mala veha Florespo taawak.

Luisa: Hmm.

M.H.: Vuitimeam amau suutohak.
Kaita Vuitimea.

Luisa: Hmm.

M.H.: Si'ime emo, emo akok.
> Emo haisa atteaka veha nau katee tea,
> ti hiia tea hunu'u Urvaleeho. "Haisa
> empo hunuka familiata empo hunuen ya'ane?" ti au hiia tea.
> "Kaa am vicha? Si'ime familiarim
> intuchi waate, intuchi waate."
> Pos si vu'uka te nau, nau . . .
> i'an veha sosiedam venasia.
> Wepulai uhteamta te veha nau yecha'ane.
> Pos hunuen veha katek uu maala,
> Paula Flores.

If they do something to you,
I will also tell all the people [*inaudible*].
It will not stay that way," he said, they said.
"And now, you all," he said, they said.
Because Mom's last name was Buitimea.

Luisa: Hmm.

M.H.: Alvarez. Then she took that surname . . .
"But do not, do not have only one [sur]name.
Ten or fifteen of you
should have one surname," he said to her.
"One surname."
Well, then, they knew each other—
I don't know who was Flores. There were twenty of them
who came together, they said.
Well, then some became cousins, others were moms,
others older sisters. "Let's see, all of them Flores, Flores, Flores."

Reyno: Hmm.

M.H.: Well, then Mom became a Flores.

Luisa: Hmm.

M.H.: She left the name Buitimea there.
No more Buitimea.

Luisa: Hmm.

M.H.: All of them became older sisters.
They became related, then went walking together, they said,
is what that Urbalejo said. "How,
if she is your wife, can you do that to her?" he said, it is said.
"Don't you see them? All the wives,
and others, and also those others."
Well, so many of us were together, together . . .
Then, now it was like the societies.
We will share surnames.
Well, that is how Mom is named now,
Paula Flores.

Luisa: Hmm.

M.H.: Mehikowi. Tarheta hunum katek.
Uu maala hunumun Mehikowi
kaa Vuitimea.

Luisa: Hmm.

M.H.: Hunuen aa ya'ak
porque hunu'u Urvaleeho
"Kaa wepul uhteam," ti au hiia tea.
"Diestaka, veintetaka emo nau tohine.
Hunak veha nau katne," ti hiia tea.
"Hunaman nee enchim voovitne Mehikowi,"
ti au hiia tea. Kaa amemak siika . . .

Luisa: Hm, hmm.

M.H.: . . . ta hiva humak am suasime,
am suasime, am hu'uneiya'asime, bwan.
Haksa humak te kom checheptek,
o si Mansania, porque empo
im Kolimapo ti hiia, hewi?

Luisa: E'e. Ite Mansaniawi.

M.H.: Nee veha tua kaa huunea . . .

Luisa: Hunum Waimampo vaporpo varkaroa
asta Puerto Mansaniau yeu tohiwak.

M.H.: Hunaman intok hitaapo? Trenpo?

Luisa: Trenpo wam vicha nuksaka'awak.
Tolukau vicha trenpo nuksaka'awak.

Luisa: Hmm.

M.H.: In Mexico. There is the card.
There in Mexico Mom is
not a Buitimea.

Luisa: Hmm.

M.H.: That is what they did
because that Urbalejo
said, "No single surnames," is what he said to them, they said.
"Ten of you, twenty of you get together.
Then you will go together," he said, they said.
"I will wait for you all in Mexico City,"
is what he said to them. He did not go with them . . .

Luisa: Hm, hmm.

M.H.: . . . but perhaps he kept checking on them,
checking on them and learning about them, well.
I do not know where we got down,
maybe in Manzanillo, because you
said here in Colima, yes?

Luisa: No. We got down in Manzanillo.

M.H.: I really do not know . . .

Luisa: We boarded the boats there in Guaymas
where we were taken to Port Manzanillo.

M.H.: And over there, in what [did you travel]? In the train?

Luisa: We were taken that way by train.
We were taken by train to Toluca.

On the Transport Ship *Progresa* (Maria Hesus and Luisa)

Luisa describes her experience on board the ship that took them from Guaymas southward, which was named the *Progresa*.[3] It was a large naval ship. When any of the captives died, they were buried at sea in a gunnysack with a railroad tie tied to their feet. Captives were kept both in the hold and on deck, and had access to toilet facilities. They were fed black beans. Luisa thought that the *Progresa* had ended its days in Veracruz, but Maria Hesus remembered that the *Progresa* was used to bring soldiers north in 1920 and had returned her mother to Guaymas on her journey back from the Yucatán. After the people had disembarked, it rolled over and sank right there in Guaymas harbor.

Maria: Varkompo kateme,
intok huname kokome o ko'okoeme,
huname intok kia veha yeu wootana?

Luisa: Bwe, kia va'au kom wootana.
Kia ori, lonampo kutti hiikna.
Lonampo namalo'ala hiikwaka veha
hunam hiiksuwak veha
koekoekti aa chaptane, wohoktane.
Hunak veha imin, veha vetukun ume durmientem, veha hunam . . .
im veeppanim veha aet suma'ane im wokpo.
Chukula veha hunum veha varkot veha inen aa tekine,
wokekamta, hewi?
Inen aa tekikai veha kampanita vahisi hihiak veha
aman kom hima'ana um va'awi.

Maria: Hmm.

Luisa: Ilitchi intok kia yo'owe huni hiva
va'au kom hima'ana, mukuko.

---

3. Progreso is the name of a port in the Yucatán to which many Hiakis were shipped for enslavement, as described by John Kenneth Turner in *Barbarous Mexico* (London: Cassell and Company, 1911). Perhaps the ship was named after the destination.

FIGURE 20 A Mexican warship in Guaymas harbor, ca. 1908. Arizona Historical Society, Places-out-of-state-Sonora-Guaymas, box 68, #62010.

Maria: Those who were traveling in the boats,
and those who were dying or were sick,
were they just thrown overboard?

Luisa: Well, they just threw them overboard.
They just, well, sewed them tightly in gunnysacks.
They were rolled in canvas, sewn, then
after being sewn in there, then,
then they would cut holes in the canvas.
Then here, down below, the railroad ties, then those . . .
this long[4] would be tied to their feet.
Then later they would lay them this way on the boat,
with their feet,[5] yes?
When they were laid this way, then a bell would ring three times,
then they would throw him or her down into the sea.

Maria: Hmm.

Luisa: And little children just the same as the adults
were thrown into the water, when they died.

---

4. Here Luisa holds her hands up to show about a meter in length.
5. She indicates that the feet would be pointing toward the sea.

Maria: Intok unna ko'okoetek huni hu . . .
 hunuen hohoa, kee muki, kee muke . . . ?

Luisa: E'e. Kokokame hiva aman kom woowota.

Maria: Kokome hiva?

Luisa: Heewi, ta kaa am e'ehso'ii'aawa.
 Kiala mukuk hiva sep partem ya'asauna,
 porque kaa tu'i, tea ti hiia . . . ume marineom.
 Porque hu'une'ea,
 haisa humak hu'une'ea.
 Porque hunuen senuk vinwa mukiataka ama weyeo,
 haivu kia nah tennine,
 hariune, nattemaine.

Maria: Hmm.

Luisa: Muku . . . havetasa mukuka'u,
 intok "Havesa aa hippueka kaa monte tea?" ti hiune.

Maria: Huname, ume hente, pos hunuen weiyawame,
 huname intok haksa hipu'uwa, vetuku?

Luisa: Wate vetuku. Huevenaik vetuk kima'ana.
 Intok huevenak intok vepa hoosakane.
 Komo vagonimmet sontaom weiyawamevenasia.

Maria: Huname intok hitaa bwa'atuawa?

Luisa: Abwe mun vakim si chirikootem venam.
 Chuku'im bwa'atuawa.
 Ori, hita gasolinae bwabwa'asawa.

Maria: And if they were very sick, even . . .
    they would do this to them, before death, before they died . . . ?

Luisa: No. Only the ones who died were thrown overboard.

Maria: Only those who died?

Luisa: Yes, but they were told not to hide them [the deceased].
    As soon as one died, they were told to notify them right away,
    because it was not good, they said . . . the sailors.
    Because they would be found out,
    I don't know how they found out.
    Because when one had been long dead and was still on board,
    they would already be running around,
    looking for it, asking questions.

Maria: Hmm.

Luisa: Die . . . when someone had died,
    "Who has it [the corpse] and is not revealing it?" they would say.[6]

Maria: The people who were taken like that,
    where did they keep them, in the hold of the boat?

Luisa: Some were below. Many were placed down there.
    And many were sitting on deck.
    As if they were soldiers traveling in the train boxcars.

Maria: And what were they fed?

Luisa: Well, boiled beans that looked like large navy beans.
    They fed us black beans.
    Well, they were cooked with some kind of gasoline.

---

6. Although the author heard many more accounts to do with the disposal of the bodies of Hiakis who died on board ship, those recordings are unfortunately lost. However, doña Luisa told of how, over the course of the voyage, the deaths would mount up so much that it became customary to simply throw corpses overboard without any covering, or ceremony, particularly those of babies and small children. Many babies died when their mothers were unable to nurse them anymore, through malnutrition. Luisa also described increasing numbers of sharks following the boat, as she saw the fins; they were there to feast on the deceased.

Bweere, ori, sisiwokim inen tuvummet cha'aka.
Hunae, hitasae humak am bwabwa'asa, lektresidad.
Ta kia hi'ito vakimvenane.
Kaa va'awane. Kia hunuen chuchukurine, roovoim.

Maria: Yumhuevaetek veha kia hunama o haksa ili lugar ama aayuk hunuevetchi'ivo?

Luisa: Heewi. Si'imeta hippue.

Maria: Aa, heewi.

Luisa: Uu varko?

Maria: Heewi.

Luisa: Si'imeta hippue. Hunu'u i'an itom aman tohakame, hu tua sontao vapor aman itom totoisuk. I'an . . .

Maria: Aa heewi.

Luisa: Progreesa tea. Hunaa bwe'u varko.

Maria: Huevena henteta nunu'e?

Luisa: Heewi. Sontao varko. Hunaa aman itom . . .

M.H.: Hunaa, hunaa Progreesa intok hakunsa ho'akan?

Luisa: Abwe, kaa tu'iriakan.
Hunaa ultimo viaheta ya'aka, veha Veracruzpo taawak.

M.H.: Progreesa?

Luisa: Heewi.

M.H.: Porque hunu'u Progreeso malata Yukatanvetana yeu tohak imin Wamamewi.

Luisa: Aa. Tua, tua sontao vapor ibwan huna'a.

M.H.: Um, hmm. Progreeso.

Luisa: Hunum, itom ama . . .

M.H.: Ta, hunaa, intok, Progreeso, havesa humaku'u,

	Well, big metal things were hanging on tubes like this.
	Maybe they were cooked with those, maybe with electricity.
	But they just looked like a tree bearing fruit.
	They [the beans] had no broth. They were just black and whole.
Maria:	If one wanted to use the toilet, did one just use any space one found for that purpose?
Luisa:	Yes. It did have everything.
Maria:	Ah, yes.
Luisa:	The boat?
Maria:	Yes.
Luisa:	It had everything. That boat that took us over there, that was a real naval ship that took us over there. Now . . .
Maria:	Ah, yes.
Luisa:	It was named *Progresa*. That was a big boat.
Maria:	Did it take a lot of people?
Luisa:	Yes. It was a naval boat. That one took us there . . .
M.H.:	That, that *Progresa*, where was it stationed?
Luisa:	Well, it was not seaworthy. That was the last voyage it made, then it remained in Veracruz.
M.H.:	The *Progresa*?
Luisa:	Yes.
M.H.:	Because that *Progresa* brought Mom from Yucatán here to Guaymas.
Luisa:	Ah. That, that was a real naval ship, well, that one.
M.H.:	Um, hmm. The *Progresa*.
Luisa:	There, when we . . .
M.H.:	But, so, that one, *Progresa*, I do not know who,

hunum katin Waimampo
kia aman yeu am tohaka si'ime henteta,
yeu viaktaka veha
haksa orapo, o si heeka
o kia a'apo wohokteka,
le entró el agua y se fue de piiki,
hunum Waimampo.

Maria: Hmm.

M.H.: Porque mil nuevesientos veintetuk hunum yeu yahak . . .

Luisa: Hmm.

M.H.: . . . de Yukatan. Hunue, ta sontao kaate.
Sesenta y kuatro vatayontukan, huna'a . . .

Luisa: Aa.

M.H.: . . . de Yukatan, hasta, hasta aquí, hasta Waimas.

FIGURE 21 The harbor at Guaymas sometime between 1904 and 1927. Records of the Compañía Constructora Richardson, S.A., 1904–1968 (bulk 1904–1927), MS 113, box 1, folder 4: Photographs. Courtesy of University of Arizona Libraries, Special Collections.

> there, remember in Guaymas,
> it just took them there, all the people,
> and then after it had rolled out,
> at some hour, maybe it was the wind,
> or maybe it had a hole,
> the water came in and it sank,
> there in Guaymas.

Maria: Hmm.

M.H.: Because in 1920, it arrived here . . .

Luisa: Hmm.

M.H.: . . . from Yucatán. That one, but it was carrying soldiers. It was the 74th Battalion, that one . . .

Luisa: Ah.

M.H.: . . . from Yucatán to, to here, to Guaymas.

Life in the Holding Center at Paraíso, in Tabasco (Luisa)

Luisa describes how she and the other captured Hiaki women were separated from the men and lived by the water in the state of Tabasco. When she arrived she was nursing a baby, Marsiel. There were many biting flies and mosquitoes that they could not escape. They ate oysters, fish, turtles, and other food eaten by the local people: cassava, yams, and squash. The

---

Luisa: Toiwakan, hunume submariinim hunum vawepo kiimun,
veha aman toiwak.
Pos hunam Paraisopo te toiwak tukaapo.
Hunum veha tukaapo na'ikimtewak ume yoeme,
Limonimmeu vicha intok Komakalkou vicha,
wokimmea na'ikim vittuawak.
Intok Limonimmeu vicha, tukaapo,
tukaapo ama yahaka hunuen naikimtewak o'owim.
Ite intok kia hunama va'a bwikola wootawak.
Hunaman te ket kia hunuen ya'awak,
kia te va'a bwikola wootawak uu familia.
O'owim ta hakunsa kia veha yeu sahak inen teakau vittuawak . . .
tia Mikeataim aa hu'uneiya.
Tua te humak senu metpo itepola ama hooka
hunama'a va'a bwikola.
Kaita, kia te ume ori,
alian veha te kia koyom hiva bwa'eka ama hooka.

Maria: Hmm.

locals made houses and raised platforms from bamboo, and ate stewed vegetables and seafood with yams. The Hiakis ate those also, but in addition they made tortillas out of the cassava or yuca. The local houses were thatched with palm leaves and did not leak, even though they were very basic, unlike the modern homes Hiakis live in now in Sonora. Luisa also mentions the names Tepesida and Matuspaana as locations where the Hiakis were taken.[7]

Luisa: We were taken there, when those submarines were launching,
then we were taken there.
Well, we were taken there to Paraíso[8] at night.
Then there at night the men were separated [from the women].
Then to Limones[9] and to Comalcalco,[10]
the men were sent their separate ways, on foot.
And toward Limones, at night,
at night when we arrived, the men were separated from us.
And we, we were just abandoned there by the edge of the water.
That's how we were treated there,
we wives were just left by the edge of the water.
But the men then were sent out to a place known as . . .
Aunt Micaela knows where.
We were there by ourselves for about one month
there by the side of the water.
Nothing, we just, well,
as they say, then, we were just there eating oysters.

Maria: Hmm.

---

7. These are Hiaki versions of Mexican place-names whose Spanish correspondents are not 100 percent clear; however, some suggestions are made in footnotes as they occur in the transcript below.

8. Paraíso is in the state of Tabasco in Mexico.

9. This may be the Limones in the state of Quintana Roo in Mexico, although there are other Limón-derived names elsewhere in Mexico as well.

10. Comalcalco is in the state of Tabasco in Mexico.

Luisa: Kooyom si vu'u um va'apo, va'ai,
va'a komiapo, kaka va'ampo.
Huname te hiva puaka ume ili usim,
am bwa'atua kechia u'usekame.
Nee intok hunak kaa usekan,
hunuu Marsiel hiva, ta ilitchiakan.
Hunaka nee puanaman; kaa, kaa yo'otukan, kaa hi'ibwa.
Hunum veha, veha huevenaka
veha kia sesenu singrem vaakne ume kooyom.
Huname veha am bwa'atua.
Intok si kurum, wo'om,
si vu'u hunama levela.

Maria: ¡Ay, qué va!

Luisa: Kia kupteo kia te aet sassa'awavenasi
yetet watwattine.
Kiale ohvoi puhtitavenane ime mamam wokpo.
Hain ee bwichiiata ya'arine intok
kia hiva enchi bwa'ane.
Intok paveyoonek huni,
tukaapo wakiam kaachin cha'ane.
Am va'apo am tuttaka am chaya'ane,
hunak veha kaa amet pasaroane.
Si ousi vu'u hume'e animaalim hunaman.

M.H.: Hmm.

Luisa: Va'apo. Intok kia inen islapo ho'ara.
Kia inen hakun,
intok kia ili islampo hooneete hunum hak ta'apo chochopo'oku.
Kaita imvenasi kaa, kaa haksa tu'ulisi ho'ak.
Intok kia hunuen, yukeo,
intok va'ata yepsau, kia ilevenasi hoarampo,
kia va'a sasabwa'ati weene.

Luisa: There were a lot of oysters in the water,
    shallow water, sweet water.
    We just picked those and fed them to the children,
    they fed them also, those with children.
    And at that time, I did not have any children,
    only Marsiel, but he was very small.
    I used to carry him; he was not grown, he did not eat.[11]
    There then, there were many of them
    who would just boil one pail of those oysters.
    This is what they fed them.
    And there were so many bedbugs, mosquitoes,
    so many in that particular place.

Maria: Ay, my goodness!

Luisa: In the evening, it seemed like we were being splashed
    as they fell on us.
    It just looked like my arms, legs were sprayed with blood.
    Even though we made a lot of smoke
    it just seemed like they kept biting us.
    And even with mosquito nets—
    at night we could not hang the nets dry.
    You would have to soak them in water and hang them,
    then they would not penetrate it.
    There were so very many of those animals over there.

M.H.: Hmm.

Luisa: And in the water, in the islands, there were homes.
    They were just here and there,
    and we would just sit there in the islands, in the sun, on the hills.
    Nothing like there is here, nothing, no good homes.
    And just like that when it was raining,
    and the water was coming in the homes just like this,
    the water just flowed by us noisily.

---

11. Luisa was probably nursing this infant child; this is what she means by saying that he did not eat (i.e., solid food).

Maria: Hmm.

Luisa: Kaa wakiaku ho'ane.
Kia tapehtim hita ya'arine bwan.
Hunama veha hikat hoone, va'ata vuiteo.
Ket hunuen ili tapehtim ya'arika ama hikat hoone
hunuen ume ama ho'akame, si'ime.

Maria: Hunamani Tavaskopo?

Luisa: Heewi, Tavaskopo.
Intok si'ime hente ama ho'akame bwan,
kaita bwa'e kechia.
Ito, poloovem, tua poloovem.

Maria: Hunuen ama hippuwaka intok kaita enchim bwa'atua?

Luisa: Um, um. Ili mochikim, ili waivilim,
hunuka hiva bwa'eka ama ho'ak,
hente poovera, kechia.
Ket itovenasi ilevenam hiva karek, vakao.

Maria: Hmm.

Luisa: Kaave ilevenasi tosaim karek.

Maria: Ama hoome?

Luisa: Ama hoome.

Maria: Aa.

Luisa: Si'ime hunulevenam ili va . . . ta waa vakao tea.
Si bweere, im hak veetchi.
Tuturui.

Maria: Oo heewi. Aman nee senuk vichak hunule venak.

Maria: Hmm.

Luisa: Where we lived was not a dry place.
We would make mats, things, well.
We would sit on top of them when the water was flowing.
We also made some little mats and sat on top of them,
every one of those who lived there.

Maria: Over there in Tabasco?

Luisa: Yes, in Tabasco.
And all the people who lived there,
they also had nothing to eat.[12]
We, they were so poor, really poor.

Maria: They had you there like that and did not feed you?

Luisa: Um, um. Little turtles, little water turtles,[13]
that is all we ate while living there,
the poor people, also.
Like us they only had houses like this, bamboo.[14]

Maria: Hmm.

Luisa: No one had white houses like us [now].

Maria: The people from there?

Luisa: The people from there.

Maria: Ah.

Luisa: Everyone has a similar bam- . . . but they call it also bamboo reed.
It is quite big, it is about this size.
Very thick.[15]

Maria: Oh yes. I saw one over there like that.

---

12. Luisa probably means that the local people had very little to eat, perhaps just the oysters and whatever little they could find in the water.

13. *Pseudemys scripta*.

14. *Bambusa vulgaris* Schrad.

15. Luisa indicates approximately two to three centimeters in diameter.

Luisa: Hunu'u. Hunaka kakaate.
Hunaa si vu'u hunamani. Ausu'uli.
Hunaka hiva kaka'ate.
Intok kia kaa, kaa am bwiabwiatua itovenasi.
Kia ilevenam kaka'ate.
Inen chapala aa yecha'ane. Kaa, kaa bwiane bwan.
Kia tako, tako, koko sawata hiva.
Hunaa hiva amet to'one. Intok kaa vavawe kechia.

Maria: Hmm.

Luisa: Bwiakamtavenasi kaa vavawe.
Vempo aa am hoa bwan.

Maria: Heewi.

Luisa: Huname karim hiva hippue.
Kaita haksa itovenasi bwiakame karek.
Kaita haksa tevahaanta karek, kaita bwan.
Kia hunulevenam hiva karek.
Ta hunuen vempo ama ho'akame kaita intok bwa'e.
Ime ili waivilim intok ume ili mochikim va'apo aneme,
mahaum, kuchum hunuka hiva bwa'e.
Porque ket itovevena kaa wawasak, kaita hippue.

Maria: Kaita hippue.

Luisa: E'e. Kia ili vem ho'arampo,
hak ili vem ili koraka'apo huname kia ili
woi, vahi mamnim hak ili tataka ili echine vachita avaimpo.
Yuukam intok kamam echine.
Huname hiva bwa'awa intok ili kamootem.
Hunaa veha tahkaim lugarpo bwa'awa.

Maria: Hmm.

Luisa: Wakavakna, otane ineni hunaa
intok kia im hak veetchi soto'i tahipo manne.
Kama momoim pettawaka ama wattana,
intuchi huname yuukam intuchi kamootem.

Luisa: That one. They make houses from that.
There is a lot of it over there. Only that.
They use only that for houses.
And they don't, don't put mud on them like us.
They just make houses like this.
They make it with a pointed roof. No, no dirt, well.
Just palm leaves, palm leaves, coconut leaves only.
That is all they laid on them. And they also didn't leak.

Maria: Hmm.

Luisa: They do not leak, as if they had dirt [as if they were sealed with dirt].
They know how to make them, well.

Maria: Yes.

Luisa: They only have those kinds of houses.
They do not have houses with dirt [roofs] like us.
They do not have houses with ramadas, nothing, well.
Only houses like that.
But those who live there do not eat anything else.
The little water turtles, little turtles that are in the water,
desert tortoises,[16] fish, that's all they eat.
Because also like us they do not have farms, they have nothing.

Maria: They have nothing.

Luisa: No. In their little homes,
that they have fenced up, there
they planted corn that has two, three, five little ears on it.
They also have cassava and squash planted.
That is all they eat, and a few yams.
This is what they eat in place of tortillas.

Maria: Hmm.

Luisa: They will make a vegetable and meat stew with bones like this,
and set it in a pot just about this size on the fire.
The ripened squash is sliced and put in the stew,
as well as the cassava and the yams.

---

16. *Gopherus agassizii.*

> Hunaa veha bwa'ahapteak veha
> kia hunaa tahkaim lugarpo ume ili pedaaso kamootem,
> kamam, hunaka bwa'eka ama ho'ak huname'e si'ime.
> Pos ite intok ket hunaka manyata nu'ula kechia. [*Laughs.*]

Maria: Hacer lo que hacen . . .

Luisa: Heewi. Ket kia chanwomvenasi hunaka vem hoowau hooa kechia.
Ume yuukam hewi, ta vempo kaa am tatahkai ibwan.
Ite intok am tatahkai, yuukam.

Maria: Hitasa huname'e?

Luisa: Ori, naawam, e'etwa kechia. Im veeppanim nanawa.
Wepul mata si vu'um nawane.

Maria: Hmm.

Luisa: Pocho'oku aayuk. Ta ket aman sik ket am hinune.
Huname veha ore'ene.
Papam venasi am kattane.
Am oreka veha am tutuhne.
Huname kia aina tahkaimvenane.
Si ili vachita auk hunaka ilikik ama kuutaka,
veha nau am kutaka am tahkaine.
Kia ainamvenane, aina tahkaimvenane
ta tutu'ulisi vovoyone . . .

Maria: Hmm.

Luisa: . . . wako'opo tahkaiwaateko. Huname veha bwa'ane.

Maria: Ta hunuka veha ume Hiakim veha hunuka hooa?

Luisa: Heewi.

Maria: Vempo intok kaa hunuen . . .

Luisa: E'e. Kialam vavakeka am bwa'e, wakavakpo.
Kia vechehtine huname'e, etahtine.

[. . .]

Maria: Tabaskou empo etehon, vehako katinia.

When they begin to eat it, then,
the little pieces of yam are used in place of tortillas,
squash, that is what they ate while they lived there, all of them.
Well, and we also learned to eat that way also. [*Laughs.*]

Maria: Do as they do . . .

Luisa: Yes. Just like monkeys, what they did, we did also.
The cassava, yes, but they did not make tortillas from them.
And we did make tortillas from the cassava.

Maria: What are those?

Luisa: Um, roots, they are also planted. The root is this size.[17]
One plant would have a lot of roots.

Maria: Hmm.

Luisa: They are in the wild. But if you go there you can also buy them.
Then you would work on them.
You would slice them like potatoes.
You do this to them, then you grind them.
Those would look like flour tortillas.
If there is a little bit of corn, then you mix in a little,
then mix it together and make tortillas.
They would look just like flour, like flour tortillas,
but would puff up nicely . . .

Maria: Hmm.

Luisa: . . . when you cook them on a hot plate. Then you would eat them.

Maria: But then only the Hiakis did that?

Luisa: Yes.

Maria: And they [the people who lived there] did not do [it] that way . . .

Luisa: No. They just boiled them and ate them in the meat stew.
They [the cassava] would just burst open, break apart.

[. . .]

Maria: You were talking about Tabasco a while ago, remember?

---

17. Luisa indicates about six inches with her hand.

Luisa: Heewi. [*Laughs.*] Tabaskou etehon.
Hak i'an . . . Hak i'an nuki, ti hiia.
Ketuni ve'e, ketun vu'uka ve'e.

Maria: Oripo . . . katin eme'e hitasa humak ama eme'e emo e'echa ti hiian?
O hitasa eme'e bwabwa'e ti hiian.

Luisa: Kamam, hita bwabwa'e.
Kaa tahkaim bwa'wa, bwan.

Maria: Ta eme'e intok . . .

Luisa: Heewi.
Ite intok ume yukam tatahkaika
am bwabwa'en.
Huya naawam.

Maria: Hunama veha eme'e haisa vinwa ama hookan?

Luisa: Hunum humak naiki wasuktiapo ama hookan.

Maria: Vinwa ama hookan hewi?

Luisa: Heewi.

Maria: Hunama humak [*inaudible*] hewi?

Luisa: Tua uu Centro Villa Hermosa, Tabasko tea.
Hunama naavuhti wam vicha veha estakamento
vittuawak si'ime uu gente.
Paraiso teau vicha, Komakalko,
Limonim tea,
Tepesidam tea, Matuspaana tea.
Hunam hak, kia huet haku'u,
ranchompo pocho'oku, va'apo,
islapo hoara.

Maria: Hunama si'imekut eme'e rehte?

Luisa: Yes. [*Laughs.*] Talking about Tabasco.
Somewhere now ... It is somewhere near, they said.
There is still some distance left, still a lot left.

Maria: There ... you had maybe planted something there, you said?
Or you all ate some things, you said.

Luisa: Squash, we ate some things.
We did not eat tortillas, well.

Maria: But you-all and ...

Luisa: Yes.
And we made tortillas from the yuca
and we ate those.
The roots of plants.

Maria: How long were you there, then?

Luisa: We were probably there for four years.

Maria: You were there for a long time, yes?

Luisa: Yes.

Maria: Maybe there [*inaudible*] yes?

Luisa: Right there in central Villahermosa, also known as Tabasco.
From there on through to the stockade
all the people were sent.
On to a place known as Paraíso, Comalcalco,
known as Limones,
known as Tepesida,[18] Matuspaana.[19]
Somewhere there, just somewhere there,
on the ranches, in the wilderness, on the water,
on the islands, there were homes.

Maria: You walked everywhere there?

---

18. Possibly referring either to the town of Tepetitán in Tabasco or to the municipality of Tepetzintla in Veracruz.

19. Possibly referring to the municipality of Macuspana in Tabasco.

Luisa: Heewi, aet estakamiento vivittuawa.
Ta kaita kamionim.
Kia kava'im konsigigiaroawa.
Hunak veha ili hita, trasteta puatine.
Ta wokimmea katne. Kaita.
Bwe vaa'am, si'ime.

Maria: Si tata humaku'u.

Luisa: Si tattaen.

Southern Plants That Cause Disease or Death (Luisa, Reyno, and Maria Hesus)

Reynaldo, listening to the discussion of locations where Hiakis were held in the south, mentions a plant that was reputed to cause disease, a kind of fig tree. Andres's little brother Chema (Jose Maria) nearly died and had nodules like spider eggs or little sacks on his legs that were associated with diabetes. They then discuss another kind of tree, called *yete*

Reyno: Hunu intok ugo tea, uu ili huya.
Ori, hunum Mehikou vicha,
chea wam vicha [*inaudible*].

Luisa: Kaa si'imekut aayuk, kompae.
Heewi. Kaa si'imekut aayuk.

Reyno: Haksa partepo hiva?

Luisa: Hunum, hunum Orizabapo, Teso Napaa teapo.

Reyno: Hmm.

Luisa: Yes, we were sent to the stockades.
 But there were no buses.
 They were just getting some horses.
 Then they would carry a few dishes, cups.
 But we walked. Nothing.
 There was a lot of water, all over.

Maria: It was probably very hot.

Luisa: It used to be very hot.

---

ougu, or "sleepy tall tree," which will bring death to one who falls asleep in its shade. It seems to shrivel and close up when you walk by it. Maria Hesus then asks Reyno about a type of big banana that they had heard his relative Fatima discuss, which was also poisonous. Luisa comments that she saw many big bananas being eaten, and they were not fatal, but perhaps in the mountains such a thing might exist. In that connection she mentions the cimmaron ash tree. Maria Hesus mentions that a cousin of hers named Isidro traveled down that way.

Reyno: And that is known as *ugo* [fig], that little plant.
 There, toward Mexico City
 and farther on [*inaudible*].

Luisa: It is not found everywhere, compadre.
 Yes, it is not to be found everywhere.

Reyno: Where is the only place [it grew]?

Luisa: There, there at Orizaba,[20] at a place named Teso Napaa.[21]

Reyno: Hmm.

---

20. Orizaba is a city in the Mexican state of Veracruz, located twenty kilometers west of its sister city Córdoba. It is understood that the name Orizaba comes from the Nahuatl name Ahuilizapan, which means "the place of pleasing waters."

21. Possibly the municipality of Tezonapa in the state of Veracruz.

Luisa: Kuno teapo.
Intuchi San Agustin tea.
Hunum partepo si vu'u porque
hunum si vinwa hookan.
Uu ili Chematukau, Antesta saira,
tua vatte amea muukuk.
Tua ime wokim kia sosovevechelaikan, imi'i.
Tua aet tapunakan.
Kakak takakamtat ha'ani hunuen hoatene tea.

Maria: Heh?

Luisa: Tua ume huvahe kavam vena,
ili lolovolai, inen iibwan, ili voosane.

Reyno: Ori, uu huya intok, katin uu huya intok si bwe'u
ket mukne tea?
Hunaa, hunaa huya intok ket ori, hunae vetuk kochok,
hekkaa, hunaa intok ket kaa tu'i tea.

Luisa: Kaa uu yete ougo?

Reyno: Ana'aka. Hunu'u. Yee sussua tea.

Luisa: Yete ougo bwan. Hunu'u.

Reyno: Hunu, huna'a?

Luisa: Porque kia inen aet wamsaka'awako
huni kia wakekamtavenasi tawane.
Kia choune, kia pattine.

Reyno: Heewi bwan, ta si uhyoisi hekka'ane teane bwan . . .

Luisa: Heewi.

Luisa: At a place named Kuno.
   Also at a place named San Agustín.
   There are so many there, at that place,
   many of [the people] were there for a long time.
   That little Jose Maria, Andres's little brother,
   almost died because of them.[22]
   His little legs were just covered with rough nodules, here [*pointing*].
   They were all over him.
   The ones that produced very sweet fruit will do this, it is said.

Maria: Heh?

Luisa: They really look like spider eggs,
   a little round, like this, and they were in little sacks.

Reyno: Well, and that tree, remember the tree that was so big
   also would die,[23] they said?
   And that, that tree, well, if you fall asleep under it,
   in the shade, that also is not good, they say.

Luisa: Is it not the sleepy fig?

Reyno: Yes, that is the one. They say it kills people.

Luisa: It is the sleepy fig, well. That is it.

Reyno: That is the one?

Luisa: Because even when one just passes by,
   even then it just seems to start to dry up.
   It just begins to shrivel up, just closes up.

Reyno: Well, yes, but it does provide a very nice shade, they say, well.

Luisa: Yes.

---

22. That is, the figs that little Jose Maria ate almost caused his death. His legs were covered with rough, jagged nodules. They say that eating the sweetest of the fruits, in large quantities, may result in fatalities to younger children.

23. It's unclear what is intended here, but from context it may be inferred that he means the big tree would cause one to die.

Reyno: Ta senu, pos inen tataeko, tata tiempotuk hewi?
Aetuk vo'otek kaa hiavihtene tea.

Luisa: Heewi. Huna'a. Bweere.

M.H.: Hakunsa aayuk hunaa huya?

Luisa: Pos inim, wam vicha auk.
Hunum, inen im teuwaapo,
Orizabapo wam vicha.

M.H.: Hakunsa intok ume bweere platanom kaa bwabwa'awa?
Hunume bwa'ak ha'ani mukne,
ti hiia katin uu em wawai.

Reyno: Havee?

M.H.: Faatima lo'i.

Reyno: Ah heewi. Plaatanom . . .

M.H.: Si bweere plaatanom.

Reyno: Plaatano machom chea bweere.

M.H.: Hunaka bwa'ako veha kaa hiapsine tea, chuyune tea.
Es peligrosa para la costa.

Luisa: Ta hunum vicha plaatano machom si vu'u o'oven,
ta kaa vehe'e,
ta gente am bwa'e,
ta kaave amea koko'okoe.

M.H.: Ta kaupo, haksa humak aayuk.

Luisa: Ah, kaupo ala humaku'u,
huyapo aukame,
simaroonim.

M.H.: Ah pos, in wawai ket hunaman hakun noitek.
Isidro . . . Alvarez . . . o . . .

Reyno: Cota.

M.H.: Ah, Isidro, kaa Sevisa?
Luis Molino, huna'a aa ase'ebwakan [*inaudible*].

Reyno: But one, well, when it's hot like this, during the hot season, yes?
If one lies down under it, one will not breathe again, they say.

Luisa: Yes. That is the one. They are big.

M.H.: Where are those plants found?

Luisa: Well, here, over that way.
Over there, where I talked about,
in Orizaba over that way.

M.H.: And where is it that the big bananas [plantains] are not edible?
If one eats those, it is said, they will die,
remember, your relative said that.

Reyno: Who?

M.H.: Fatima, the crippled one.

Reyno: Ah yes. Bananas . . .

M.H.: Very big bananas.

Reyno: The plantains are larger.

M.H.: When one eats it, one will not live, it gives indigestion, they say.
It is dangerous toward the coast.

Luisa: But over that way the plantains are quite numerous,
but they are not expensive,
but the people do eat them,
but no one falls ill [from eating them].

M.H.: But in the mountains, I don't know where they would be.

Luisa: Ah, in the mountains, perhaps there
they are in the wilderness,
the cimarron ash tree.

M.H.: Ah, well, my relative also visited over there.
Isidro . . . Alvarez . . . or . . .

Reyno: Cota.

M.H.: Ah, Isidro, isn't it Sevisa?
Luis Molina, that one was his father-in-law [*inaudible*].

CHAPTER 6

LIFE, LABOR, AND DEATH IN THE SOUTH

The Sale of Hiakis as Slave Labor (Maria Hesus)

Maria Hesus describes how her mother, after walking to Guadalajara, was taken to Veracruz on a train. Some of those with her had been badly hurt by the forced march. They were transported in bondage. From Veracruz they were loaded onto boats and taken to Yucatán, where they were sold to henequen plantation owners in groups of twenty or twenty-five, at $0.25 each. Some were taken by boat to San Lorenzo, and others to the Campeche area, among other places—anywhere there were henequen plantations. An excerpt of a later discussion mentions that some people from another Indigenous group were also brought there with them, called Labwes.

M.H.: Hunum veha Wadalahaarau yahak
tea uu maala. Wate, pos ya ves,
wate pos kate'etek pues wok vahiane.

Luisa: Hee.

M.H.: Pos hunuen veha wate veha kaa,
kaa nappat aa katee tea.
Wok kotte.
Hunum trenpo veha emo nuksaka'awak ti hiia
asta Veracruz, trenpo.

Luisa: Hm, hmm.

M.H.: Ta hiva hunuen suma'itaka katee tea ume yoeme.
Hunaman tohiwaka veha varkopo veha nuksaka'awak tea,
asta Yukatan.

Luisa: Hunum veha katin am hinuk
tea ume yoorim.

M.H.: Hunum veha Yukatanpo veha,
yeu tohiwaka veha,
kaa haksa hoara . . .
hunama vem kom hote'u,
hunama veha hiva peronim am sua tea.
Ume asiendata hippueme,
ume, haisa teak? Ume, henekeneerom . . .

Luisa: Hmm.

M.H.: . . . henekenta tekipanoa.
Huname veha am hinu tea,
animaalimvenasia, chikti ili usimmake, ho.
Veintisinko, hombres y mujeres.
Veintisinko. Woi tomi uu kova.
Una persona, veintisinko, ti hiia uu maala.

M.H.: That's where Mom arrived in Guadalajara,
said my mom. Some, well, you see,
some, when they were walking their feet would swell.

Luisa: Yes.

M.H.: Well, that way, then some could not,
could no longer walk, they say.
Their legs were breaking.
Then they were taken by train, they said,
to Veracruz, on the train.

Luisa: Hm, hmm.

M.H.: But the Hiakis were still tied up and walking, they said.
They took them over there, then they were shipped out, they said,
to Yucatán.

Luisa: That's where, remember, they brought them,
the Mexicans, they said.

M.H.: Then there in Yucatán,
when they were taken there,
but not to any type of house . . .
there where they got down,
there the bald ones were still guarding them, they said.
The hacienda owners,
the . . . what are they called? The . . . henequen planters.

Luisa: Hmm.

M.H.: . . . the owners of the henequen plantations.
Those are the ones who were buying them [Hiakis], they say,
just like animals, right along with their children, see.
Twenty-five cents, men and women.
Twenty-five cents. Two bits a head.[1]
One person, twenty-five cents, my mom said.

---

1. These amounts differ from one source to another. Some sources say that men were bought for seventeen cents a head, while the women were ten cents a head. Older men and women, as well as children, were also cheaper, but a price was not mentioned.

Luisa: Hmm.

M.H.: Hunum kanoapo, veintisinkotaka
emo nuksaka'awak, ti hiia, ho?
Hunum San Lorenzo, Yukatan.
Wate intok hunum hakun i'an veha Kampecheo vicha
hunumun veha henekenta aukau luula.

Luisa: Hm, hmm.

M.H.: Ume yoim veha,
hunuka henekenta echime veha
am hinuu, bwan.
Nekrom venasia ama tekipanoane.
Aa hunaman intok si ousi tata'a tea . . .
. . . ousi tata ti hiia uu maala.

[. . .]

M.H.: Huname veha, huname veha ume asiendata hippueme,
huname veha am hinune tea.
Woi tomi tea cada persona.

Luisa: Heewi. Hunuen hiian hunu'u ako Simoonatukau . . .

M.H.: I'an ini'i papata maala intok aa achaiwa,
hunuen ya'awak.

Luisa: Hm, hmm.

M.H.: Ume Labwemmak[2] veha nuksaka'awakan.

Luisa: Hmm.

M.H.: Hunum hakwo, vattuka he'ela.

Luisa: Heewi.

M.H.: Labwe teame.

---

2. Another Indigenous group; actual name of tribe unknown.

Luisa: Hmm.

M.H.: There in the canoe, twenty-five of them
said they were taken, they said, see?
There at San Lorenzo, Yucatán.
And others, over there somewhere, now toward Campeche,
over there, toward where there are henequen plants.

Luisa: Hm, hmm.

M.H.: Those Mexicans,
those who planted henequen,
well, they were buying them [Hiakis].
They were making them work like the black people [as slaves].
And over there it was very hot, they say . . .
it was very hot, said my mom.

[. . .]

M.H.: Then those, then those who had the haciendas
would buy them, they said.
Each person cost twenty-five cents.

Luisa: Yes. That is what my late older sister Simona said.

M.H.: Now, this one, my father's mother, and his father,
they did this to them.

Luisa: Hm, hmm.

M.H.: They took them away with the Labwes.

Luisa: Hmm.

M.H.: There, a long time ago, it just seems like the day before yesterday.

Luisa: Yes.

M.H.: Those known as Labwes.

The Black Beans and the Hiaki Cook (Maria Hesus)

Maria Hesus tells the story of her mother's arrival on the ranch she would live and work on in the Yucatán. There was a man waiting there, a soldier in the Mexican army, and he had many large pots in which black beans were cooking to be fed to those who were arriving. There was also cinnamon water in another pot, which they drank eagerly. However, the

---

M.H.: Uu, hunaman veha ume, i'an veha en ...
aman veha aman Yukataneo veha
yoeme, yoeme ama katek,
ta peron ya'ari, tea.

Luisa: Aa.

M.H.: Aman am yahako,
si ousi ume, haisa humak ...
perolim ti hiune, uu maala.

Luisa: Aha.

M.H.: Si bweere tea ume kaasom, perol ti hiune.
Aman ume mun chukuim kia haisa pohte tea.
Mun chukuim.

Luisa: Aa.

M.H.: Hunaa peron am bwasa'a tea,
ume yahakamevetchi'ivo.
Aa, intuchi senu perol intok uu kanela.

Luisa: Aa.

M.H.: Ho, intok wepul ili piesa paanim emo makwak, ti hiia.

Luisa: Tsk.

Reyno: Hm.

M.H.: Pos ume, kaa am bwa'a ta'a.

beans were so strange and unfamiliar that they did not seem edible at all, and the women just stared at them. They were surprised to hear the man address them in the Hiaki language. He urged them to eat, saying that this was the only food that would be available. They asked, Are you a Hiaki also? He said he had been brought there ten years before. All those who had been brought with him had died since. He said he was a witness.

M.H.: The, there, well, the, now then . . .
well, over in Yucatán,
a man, a man was there,
but he was made a Mexican soldier, they say.

Luisa: Ah.

M.H.: When they arrived there,
there were so many, I don't know how . . .
pots, she used to say, my mom.

Luisa: Aha.

M.H.: The bowls were very big, they say, pots they call them.
There the black beans were really boiling, they say.
Black beans.

Luisa: Ah.

M.H.: That bald one was cooking them, they say,
for the ones arriving.
Ah, also in another pot, the cinnamon.

Luisa: Ah.

M.H.: See, and they were given a small piece of bread, they said.

Luisa: Tsk.

Reyno: Hmm.

M.H.: Well, they did not know how to eat them.

| | Pos haisa am bwa'ane?
| | Pos mun chukuim.
| | Haisa maachi?
| | Pos kia emo am vitchu ti hiia, muunim.

Luisa: Hmm.

M.H.: Kanelata into pos
va'am venasi te aa he'eka,
ti hiia uka kanelata.
Munim intok kia tua vitchuk ti hiia. [*Chuckles.*]

Luisa: [*Laughs.*]

Reyno: Hmm.

M.H.: Kaa am bwa'a ta'a, ti hiia, ume muunim.
Hunak intok . . . hunuen au hiia tea.
Uu yoeme intok, pos,
kaa a yeu bwi'ibwise bwan.
Vempo intok aa,
aa yoi ti hiiaka veha
"Haisa itepo inika bwa'ane?" ti emo hiia,
ti hiia ume haamuchim.
"Maalam," ti ameu hiia tea.
"Akem am bwa'e.
Ini'i hiva inim bwa'awa," ti ameu tea.
"Au hoiwane," ti ameu tea.
Hunaa yoeme veha,
hunuen aa eteho hunua yoemtawi:
"Haisa empo ket Hiaki?"
"Hmm, nee ket emovenasia
hunuen ya'awaka a'avo tohiwak," ti hiia tea.
"Nee veha inim lugarpo
em nee vicha'apo,
dies wasuktiapo,
nee inim katek," ti hiia tea.

Luisa: Tsk. Ay.

Well, how could they eat them?
Well, they were black.
How do they taste?
Well, they were just looking at the beans, they said.

Luisa: Hmm.

M.H.: And the cinnamon, well,
we drank it like water,
they said, the cinnamon.
And the beans, we just looked at them, they said. [*Chuckles.*]

Luisa: [*Laughs.*]

Reyno: Hmm.

M.H.: They had never tasted them, they said, those beans.
And then . . . then he said to them, they said.
The man, well,
he did not reveal himself, well.
And they thought
he was a Mexican, they said, then,
"How can we eat this?" they said to themselves,
the women said.
"Mothers," he said to them, they said.
"Do eat them.
This is all there is to eat here," he said to them.
"You will get used to them," he said to them.
That man, then
said this to the man:
"Are you also a Hiaki?"
"Hmm, they did that to me, just like they did to you,
and here I was brought," he said, they say.
"Here in this place,
where you see me,
for ten years,
I have been here," he said, they said.

Luisa: Tsk. Ay.

M.H.: "Ho, ume nemak a'avo tohiwakame,
si'ime kokok," ti hiia tea.
"Nee im taawak," ti hiia tea.
"Testigo humaku'u," ti hiia tea.
Hunaa veha peron taho'oreka veha
bwa'amta hooa tea . . .

Luisa: Hmm.

M.H.: . . . ranchopo. Hunuka hooa tea.

Labor on the Henequen Plantations (Maria Hesus)

Maria Hesus describes her mother's experience of working on the henequen plantation. The enslaved Hiakis did not go anywhere or do anything except work. With time, her mother became skilled. She was able to cut one thousand leaves per day, knocking the thorns off and throwing them in a canoe. It would only take her two strokes to knock the thorns off. She said her coworkers were surprised at how quickly she worked. The overseer would instruct them which leaves to cut. It seemed that the henequen was endless. None of the workers were there voluntarily; even those people who were born down there had been forced into labor, sold against their will.

M.H.: Kaaveta hu'uneiya
intok kia kaakun huni emo yeu nuksasakawa ti hiia.
Hunama hiva. Tekil vetana aa hoarapo.
Yokoriapo, tekil. Hunuen hiva.

Luisa: Kia ama yeu matchuk hiva . . .

M.H.: Kia ama yeu matchu aman tekileu.
"Aa chukula intok veha nee

M.H.: "See, those who were brought here with me
are all dead," he said, they said.
"I stayed here," he said.
"Maybe I am a witness," he said.
He was wearing a Mexican soldier's uniform
and was cooking, they said . . .

Luisa: Hmm.

M.H.: . . . on the ranch. That's what he did, they said.

FIGURE 22 A man cutting henequen between 1883 and 1930. 2A051068 Fototeca Pedro Guerra, Facultad de Ciencias Antropológicas, Universidad Autónoma de Yucatán.

M.H.: She did not know anybody
and they were never taken anywhere, she said.
Only there. From work to home.
In the morning, work. Only that.

Luisa: They just woke up there in the morning . . .

M.H.: They just woke up to work, there.
"Ah, and then later I

hoiwataitek humaku'u," ti hiia.
"Kia, kia nee senu wechiapo
ume senu millim chuktaka,
am wicha yohtaka am sumaka,
pangau am hima'ane," ti hiia.
"Haivu nee in hoau vichaa weene," ti hiia.

Luisa: Aa.

M.H.: Chukula au hoiwak ti hiia . . .

Luisa: Hee.

Reyno: [*Chuckles.*]

M.H.: . . . tekipanoataitek. Kia hunuen haisa humaku'u,
kia wosa aa veevak
haivu kaa wichane tea.

Luisa: Aa.

M.H.: Hoiwak ti hiia.
Hunuka senu milta kia kaitapo au aa hohoa ti hiia.

Luisa: Hmm.

Reyno: [*Chuckles.*]

M.H.: Wate humak veha hunen hiune tea, ume wate haamuchim.
"Haiki, haisa, haisa empo am hoaka
haivu hunume penkam suma?"
"Bwe, am chuktasime," ti au hiune a'apo intoko.
Kaa emo vitne ti hiia ala, porque pos
humak turuu, chuktawa'apo.

Luisa: Hm, hmm.

M.H.: Intok u'u, u'u, hunu'u, hita,
kapatas teame veha am tehwane hita

began to get used to it, maybe," she said.
"I just, just very quickly
would cut one thousand[3] henequen leaves,
knock off the thorns, tie them,
and throw them in the canoe," she said.
"Then I would already walk home," she said.

Luisa: Ah.

M.H.: Later she became used to it, she said . . .

Luisa: Yes.

Reyno: [*Chuckles.*]

M.H.: . . . having to work. Just like that, she didn't know how,
she would just hit it twice
and already the spines would be gone, she said.

Luisa: Ah.

M.H.: She got used to it, she said.
She could do those thousand very easily, she said.

Luisa: Hmm.

Reyno: [*Chuckles.*]

M.H.: Some of the women would then say this, she said:
"How many, how, how do you do it
that you are already tying those leaves?"
"Well, I am going along cutting them," she would say.
They would not see each other since
the plants were thick, where they were cutting.

Luisa: Hm, hmm.

M.H.: And that, that, that one, something,
the one called the overseer would tell them

---

3. This seems highly unlikely, since most men usually cut only two hundred leaves per day. But then again, Hiaki men and women were there as slaves and were perhaps obligated to cut one thousand leaves per day. Hiakis were also known for their ability to work hard under the most adverse conditions.

| | penkata chuktane, hita intok kaa chuktane.
Woi, vahi penkata huni ama yeu
wikek intuchi seenu.
Asta hunuen veha am yuma'ariane ume senu millim. |
| --------- | --- |
| **Luisa**: | Hm, hmm. |
| **M.H.**: | Uu, kia kaa nuklak uu heneken ti hiia.
Si vu'uriakan ti hiia.
Por eso, por eso hunuu hente,
hunaman hakun hoosukame,
hunaman yo'otukame, wate aman yeu tomtek,
kaa vem e'apo. |
| **Luisa**: | Hm, hmm. |
| **M.H.**: | Utteapo hunaman yeu tom . . .
Utteapo hunaman hakun tohiwakame.
Utteapo, nenkiwak.
Yukataaneu nenkiwak, ho. |

Her Mother's Depression in the Yucatán (Maria Hesus)

Maria Hesus's mother had been brought to the Yucatán in a group with her brother, but he was sold off to some other plantation owner when they came in their boats to select slaves, and she never saw him again. She fell into a depression and would not eat anything. Instead, in the evenings after work on the plantation, she would go sit under a tree by the ocean where she had disembarked, and cry. She hoped some of her other rela-

| **M.H.**: | Ho pos, chuvvatuk hunu'uvotana
kia haisa katee tea, ume hitam,
ume ili kanoam,
am hinuvaeme, animalim hinuvaeme.
Kia haisa tenne tea. |

> which leaves to cut, and which not to cut.
> Even just two or three leaves would be
> removed [from one plant], then another.
> Until they reached one thousand [leaves].

Luisa: Hm, hmm.

M.H.: It had no end, the henequen, she said.
> There was a lot, she said.
> That's why, that's why those people,
> those who were over there,
> they grew up over there, some were born there,
> not because they wanted to.

Luisa: Hm, hmm.

M.H.: They were forced to be . . .
> They were forced to go over there.
> They were sold against their will.
> To Yucatán they were sold, see.

---

tives might someday also be brought there and that she would see them. A local woman who liked her wanted to bring her out of her depression. She told her not to sit by the ocean, as a crocodile had eaten someone in that spot not long ago (which wasn't true). At first Maria Hesus's mother wished a crocodile would eat her. Then the idea that she might be eaten, and that her family might arrive and not find her, gave her the strength to stop going to sit by the ocean. She still did not feel like eating, but she was able to work.

M.H.: See, then later, from that direction
> they were coming, those things,
> those little canoes,
> the ones who were going to buy them, buy the animals [Hiakis].
> They were really racing toward them, they say.

"Pos hunume nee . . ." i'an ini'i tia Hoanata:
"Hunama hiva nee aa vichak," ti hiia.
"Intok uka avachi Hoanta," ti hiia.
"Hunum vicha nuktenniwa," ti hiia.
"Itepo intok im vichaa.
Haksa intok nee am vichak?" ti hiia.
"Kan nee am vichak," ti hiia.
Im vicha vem nuksaka'awak, veintisinkopo.
Kaa, kaa hu'unea o si aemak weri.
Kia veha "Waka nee waata intok waka'a."
Utteapo veha ameu yu'una tea . . .
[. . .]
. . . veha tatapna, tea.

Luisa: Hmm.

M.H.: . . . ho, kaa aa chupakame.
Hunuen hoowa tea.
Intok hakwo huni te kaa hunume, hita mache'etam,
katin perikom venak yekak . . .

Luisa: Heewi.

M.H.: . . . hunue veha aa chuktane tea.
Hunae veha aa chuktane tea vempo.
Hunak veha mala veha, pos,
"Pos, kia nee, kaa nee hi'ibwapea," ti hiia.
"Intok kia kaita neevetchi'ivo.
Haz de cuenta que kia si'ime . . ."
[. . .]
. . . ameu kikkivake, tea,
chukui munimmeo.
Pos hunumun emo hookae veha
kaa hi'ibwa'apeene ti hiia, bwan.
Chikti ta'apo, kupteo yepsak huni'i.
Hitasa, hitasa humak, hunaman haksa
vatte vawe mayoat weyek, hunaa seiva,
o haisa humak teak.
"Si bwe'u huya," ti hiia.

"But those I . . ." Juana spoke in this way:
"That is the only place I saw him [her brother Juan]," she said.
"Then my older brother, Juan," she said,
"he was taken over that way," she said.
"And we were taken this way.
Where would I ever see them again?" she said.
"I never saw them again," she said.
This is how they were taken, in 1925.
They did not care if they were related.
It was just, "That one I want, and that one."
They would be forcefully pushed toward them . . .
[. . .]
. . . then they would be knocked down, they said.

Luisa: Hmm.

M.H.: . . . see, those who did not finish it.
That's what they did to them, they said.
And we never, not, those things, machetes,
remember they are curved like a parrot's nose . . .

Luisa: Yes.

M.H.: . . . with those, then they would cut it, they said.
With those they would cut it.
Then Mom, then, well,
"Well, I just, I didn't feel like eating," she said.
"And for me, there was nothing.
It just seemed like everything . . ."
[. . .]
. . . went in there, they say,
where the black beans were.
Well, while they were there
she did not feel like eating, she said, well.
Every day, in the evening when she came back.
What, what maybe, over there,
close to the coast, that ceiba,
I don't know how it's named.
It was a very big tree, she said.

Luisa: Hmm?

M.H.: "Hunama hiva nee yehne," ti hiia.
"Itom nu'upawatpo
luula nee vitchune," ti hiia.
"O Maala, o in wai, o avachi
a'avo weene," ti au eene ti hiia.
"Haksa? Kia vo'oka uu vaawe," ti hiia.
"Haksa nee am vitne?" ti hiia.

Reyno: Hmm.

M.H.: Hunama hiva kateka au bwanne, ti hiia.
Haksa weeka veha uu Yukateeka hamut
humak pos au tu'u hiapsek malatawi.
Papa intok pos haivu amemak amistaata bwihla,
Yukateekommake.

Luisa: Hmm.

M.H.: "Paula, Paava[4] intok haiseaka hiva bwabwana?" ti au hiia tea.
Huna'a Inessa tea . . .

Luisa: Hmm.

M.H.: . . . uu Yukateeka hamut.
"Pos kaa nee hikkaa," ti hiiune tea uu papa.
"Kaa hi'ibwavae intok
kia hiva bwaana."
"Veras, nee ala aa womtavae
uka Pavata," ti hiiune tea.
"Kaa lutu'uria, ta hunuen nee
au hiuvae," ti au hiiune tea.

Luisa: Hmm.

M.H.: "Kupteo aman aa hoawau vichaa aa weiya," ti au . . .
hunuen au weene tea hunaa Yukateka hamut.

---

4. Paava was the nickname that was given to Maria Hesus's mother. Her true name was Paula, but since the lady who was a native of Yucatán liked her, she gave her the nickname Paava.

Luisa: Hmm?

M.H.: "I would always sit there," she said.
"From where we were brought,
I would look straight out there," she said.
"Perhaps my mom, or my younger sister,
or my older brother might arrive," she would feel, she said.
"Where? The ocean was so vast," she said.
"Where will I see them?" she said.

Reyno: Hmm.

M.H.: She would sit there and cry, she said.
Then one day, a woman from Yucatán
had a warm heart for Mom.
And Father had already made friends with them,
with the people from Yucatán.

Luisa: Hmm.

M.H.: "Paula, why is Paava always crying?" she said to him.
She was named Inessa . . .

Luisa: Hmm.

M.H.: . . . the woman from Yucatán.
"Well, she does not listen to me," my father would say.
"She does not want to eat and
she is always crying."
"Look here, I am going to scare her,
that Paava," she said.
"It is not true, but that's what I
am going to say to her," she said to him, they said.

Luisa: Hmm.

M.H.: "In the evening, bring her to my house," she said . . .
that's how she came to her, they say, that woman from Yucatán.

"Paava," ti au hiune tea. "Mande."
"Yu, Paava," ti au hiune tea.
"Kattee hunum vaweo vichaa sisime," ti au hiine tea.

Luisa: Hmm.

M.H.: "Haiseakai?"
"Hunum chea animaalim yeu sahaka
yee bwabwa'e," ti au hiiune tea uu Yukateeko.
"Kaa tu'i. Kat aman yeepsa," ti au hiune tea.
"Hunum chea animaalim
hunuen bwaname kaa tuttu'ure," ti au hiune tea.
"Empo kaa vawe mayoat ho'akan?"
"E'e," ti au hiia tea.
"Aa pos kat aman yeepsa.
Hunum chea sestul hamut hunum katekasu veha
kaa, kaa ama teuwak," ti hiia tea.
"Bweituk kama,
kama aa bwa'aka," ti au hiia tea.
"Kat aman yeepsa."
"Ohala kee nee bwa'a'ean," ti hiia tea uu maala.
"Kaita intok pensaroa'ean."
"Ay! Chukula intok maala o in avachi
yepsak intok kaa nee teune," ti au eene
ti hiia intoko, ou vuhvuhtaka veha
kaa intok aman au sikaa, ti hiia . . .

Luisa: Aa.

M.H.: . . . hunamani. Uu, pues hunama
veha ave au me'a ti hiia uu maala.
Hiva kaa au hi'ibwapea, ti hiia.
Kaa au hi'ibwapea, ti hiia.
Pos hunum, hunum veha
au rohikte ti hiia,
bwan, a'apo uu maala,
rohikte, ti hiia.

"Paava," she would say to her, they said. "Tell me."
"Look, Paava," she would say to her, they said.
"Do not go to the ocean," she would say to her, they said.

Luisa: Hmm.

M.H.: "Why?"
"There are animals that come out
and eat people," the Yucatán woman said to her, they said.
"It is not good. Do not go there," she said, they said.
"There are animals there
that don't like people who cry that way," she said, they said.
"Haven't you lived by the seacoast?"
"No," she said, they said.
"Ah, then do not go there.
One time, a woman was sitting there, then
she was not found there," she said, they said.
"Because a crocodile,
a crocodile ate her," she said to her, they said.
"Do not go there."
"I hope that it will eat me," my mom said, they said.
"That way I shall not think of anything else."
"Ay! Later Mom or my older brother
may come and they won't find me," she thought,
she said, and she found courage
and did not go there anymore, she said . . .

Luisa: Ah.

M.H.: . . . over there. The, then, there
my mom almost killed herself, she said.
She still did not feel like eating, she said.
She did not feel like eating, she said.
Then there, there
she was depressed, she said,
well, she, my mom,
was depressed, she said.

Luisa's Sister's Life in the South (Luisa)

Luisa tells the story of her older sister's life as a captive in the south. After arriving, the men were assigned an amount of henequen harvesting, eight bundles, that was impossible to do without training, and when they failed to do it they would be beaten. They eventually were freed by Madero, who brought all the enslaved Hiakis to Mérida and put them on a train north. The freed Hiaki men were given the opportunity to enlist in the

---

Luisa: ... si'ime, ti hiiaa,
o'owim huni hunuen hoowan tea,
pos hu'ubwa aman yahaka
pos kaa aa tekipanoa ta'a,
heewi, huevenakai.

Heera: Heewi.

Luisa: Haisa aa ya'ane,
kai-, kaivu aa chupa'ane.

Heera: Kaivu.

Luisa: Hmm. Vem tekia[5] makri,
haiki ocho manohota veha makritune,
aa teekia maktune, tea.

Heera: Heewi.

Luisa: Hunaka kaa kompletaroak veha
hunuen ya'ana tea,
vepsuna tea.

Heera: Vepsuna?

Luisa: Heewi. Si hiokot itom hohoan, ti hiia.

Heera: I'an tahti, veha ume yoi,
yoim veha am omta, hewi?

---

5. *Teekia*: a certain amount of work to be done in a certain period of time. This term is derived from the Hiaki term *tekia*, which means a duty, an assigned task, an office.

Mexican army and sent back to Sonora with their wives. Luisa's sister and another relative were put with the soldiers' wives on the train. During their time in the south, they had to scavenge for food, collecting rotten tomatoes at the dump and rotten avocados and other discarded items in the market. As unmarried women, they had no other recourse and no one to support them, but despite this they were still deported to the same place and had to scavenge. They were returned to Hiaki territory, then recaptured and taken south again, three times.

Luisa: ... everyone, she said,
  even the men were treated that way,
  since they had only just arrived,
  well, they did not know how to do the work,
  yes, many of them.

Heera: Yes.

Luisa: How could they do it,
  ne-, never could they finish it.

Heera: Never.

Luisa: Hmm. They were given this work to do,
  eight bundles were given to them,
  they were supposed to do that work, they say.

Heera: Yes.

Luisa: If they did not finish that work,
  then they would be treated this way, they say,
  they would be beaten.

Heera: They were beaten?

Luisa: Yes. "They treated us very badly," she said.

Heera: And even now, the Mexicans,
  the Mexicans hate them [the Hiakis], yes?

Luisa: Heewi. I'an tahti.

Heera: Kaa amemak tuttu'imme.

Luisa: Hunuen am hooan.
Hunuman hak,
nau am tohaka veha
hunum vicha am totoha.
Ta hunu'u veha intuchi
uu mismo Madero, veha hunum, veha
aman nau am tohak uchi,
um Yukataneo nau am tohak, tea
huet Meridapo.
Huet si'imen nau tohaka veha
uchi ume vatayoonim
pa'akun yeu am tohak tea.
Hunama veha si'imem uchi sontao ya'ak tea,
ume yoemem huni'i, o'owim.
Vempo intok ume familiam,
veha hunuu sontao familiammak
veha ama hoosasaka, ti hiia.

Heera: Heewi.

Luisa: "Kia te hunuen ili ito tatahkaika amemak
ama cha'asasaka
ume sontaommake," ti hiia.
Hunen e'etehon akotukau, poloove.

Heera: Heewi.

Luisa: Um vasureo intok
emo si'ime emo nau tohaka

Luisa: Yes. Even now.

Heera: They do not treat them well.

Luisa: That's what they did to them.
Over there,
somewhere they picked them up,
they took them over there.
But that one, again,
that same Madero, then there,
he gathered them again over there,
he gathered them there in Yucatán, they say,
somewhere in Mérida.
Somewhere there, all of them were gathered
and again the army battalions
took them out of there, they say.
Then all of them were made soldiers there, they say,
even the Hiakis, the men.
And they[6] were sitting with the wives,
with the soldiers' wives
sitting there [on the train], they say.

Heera: Yes.

Luisa: "We would just do a little work with them
and we hung around there
with the soldiers," she said.
That's what my late older sister used to say, poor thing.

Heera: Yes.

Luisa: And at the trash dump,
they all gathered together

---

6. "They" refers to Luisa's older sister and another relative who had been captured and taken to the henequen plantations in Yucatán. When President Francisco Madero freed the Hiakis who were forced to work on the plantations, the men were given the option of joining the military forces. The men who joined the military and their wives traveled by train back to Sonora, to Hiaki territory. Luisa's sister and relative joined the wives of the Hiaki soldiers on the train to Sonora.

intok hunaman
ili tomaatem vikaam emo puane, ti hiia,
ume kaa totomekame.

Heera: Hee.

Luisa: Merkao vichaa veha emo nuksaka'ane, ti hiia.
"Hunait veha te, hitasa
awakaate vikam, hita wait,
emo nau tohine," ti hiia.

Heera: Bwa'avaekai.

Luisa: Heewi. Hunuen au e'etehon
kechia maa hunaa ket aman toitakai, ti hiia.

Heera: Hee.

Luisa: "Pos te kaa kukunak.
Havesa itom aniane?" ti hiia.
"Kaave. Kia ama cha'asasaka," ti hiia.
Ta chukula veha
ket uchi itom ya'awakaavenasi.
Uchi nau toiwaka veha
uchi in wain emo vittuawak, ti hiia,
si'ime kaa kukunakame.

Heera: Hee? Kaa kukunakame huni
kaupo bwihwaka
aman tohina?

Luisa: Heewi, huevenakai.
Kaa kukunakame.

Heera: Hm, hmm.

Luisa: Huevenaka aman tohiritukan kaa kukunakai.
Ta katin i'an ket hiva hunueni, bwan;
ume, ket vahisi aman vem tohiwakamevenasi a'avo,
vittuawak vahisi.

Heera: Vahisi?

LIFE, LABOR, AND DEATH IN THE SOUTH

and there
they would pick little rotten tomatoes, she said,
those who had no money.

Heera: Yes.

Luisa: They would gather together and go to the market, she said.
"Then there we, some things,
rotten avocados, some things around there,
we would gather," she said.

Heera: To eat them.

Luisa: Yes. That's what she said about herself,
since she was also taken over there, she would say.

Heera: Yes.

Luisa: "Well, we were not married.
Who would support us?" she would say.
"No one. We were just hanging around," she said.
But later then,
they also did to them as they had done to us.
Again they were gathered and
sent over here, she said,
all of those who were not married.

Heera: Yes? Even the ones who were not married
and were captured in the mountains
were taken over there?

Luisa: Yes, many of them.
The ones who were not married.

Heera: Hm, hmm.

Luisa: Many were taken over there, those who were not married.
But remember, even now it is that way, well,
like those who were taken over there three times,
they were returned here three times.

Heera: Three times?

Luisa: Heewi. Vahisi a'avo vittuawak
intok vahisi aman tohiri.
Huname si'ime.

The Ration Cards (Maria Hesus and Luisa)

Maria Hesus and Luisa discuss the pay cards the soldiers' wives were issued. Each woman would receive six pesos every five days, plus a supplement if they had an older child. Many women supplemented their income by using their pesos to buy supplies, then making tortillas and selling them. Maria Hesus has her mother's card with her photograph

M.H.: Hunama, hunama Toluukapo.
Hunama . . .

Luisa: Bwe'u patiotukan inen katinia?
Pader ilevena, korak, sami korak.

M.H.: Sami korak.

Luisa: Hunue veha hekkateika ama hooka.
Wate veha ili waka nonoha, ili paanim hoaka
am nenenka nawi.

M.H.: Tahkaim.

Luisa: Tahkaim. Wate kaa, kaa o'ove bwan, hewi?
Ili tatahkaika nau am nenenka,
alian veha. [*Chuckles.*]

M.H.: Hunaka, hunuka veha hooka
para venirse desertados. Hm, desertados.

Luisa: Yes. They were sent here three times
and taken over there three times.
All of them.

on it. The older children were photographed with their mothers to show that a supplement was required. However, younger children were not included in the photograph, and nothing was provided for them. Luisa also was there and had an older child who was photographed with her for her pay card, though her younger child was not. (We learn later [pp. 364–65] that her younger child later died in the south.)

M.H.: There, there in Toluca.
There...

Luisa: It was a big patio like this, remember?
A wall like this, fenced, an adobe fence.

M.H.: An adobe fence.

Luisa: They made a shade with that and sat there.
Then some would make a few meat tamales, a little bread, and sell those together.

M.H.: Tortillas.

Luisa: Tortillas. Some were not, not lazy, well, yes?
They made a few tortillas and sold them together,
as one would say. [*Chuckles*.]

M.H.: Then that, that's what they did
to come [back] as deserters.[7] Hm, deserters.

---

7. The women were very enterprising in order to collect enough money to make the return trip back to their homeland. Maria Hesus refers to them as deserters, even though these women were not inductees in the military but had been captured

Hunama, hunama havoneera,
havoneerapo veha ume haamuchim veha
rettrataroa para darles la, la, la tarjeta donde van a pagar.
No se, haiki humak mamakwa, komae?

Luisa: Vusan pesota hiva.

M.H.: Vusan peso? ¿Diez o quince? ¿Diez días o quince días?

Luisa: Mamni ta'apo.

M.H.: Aa, heewi. Hunaka, empo uka tarhetata kaa nu'ubwa?

Luisa: E'e.

M.H.: Nee ala aa nunu'ubwa, malata tarheeta.

Luisa: Hee?

M.H.: Hunama katek uu maala.
Con el pelo así, sin rebozo.
Im tahti ya'ari.
Hunaa veha seeyok, ho, donde está firmado.
Hunaa tarheta, cada vez que le dan el dinero
le checan. Le . . .

Luisa: Hiva i'an, hiva i'an o'owim pensionaroarivenasi.

M.H.: Hmm.

Luisa: Hiva.

M.H.: Hm, hmm. Ketuni, rettratota hiva nee nunu'ubwa,
malata rettrato.
Hmm. Hunuen, hunuen te ya'awak.

Luisa: Kada mamni ta'apo aa mamakwa.
Hunama veha ili—kaa o'oveme hewi?
—waka nohine, tahkaim,

> There, there at the soap factory,
> in the soap factory then the women
> were photographed to give them the, the, the pay card.
> I don't know, how much was given, comadre?

Luisa: Only six pesos.

M.H.: Six pesos? Ten or fifteen? Every ten days or fifteen days?

Luisa: Every five days.

M.H.: Ah yes. Don't you have that one, that card?

Luisa: No.

M.H.: I do have Mom's card.

Luisa: Oh?

M.H.: That's where Mom's photo is.
With her hair like this, without her shawl.
It came down to here.[8]
That one has a seal, see, where it is signed.
That card, every time they were given money,
they would check it off. They . . .

Luisa: Like now, like the men who receive a pension.

M.H.: Hmm.

Luisa: Just like that.

M.H.: Hm, hmm. Still, I only have the picture,
Mom's picture.
Hmm. That's, that's what they did to us.

Luisa: It was given every five days.
Then from that little—it wasn't a lot, yes?
—they would make beef tamales, tortillas,

---

along with the men. They simply wanted to return home, as their living conditions were intolerable.

8. Maria Hesus indicates about two inches below her chin.

tiiko paanim, hita hoaka am nennenka,
ili hita, tahkaim.

M.H.: Hunuen, hunuen, hunuen,
hunuen te hoosuwak.
Chukula intok katin,
segundapo intuchi rettrataroakame . . .

Luisa: Heewi.

M.H.: . . . ta hunak veha nemak,
mala veha nee pua weyekan veha
nee au ya'ak.
Ta peronim hunuen itom ya'aka, bwan,
para que nehpo ket hiva ket mikna
tea ti hiian uu peron.

Luisa: Ta hiva kaa mikwak ume ili uusim.
Nee ket wepu'ulaik ili yo'otu usekan, wepu'ulaik hiva.
Hunaa nemak ya'awakan. Kaita.

M.H.: Heewi. Hunuen, hunuen nee ya'ak.

FIGURE 23 A family selling food on the street in Guaymas at night in 1902. Arizona Historical Society, PC 078, Mathews Photograph Collection, box 3, DU 43.

	wheat bread, make things and sell them, little things, tortillas.

M.H.: That way, that way, that way,
that way they did to us.
And later, remember,
they were photographed again, a second time . . .

Luisa: Yes.

M.H.: . . . but that time [she was photographed] with me,
Mom was holding me and
I was photographed with her.
But that's what the bald ones did to us, well,
so that I would also receive something,
they said, said the bald one.

Luisa: But the small children never received anything.
I also had an older child, only one.
That one was photographed with me. Nothing.

M.H.: Yes. That way, that way they did me.

Nacha Mayo and the Drunk Women at the Soap Factory (Maria Hesus and Luisa)

Maria Hesus and Luisa discuss a time when Luisa and Maria Hesus's mother were required to work in a soap factory. There was a big woman who was in charge of the Hiaki prisoners, Nacha Mayo. She had a big pistol, and Maria Hesus remembers her wearing a hat. On one occasion, she called the women in and made an announcement. Maria Hesus was playing somewhere and didn't understand what was being said, but afterward she heard the women laughing and joking. They said if they did get

---

M.H.: Pos hunama te, hunama veha nee kaa hu'unea.
Aa hunaa intok, hunaa intok waa bwe'u hamut.

Luisa: Naacha, komae Nacha Maayo.

M.H.: ¡Ándale! Ta si bwe'u hamut.

Luisa: Heewi. Hunaa katin ameu weekan ume haamuchimmeu.

M.H.: Hunaa, hunaa . . . hunak nee au waate
porque pa'akun vichaa te yeu kaaten.

Luisa: Hmm.

M.H.: Hunaa intok puetapo aman kivakek,
hunaa hamut, si bwe'u hamut.

Luisa: Hm, hmm.

M.H.: Una brujota y una pistolota de este lado.

Luisa: Hmm?

M.H.: Una tejana.

a pay increase, as had apparently been announced, they would buy wine and tequila and get drunk to celebrate. Maria Hesus asked her mother if she intended to get drunk with those women too. She did not want her mother to socialize with them and get drunk, so she would watch her very closely to see if she had any alcohol on her, and would stay with her everywhere, to prevent her from drinking. Luisa and Maria Hesus remember that when the women would get drunk, they would be lowered into the soap vats by the Mexicans. Luisa remembers there were mainly four women who suffered that fate: Rita Choparau (Rita Raccoon), Hoana Chooki (Jenny Star), Luz Amarillas, and another woman named Nacha.

M.H.: Then there, we, then there I do not know.
Ah, and that one, and that one, that big woman.

Luisa: Nacha, comadre Nacha Mayo.[9]

M.H.: Yes, that one! But she was a very big woman.

Luisa: Yes. Remember, she was in charge of the women.

M.H.: That one, that one . . . I remember her
because we were going outside.

Luisa: Hmm.

M.H.: And that one went in through the door,
that woman, very big woman.

Luisa: Hm, hmm.

M.H.: A big witch and with a big pistol on her side.

Luisa: Hmm?

M.H.: A Texan.

---

9. The Mayo Indians live southeast of the Hiaki territory in the state of Sinaloa. Their language and culture are very similar to the Hiaki language and culture. Evidently Nacha was not a very well-liked person there in her homeland, so, because of her imposing figure, she was recruited by the Mexican government to oversee the Hiaki women prisoners in Toluca.

Luisa: [*Chuckles.*]

M.H.: "Hu intok haisaaka moove'ek,
intok haisaaka hunuka hita wikosak?"

Luisa: Hmm.

M.H.: Hunaa veha itot wam weye,
hunaa hamut. Como una oficial . . .

Maria: ¿Sí?

M.H.: . . . como una oficial. Yoi ya'ut. Pistolak.

Luisa: Ket si aa etehoka teaka.
Katin um Mayompo omtawa teaka veha
ume haamuchim kaupo nu'urimmak aman toiwak.

M.H.: Oo.

Luisa: Heewi. Hunuen ya'awak.

M.H.: Hunum veha, hunum veha nee aa ta'ak hunaka hamutta.
Hunaa veha, "Katem yeu sasaka komaem," ti hiia.
"Hamut etehovae," ti hiia.
Hunama veha nottek intuchia.
Hunaa korau, hunaman veha kiimuk.
Aa pues, yo qué voy a saber de quién es,
o hita, katin haisa maachi ume ili uusim.
Im vichaa weene, waimmak yeune.
Pos imin veha nee weama, ho.
Hitasa etehowa'apo nee kaa hu'unea.
Hunen, hunen yeu sik veha uu, uu, uu . . .
Hu, hunaka ansuk veha te yeu sahak.
Pos ume haamuchim veha nau etehosaka.
"Pos tu'i," ti hiia.
"A ver, a ver si lutu'uriapo
itom, itom intuchi ili aumentaroane," ti hiia.
Ya ves ume haamuchim hunuen bwan nau rehte'eteko,
katin wate ket si vasiloonim.

Luisa: Hmm.

Luisa: [*Chuckles.*]

M.H.: "And why is she wearing a hat,
and why does she have that thing on her waist?"

Luisa: Hmm.

M.H.: Then that one was walking past us,
that woman. Like an official . . .

Maria: Yes?

M.H.: . . . like an official. A Mexican authority. With a gun.

Luisa: Because she was also a good speaker, they say.
Remember, in Mayoland they did not like her, they said, so then
she was taken there with the women captured in the mountains.

M.H.: Oh.

Luisa: Yes. That's what they did to her.

M.H.: Then I got to know that woman there, there.
Then that one said, "Don't go out, comadres."
"The woman is going to speak," she said.
Then we went back in again.
At that fence, there we entered.
Ah, well, what would I know of who she is,
or what, you know how little children are.
Go this way, play with that one.
Well, I was over here, see.
Whatever was going on I did not know.
That way, that way, what happened, the, the, the . . .
When she was done [talking], then out we went.
Well, the women were talking to each other.
"Well, good," they said.
"Let's see, let's see if it is true
that our, our money will be increased," they said.
You see, when the women were together,
remember how they really joked about things.

Luisa: Hmm.

M.H.:	"Heewi komae," ti hiia.
	"Ojala kee itom intuchi itom aumentaroae'an," ti hiia.
	Hunaa veha "Siquiera," ti hiia,
	"intuchi ili pesota ama hikat yechak huni,
	sep te, sep te aa, aa festeharoane," ti hiia.
	"Sep te si ume woi hita, ume vinom, tekiilam,
	sep te hunaka nu'uka, si te naakone," ti hiia . . .
Luisa:	[*Laughs.*]
M.H.:	. . . ume haamuchim. Mala intok ama weye.
	"Maala, haisa empo ket aa hi'ine?"
	"Hitaa?"
	"Pos ume haamuchim . . ."
	"Hakuni? Kia veha ha'aniamme!" ti kia neu hiia uu maala.
	Pos hunak naateka
	nee tua malata ilitchisi huni nee kaa apela hakun aa . . .
	porque nee kaa aa vino hi'i'ii'aa, ho.
	Si nee aa naitvuken. Hamuttamak aa katek,
	haivu nee au yehne.
	Tua nee aa vitchune.
Luisa:	[*Laughs.*]
M.H.:	"Ay Maala. Nee bwan im puhpo si ko'okole."
	Por a ver si, por casualidad,
	tenía por ahi la tequila escondido.
Luisa:	[*Laughs.*]
M.H.:	Hunuen nee aa hohoan uka malata . . . [*Laughs.*]
	. . . por tal de que no se emborrachara.
	Pos chukula ume haamuchim con aumento, sin aumento,
	pos se emborrachaban, ho. Haisamaisi hunum
	havoneerapo kom hohoanwan ume hamut nakooriam . . .
Luisa:	. . . am e'etan.
M.H.:	Heewi.
Luisa:	Varillimpo kom am hohoan.

M.H.: "Yes, comadre," she said.
"I hope that they will increase our pay again," she said.
Then she said, "At least,
if they increase it by a peso,
right away we will celebrate," she said.
"Right away the two things, the wine, tequila,
right away we will get that and we will really get drunk," they said . . .

Luisa: [*Laughs.*]

M.H.: . . . the women. And Mom was walking there.
"Mom, will you drink also?"
"What?"
"Well, the women . . ." [said M.H. to her mother].
"Where? They are just saying silly things!" Mom said to me.
Well, from then on
I really did not let Mom go anywhere alone . . .
because I didn't want her to drink wine, see.
I was very jealous of her. When she was with some woman,
I would already be next to her.
I would really watch her.

Luisa: [*Laughs.*]

M.H.: "Ay, Mom. My eye is really hurting."
Well, to see, well, perhaps
she had some tequila hidden somewhere on her.

Luisa: [*Laughs.*]

M.H.: That's what I used to do to my mom . . . [*Laughs.*]
. . . well, so that she would not get drunk.
Well, later the women, with or without the raise,
well, they got drunk, see. There then,
then those drunk women were lowered into the soap vats . . .

Luisa: They used to lock them up . . .

M.H.: Yes.

Luisa: They used to put them down in the barrels.

M.H.: Hunaman kia kom am hohoan ume peronim,
por tal de que no anduvieran en la calle borrachas.
Hunuen am hohoan.
Ta pos haboneerapo kom am hohoan.

Luisa: Ta hunak kaa tua vu'uka aa he'en komae.
Havesa hiva tua aa he'en,
waa Rita Chooparau intok Hoana Choki
intok Lus Amarillastukao intok,
intok wa'a Naacha im mukukame.
Hunume hiva tua aa he'en hunako.

M.H.: Naiki?

Luisa: Heewi. Hunamesan kia hiva ama kom hohoawan.
Aa intuchi uu Ritatukao, ket hiva Chooparau tea,
chikti aa asoawakame. Intuchi . . .
hunume hiva tua ousi aa he'en
hu'ubwa ama yahakai.
Kia ama yahaka hiva sepi.

M.H.: Pos huname veha nee vivichakai
nee malata tua nee kaa yoem eiyan.
Huname haamuchim.

Luisa: Hmm. Huname si ousi . . .

M.H.: That's where the bald ones used to put them
so that they would not be walking around drunk in the streets.
That's what they did to them.
But, well, they used to put them in the soap vats.

Luisa: But then not too many would drink, comadre.
You know who really used to drink,
that Rita Raccoon and Jenny Star
and the late Luz Amarillas and,
and Nacha, the one who died here.
Those are the ones who really drank then.

M.H.: Four?

Luisa: Yes. Those are the ones they always put down there.
Ah, and also the late Rita, she was also named Raccoon,
along with her daughter. Also . . .
those are the ones who really used to drink
when we first arrived there.
Just as soon as they arrived, right away.

M.H.: Well, I used to see them
and so I really did not trust Mom.
Those women.

Luisa: Hmm. Those really . . .

Maria Hesus Learns About Lent in Toluca, and Her Sister Dies (Maria Hesus)

Maria Hesus speaks of learning about Lent (Waehma) from her mother in Toluca, where she, her younger sister, and her mother were kept captive. She doesn't have a good sense of the time, she says, because she was

---

M.H.: Ta nee kaa hunea hitaa mechatsu
hunum veha te aman toiwak
o haiki semaana o haiki meecha veha;
kia nee veha hiapsa.
Hunum veha in wai ketun itomak weama,
Toluukapo.

Luisa: Heewi.

M.H.: Clemta veetchi.

Luisa: Hmm.

M.H.: Sietemmeu kivakla kechia. Ta wo'ori.

Luisa: Hm, hmm.

M.H.: Hunum veha, hunum o empo aman ket noitek,
katin konventopo tohiwak.

Luisa: Heewi.

M.H.: Hunum Toluukapo.

Luisa: Hm, hmm.

M.H.: Hunama konventopo veha te tohiwak.
Hunak veha ili huyam vetuk
katin si'ime haamuchim hooka.
No sé si semana o dos días.

so little. She remembers learning about the Lenten ceremonies that occur in the fifth week, asking her mother about the covered faces of the saints in the church, and asking why her mother was unbraiding her hair. From the church they were taken to work in the soap factory, where her sister, who was about seven, died. There were many fleas there. The women would hang up sheets and sit behind them.

M.H.: But I do not know in what month
we were taken over there
or how many weeks or how many months;
I just existed.
My younger sister was still with us there,
in Toluca.

Luisa: Yes.

M.H.: She was about Clem's[10] age.

Luisa: Hmm.

M.H.: She was also seven years old. But she was a twin.

Luisa: Hm, hmm.

M.H.: There then, you [Luisa] also went there,
remember, we were taken to the convent.

Luisa: Yes.

M.H.: There in Toluca.

Luisa: Hm, hmm.

M.H.: We were then taken to the convent.
Then under the little trees,
remember, all the women were sitting there.
I do not know if [we spent] one week or two days.

---

10. Clem is Maria Hesus's grandchild. At the time of our visit to Maria Hesus, Clem was about six years old, almost seven.

          Hunum veha nee tua kaa . . .
          hunum veha in, inen te yeu sahak,
          um pocho'okun aanen.
          Notteka veha mala, veha
          teopou te kiimuk . . .

Luisa: Hm, hmm.

M.H.: . . . en las casas de las monjas. Hunaman te kiimuk.
        Santom veha haivu patti.

Luisa: Hmm.

M.H.: Lila tahoorimmea veha patti;
        haiki konti humaku'u.
        Vempo ala haivu patti. Hivatua mamni, hewi?

Luisa: Heewi.

M.H.: Mamni konti. Pattimme.
        Hunaa mala veha ama weeka veha nee chon woita.
        "Mala, haiseaka empo nee chon woita?"
        "Haisa Itom Aeta kaa vicha?" ti hiia.

Luisa: Aa.

M.H.: "Haisa hiuvae hunuu? Haisa, haisa intok nee anne?"
        "Pos hunuen weamne,
        chon woitilatakai. Hiowa," ti neu hiia.
        Hmm. Hunum veha nee kaa . . .
        hunum veha te kiimuk, itom hokau luula.
        O si te ama semaanak o ama woi mechak,
        hunum veha nee tua kaa hunea, bwan.

There then, I really do not...
there then in this, this way we went out,
we had gone to the bushes.[11]
Then when we returned, Mom, then
we entered the church...

Luisa: Hm, hmm.

M.H.: ...at the homes of the nuns. We went in there.
Then the saints were already covered.[12]

Luisa: Hmm.

M.H.: They were covered with lilac cloths;
I don't know how many processions had taken place.
But they were covered. It was probably five, yes?

Luisa: Yes.

M.H.: Fifth procession. They were covered.
That one, my mom, was standing there unbraiding my hair.[13]
"Mom, why are you unbraiding my hair?"
"Do you not see Our Holy Mother?" she said.

Luisa: Ah.

M.H.: "What does that mean? And what, what shall I do?"
"Well, you will walk around like that,
with your hair loose. We're in mourning," she said to me.
Hmm. There then I did not...
then we went in there, toward where we were staying.
Or maybe we were there for one week or there for two months,
that I really do not know, well.

---

11. This means that they had gone to relieve themselves out by the bushes. Some older Hiakis and Arizona Hiakis still say this even though they have homes with outhouses or indoor plumbing.

12. In Sonora and Arizona, during the fifth week of Lent the religious figures are covered with dark or purple cloths. The dark cloths signify a period of mourning.

13. Also during the fifth week, the women and young girls wear their hair unbraided and loose as a sign of respect for Our Holy Mother, and to join her in mourning as she awaits the crucifixion of her son.

Luisa: Katin chukula hunama toiwakan.
Ranchito tean hunaa teopo.

M.H.: Hmm?

Luisa: Ranchito tea.

M.H.: Hmm.

Luisa: Hunaman teopowi.
Ume wate intok imin bwe'u ori galeera ori,
savum hoowa'apo hookan,
hume vat aman toiri.

M.H.: Oo. Hmm. Hunama veha, hunama veha, hunum te yeu sahak,
hunum veha nee kaa hunea, o si de día o
de noche, hunum havoneerau vicha.
Hunaman yeu matchuka veha nee vusak.
"Ii intok hitasa maala?"
"Hunuu ti havoneera. Inim saavum hohoowa."
Si bweere hita tankemvena hewi? Komo . . .

Luisa: Varrillim, tapla.

M.H.: ¡Ándale! Como unos barriles.

Luisa: Varrillim, bweere.

M.H.: Ta hunama havon, hita,
savum ha'ani pohpohtiawan tea hunama'a.
Hunama veha te hooka,
hunama muukuk in wai.

Luisa: Oo.

M.H.: I'an, i'an nemak weri, woori hunama muukuk.
Ili hikat te hooka, ineni.
Pos si vu'u hente bwan.

Luisa: Hm, hmm.

M.H.: Ni modo que con muebles, kia . . .
Hunaman te tohiwak. Hunama muukuk.

LIFE, LABOR, AND DEATH IN THE SOUTH

Luisa: Remember, we were taken there later.
That church was known as "Little Ranch."

M.H.: Hmm?

Luisa: Little Ranch, they say.

M.H.: Hmm.

Luisa: At that church.
And the others over here at the big gallery,
there where they made soap,
those who had been taken there first.

M.H.: Oh. Hmm. Then there, then there, we left from there,
there, I do not know if it was in the daytime or
in the nighttime, toward the soap factory.
I woke up at dawn after I spent the night there.
"And what is this, Mom?"
"That is called a soap factory. They make soap here."
They looked like huge tanks, yes? Like . . .

Luisa: Barrels, wooden.

M.H.: Yes, that's it! Like barrels.

Luisa: Barrels, big ones.

M.H.: But there, soap, something,
soap supposedly was boiled there, they said.
Then that's where we were,
that's where my younger sister died.

Luisa: Oh.

M.H.: Now, now, my relative, the twin died there.
We were up on top, like this.
Well, there were so many people, well.

Luisa: Hm, hmm.

M.H.: It's not as if we had furniture, just . . .
That's where they took us. There she died.

Luisa: Pos si tepuchim vu'u kati'ini?

M.H.: Vu'ureakan?

Luisa: Si tepuchim vu'u.

M.H.: Intok wate katin inen, inen,
bwe'u kora, katin inen katek,
hunaman hooka ume wate haamuchim.
Ili savanam inen cha'arika ama hooka.
Hunama, hunama Toluukapo.

Disease, Death, and the Ceremonies in Xochimilco (Maria Hesus and Luisa)

Maria Hesus and Luisa discuss the period when they were kept captive together in the south, in Toluca and Xochimilco. Maria Hesus was a child, held with her mother and sister, and Luisa was a young woman with children. Luisa says they were kept at the soap factory in Toluca for a long time, until the peace treaty ransoming the women and children was agreed to. The men came south to sign the treaty, and after spending a couple of days in Mexico City, they traveled to Toluca and stayed in the barracks nearby. After that, all the Hiakis were taken by train to Mexico City. From the train station they walked to a place Luisa called Kavayito (Caballito), with a statue of a horse. She says it was the Zócalo, where the buses stop. Eventually they arrived at Xochimilco and were

M.H.: Huname, hunama, hunama havoneerapo intok haiki metpo, o semaanapo te ama hookan?

Luisa: Vinwa.

M.H.: Vinwa?

Luisa: Vinwa. Yoemem im, im waim paasta makwau

LIFE, LABOR, AND DEATH IN THE SOUTH   357

Luisa: Well, there were so many fleas, remember?

M.H.: There were many?

Luisa: There were so many fleas.

M.H.: And some, remember, like this, like this,
remember, a big fence was there,
some of the women were there.
They sat there with little sheets hanging.
There, there in Toluca.

---

held in a church with a cemetery. Maria Hesus remembers sitting with her mother, who had hung a sheet behind a fence. There a disease killed many children, sometimes ten in a day. Luisa also remembers two adult women who died. The disease caused a dense red rash on the skin, which then turned purple, and it killed very quickly. The local people, whom she calls "Labwe," said it was not measles, but she did not know what it was. Because the Hiakis were dying, General Mori requested that they be transferred to Perote. They stayed in Xochimilco for less than three months. This was where Luisa's youngest child died. Because the men were there, including many ceremonial officials, ceremonies were held for the dead, including Maria Hesus's younger sister and Luisa's child. Maria Hesus remembers running after her mother, who was holding a candle and looking for the ceremonial participants. Luisa mentions one of the participants, Luis Tonopoa, and his father.

M.H.: And those, there, there at the soap factory, how many months or weeks were we there?

Luisa: A long time.

M.H.: A long time?

Luisa: A long time. Until the Hiakis, here, were given the peace treaty

tahti te ama hooka.
Intuchi aman am yahao tahti te ama hooka.
Ume yoemem, hunumun wanna'avo,
katin inen kuartel katek?
Kaa au waate? Kaa hu'unea?
Hunaman veha yahak, ume yoeme.
Mehikou hokaa veha
woi, vahi ta'apo aman hookan um Mehikou yahakai.
Huntuen veha uchi im yahakai veha
Tolukau yahak.
Hunum veha hunaman kuarteleu yahak.
Huname yahaksu veha
si'ime am vicha ameu sahak, ume haamuchim.
Si'ime hittoi haptek.
Hunait ta'ewai veha si'ime am vicha sahak
hunaman kuarteeleu vicha.

M.H.: Pos hunuen veha nee kaa . . .
bueno pos . . . maala huni bwan,
reeve pues humak kaa pensasaroan,
kaita haksa bwan, pos o
inen ta'apo te im yeu sahak . . . kaita.
Hunum veha te, hunum veha te . . .
Hitaapo te veha Tolukao sahak,
Sochimilkou vichaa sahak, hitaapo?

Luisa: Abwe tren . . .

M.H.: Trenpo?

Luisa: Trenpo. Hunum te veha katin Mehikou kom toiwak.
Estasionpo. Hunum veha intuchi ume gondulam, ume'e,
kia ume lataformampo veha, katin . . .
ta hunum estasionpo veha wokimmea aman vittuawak,
hunaman kavayiito teawi.
Katin kava'i ama hikat week.
Sokalo tea.
Hunama hahapte ume kamionim.
Hunaman veha si'ime hittoha.
Kaa . . . wokimmea aman hittoisuka veha . . .

         we were there.
         And again until they arrived, we were there.
         The men, there, on the other side,
         remember where the barracks were?
         Don't remember? Don't know?
         That's where they arrived, the men.
         They were in Mexico City
         two, three days after they arrived there.
         So then, when they had arrived here again, then,
         they came to Toluca.
         Then they arrived there at the barracks.
         When they arrived then
         all the women went over to them.
         Everyone started to take their things.
         On that day then everyone went there,
         over there to the barracks.

M.H.: Well, then, that's how I did not . . .
         good, well . . . even Mom, well,
         half the time, well, she did not think,
         nothing there, well, well, or
         like on that day we will leave here . . . nothing.
         There then we, there then we . . .
         How did we go to Toluca,
         to Xochimilco, in what?

Luisa: Well, on the train . . .

M.H.: On the train?

Luisa: On the train. Then, remember, we arrived down in Mexico City.
         At the station. Then there again the gondolas, the,
         just the flatcars then, remember . . .
         but at that station then we were sent on foot,
         to the place known as Kavayito.
         Remember, there is a horse standing up there.
         It is known as Zócalo.
         That's where the buses stop.
         Then everyone took their things over there.
         Not . . . once we had taken our things over there, walking, then . . .

M.H.: Así de modo que de, de, de Toluuka a Mehiko, ili mekka?

Luisa: Mekka.

M.H.: De Mehiko a Sochimilko?

Luisa: Ha.

M.H.: Ili mekka kechia?

Luisa: Mekka komae, ili mekka.

M.H.: Pos hunum veha nee tua . . .
hunum veha, ay sí, sí se cierra el mundo.
Kaa nee hu'unea. Asta . . .

Luisa: Hunum ket katin te teopopo toiwak.

M.H.: Sochimilkopo?

Luisa: Heewi. Katin inen mercao katek, vichapo.
Uu teopo intok inen katek.
Hunama te katin toiwak.
Katin te hunama teopopo waiwa hookan.

M.H.: Aa.

Luisa: Ket teopotukan, katin . . .

M.H.: Porque, mala, mala, katin im,
im vicha katek uu pueta?

Luisa: Hmm.

M.H.: Uu pueta, peronim ama . . .
mala intok in, inen kaa, kaa kora vo'oka?

Luisa: Heewi.

M.H.: Pos imin katekan uu maala detrás de un . . . de la barda.
Ili savanam ama chayaka ama hooka.
Ta hunum veha nee kaa hu'unea o haksa wate hente . . .
kia veha nee . . .

Luisa: Katin vooveram kia ama . . .

M.H.: So then from, from, from Toluca to Mexico City, is a bit far?

Luisa: It is far.

M.H.: From Mexico City to Xochimilco?

Luisa: Ha.

M.H.: Is it a little far also?

Luisa: It is far, comadre, a little far.

M.H.: Well then, there, I really . . .
there, then, ay, yes, yes, the world closed around me.
I don't know. Until . . .

Luisa: Remember, they also took us to the church there.

M.H.: At Xochimilco?

Luisa: Yes. Remember where the market is, in front.
And the church is this way.
Remember, they took us there.
Remember, we were inside the church.

M.H.: Ah.

Luisa: It was also a church, remember . . .

M.H.: Because, Mom, Mom, remember,
toward here, here was the door?

Luisa: Hmm.

M.H.: The door, the bald ones there . . .
and Mom like, like where the fence is?

Luisa: Yes.

M.H.: Well, Mom was here behind the . . . the fence.
She hung a sheet there and there we sat.
But there I don't know or if some people . . .
I was just . . .

Luisa: Remember the graves were just there . . .

M.H.: Las bóvedas de los . . .

Luisa: . . . aayuk. Otam, huni kia ama momoyo weyek.
Panteom iibwan, teopo. Hunama hookan.
Hunama hoowaksu katin ume ili uusim kaa kokoka'um,
hunama veha si ousi kokok.
Senu ta'apo, sietetaka, ochotaka ma'awa; nuevetaka, diestakai.
Hunama veha tua luutek ume ili uusim.

M.H.: Hmm.

Luisa: Um Sochimilkopo si taawak, panteompo ume ili uusim.
Tua si'ime.
Intok woi hamut yo'owe kechia.
Senu Hakaa
Antonia Yoomaisatatuka'u havorai,
intuchi wa Chaveerata wai, Ferisiana.
Sarampionimvenaka, huname hunen am suak.
Kia amet yeu vo'otene, sik turu yeu vo'otene,
yoko intok kia moraotaka matchune.
Hunae veha kia luula ka,
keesan luula yehteu haivu muksune.

M.H.: Ay Dios!

Luisa: Ta hita ko'okoasu humaku'u.
Hunama ho'akame, Rabwem[14] inen,
kaa am sarampionle, ti hiia.
Hunaksan hunuen ama am kokoususan,
veha Peroteu vicha aa a'awak.
Uu heneral Mori veha nattemaiwaka veha hunen veha te . . .
Hunum veha tu'i lugar ti hiia tea Peroteu vicha.
Hunumun veha aa a'awak.
Hunum vicha veha nuksaka'awak.

---

14. "Rabwe" is also pronounced "Labwe" by some Hiakis. Evidently some of the Indigenous people in Xochimilco refer to themselves as Labwe or Labue. However, this writer did not locate any Indigenous people in the Mexico City or Xochimilco area by that name.

M.H.: The graves of the . . .

Luisa: . . . were there. The bones were just stacked up.
It was a cemetery, well, a church. That's where we were.
Remember how the little children who had not died, then, there,
then there many died.
In one day, seven, eight were buried; nine, ten.
That's where the children really were finished.

M.H.: Hmm.

Luisa: The little children stayed in Xochimilco, in the cemetery.
Really all of them.
And two older women also.
One was my late paternal grandmother,
Antonia Yoomaisa's daughter-in-law,
and also that younger sister of Isabel, Feliciana.
It looked like measles, that [disease] which killed them.
It would just appear on them, red, densely,
and the next day in the morning they would be purple.
With that then just by noon,
before noon they would already be dead.

M.H.: Oh God!

Luisa: But I don't know what sickness it was.
Those who lived there, the Labwes,
it was not measles, they said.
Then when they were dying like that there,
they then asked to go to Perote.
General Mori was then asked, then we . . .
Then there he said, they said it was a good place toward Perote.
That's where he requested to go.
Then that's where they took us.

M.H.: Hunum veha Sochimilko haiki metpo ama hooka?

Luisa: Katchan vahi metpo ama hookan.

M.H.: Aa no?

Luisa: Kaa vinwa ama hookan komae. Hak humak woi ...

M.H.: Porque mala, mala hunum, hunum,
hunum Sochimilkopo yeu siika ...

Luisa: Ha.

M.H.: Ume yoemem yahako.
Ume yoemem yahao katin
mala pahkon.

Luisa: Heewi.

M.H.: Ili usita ama tekiakan.

Luisa: Hmm.

M.H.: Imin veha ume yoim ...
malata sik nee intok aet cha'aka vuite.
Mala kantelam weiya.
Pahko'olam haiwa,
tampareom intok laveleom.
Hunak veha yahak ...
"Si'ime ofisiom im kaate maala," ti au hiia uu yoeme, malatau.
Pos hunum veha mala veha am hahase.
Nee intok aamake.

Luisa: Ume chukula yahakame.

M.H.: Huname bwan, chukula.

Luisa: Huname'e. Huname apareoka kaaten.
Nee intok ket hunae taiwai,
nee ket uka ili usita mucha'alatukan.

M.H.: There in Xochimilco, how long were we there?

Luisa: Not even three months we were there.

M.H.: Ah no?

Luisa: We were not there for a long time, comadre. Perhaps two . . .

M.H.: Because Mom, Mom, there, there,
there in Xochimilco she left there . . .

Luisa: Ha.

M.H.: When the men came.
When the men came, remember,
Mom was sponsoring a ceremony.

Luisa: Yes.

M.H.: She was having a wake for her little child lying there.

Luisa: Hmm.

M.H.: Then over here the Mexicans . . .
when Mom left I ran after her.
Mom was carrying a candle.
She was looking for the ceremonial dancers,[15]
the drummer and the violinist.
Then they arrived . . .
"All the officials are here, mother," the man said to Mom.
Well, that's when Mom followed them.
And I went along with her.

Luisa: The ones who arrived later.

M.H.: Those, well, later.

Luisa: Those. They came with a harpist.
And on that day, I also,
I had also lost my little child.

---

15. In Hiaki culture, it is customary to have the *pahko'ola* and deer dancers, as well as the musicians—violinist, harpist, drummer, and deer dance singers—at the funeral wake of a young child or unmarried person.

M.H.: Hmm.

Luisa: Tokti haikika ama to'okan.
Huname veha si'ime pahkoriawak hunae, hunae tukaaria.

M.H.: Hmm. Mala veha inen pahkok, ivotana.

Luisa: Heewi. I'an uu Luis Tonopoatuka'u ama weyen.
Intuchi waa aa achaiwa.

M.H.: Pos hunum veha nee . . .

Luisa: Si'ime, si'ime ume tetekiakame ama kaaten.
Heewi, si'ime . . .

M.H.: Pahko'olam . . .

Luisa: Heewi, si'ime.

M.H.: . . . maasom intok . . .

Luisa: Si'ime hunume chukula yahakan.

M.H.: . . . laveleom, tampareom.

Micaela and the Dolls (Luisa)

Luisa describes the experience of Micaela, who had been deported to the Yucatán with her father. There was an attack, and the Hiakis took advantage of the chaos to loot the hacienda. Micaela, as a child, not conscious of the danger, joined in and ran around in the hacienda collecting dolls

Luisa: Totoiwa, ho. Aman Yukataaneu
chukti nau am tohak ti neu hihian uu Mikailatukao.
Hunaa kaa yo'otukan, papaawamake.
Hunuu ket hiva hunuka si'imeta neu etehone, poloove.
Hunaman te hookan, ti hiune Yukaataaneu ti hiune.

Maria: Hmm.

M.H.: Hmm.

Luisa: There were quite a few [babies] lying there.
They had a ceremony for all of them on that night.

M.H.: Hmm. Mom had a ceremony, on this side.

Luisa: Yes. Now, the late Luis Tonopoa came there.
Also his father.

M.H.: Well, there, then, I . . .

Luisa: All the ceremonial people came there.
Yes, all of them . . .

M.H.: The ceremonial dancers . . .

Luisa: Yes, all of them.

M.H.: . . . and deer dancers . . .

Luisa: All of those came later.

M.H.: . . . violinists, drummers.

---

even during the gunfire. The Mexican leader Madero gathered all the Hiaki men and took them off to form a battalion. The unmarried girls were left behind. Maria remembers that Micaela had told her that the girls would hide from the Mexican soldiers in trenches that had been dug there, but would nonetheless be found. Luisa says that although she heard of such things happening, she herself did not experience them.

Luisa: Deported, see. There in Yucatán
also they were gathered, the late Micaela used to say to me.
She was not very old, with her father.
She also used to speak about all that to me, poor thing.
We were there, she would say, in Yucatán, she would say.

Maria: Hmm.

Luisa: Chukula veha Maderota aman yepsak intok wiko'ota,
um asiendapo veha si am mumuhe tea, ti hiia.
Pos usituk veha kaita pensaroane, hewi?

Maria: Heewi.

Luisa: Hunaa ma hunen hiia.
"Kia nee si am vichaa vuite," ti hiia.
"Si henteta ama aneu. Ta wiko'i intok hiia," ti hiia.
Hunume intok ama kimuk um asiendapo
kia hita bwa'amta yeu woota tea, moonom, hita, ti hiia.
A'apo intok hunamet kia si au nah vuiteka nau tohaa ti hiia, bwan.

Maria: Kia kaa hain ea.

Luisa: Heewi. Kia kaa au mahai ti hiia bwan.
Chukula veha aman aa malatau au yepsak, ti hiia.
"Yu ma'ala. Nee chea monom si nau tohak," ti au au hiia, ti hiia.
Kia inen au am iva'ate ti hiia bwan. Heewi, hunueni.
"A'e, haksa empo am nu'uka?" ti au hiia tea aa malawa.
"Kaa suak. Veras eu . . . polesiam
enchi nuksaka'ane," ti au hiia, tea.
"E'e, ta yoeme ama aane," ti au hiia ti hiia.
Hunak veha am vichaa sikaa tea aa papawa, ti hiia.
Hu'ubwa hiva tekipanoaka yepsan tea, ti hiia.

Maria: Um, hm.

Luisa: Hunak veha am vichaa sahak tea, ti hiia.
Ta hunak veha huname yoemem veha,
hunaa Madero veha si'imem nau tohak tea.
Si'imem nau tohaka veha imin Mehikou,
vatayoonimmeu veha yeu am tohak tea ti
neu e'etehon a'apo uu Mikaila.

Maria: Hm, hmm.

Luisa: Hunaman veha si'ime sontaopo,
vatayonpo kimuk tea, ti hiia.
Intok kia haamuchim, kaa kukunakame,
veha hunama veha kukunak, tea, ti hiia, heewi.

Luisa: Later when Madero arrived there and with a weapon,
at the hacienda then they were really shooting at them, she said.
When you're a child you do not think, yes?

Maria: Yes.

Luisa: Like that one, she said that.
"I just ran over that way," she said.
"So many people were there. But the weapon was firing," she said.
And those [Hiakis] entered the hacienda
and just took things, food, she said, dolls, things, she said.
And she was running around collecting them [dolls], she said, well.

Maria: She was not worried about anything.

Luisa: Yes. She was not afraid, she said, well.
Later she arrived where her mother was, she said.
"Look, Mom. I collected a lot of dolls," she said to her, she said.
She was just carrying them this way, she said, well. Yes, that way.
"Hey, where did you get those?" her mother said to her, it is said.
"You're crazy. You will see . . . the police
will take you away," she said to her, it is said.
"No, but there are Hiakis there," she said to her, she said.
Then, then her father went over there, she said.
He had just then arrived from work, she said.

Maria: Um, hm.

Luisa: Then they went over there, it is said, she said.
But then those men then,
that Madero then gathered all of them, they say.
He gathered all of them then here to Mexico,
he took them to a battalion, they say,
she used to tell me, she, that Micaela.

Maria: Hm, hmm.

Luisa: Over there, then all of them as soldiers
went into a battalion, they say, she said.
And just the women, the single ones,
then there they were married, they said, she said, yes?

Maria: Oo.

Luisa: Hunaa ket hunaman chukti weamlatukan, Mikaila poloove.

Maria: Muksuk?

Luisa: Heewi, muukuk i'ani. Potammeu muukuk.
Hunaa ket hunum chukti etehola, poove.

Maria: Ori, hunak ket ori senu ket hunak neu etehok
kee ume haamuchim, hu'ubwa yo, bwe, veeme, hewi?
Huname am asoakame
kaa, kaa ume yoi sontaom am nu'u'ii'aakai veha ori.
Ume bweere orim veha bwebwehen, tea,
katin ume bweere hitam . . .

Luisa: Huukim.

Maria: Heewi. Hunama veha kom kimune tea ume haamuchim.

Luisa: Hmm.

Maria: Huname vepa intok kia [*inaudible*] ori.

Luisa: Hunueni bwan. Hunuen, hunuen aanen hunak . . .

Maria: Ta empo veha hunuka veha kaa pasaroak?

Luisa: E'e.

Maria: Kaa hunuen ya'awak.

Maria: Oh.

Luisa: That one had been over there too, Micaela, poor thing.

Maria: She is deceased?

Luisa: Yes, she died here lately. She died in Potam.
That one, she also spoke about that place, poor thing.

Maria: Then, also, one also then spoke to me before
the women, just then, well, young girls, yes?
Those, the mothers,
didn't, didn't want the Mexican soldiers to get them.
Then they dug those big trenches, they say,
remember the big things . . .

Luisa: Dugouts.

Maria: Yes. That's where the girls would go down, they say.

Luisa: Hmm.

Maria: On top of those then just [*inaudible*].

Luisa: That way, well. That way, that way, they did it then . . .

Maria: But you then, then you did not experience that?

Luisa: No.

Maria: They did not do this to you.

FIGURE 24 Hiaki warriors en route to peace conference, 1920. Arizona Historical Society, PC 078, Mathews Photograph Collection, box 3, album #54473, page 19, #BF.

CHAPTER 7

MILITARY SERVICE

Traveling South to Sign a Peace Accord (Reyno and Luisa)

Luisa and Reyno describe how two groups of Hiaki men were taken south to sign a peace accord. The Hiaki men were not physically coerced; no soldiers went with them or attended their arrival; they went to get their wives who had been taken. Luisa and other women were already there in Xochimilco. Luisa lists the names of some of the men who came.

Reyno: Hunuen yeu sika'apo veha haksa weeka'apo,
veha uu vehak enchim eteho'u . . .

Luisa: Hmm.

Reyno: . . . ume yoeme veha inika paasta firmaroane'e
teakai ti, nuksaka'awak. Woosa.

Luisa: Hmm.

Reyno: Ume, ume, ume, ori,
primerpo am vicha sahakame huni huevena . . .

Luisa: Huevena. Hm, hunueni bwan.

Reyno: Ta huname veha si'ime sahak.
Chukula intuchi ume waate.

Luisa: Hmm.

Reyno: Ta hunum hakunsu veha ameu yahak,
um aman tohirimmewi.

Luisa: Hmm. Haivu hunaman Sochimilkopo itom hok
aman yahak.

Reyno: Hee?

Luisa: Hunum te hookan.
Chukula hunume aman yahak.

Reyno: Hmm.

Luisa: Katin uu kompae Antonio Ania
aman yepsak, chukula.

Reyno: Oo . . .

Luisa: Norita mooneka'u.

Reyno: Hee?

Luisa: Wate hentemmake intok
aa familiawa intok wate familiam
huevenaka aman kia amemak yahak . . .

Reyno: At one time, when that happened, then,
    then, what you-all were talking about . . .

Luisa: Hmm.

Reyno: . . . the men then were to sign this peace accord,
    they said, so they were taken away. Twice.

Luisa: Hmm.

Reyno: The, the, the, um,
    the first [group] to go over there was also many . . .

Luisa: Many. Hm, that is the way it was.

Reyno: But they all left, then.
    Later, also the others.

Luisa: Hmm.

Reyno: But somewhere over there they came to them,
    to the ones who had already been taken there.

Luisa: Hmm. When we were already there in Xochimilco,
    they got there.

Reyno: Oh?

Luisa: We were there.
    Later they arrived.

Reyno: Hmm.

Luisa: Remember, compadre Antonio World
    arrived there, later.

Reyno: Oh . . .

Luisa: Nori's late son-in-law.

Reyno: Oh?

Luisa: With some people and
    his wife and other wives,
    many just arrived there with them . . .

Reyno: Hee?

Luisa: ... Pitaayat ho'akame, hunume,
Antesta maalam, akowam intok hunu
komae Lus weeratukautaim ...
hunume si'ime kia aman yahak.[1]
I'an chukula ultimopo aman yahau.

Reyno: Heewi.

M.H.: Aa, kia vempo voluntariom?

Luisa: Kia vempo voluntaa porque
ume yoememmak kaave amemak sahak, o yahak.

M.H.: Kaa mampo ... kaa, kaa bwihri?

Luisa: E'e.

Reyno: Kia voluntaa.

---

1. Remember that "Antes" is how Hiaki people refer to men named Andres, or Andrew in English. So here Luisa is describing how her own in-laws, Andres's family, voluntarily left to witness the signing of the peace accord; however, they were also captured and imprisoned.

Reyno: Oh?

Luisa: ... the ones who lived in Pitaya, those ones, Andres's mom, [his] older sisters and that one, the late comadre Luz, the fair-skinned one ...
... all of them just arrived there.
Now later, they were the last ones to arrive.

Reyno: Yes.

M.H.: Ah, they were just volunteers?

Luisa: They were just volunteers because no one left or arrived with the men.

M.H.: They were not captured ... not caught?

Luisa: No.

Reyno: Just volunteers.

Hiakis Are Enlisted in Pitaya and Toluca (Luisa and Maria Hesus)

Luisa and Maria Hesus discuss what happened when the men arrived in Toluca to collect the women. Luisa says that the Hiaki leaders who brought the men on behalf of the Mexican authorities were Antonio Ania (Antonio World) and Poori (Paul). After the transfer to Xochimilco, those two came again and took the men away again. Another Hiaki man charged with moving Hiakis around for the Mexican authorities was Lazaro Bule. Maria Hesus also mentions that her mother left with a group led by Lauro Weero, "Light-Skinned Lauro." Others who were part of that group were Pooli (Paula); Hoan (Juan); all Hoan's family including his wife, siblings, and mother; another woman who had lost a child; a man named Pori Soso'oki (Pockmarked Paul, who was a ceremonial society horseman in Vikam); and Maria Hesus's father's older brother, father to Nacha Kome'ela (Short Nacha). These men, including Paul, were serving as auxiliaries for the Mexicans, though later they became regular soldiers. That's why they arrived separately from the big group led by General Mori. Paul, Maria Hesus's father, a man named Antes (Andres), and another younger man named Xavier were all together in Mexico City. They began to follow Rodríguez Lara. They had become soldiers. Maria Hesus comments that, although they at first thought they would be sent to Sonora, in fact they were taken to Veracruz from there. Luisa mentions that a man named Chayo Loco (Crazy Rosario) was also with them but deserted in Querétaro and got on the train to Perote with Luisa's group;

Luisa: Hunuu hefe ama weyen, ori
kompae, Antonio Aniatuka'u. Intuchi uu Porituka'u.
Hunume veha am weiya ume hentem.
Chukula huchi a'avo am nu'uka huchi aman am tohak.

M.H.: ¿A poco?

Luisa: Heewi. Chukula huchi a'avo nu'uwaka aman toiwak,
haivu hunum Sochimilkopo itom hooko.

his mother was with them. Another man named Hoan Sivame'a (Hoan Killed on a Cliff) also deserted and joined them. Luisa says that her husband Andres told her that the men were asked to join the military as soon as they came to Pitaya. Those who agreed were immediately given gray hats and sent to the barracks. Thus some were already soldiers when they arrived to get the women in Toluca. Andres said that in Pitaya, those who declined to join, including him, were sent in a different direction, to a ramada where they were given food. Another Hiaki who joined up at that time was Antonio Soto'oleo (Antonio Potmaker), though he later split off to go with General Mori. Maria Hesus calls those who enlisted right away traitors and comments that there was a lot of treason at that time. Luisa replies that many of them were following Obregón, joining up to serve his cause. Maria Hesus feels ashamed of this behavior, and feels that such service should not be celebrated. She does not respect Obregón, and she mentions another figure, Father Lázaro, whom some Hiakis welcome but whom she sees only as someone who stole Hiaki land. Luisa again mentions that the enlistees were following other Hiakis and Mayos, such as the Mayo general Verdusko,[2] who went with the battalion to Tabasco. When the authorities were making a list, Verdusko exhorted the Hiaki soldiers not to desert. He appealed to their esprit de corps, saying that they must stick together, go together, and return together, and that they must all spit on any who deserted. Then they arrived in Veracruz. Verdusko traveled alone with Lazaro Bule and José Pérez. Pérez came back and then left again for Tabasco, working as a Mexican authority the entire time.

Luisa: That boss was with them, ah, um,
the late compadre Antonio World. Also the late Paul.
They were leading the people then.
Later they again came here for them and again took them there.

M.H.: Really?

Luisa: Yes. Later, again, they got them and took them over there,
when we were already there in Xochimilco.

---

2. In Spanish this name might appear as Verduzco or Verdugo.

Huname pahko'oraka, apareoka yahak.
Ume intok haivu ama yahilatukan,
heneral Moritamake waate vu'ukai, chea vu'ukai.

M.H.: Pos hunum veha . . .

Luisa: Katin i'i kompae Lasaro Buli,
katin a'avo am nu'uka.
Hunuu a'avo am nu'uka ta ket huchi, huchi,
watem chea vu'um nu'upak, nu'upasaewa tea.
Para que hunak veha hunamemak huname yahak veha
si'ime nau saka'ane ti hiupo.
Ta kia veha politikapo . . .
Hunuen hiuwaka veha huname a'avo nu'ukan.
Ta kaa . . .

M.H.: Porque huname, hunume yoemem a'avo, a'avo . . .
hunum hokame, huname, huname yoemem,
katin hunum Mehikou yeu tohiwakame,
i'an hunuu . . .

Luisa: Heewi.

M.H.: Hunaamak yeu siika uu maala, Lauro Werotamake.

Luisa: Heewi. Ta inime veha oritukan . . .
Havee ket siika hunako?
Inime komae Pooli, Hoan,
pooveta huuvi, emo waikai, si'ime.

M.H.: Aa malawa.

Luisa: Heewi, aa malawa. Si'ime hunume hunak sahak.

M.H.: Maala, maala.

Luisa: Heewi. Huevenaka sahak.
Intuchi wa komae ori ket wo'ori, wo'olim asoak, woim.
Wa, kia hunama uka ili usita ma'ak hiva siika.
Kaa . . . au simvae ti hiakai vinavicha,
katin am saka ti hiuwau amemak sahak.
Intok wa, Poori, yoeme Pori Soso'oki tea,

They arrived with the pascolas and with a harpist.
And those had already arrived there,
some with General Mori, many of them, a lot more.

M.H.: Then there . . .

Luisa: Remember compadre Lazaro Bule,
remember, he came here for them.
He came here and got them, but also again, again,
he brought more, he was told to bring more, they say.
So that with them, when they came, then,
everyone would leave together, as they said.
But it was just politics . . .
They said that then they were taken from here.
But not . . .

M.H.: Because they, those men, here, here . . .
those who were there, those, those men,
remember those that were taken to Mexico,
now that . . .

Luisa: Yes.

M.H.: My mother left with that one, with Light-Skinned Lauro.

Luisa: Yes. But these then were . . .
Who also left then?
These: comadre Pooli, Juan,
the poor one's wife, they were sisters, all of them.

M.H.: Her mother.

Luisa: Yes, her mother. All of them left then.

M.H.: Mother, mother.

Luisa: Yes. Many left.
Also comadre, also a twin, her children are twins, two of them.
That one, she buried her little child there and then she still left.
Not . . . she said she was not going to leave.
Remember, when they said they were leaving, she left with them.
And that one, Poori, the man called Pockmarked Paul, they said,

katin ket kavayeriatukan im Vikampo.
Kaa aa ta'ak?

M.H.: Pos hunaka papa aa saekan.

Luisa: Heewi, hunaa bwan.

M.H.: Hunaka saekan uu papa.

Luisa: Poori.

M.H.: Ii, Nacha, Nacha Kome'ela aa papakan.

Luisa: Heewi. Hunuu bwan aa papak.

M.H.: Papa bwan aa saek, hunuka'a . . .

Luisa: Heewi, huna'a . . .

M.H.: Poorita.

Luisa: . . . huna'a. Ta huna, huname veha
si'ime ya'uchimtaka kaaten hunako.

M.H.: ¿A poco?

Luisa: Heewi. Si'ime ya'uchimtaka kaaten.
Im yeu yahiwak veha sep peronimtuk, tea,
ta komo ausiliarim, hewi?
kialikun kaa uu Moritamak aman yahak, wa'ami.
Im Mehikopo yahak, intok uu Haviel i'an aman tawala,
hunume veha si'ime nau kaaten.

M.H.: Aa entonces hunu, hunu Pori veha hunum,
hunum veha ya'uttaka weeka intok
chukula intok kia, kia, kia peron?

Luisa: Heewi. Ya ves . . .

M.H.: Musa'ala ya'awak hewi?
Peron, porque papaa, papatamak weaman hunu'u . . .

Luisa: Kia veha . . .

remember he was in the cavalry[3] here in Vikam.
You didn't know him?

M.H.: Well, he was Father's older brother.

Luisa: Yes, well, that one.

M.H.: That one was Father's older brother.

Luisa: Poori.

M.H.: Nacha, Nacha, the short one, he was her father.

Luisa: Yes. He was her father.

M.H.: He was Father's older brother, that one . . .

Luisa: Yes, that one . . .

M.H.: Poori.

Luisa: . . . that one. But that, then, those,
they were all being leaders, then.

M.H.: Truly?

Luisa: Yes. All the leaders were going.
When they arrived here they became bald ones, they say,
but because they were auxiliaries, yes?
That is why they did not get there with Mori, over there.
They arrived here in Mexico City, and Xavier who had stayed there,
then all of them were traveling together.

M.H.: So then, that, that Poori then there,
there then he stood as a leader, and
later he was just, just, just a soldier?

Luisa: Yes. You see . . .

M.H.: They did a funny thing to him, yes?
Bald one, because Father, he was with Father . . .

Luisa: Then just . . .

---

3. This refers to the ceremonial *chapayeka* group called the *caballeros*.

M.H.: . . . Poori. Hunuu Haviel intok
haksa humak veha taawak hunuu uusi. Papa ama weyen.

Luisa: Pos hunaman kechia, oriwi
Rodrigez Larau, katin, ume yoeme kwaktek.

M.H.: Porque hunuu, hunuu, hunuu Poori,
papa aamak weyen intok
hunuu ako Mariata kuuna, Andres.
Ho, huname nau rehtekas hunum Mehikopo
haksa humak peron ya'awakamme.

Luisa: Heewi, imin . . .

M.H.: Haivu listo.

Luisa: I'ivo haivu peronimtaka katen tea hunume'e, si'ime.

M.H.: Peronimtaka kaaten.
Hunama veha papa veha hunum Mehikopo taawak.

Luisa: Hmm.

M.H.: Hunama tawaka veha, mala haivu aemak weama,
papatamak weama.
Hunum veha hunum vichaa emo katee,
ti hiia tea, Sonorao vicha.
Ta katchani, yantela Verakruseo vicha nuktenniwak.

Luisa: Heewi.

M.H.: Ho. In mala . . .

Luisa: Ii Chayotuka'u ket amemak weaman,
Chayo looko.

M.H.: Aa, hunuu . . .

Luisa: Ta hunuu, Kereetaro teapo
katin veha uka aa malawa itommak weyeo
veha hunum veha desertaroaka
ama ha'amuka veha itommak siika Peroteu vicha.

M.H.: Hunum veha nee kaa hu'unea.

M.H.: ... Poori. And that Xavier,
I don't know where that child stayed. Father was with them.

Luisa: Well, over there also, um,
[turning] to Rodríguez Lara, remember, those men became traitors.

M.H.: Because that one, that one, that one Poori,
Father was with him and
older sister Maria's husband, Andres.
See, they were together there in Mexico City;
I don't know where they made them Mexican soldiers.

Luisa: Yes, here ...

M.H.: Already ready.

Luisa: From here they were already marching as bald ones, all of them.

M.H.: They were already marching as Mexican soldiers.
Then, Father then stayed there in Mexico.

Luisa: Hmm.

M.H.: When he stayed there, Mom was already with him,
she was with Father.
Then there, they were walking toward there,
they said, to Sonora.
But no, instead they were taken to Veracruz.

Luisa: Yes.

M.H.: See. My mom ...

Luisa: The late Chayo [Rosario] was also with them,
Crazy Chayo.

M.H.: Ah, that one ...

Luisa: But that one, in the church in Querétaro,
remember then when his mother was with us,
then, there, he deserted,
there he climbed on and then went with us toward Perote.

M.H.: I do not know about that, then.

Luisa: Intuchi uu kompae Hoan Sivame'atuka'u huni'i.
Ket hunum itomak siika uchia, desertaroaka.
Hunuu huni ket amemak weaman.

M.H.: Pos hunuen iibwan. Nee, nee veha im partepo
kia reeve bwan inen bwan au wauwaate.
I'an intok nee kia kochok simetavenasi
tawasime.

Luisa: Huna'a. Hiva sontao...
Im yeu yahiwak sep sontaomtaka kaaten tea.

M.H.: Aa, haivu?

Luisa: Heewi. Katin, katin hiva temaiwa tea
ume yeu yahame
"Empo perontuvae
o empo kaa perontuvae?" ti hiuwau veha,
he, perontuvae ti hiuwau
veha aman vicha weene, ti au hiuna tea.
Sep to'oko move'im makwan tea, ti hiia Antes,
hunen hiia, im yeu yepsakame.
A'apo'ik ket tetemain tea, "Empo perontuvae?"
"E'e," ti au au hiia ti hiia. Hunae veha,
"Pos aman bwa'amta nu'use," ti au hiia tea.
Ili kari ama katek tea, ramaa.
Hunaman veha bwa'amta makwa tea ume kaa peronim...
Ume perontuvae intok
sep kuartelleu vicha veevia tea.

M.H.: Bwe!

Luisa: Ti hiia, hunum Pitaayapo yeu yaiwau.

M.H.: Hmm. Hunuen, iibwan.

Luisa: Hmm. Uu kompae Antonio Soto'oleo
huni ket perontukan tea.

M.H.: Im yeu sikaa?

Luisa: Heewi.

Luisa: Also even Compadre, the late Juan Silvame'a, also.
He also went with us, after deserting.
Even he was also with them.

M.H.: Well, that's the way it was. I, I, for my part then,
just halfway, well, this way, remember it.
And now it seems I was like a sleepwalker
going along like that.

Luisa: That one. Always a soldier . . .
When they arrived, they quickly became soldiers, they said.

M.H.: Ah, already?

Luisa: Yes. Remember, remember they kept questioning them, they said,
the ones who were arriving,
"Do you want to be a bald one
or do you not want to be a bald one?" they said.
Heh, when one said he wanted to be a bald one
then he was to go over there, they said.
Right away they were given gray hats, said Andres,
the one who arrived here said this.
He also was asked, they say, "Do you want to be a bald one?"
"No," he said to him, he said. Then with that,
"Well, go over there and get some food," he said to him.
And there was a little house there, a ramada.
There then food was given to the ones who were not bald ones . . .
And the ones who were going to be the bald ones
were immediately sent to the barracks, they said.

M.H.: Well!

Luisa: He said, when they were arriving in Pitaya.

M.H.: Hmm. That is how it was, well.

Luisa: Hmm. Even that compadre Antonio Potmaker
was also a bald one, they said.

M.H.: He left from here?

Luisa: Yes.

M.H.: ¿A poco?

Luisa: Tua. Ta pos hunaman ket au naikimteka veha Heneral Moritaimmak veha siika tea. Siika.

M.H.: Aa pos uvo mucha traición.

Luisa: Heewi.

M.H.: Mucha traición.

Luisa: Tua. Katin hunensan veha humak kia hunuen, katin tu'uwampo aman am toisuvaen tea, uu Obregon . . .

M.H.: Aa hiva, heewi.

Luisa: Obregon, heewi, hunak huni'i . . .

M.H.: Por eso nee Mariatau hunen hihiia i'an . . .

Luisa: Heewi.

M.H.: . . . neu aa yepsako. Ime yoemem, kaita [*inaudible*].

Luisa: Hmm.

M.H.: Nee kaa yo'otaka hunum nee malatamak hihiokot ansisimem.
Ta hunuka Obregonta nee kaa aa yo'ore.
I'an intok nee ili tiune.

Luisa: Heewi.

M.H.: Ay, qué Obregón. Ahi va el montón.
¿Por qué van a ver al traicionero?
Itom yo'owam itom, itom ta'aruk
huni'i veha ketunia vempo aa hahhane?

M.H.: Really?

Luisa: Really. Well, but he also separated from them, then he left with General Mori, they said. He left.

M.H.: Ah, well, there was a lot of treason.

Luisa: Yes.

M.H.: A lot of treason.

Luisa: Really. Remember, that is how they just, remember, in good faith, Obregón was going to finish taking them over there, they said . . .[4]

M.H.: Ah, always, yes.

Luisa: Obregón, yes, just, even then . . .

M.H.: That's why I say that to Maria, now . . .

Luisa: Yes.

M.H.: . . . when she comes here. These men, nothing [*inaudible*].

Luisa: Hmm.

M.H.: I wasn't very old when I was suffering there along with Mom.
But I do not respect that Obregón.
And now I feel a little ashamed.

Luisa: Yes.

M.H.: Ay, that Obregón. There goes the whole bunch.
Why do they go to see the traitor?
Even though we lost our, our elders,
they would still follow him, then?

---

4. Álvaro Obregón was a Mexican general who convinced some of the Hiakis to join forces with him to do battle against the regime of Victoriano Huerta. In 1920 he won the presidency of Mexico. In 1924 he handpicked Plutarco Elías Calles to succeed him as president of Mexico. In 1928 Obregón again ran as a candidate for the presidency and was reelected. Before he could begin his term, however, he was assassinated by an individual who was incensed by the Calles government's treatment of Catholics. The city of Ciudad Obregón is named after Álvaro Obregón.

Luisa: Hmm.

M.H.: Eso es la cosa, ves.
Kaa, kaa aa festeharoak huni tu'ine.
Hunuka, hunuka Lasarota
huni hitaa tu'ik itom yarialataka ume yoemem,
"Ay, achai Lasaro a'avo weye." ¿Qué bien nos ha hecho?
Nos ha quitado la tierra. Hunuka im kaa mammatte.
"Ay, achai Lasaro" [*inaudible*].

Luisa: Kialikun hunuu, hunuu, hunuu heneral Verdusko, hewi komae?
Uu Maayo; katin heneral Ver-,
Verdusko katin vatayonpo weaman amemake.
Intok amemak Tavaskou noitek.
Intok hunum, Tavaskou vichaa
sakava'awau, veha listawa'apo,
veha amemak eteho, tea.
Listaho'owa'apo veha amemak etehoka veha
hunen ameu hiia tea.
"Katem desertataroa intok katem nee tiusi ve'a," ti ameu hiia tea.
"Hunumun te noitek, veha yahak te si'ime mochila te nau saka'ane.
Nau te saka'ane si'ime mochila," ti ha'ani hiia tea.
"Desertaroakamtat te kia si'ime aet te chitwattine,"
ilen ha'ani ameu hii tea, ho.
Hunum Verakruspo yaiwak, hewi?
Pos katchansan hu'uneiya'awa vinavicha sahakai.
Vempola sahak uu heneral Verdusko
intok kompae Lasaro Vuuli, kompae Hose Perez.

M.H.: Hose Perez?

Luisa: Heewi, heewi.

M.H.: Aa. Hunuu Hose Perez intok a'avo yepsaka intuchi siika?

Luisa: Hmm. Katin uchi Tavaskou vittuawakan, tea.
Aman katekan tea.

M.H.: Ta, ta hiva yoi ya'uttakai?

Luisa: Heewi.

Luisa: Hmm.

M.H.: That is the thing, see.
If it is not, not celebrated, it is all right.
That, that Lázaro.
What good has he done for us that the men,
"Ay, Father Lázaro is coming here." What good has he done for us?
He took away our lands. That's what they do not understand.
"Ay, Father Lázaro" [*inaudible*].

Luisa: That's why that, that, that General Verdusko, yes, comadre?
The Mayo; remember General Ver-,
Verdusko. Remember he was in the battalion with them.
And he visited Tabasco with them.
And there, toward Tabasco,
when they were going to leave, when they were making a list, then he was talking to them, they said.
Then when they were making the list he spoke to them, then,
this is what he said to them, they said.
"Don't desert, don't leave me in shame," he said to them, it is said.
"When we go there, then when we return we will all leave together.
We will all leave together," is what he said, they said.
"We will all spit on anyone who deserts."
This is what he is supposed to have said to them, they said, see.
They arrived there in Veracruz, yes?
Well, they did not even know when they came this way.
They left by themselves, that General Verdusko
and compadre Lazaro Bule, compadre José Pérez.

M.H.: José Pérez?

Luisa: Yes, yes.

M.H.: Ah. And that José Pérez came here and left again?

Luisa: Hmm. Remember, they sent him to Tabasco again, they say.
He was over there, they say.

M.H.: But, but he was still a Mexican authority?

Luisa: Yes.

The Hiaki Battalion (Luisa and Andres)

[*N.B.: This section repeats a portion of the section "Coercing Hiaki Men to Enlist by Holding Families Hostage" from chapter 3.*] Luisa and Andres discuss the beginnings of Andres's time in the military. At first they were auxiliaries, not soldiers, called *papalores*. They earned 140 pesos at the time. It was enough to buy a few things, including clothes and shoes, as

Luisa: Ausiliarimtukan.

Andres: Ausiliarimtukan.

Luisa: Kaa sontaomtukan.

Andres: Si'ime huniat itom nahsahaka'apo, Papaloorimtukan vachia.
Uno kuarentata koovan, si'ime hunako.
Sontaom si'ime aa koovan.
Uno kuarentata hunak tiempopo.

Luisa: Kaakun intok aa koovan.

Andres: Hunak kaa vehe'en,
si'ime kaa vehe'en, taho'ori, bwa'ame.

Maria: Heewi.

Andres: Sentavoe veha im huevenak hinune Mehikopo,
huet in weamapo.

Maria: Aa, ha.

Andres: Kaa... varaato bwan taho'ori.
Si'ime varaato sapa'atom.
Kaa i'an venaikan.

Maria: Heewi. I'an si'ime vehe'e.

goods were not expensive then. But then they were sent to Mexico City, and there they became soldiers. Luisa says that Aguirre lied to them, saying that they would go and return, but then taking them out to the wilderness to fight. The wives were brought along in boxcars, homeless. Andres says there were hundreds of Hiakis in the battalion, which was made up only of Hiakis. General Mori and General Wicha were sent with them, but they died there in the south.

Luisa: They were auxiliaries.

Andres: Auxiliaries.

Luisa: They were not soldiers.

Andres: There, everywhere we went, we were *papalores*[5] first.
    140 [pesos] is what we were paid, all of us, at that time.
    All the soldiers earned that.
    140 [pesos] at that time.

Luisa: They were earning no more than that.

Andres: At that time, things were not expensive,
    everything was inexpensive, clothing, food.

Maria: Yes.

Andres: With the money one could buy a lot here in Mexico,
    around there where I was.

Maria: Ah, ha.

Andres: Not . . . well, it was cheap, well, clothes.
    Everything was cheap, shoes.
    It was not like now.

Maria: Yes. Now everything is expensive.

---

5. Like *peronim* and *toroko yoim* ("gray Mexicans"), this is another term for those enlisted in the Mexican military.

Andres: I'an si vehe'e si'ime.
　　　　　Hunuen auka Mehikou nee tata'ak kechia.
　　　　　Vinwa aman nah kuaktek.

Luisa: Hunum sontao ya'awak ...

Andres: Heewi.

Luisa: ... intok hunum Aguirrestamak chaketiaroaka
　　　　　hunaman hak aniapo,
　　　　　pocho'okun nunupsuwak, kaa itom ta'aku.

Andres: Heewi.

Luisa: Konila a'avo tohina tiupo
　　　　　hunu'u veha Aguirres hunuen am vaita'aka
　　　　　veha hunaman hak am nunu'ubwa.
　　　　　Si'ime henteta, uka ...

Andres: Si'imem.

Maria: Hm, hmm.

Luisa: ... familiata vagonnimpo kima'itaka
　　　　　nunu'ubwia hunait pocho'okun
　　　　　kaa ... kaa ho'aka ...

Andres: Ite ori vahi siento o'ow Hiak,
　　　　　vahi siento porque te sontao [*inaudible*] ...
　　　　　mamni, naiki siento, vahi sientota
　　　　　ori kompletaroak vatayon entero.
　　　　　Tua Hiak emo [*inaudible*].

Maria: Ii ...

Luisa: Si vu'uriakan,
　　　　　im aman yahakame ...

Andres: Kada pueplompo yeu saka'awak,
　　　　　yeu wikwaka'a bwan.

Maria: Hm, hmm.

Andres: Now everything is so expensive.
When I did that, I also got to know Mexico.
I was there for a long time.

Luisa: That's where they made him a soldier . . .

Andres: Yes.

Luisa: . . . and there when they fought with Aguirre,
somewhere in that world,
they took us to wander in the wilderness, a place we did not know.

Andres: Yes.

Luisa: That we would circle around [and return] here, is what they said.
That Aguirre lied to them that way, then,
then he took them over there somewhere.
All the people, the . . .

Andres: Everyone.

Maria: Hm, hmm.

Luisa: . . . the wives were in boxcars
and were taken around in the wilderness
not . . . not having a home . . .

Andres: We were three hundred Hiaki men,
three hundred because we soldiers [*inaudible*] . . .
five, four hundred, three hundred
were in the complete battalion.
Only Hiakis themselves [*inaudible*].

Maria: This . . .

Luisa: There were so many
from here that arrived there . . .

Andres: They came from each pueblo,
they were taken, well.

Maria: Hm, hmm.

Andres: Heneralim intok hunu heneral Mori
intok uu Wicha, hunume woika
aman vittuawak.

Luisa: Kompae Lasaro Vuuli.

Andres: Huname intok aman kokok.

FIGURE 25 The Hiaki general Mori sits between two men. Arizona Historical Society, PC 078, Mathews Photograph Collection, box 3, album #54473, page 19, #BD.

Andres: And the generals, that general Mori and Wicha [Thorn], those two were sent over there.

Luisa: Compadre Lazaro Bule.

Andres: And they died over there.

The Hiaki Battalion in Battle During the Escobar Rebellion (Maria Hesus)

Maria Hesus describes her father's experiences as an enlisted soldier in a unit made up entirely of Hiakis during the Escobar Rebellion. At first his regiment had the number 86, and it was deployed with the 29th in Michoacán. Maria Hesus describes how he was caught in a very dangerous battle in which his unit was intermingled with the enemy units, and it was not clear who were the enemy and who were his allies. He had a horse, and he was caught in a closed arroyo looking for an exit. As he was escaping, he saw an officer from his group, Lt. Valles, and together they ran through the sand under fire from the Escobaristas. He was sure he would be killed, but they succeeded in escaping. After they arrived in a safe place, the exhausted horse was given water to drink, but it got diarrhea and died within a few hours. Luisa comments that often when there was close fighting the soldiers used bayonets on each other.

Maria Hesus says that her father was in the Pénjamo jurisdiction but was deployed to somewhere in Michoacán where the battle with the Escobaristas was fought. Maria Hesus saw the battlefield afterward with her father; she saw the empty coats and helmets of the dead, and feet sticking out of graves. She said there were thousands killed. When the Hiakis were ordered to attack, the Escobaristas had buried themselves in the ground and could not be seen; she says the attackers dropped like wood as they were fired on. Three units went in and were destroyed: an infantry unit, a covering unit, and a cavalry unit. Maria Hesus's father was with a Mexican from Vahkom named Luis, and discussed with him how far they should advance. Luckily, the retreat was eventually sounded and the Escobaristas surrendered. They raised white flags,

---

M.H.: Pos hunum veha, nee veha in partepo,
ii papaa veha im vicha vittuawak con la gente de . . .
mal de cuentos que, nee kaa tua hu'unea,
pero tenía un ocho y un seis, ochenta y seis, hewi?
Hunaka veha im nunu'ubwa uu papaa,

FIGURE 26 Mexican soldiers in a foxhole. Arizona Historical Society, PC 235, Douglas, Arizona Photograph Albums, box 3, album #4, AW.

came out of the ground like worms, and were captured. Some may have been killed.

After the battle was finished, the Hiaki soldiers were sent to Ciudad Juárez. The wives and families of the soldiers were left there in Michoacán, not knowing where their men were or whether they were alive or dead. When the battalion arrived in Ciudad Juárez, their regimental number was changed to the 24th. The journey was hard and the soldiers were not adequately supplied; Maria Hesus's father became very hungry. At one point he toasted some corn that he had saved out of his horse's corn ration and ate it; it made him very sick. Maria Hesus says that the unit commander, Colonel Badillo, was promoted to general at that point. He credited the Hiakis for winning the battle and earning him his promotion.

M.H.: Well, there then, I, on my part,
then Father was sent this way with the people of . . .
the bad thing is that, I don't really know,
but he had an eight and a six, eighty-six, yes?
That is what my father had here,[6]

---

6. She points to her shoulder to show where the number was sewn.

henompo, ochenta y seis rehimiento.
Hunum katek. Chukula intok rehional tea.
Hunum veha nah kaate haivu.
Con el veintinueve hunum rehte en el estado de Michoakan.
Hunum weaman ii papaatuka'u,
ta kia Hiakim ausu'uli, Hiak ausu'uli.

Luisa: Heewi.

M.H.: Cuando la "Revuelta de Escobar" hunum veha, ho,
Dios kaa aa waata uka papaata.
Hunum, hunum, ume peronim
veha hiokot aa ya'ane uka papaata, haivu bwan.
Haivu bwan amemak au weiyan, ti hiia bwan.
Pos wame huni kava'ek, vempo huni kava'ek.
Ta pos kaa au hu'unea ti hiia bwan o si in hente o ta'abwi.
"Veha nee kaa am ta'a," ti hiia.
"Ivotana intok nee kaa am ta'aka
intok nee ameu vichaa sikaa uka kava'ita nee pentak," ti hiia.
Hitaa, haisa teak ume'e, un, un,
un como un arroyo sin salida, como encajonado.
"Hakun vichasa nee vuitine?" ti hiia.
"Pos tua hunum nee pa'akun vicha yeu vuiteo intok
hunuu teniente Vaayes: '¡Córrele, Juan! ¡Córrele, Juan! ¡Ahi vienen!'"
Pos ume intok am mumuhe tea ta pos papaa intok
"Kia nee mukiataka vuite," ti hiia.
Pos kava'i veha haivu kaa vuite, tea.
Lottila se'epo vuiteka ti hiia.
Pos hakun yeu yahaka veha papaa veha
"Ah, Juan, nos salvamos,"
ti hiia tea huna'a kapitan, i'an.
Pos vatte emo suawak en la Revuelta de Escobar.
Nau emo kuutek ti hiia, ho.
Wame huni peronim, ime huni peronim.
Soldados con soldados.
Hunum yeu tenneka veha hunum veha . . .
wame intok bwan ume, hunuu,
hunuu ochenta y seis rehional am tootenneka bwan.

on the shoulder, 86th Regiment.
That's where he was. And later it was known as a regional.
Then that's where he was already.
With the 29th in the state of Michoacán.
That's where he was, my late father,
but they were Hiakis only, Hiakis only.

Luisa: Yes.

M.H.: During the "Revolt of Escobar" there then, see,
God did not want my father.
There, there, the bald ones
then will treat my father badly, already, well.
Well, already he was mixed with them, he said, well.
Well, some even had horses, they even had horses.
But, well, he did not know, he said, if they are my people or others.
"Then I do not know them," he said.
"And on this side I did not know them,
and I went to them and I pawned the horse," he said.
What, how are they named, one, one,
one like an arroyo without an exit, like boxed in.
"Which way will I run?" he said.
"Well, and just as I was running out,
that Lt. Valles: 'Run, Juan! Run, Juan! They are coming!'"
And, well, they were firing at them, they say, and, well, but Father,
"I was just running like a dead man," he said.
"Well, then, the horse already could not run," he said.
He was tired from running in the sand, he said.
Well, when they had gotten far away, then, Father, then,
"Ah, Juan, we have saved ourselves,"
is what the captain said, now.
Well, they were almost killed at the Revolt of Escobar.
They got mixed up together, he said, see.
Those were the bald ones and even these were the bald ones.
Soldiers with soldiers.
When they ran from there then . . .
and those, well the, that one, well,
that 86th Regional ran away from them, well.

Luisa: Tsk, aa.

M.H.: Ime veha amau taawak intok kaa hu'unea,
bwan haksa tawane,
pos kia tennek pos wame huni hahawa,
ume Escobarim am hahase.

Luisa: Aa ha.

M.H.: Aman veha . . . pos kia laauti emo katee ti hiia porque uu,
aman veha hunaman si'imem, si'imem ane'epo
veha kaa yoem e'a tea yoi ya'ut,
peron, no sé si im nah rehte,
tea, ume itommak sontaom.
Hunak veha aman emo yahak, ti hiia.
Pos uu kava'i intok pos va'ai hi'ipea, hi'ibwapea,
pos humak he'eka, uu kava'i.
Chuvvatuk kia haisa voohte tea uu kava'i,
papaata puateka vuitekame.

Luisa: Aa.

M.H.: Voohte tea. Pos kia woi, vahi horapo
vohteka mukuk, tea uu poloove kava'i [*inaudible*].
Pos si tevesi se'epo aa nukvuite,
intok haivu lottila, ti hiia.
Pos hakwo naateka te hahawa, ti hiia.
Ta komo valampo emo kuutaka veha,
kaa hu'unea o wame o ime'e, pos kia ama taawak.
Cheaneaka kaa ama aet mammattekamme.
Hunum aa me'ean uka papaata.

Luisa: Ya ves que kia hunuen nau kuutek,
kia wiko'i puntammake emo ore'ine,
kia pehpehti amea emo sossoane.

M.H.: "Penhamo ti hiiamta vena," uu papaa.
"Penhamo, Penhamo huridihionpo
nee tawa'e'an," ti hiia.
Ta hunuu yoi veha aa tehwak.

Luisa: Tsk, ah.

M.H.: And these stayed behind and did not know,
well, where they would stay,
well, they just ran since they were being chased,
the Escobaristas were chasing them.

Luisa: Ah ha.

M.H.: Then there ... well, they were walking very slowly, he said, because
over there then, over there where everyone, everyone was,
well, the Mexican authority did not trust them,
the bald one, I don't know if they are around here,
they said; the soldiers who are with us.
Then they arrived there, he said.
Well, the horse was thirsty, hungry,
well, I guess the horse drank.
Later he had diarrhea, they say, the horse,
the one who carried Father and ran.

Luisa: Ah.

M.H.: He had diarrhea, he said. Well, just two, three hours with
diarrhea, he said, the poor horse died [*inaudible*].
Well, he [the horse] carried him for a long time in the sand,
and he was already tired, he said.
Well, they were chasing us for a long time, he said.
But in between the bullets, they got mixed up, then,
not knowing if it was those or these, well, they just stayed there.
Thank goodness they did not recognize him.
They would have killed him there, my father.

Luisa: You see that they just got all mixed up,
just with the bayonets,
they just stabbed each other with those.

M.H.: "Pénjamo, it sounds like," my father said.
"In the Pénjamo, Pénjamo jurisdiction
I should have stayed," he said.
But that Mexican told him,

"Vámonos, Juan, son contrarios."
Hunak emo tennek ti hiia, bwan.
Ta pos, ume, bwan pos . . .
wame, ime im vicha mumuisaka,
wame intok pos am mumuhe,
ta pos kaa hu'unea wame o ime'e.
Haisa humak nau auka emo kuutaka, bwan,
ume peronim Rehional con los Escobaristas.
Hunum veha vuitek ti hiia.
Chukula veha senu kava'ita au makwak ti hiia uu papaa.
Hunama taawak uu poloove kava'i ti hiia.
Nee yeu nuksikame aman taawak, ti hiia.
Hunaman hakun veha Michoakanpo,
haksa lugarpo, haisa humak aa teuwa.
Hunama veha nau kiimuk.
"Ay, qué feo, Mari," ti hiia.
Chukula te aa vitchusaka ama wam katekai.
Mira los capotes en los mesquites, en los postes;
ume kapo'otem ketun ama kokowe. Los, esos cascos
. . . del . . . Hunaa intok, hunaa intok, ama veha,
ume, ume peronim, o si ivotana o
wanna'avotana en los postes de la luz,
hunama kia, kia husamoyo weyek ume kartucham.
Y todavía los soldados con los pies
para afuera en los hoyos. Hm.
Pero no creas que mataron un, un hombre—
miles y miles de soldados.

Maria: Yoorim?

M.H.: Yoorim. Pos inii, inii rehimiento papaata ama weama'u huname,
intok kia, kia Hiak ausu'ulim tea,
Hiak ausu'uli ti hiia uu papaa.

Luisa: Hmm.

M.H.: Primero entró un batallón.
Hunak kia kutamvenasi tawakamme.
Pos hunama, huname wattek. Va el,

"Let's go, Juan, they are the enemy."
Then they ran, he said, well.
But well, those, well . . .
those, these were shooting this way,
and they were firing at them,
but, well, they did not know if it was those or these.
What they did to get all mixed up with each other, well,
the bald ones, regional, with the Escobaristas.
That's when he ran, he said.
Later, then, a horse was given to him, my father said.
The poor horse stayed there [died], he said.
"The one who took me out stayed there," he said.
Over there somewhere in Michoacán, then,
in some place, I do not know what he called it.
That is where they fought.
"Ay, it was so awful, Mari," he said.
Later we were looking at it as we went by.
We saw the capes in the mesquites, on the poles;
the capes were still swaying there. The, those helmets
of . . . and that, and that, then, there,
the, the bald ones, whether on this side or
on the other side on the light poles,
there, just, just brown stacks of ammunition.
And still the soldiers with their feet
sticking out from the holes [graves]. Hm.
But do not think that they killed [just] one, one man—
thousands and thousands of soldiers.

Maria: Mexicans?

M.H.: Mexicans. Well, this, this regiment that Father was with,
those were only Hiakis, they said,
only Hiakis is what my father said.

Luisa: Hmm.

M.H.: First a battalion went in.
Then, just like wood, they remained there [dead].
Well, there they fell. They went,

va el segundo tapador huname,
intok pos ket wokimmea,
con kanyon, con metrayadooram.
"Ta pos haisa am suane Maari?"
pos ume emo ma'ari bwiapo,
pues ume Escobaristam bwiapo emo ma'ari.
Haisa am ya'ane? Ni los ba-,
ni las balas de las, de los [*inaudible*]
porque no los ven en qué lugar están.
Antes no había como la, la,
la que hay ahora para verlos en donde están.
No, ahora no.
Si se meten allí los miran y los matan.
Antes pues, nomás, no, no están.
Pues síguele adelante. Uu hente intok kia hiva ama lu'ute.
Tres, una de infantería, una de tapadores
y una de caballería. Hunama lu'utek, ho.

Maria: Hiakim?

M.H.: Yoim. I'an veha hunu Koronel Badiyota hente veha
hunen, hiia tea. "¿Y los generales pues?
Mandarlos a la línea y ellos se quedaron
en campaña la entre medio."
Ama hokaa veha nesawe . . . Haisa humak teak uu general.
Le toca al General Badillo que meta . . .
Pos ume waate, i'an uu Reyno aa ta'a hunaka peronta.
Hunaa Luis tea.
Pos, papaa intok . . . Kia emo . . .
"Hitaa wataka itepo puttine?" ti hiia tea ume waate.
"Pos ume kattee am vicha, estarán tapados."
[. . .]
Hunaa, hunaa veha, o papaa veha hunuen au hiia tea.
Uu Luis—hunuu im Vahkompo yoi.
Hunuen au hiia tea, a'apo uu papaa,

the second cover charge went,
and they were also on foot,
with cannons, with machine guns.
"But how could they kill them, Mari?"
Well, they had buried themselves in the dirt,
well, the Escobaristas had buried themselves in the dirt.
What could they do to them? Not even the bu-,
not even the bullets of the, of the [*inaudible*]
because they could not see where they were.
Before, there was nothing like the, the,
the things available today to see where they were [hiding].
No, not now. If they go into the foxholes,
they would see them and kill them.
Before, well, they weren't, weren't there.
Well, go forward. And the people just kept dying there.
Three [units], one infantry, one who covered them,
and one of the cavalry. They were finished [off] there, see.

Maria: Hiakis?

M.H.: Mexicans. Now, the people of Colonel Badillo then said this,
they said, "And the generals, well?
They sent them to the front and they stayed behind
in the middle of the campaign."
They sat there giving orders . . . I do not know the general's name.
It was his turn, General Badillo's, to send . . .
Well, the others, now Reyno knew that bald one.
His name was Luis.
And Father, well . . . They just . . .
"What do we want that we have to shoot?" they said, the others.[7]
"Well, we can't see them, they are probably covered."
[. . .]
That one, that one, or Father then said to him, he said, then,
that Luis—he is a Mexican here from Vahkom.
This is what he [Luis] said to him, they said, him, Father,

---

7. That is, the soldiers were questioning their orders, asking why they should be ordered to shoot at the enemy.

"Oye, Juan," ti au hiia tea.
"Hasta aquí nomás."
"Pues sí," ti hiia tea uu papaa.
"Hasta aquí. Hasta aquí," ti au hiia tea uu papaa.
Pos hunaa yoi ti hiia,
pues nee huni mahai ti hiia tea.
Ta pos haisa anne? Ta hunuu bwan . . .
riendam huni kaa aa wike.
Inen anee tea uu yoi.
Haivu kuhwa bwan ume toorom.

Luisa: Hmm?

M.H.: Luis kia inen ane'e tea uka kava'ita bwisikai.
"Ahora sí, Juan."
"Pos ni modo," ti hiia tea uu papaa. Si'ime.
Ho, haisa? Pos bueno, uu yoeme kaa kia kivakne.
Siempre le habla a la Virgen de Guadalupeka aman kivakek.

Luisa: Hmm.

M.H.: Hunak veha inen hiia, tea uu Luis. "Ahora sí."
Chuuvatuk im veha kuhwa tea aman eskinapo inen.
Vanteam totosaem haptek tea emo ma'aripo.

Luisa: Aa.

M.H.: Haptek tea ume vanteam.
Hunak veha atala emo sahak, ti hiia.
Lutula ha'abwek ti hiia.
Ta haisa bwan, pos.
Ya pos Dios humak kaa intok ime . . .
Hiakim kaa aman am kimu'ii'aa haptekame.
"Pos haisa itepo am teune?" ti hiia.
"Posi bwiapo emo ma'arimme," ti hiia.
Haiki metpo huni,
pos wame hi'ibwa intok va'a he'e,
ite intok kaa hi'ibwa intok kaa he'e ti hiia.
Chukula veha kia bwichiamvenasi yeu kattaitek tea,
ume peronim emo ma'arime.

"Listen, Juan," he said to him, he said.
"Up to here only."
"Well, yes," my father said.
"Up to here. Up to here," my father said to him.
"Well, that one is a Mexican," he said.
"Well, I was scared too," he said.
But, well, what could they do? But that one, well . . .
he could not even pull the reins.
This is what that Mexican was doing, they said.
They were already blowing the retreat.

Luisa: Hmm?

M.H.: Luis was just doing this as he held the horse.
"Now then, Juan."
"Well, what can we do," my father said. "Everyone?
See, how? Well, good, the Hiaki does not just attack.
He always speaks to the Virgin of Guadalupe, then attacks."

Luisa: Hmm.

M.H.: Then that Luis said this, they said: "Now then."
Later, here, then, was heard the bugle over at that corner, like this.
White flags rose up, they said, where they had buried themselves.

Luisa: Ah.

M.H.: The flags rose, they said.
Then they were placed right side up, he said.
Then they were standing up straight, he said.
But how, well, well?
Enough. Well, maybe God did not want these . . .
did not want the Hiakis who stood up to go in.
"Well, how could we find them?" he said.
"Well, they were buried in the dirt," he said.
Even though for several months,
well, they were eating food and drinking water,
and we were not eating food or drinking water, he said.
Then later just like worms they begin to come out, they said,
the bald ones who had buried themselves.

Yeu sahak tea, ho.
Pos ii, ii veha rehimiento papaata vetana
veha am bwisek tea huname'e
... Am bwisek hunume Hiakim.
Asta hunuu Koronel Baldio huni allea tea,
bwan pos a'apo huni pos ...
si ume aa hentewa tatapwak, pos a'apo huni pos wetne, ho.
Es mejor, pos ume heneraalim taawa.
Pos huname ulti-,
pos hunume yeu sahak pos,
kia kaitapo am ya'a'e'an
pos hunama am sua'e'an.

Luisa: Heewi.

M.H.: Pos, "Ay, muchachos," ti ameu hiia tea.
"Gracias a Dios que allí vienen ya," ti hiia tea.
Ta pos ume wiko'im haivu kom kovak,
kom kovaka katee, ho.
Kaa nahsuavae.

Luisa: Heewi.

M.H.: Hunama veha haisa humak am ya'ak,
o si hakunsa am vittuak o
watem suak ume Escobarim.

Luisa: Aa.

M.H.: Porque si henteta suak tea ti hiia uu papaa.

Luisa: Tsk.

M.H.: Pos ume emo ma'ari, haisa am vitne?
Kaachin am vitne. Pos hunama yeu sahaka,
veha asta Ciudad Huaresseu yeu yahak hunume'e.

Luisa: Hmm.

M.H.: Hunaman yahaka veha numero nakuliawak,
24 rehimiento, hunuu papaa.
Pos inii, ume haamuchim
intok hunum tawala, Michoakanpo.

They came out, they said, see.
Well then, this, this regiment that Father was a part of,
then they captured them, they said . . .
The Hiakis captured them.
Even that Colonel Badillo was also happy, they said.
Well, well, even he, well . . .
if they defeated his people, well, even he would fall, see.
It is better, well, that the generals stayed.
Well they la-,
well, when they went out, well,
they would have made nothing out of them,
well, they would have killed them there.

Luisa: Yes.

M.H.: Well, "Ay, boys," he said to them, they say.
"Thanks to God that they are coming already," he said, they said.
But, well, the rifles were already pointing down,
they were pointing down, see.
They did not want to fight anymore.

Luisa: Yes.

M.H.: There, I don't know what they did to them, then,
where they were sent, or
if the Escobaristas killed some of them.

Luisa: Ah.

M.H.: Because they killed a lot of people, it is said, my father said.

Luisa: Tsk.

M.H.: Well, they had buried themselves, how could they be seen?
There was no way to see them. Well, when they left from there,
then they went all the way to Ciudad Juárez, those ones.

Luisa: Hmm.

M.H.: When they arrived there, then their number was changed,
the 24th Regiment, that one, Father.
Well, and these, the women
had stayed over there in Michoacán.

Luisa: Hmm.

M.H.: Huname familia ama tawakame o hu,
o kaa hu'unea o si hiapsa o kaa hiapsaka
kaate, hunum vicha, Ciudad Huareseu vicha.
Kaa hu'unea, pos kia veha te am hahase [*inaudible*].
Hunaa pos . . .

Luisa: Hmm.

M.H.: . . . pero kaa hu'unea o si hunama taawak
o ketuni ket kaate. Kaita, kia veha kaate.
Hunaman haksa veha papa
huma pos tevaure, poloove.
Vachita intok makwak kava'itavetchi'ivo, senu kiilo.
Ili moralpo aa to'aka veha kava'itat aa chayak.
Pos uu humak kee kava'ita aet tenteu,
aa nu'une voosapo aa kivachane, woi ili puntom.

Luisa: Aa.

M.H.: Aa ansuk veha aman,
ili tahita ya'ak
hunama aa tootaka aa bwa'ane.
Pos hunamea pottek uu papaa.

Luisa: Tsk.

M.H.: Pos, si kaa tu'isi aa sakne, ho.

Luisa: Kia veha napohpo aa . . .

M.H.: Haksa va'am teune pos kia veha napohpo aa tootaka
aa bwabwa'e.
"Pos hiva nee hunuen a'ane,
pos nee tevaure intok kaa tomek."
Hunuen am hoosuk uu Mehiko.
Hunaman Ciudad Huaresseu yahaka
veha ave muuke uu papaa.

Luisa: Tsk.

Luisa: Hmm.

M.H.: Those wives who stayed there knew,
or did not know, if they were alive or not alive,
just walking that way, toward Ciudad Juárez.
We did not know, well, we were just following them [*inaudible*].
Well, that one . . .

Luisa: Hmm.

M.H.: . . . but we did not know whether they stayed there
or were also still walking. Nothing, then, just walking.
Somewhere out there, then Father
was, well, probably hungry, poor thing.
And he was given some corn for the horse, one kilo.
He poured it into a small bag, then hung it on the horse.
Well, maybe, before the horse put his mouth on it,
he would take some, put it in his pocket, two little pinches.

Luisa: Ah.

M.H.: When he [the horse] finished [eating],
he [Father] would make a small fire there
and he would toast it and eat it.
Well, Father got indigestion.

Luisa: Tsk.

M.H.: Well, he did not cook it right, see.

Luisa: In the ashes he just . . .

M.H.: He just toasted it in the ashes
and ate it.
"Well, I always did that.
Well, because I was hungry and had no money."
That is what Mexico did to them.
When they arrived over there in Ciudad Juárez,
then my father was about to die.

Luisa: Tsk.

M.H.: Ya se había . . . ta, haivu, haivu bwan hunaa,
uu numero nakuliari.

Luisa: Hmm.

M.H.: Hunaa veha, imin yepsaka veha uu,
uu mensaje aman vittuawak Mehikowi.
Hunaa veha kaa, kaa nahsua porque
ume Escobardistam veha au emo nenkak.

Luisa: Hmm.

M.H.: Hunaman orden yepsaka veha
ii, veha heneraltuk, Miguel Badiyo.

Luisa: Aa.

M.H.: "Pero les agradezco, muchachos," ti hiia tea.
"Por ustedes, los indios yaquis de Sonora,
por ustedes [me] hacen de general," ti hiia tea.

Luisa: Aa.

M.H.: Por los indios pos kaa kiimuk.
Ume Escobaristam au, au, emo nenkak.
Hunuen veha, bwe, si am naken
hunaa heneral . . .

Luisa: Tsk. Hmm.

M.H.: . . . hunume Hiak ausu'ulim.

M.H.: He had already . . . but, already, already, well, that, the number had been changed.

Luisa: Hmm.

M.H.: Then that one, when he arrived here, then the, the message was already sent to Mexico. Then that one was not, was not fighting because the Escobaristas had surrendered to him.

Luisa: Hmm.

M.H.: When that order arrived there, then this one, then, became a general, Miguel Badillo.

Luisa: Ah.

M.H.: "But I appreciate you boys," he said, it is said. "Because of you, the Hiaki Indians of Sonora, because of you they made me general," he said, it is said.

Luisa: Ah.

M.H.: Because of the Indians, well, they did not attack. The Escobaristas surrendered to him. That way, then, well, he really cared for them [the Hiakis], that general . . .

Luisa: Tsk. Hmm.

M.H.: . . . those were Hiakis only.

FIGURE 27 Hiaki "Constitucionalistas." Arizona Historical Society, PC 041, Elsing Photograph Albums, box 1, page 47, #21520.

M.H.: Michoakanpo. Estado Michoakan.
Ho, itepo intok hunaman hooka,
Moreliapo, Michoakan.

Luisa: Hmm.

M.H.: Kaita haksa waa ili sentaavo, familitau,
ili hita, kaita.
Quince, veinte días.
Poloove ume haamuchim . . .
pos nee huni poloove porque pos nee
tevaureka malatamak cha'asisime.
Hunumun te katne . . .
Hunak veha inen hiune poloove haamuchim.
"Hante Paula," ti au hiune.
"Haisa, por casualidad,
ume itom o'olam hunum hak yeu katne?
Kaa tu'ika a'avo toina.
Estasioneu vicha te tennine.

Searching for Her Father Among the Wounded (Maria Hesus)

Maria Hesus describes how the wives and children of the soldiers would wait for news and mail from the front. Some received a little money in the mail now and then. The wives would beg for money and food for their children at the train station, while waiting for the trains with casualties from the front to arrive. Maria Hesus's mother asked her to check the cattle cars, where the wounded were, to see if her father was there. The little girl saw terrible things: men with no limbs, dying men, a man with an eye hanging out. There were too many casualties for the Mexicans to cope with. A train like that would arrive every two or three days. The official distributing the mail would confirm that her father was still alive, but there was never a letter or money for them. The official said that those on the front were starving too. The starving Hiaki soldiers would take whatever they could from the dead on the battlefield.

M.H.: In Michoacán. The state of Michoacán.
See, and we were there,
in Morelia, Michoacán.

Luisa: Hmm.

M.H.: Nothing. Where were a few cents for the family,
a little something; nothing.
Fifteen, twenty days.
Those poor women...
Well, I was also poor because I was
hungry while hanging on to my mother.
We would go over there...
Then they would say this, the poor women.
"Let's go, Paula," they would say to her.
"What if, by chance,
our husbands maybe show up there, somewhere?
Gravely injured, they will be brought here.
We will run to the station.

Kaita huni te tompo weiyaka katne.
Pos, ume ili usim tevaure.
A ver qué nos dan."
Mala ili sinkota[8] ama . . .
[*inaudible*] hunuen limohnane, ume haamuchim.
"Por favor, una tortilla,
un peso de frijol pa las criaturas."
Wepulaika noksimne.
"O una plancha o un plato.
Pos te tevae kokoka rehte. Heitu."

Luisa: Hunuentaka huni wate yee omta ume senyoam.

M.H.: Yee omta.

Luisa: Heewi, yee omta.

M.H.: Hunak veha, hunak veha . . .

Luisa: [*Chuckles.*] Nee ket hu'uneaka hunen hiia.

Reyno: Hmm.

M.H.: . . . aman te, aman te veha yahine.
Kaita nee pensaroane o,
o papaata nee ama vitne. Kaita.
Hunen hiune waate, chea ili nee vepa yo'owe.
"Vanse'e, Hesus. Aman te hiune."
Karay, vagonnimpo te hiune . . .
Ay Dios! Haisamaisi . . .
wate im kaita hippu'une imi'i;
la vaala los fregó, ho.
Sin brazo, sin pierna, con la panza de afuera.
Ay. Aa, malata nee tehwane.
"Maala, yoeme bwan aman te'ine."
"Haivu ha'ana hiune.
Empo aman am vichak?"
"Ay, si vu'umme to'oka
vagonnimpo," ti nee au hiune.

---

8. *Sinco*: a nickel.

We will have nothing in our stomachs as we walk.
Well, the little kids are hungry.
Let us see what they give us."
Mom would have a nickel.
[*inaudible*] that is how the women asked for donations.
"Please, a tortilla,
a peso's worth of beans for the children."
One would do the talking.
"A grill or a plate."
Well, we were starving, walking around. I do not know.

Luisa: And even then some of the Mexican women disliked us.

M.H.: They disliked us.

Luisa: Yes, they disliked us.

M.H.: Then, then . . .

Luisa: [*Chuckles.*] I also knew it, so I said it.

Reyno: Hmm.

M.H.: . . . over there, we, over there, we would then arrive.
I thought about nothing or,
or that I would see Father there. Nothing.
This is what some of those that were older than me would say:
"Come, Jessie. We will take a look."
Damn! We would look in the freight cars . . .
Ay, God! What a sight . . .
some would have nothing, here,
the bullet severely injured them, see.
No arm, no leg, with their guts hanging out.
Ay. Ah, I would tell Mom.
"Mom, there's a man moaning over there."
"You are already saying foolish things!
You saw them there?"
"Ay, there are a lot of them lying
in the freight cars," I would say to her.

Poloovemme, kia haisa te'inine
ultimo revueltapo nu'upawakame.
Ospitalim, ni se diga.
Wate koko, wate, convalescente,
sin brazos . . . [*inaudible*]
Hmm, Maari. Era el fin de
la gente en esos años, i'an ti nee e'e'an.
"Ay," ti hiune uu maala.
"Em papaata ama vitnanna.
Hak humak ket vo'oka."
Hunak veha nee aman kivakne.
"Pos hunama nu'upana, Maari."
Trenpo, vagonnimpo nu'upana.
Pos ume peronim kaa, kaa am yuuma
porque son un montón.
Los meten a una camilla.
Imin toina, intuchi seenu.
Kia hana am bwiseka aman
am wootaka, imin am tohine.

Reyno: Heewi.

M.H.: Hunak veha hunen am ya'ane.
Polovemme. Haksa weeka veha [*inaudible*].
Hunum senu veha tua nee womtak uu peron.
Tua pusim yeu tatapla.

Maria: Ay!

Reyno: Hmm.

M.H.: "Hunu'u chea tua papata vena," ti nee . . .
tua nee aa vitchu.
Kia um yeu wokek.
Wate kaa, kaa wokek; tua hamtila.
Ume valam am hamtala ume wokim.
Wate kaa hihiavihte.
Pos haksa, ho.
Pos si hakun am nu'une, ho.

"Poor things, they are just moaning a lot,
those who were brought in, in the last battle."
In the hospitals, do not even mention it.
Some dying, some convalescing,
without arms . . . [*inaudible*]
Hmm, Maari. It was the end of the
people in those years, I used to feel.
"Ay," my mom would say.
"Peek out to see if your father is there.
Maybe he is also lying there somewhere."
Then, then I would go in there.
"Well, they will bring them in those, Maari."
In the train, in the freight cars they were brought.
Well, the bald ones could not, not handle them
because there were so many.
They put them in the stretchers.
They would bring them here, again, then another.
They would just grab them any way,
throw them over there, bring them here.

Reyno: Yes.

M.H.: Then, they would do that to them.
Poor things. Then one day [*inaudible*].
There, then, one really scared me, a bald one.
One of his eyes was hanging out.

Maria: Ay!

Reyno: Hmm.

M.H.: "That one really looks like Father," I . . .
I really stared at him.
He just had his foot out.
Some had no legs; they were really pulverized.
The bullets destroyed their legs.
Some were not breathing.
Well, where, see.
Well, so where would they take them, see.

Hunaman intok ume enfermerom
kaa ameu yuma'ane.
Haisa am hittone?
Pues kaavaekai
imin, imin vittuana.
Pos haikika kokoka matchuk.
Cada woi, vahi ta'apo aman te yaaha.
Hiva te hunuka vitne, bwan.
Wate haamuchim [*inaudible*]
haksa yoi ya'ut imin yevihne,
kuarteleu, Moreliawi. Hunaman yevihne.
Pos aet cha'aka tennine,
ume haamuchim, totoimvenasi.
"A ver si por casualidad,
in kuuna o ili sinkota neu vittuak."
"Ay, señoras," ti hiune ume yoim,
"pues nee kartam weiya."
Si senu moraalim weiyane.
Pos hunak veha am teuwane ume haamuchim.
Mala intok inen hiune,
"¿Y a mí no me mandaron carta?"
"No," ti hiune. Aa tatakne uka voosata.
"Kaita," ti hiia. "Ho."
Si'ime kaartam mavetne;
wate tomeka katne, ume kartam.

Luisa: Hmm.

M.H.: Waate pos, ili viivom ume Hiakim.
Peronta wechek aa volsiaroane.
Aa u'uraka veha a'apo aa nu'une.
Inen am hohoan ume kontrariom.
Am suaka veha am volsiaroane.
Pos hunum veha te, kaita.

And over there, the nurses
could not tend to all of them.
How would they nurse them?
Well, they had no choice
but to send them here, here.[9]
Well, many of them died during the night.
Every two or three days we used to go over there.
We always saw the same thing, well.
Some women [*inaudible*]
where the Mexican official would arrive,
at the barracks, in Morelia. He would arrive there.
Well, they would run after him,
the women, like chickens.
"Let me see, perhaps, by chance,
my husband has sent me a nickel."
"Ay, ladies," the Mexicans would say,
"well, I am bringing letters."
He had a whole bag full.
Well, then, he would call the women's names.
And Mom would say,
"And I did not get a letter?"
"No," he would say. He would shake out the bag.
"Nothing," he said. "See."
Everyone would receive a letter;
some had money in them, the letters.

Luisa: Hmm.

M.H.: Some, well, the Hiakis were kind of smart.
When a bald one fell, they would pick his pockets.
They would take things from him and take it for themselves.
This is what they did to their enemies.
They would kill them, then pick their pockets.
Well, there, then, we, nothing.

---

9. To the cattle cars. It was common practice for medical personnel to tend to the soldiers who had a better chance of recovering from their wounds. Those who were gravely injured were set aside, or, as in this case, placed in the cattle cars, there to die a slow and agonizing death.

Surviving While the Men Were in Combat (Maria Hesus)

Maria Hesus describes how, although her father was serving in the military and the officials could confirm he was alive, they did not give any money to support his family—indeed, the officials said the soldiers were also starving, and Maria Hesus says they did not get paid. During this time Maria

---

M.H.: Veha mala hunuen au hiune yoi ya'utawi.
"Hunu'u, veha in, in, in o'ola veha hiapsa?"
"Heewi," ti au hiune.
Hunak veha listapo aa vitne.
"Heewi, hiapsa, hunum listapo. Ta pos kaa,
kaita bwan uu ili sentavo," ti au hiune malatawi.
"Iteposu huni ave tevae koko," ti hiune.
Si kaa sosotan, hunume pleitopo rehte.
Hunen hiva katne, katne.

Reyno: Kaa tu'uwampo.

M.H.: E'e. Kaa tu'uwampo katne, ho.
Haksa weeka mala veha hunuen hiia
senu hamuttau, i'an ini'i Antonia.
"Nana," ti hiia.
"Nee si kaa intok hunum vichaa weepea," ti hiia.
"Haisa inim, inim itom hoka'apo Sonorau?
Tahti mekka ha'ani?"
"Ako ala," ti au hiia.
"Si mekka inimi'i," ti au hiia.
"Hitasa intok empo im hoovae?
Saka'aneete.
Nee huni Santosta kaa hu'uneiya.
Kia veha nee aa hahasek.
Saka'ane'ete. Kat tatawa," ti au hiia.
"Hita empo im hoovae? Saka'ane'ete."
Hunuen kaa montine uu in maala.
Yokoriapo ume senyoam:

Hesus and her mother were in Morelia, Michoacán, waiting for the return of her father. Her mother would go with the Mexican wives to find food. She had to trade some of their possessions, two plates, for a small cup of wheat and a handful of beans to feed them. She could not take Maria Hesus with her because the trip was too dangerous. It felt to Maria Hesus as though the revolution that kept her father fighting went on forever.

M.H.: Then Mom would say to the Mexican official,
"That one, then, my, my, my old man, then, he is alive?"
"Yes," he would say.
Then, then, he would look at the list.
"Yes, he is alive, there on the list. But there is not, well, there is no money," he would say to Mom.
"We are also about to die of hunger," he would say.
They did not earn any money, the ones in battle.
That was the only way, keep walking, keep walking.

Reyno: Not with good intentions.

M.H.: No. They did not go with good intentions, see.
One time, Mom said this, then,
to another woman, now, this one, Antonia.
"Young girl," she [Mom] said.
"I do not feel like going over there again," she said.
"How far is it from where we are to Sonora?
Is it far, perhaps?"
"My older sister, silly," she [Antonia] said to her.
"It is very far, here," she said to her.
"And what do you want to do here?
We will leave."
I also do not know about Santos.
Then, I just followed her.
"We will leave. Don't stay," she said to her.
"What are you going to do here? We will leave."
Then my mom would not reply.
Another time, in the morning, the Mexican women:

"Paula," ti au hiune.
"Aman te rehtine," ti au hiune.
"Nee planchata weiya.
Empo intok hitaa weiya?"
"Nee woi puatom huni weiya'ane,"
ti hiune uu maala.
Ili taho'orimpo am vihtaka saka'ane.
Nee ala kaa nunnu'ubwan uu maala,
porque mekka intok
kaa seguro Haksa . . .
Hunak veha nee tawane ili usimmake.
Nee tawane.
Hunaman hakun veha haksa,
ili tiikomvetchi'ivo la plancha.
Una tacita de trigo.
I'an ini'i Don Peo hunaman home,
hunam Morelia, Michoakanewi
si tevaa, si tevaa!

Reyno: Hmm.

M.H.: "Te dejo esta plancha
para que nos siquiera dan
un platito de trigo o de frijol," ti au hiune,
ume senyoam.
"Ay i'i in asoa pues
no tenemos qué comer," ti hiune.
Pos kia bwanaka huni kia
senu ili tasa tiikom am mikne.
"Llévate la plancha," ti hiune.
Chea wam he'ela veha mala veha puato
ama vi'ine por un poquito de frijol.
Senu punyom am mikne.
"Llévate el plato." Aa, aa hunaa
revolusion hiva weye, hiva weye.
Haiki semana
o meecha hunama te hooka.

"Paula," they would say to her.
"Let's walk around over there," they would say to her.
"I will take the iron.
And what are you going to take?"
"I will take at least two plates,"
Mom would say.
She would wrap them in a small cloth and they would leave.
But Mom did not take me with them,
because it was far and
not very safe. Where . . .
Then I would stay with the other children.
I would stay.
Somewhere over there then,
a little bit of wheat [was received in trade] for the iron.
A small cup of wheat.
Now, this one, don Pedro is from over there,
there in Morelia, Michoacán,
so much hunger, so much hunger!

Reyno: Hmm.

M.H.: "I will leave you this iron
so that you can give us
a small plate of wheat or beans," they would say to her [Mom],
the Mexican women.
"Ay, well, my child,
we have nothing to eat," she would reply.
Well, even as she was crying, she just
gave them a small cup of wheat.
"Take the iron," she would say.
Later on Mom would leave a
plate for a little bit of beans.
She would give them a pinch [of beans].
"Take the plate." Ah, ah, that
revolution kept going, kept going.
I do not know how many weeks
or months we were there.

Luisa: Hm.

M.H.: Por eso nee inen hiune.
Inime vato'oim inim
Hiak vatwepo hooka, heewi?
Vempo aa pasaaroak.
Itepo huni aa pasaaroak.
Mekka te aa pasaaroak, kechia.
Kaa haksa itepo sentaditos esperando, no.

Luisa: Pos uu sontau familia
chea im huni doblepo aa pasaaroak.

The Suffering of Hiaki Soldiers and Their Families (Luisa and Maria Hesus)

Maria Hesus and Luisa comment on the fate of many former soldiers, on how they were not taken care of when sick and dying. They emphasize that the enlisted Hiakis did not serve willingly; they were coerced,

M.H.: Hunuen ibwan.
Ta Hiak, Hiak sontaum huni hiva hiokot aa pasaaroak
porque vempo kaa vem e'apo hunuen auka bwan.
Kaa haksa vem, vem aa tu'ule'epo veha hunuen yaawak.

Luisa: Utteapo si'ime . . .
Utteapo, utteapo sontau ya'awakamme.
Si'ime hunuen utteapo sontau ya'ari, hakwo kaa . . .
i'an veintetuk im hoowak ket
kumui Ilaario im kavayeriampo weaman kechia,
papatam sae yo'owe. Ket te wosa ama au noitek,
Kokoimpo aa kateka'apo.
Chukula uchi itom ama aneu veha haivu kaa ama hooka . . .
Huna'a ket si vinwa ama sontautukan.

MILITARY SERVICE

Luisa: Hm.

M.H.: That is why I will say this.
These baptized ones
are here in the Hiaki River, yes?
They went through it.
We also went through it.
We also went through it far away.
We did not sit around waiting, no.

Luisa: Well, the wives of the soldiers
really went through it twice.

---

forced into service by threats. During their service families were never notified when their husband and father was sent away. News was never sent back to families about how the unit or the individual was. Supplies were uncertain and sometimes unavailable, so both soldiers and their families would lack food.

M.H.: That is the way it was, well.
But even the Hiaki, Hiaki [soldiers] also always suffered pitifully,
because they did not do it because they felt like it, well.
Not where they, they felt like doing it; it was done to them.

Luisa: Forced, all of them . . .
Forced, forced, into the military.
They were all forced into the military, long ago, not . . .
In 1920 when they were here,
Uncle Hilario was also a *caballero* here,
Father's older brother. We also went there twice to visit him,
there in Ko'okoim where he was living.
Later, when we went there again, they were already not there . . .
That one was also a soldier for a long time.

Wepu'ulaika intok im itommak
yepsak intok lauti muukuk. Ho.
Chea chukula weeme . . .

M.H.: Hunuen ibwan, kaa, kaa tu'i.
Hunak veha . . . itepo veha papatamak si hiokot ansuk
hunum peronimpo aa weamau.
O si te hi'ibwa o te kaa hi'ibwa.
Haksa toosaka'awak hunama te aa voovitne
o si itou yepsa, o kaa itou yepsa.
Ta voovitne.

Luisa: Katchansan hu'une'ene heewi?

M.H.: Hmm, hmm.
Reeve, chea te tua katchansan am hu'une'iya'ane.
Lonchita ameu weiya . . . haksa?
Have huni kaavetune.
Hiokot, hiokot ibwan am hoosuk, uu Govierno mehikano.

Luisa: Tua ousia.

M.H.: Heewi. I'an intok pos hiva . . . govierno . . .

Luisa: Kia hak orapo yukeu huni yeu vittuana.
Kaita yuku amevetchi'ivo, kaita, kaa tomek,
kaita lonchek ti kaa hiune.
Kia veha hak horapo huni yeu saka'ane.

And one of them arrived here with us
and he quickly died. See.
The one who came much later . . .

M.H.: That way, well, it was not, not good.
Then, then . . . we suffered terribly with Father
when he was a Mexican soldier.
If we ate, we ate, if not, we did not eat.
Wherever we were left, there we would wait for him
whether he returned to us or did not return to us.
But we would wait.

Luisa: One never knew, yes?

M.H.: Hmm, hmm.
Half of the time, we really did not know about them.
Taking lunch to them . . . where?
No one would even be there.
They were treated horribly, horribly, by the Mexican government.

Luisa: Truly, very bad.

M.H.: Yes. And now, still . . . government . . .

Luisa: They would be sent out just at any hour, even if it was raining.
There was no rain for them, nothing, they had no money,
no lunch, they could not say.
Then they would just go out at any hour.

Escaping Mexican Military Service (Maria Hesus)

Maria Hesus describes how many conscripted Mexican soldiers, including her father, were assembled in Casa Grande in 1929 for review, and a reduction was made in the size of the forces. Some who had come up from the south were allowed to leave, and some who were too short or otherwise did not meet regulation standards for military men were also dismissed. Many Hiakis, including her father, were kept, however. Some talked among themselves, missing their comrades-in-arms and their families, and initiated an escape, walking to Navojoa. Subsequently General Badillo came to oversee the remaining Hiaki soldiers, locking them up and posting guards so no one else could desert. However, when the guards' attention wandered, more would escape. Many times Hiakis planning their escape would come to Maria Hesus's mother and ask her to make them a lunch to take with them. Some escapes happened when a contingent of soldiers was sent out on an assignment—to Chihuahua to build a hospital, for example. Even a woman, Cuca, and her children escaped from Casa Grande. Her father would sometimes have an opportunity to escape but would not take it, even when encouraged by others, since deserters were executed if they were caught. Finally there were only four Hiakis remaining: Maria Hesus's father Juan, a man

M.H.: Rohitiachi.
Na veha, na veha hunum Kasa Grandepo veha te si'ime yeu yahak. Si'ime ume sontaum, si'ime.
Hiak ausuli, ausuli; nama veha veinti nueve.
Veinti nuevetuk hunama si'ime yeu yahak
Ciudad Juarezpo, Casa Grandepo.
Huna'a veha katin rekorte ya'awak?
Rekorte.

Luisa: Heewi.

M.H.: Rekorte.
Ume chea kokome'ela huname veha vaahata makwak, intok ume chea ili o'olam.

named Mike Buitimea, a man named Florentino, and a man named Luis. Maria Hesus would beg her father to leave and take their family to Sonora, pointing out that this was not their country or people. She even volunteered to walk the whole way disguised as a boy. He finally agreed to leave after many years. She was so excited that she told their three dogs that they were going to be left behind. However, when her father went to inquire about a discharge, Captain Tachi convinced him to stay, noting that he had served nineteen years and if he stayed just a little longer he would be eligible to receive a pension. Maria Hesus was very disappointed. However, to receive the pension, a great deal of paperwork was necessary: baptismal records, records of service, and so on. A flood had destroyed some of the papers; others had been moved from one repository to another in Mexico City. It took a long time for documents to be mailed back and forth, but finally, in 1945, the final papers arrived, with train tickets to take the family back home. They left from Chihuahua on October 12. Maria Hesus's father had served in the Mexican military since 1910. There was difficulty in showing this, though; those papers from his earlier service had been left in Hermosillo or Tampico. If he could have found those, he would have been entitled to a sergeant's pension, but he wasn't interested in papers and had a terrible time keeping track of them.

M.H.: It is depressing.
Then, then, then, there in Casa Grande, then we
all arrived. All the soldiers. All of them.
Only Hiakis, only; there, then, it was 1929.
In '29 everyone arrived there,
in Ciudad Juárez, in Casa Grande.
It was then, remember, that they made the reductions.
Cutbacks.

Luisa: Yes.

M.H.: Cutbacks.
The very short were excused
and the very elderly.

Luisa: Ummm . . . vaahata makwak.

M.H.: Ho, pos Hiakim vetana pos kaa unna yeu sahak
porque hiva ili estaturata hippueme ama taawak.
Ume Mehiko vetana amemak yeu sahak
huname veha yeu saka'atuawak.
Tren veha ama katek estasionpo, vagonim.
Hunaman veha kiimu
ume peronimtuka'um.

Luisa: Ahh.

M.H.: Hunaman kiimuk
con cualquier cosita de dinero.
Kaa haksa kantidaata makwak.
Sahak vem bwiarau vicha, sahakamme.
Ime Hiakim intok pos con ganas
de que itom lisensiane. Kaita.
Yantela tamachiawa
firmetusaekai, ho.
Hunama taawak, hunama taawak.
Hunama yeu sahaka veha,
ume vem amigom, vem wawaim sahak.
Pos ume rohikteka taawak.
Pos hakwo naateka nau kaate,
nau kaate.
Hunak veha emo partaroakamme, Kasa Grandepo.
Ho, hunama taawak.
Haksa weeka veha nau etehotaitek ume yoeme.
Emo saka'avae ti hia horau vicha, ho.
Primer remesa veintetaka yeu sahak.
Veintetaka sahak hunum Kasa Grandepo a'av o vicha.
Ta hunum hak emo Navohoau yeu yahak ti hiia,
wokkimmea hunaman yeu tennekai.
Ho, pos hunuen am teak uu Heneral Badillo.
Am etak. "Kaave intok yeu katne," ti hiia.
"Porque, hunume usimvetchi'ivosu

Luisa: Ummm . . . They were excused.

M.H.: As for the Hiakis, not too many were excused
because those who were a little tall stayed in.
Those who came with them from Mexico City,
they were made to leave.
The train was at the station, the freight cars.
Then, they climbed in there,
the ones who had been Mexican soldiers.

Luisa: Ahh.

M.H.: They climbed in,
with whatever little money [they had].
They were not given any large sum of money.
They left for their lands, they left.
And these Hiakis were hoping
that they would be allowed to leave. Nothing.
Instead they begin to measure them[10]
to make them reenlist, see.
They stayed there, they stayed there.
Those [the others] left there, then,
their friends, their relatives left.
They stayed and became very sad.
Well, they had traveled together for a long time,
traveled together.
Then they became separated, in Casa Grande.
See, they stayed there.
Later on the men began to talk to each other.
They were going to go home, they said, see.
The first group of twenty left.
Twenty of them left from Casa Grande to come this way.
But they arrived somewhere there in Navojoa, they said,
on foot, after they escaped from there.
See, well, so this is how General Badillo found them.
He locked them up. "And no one else will escape," he said.
"Because it is for those children

---

10. For military uniforms.

nehposu inilevenaka inim katek," ti hiia.
"Ah vempo intok hunuen nee ya'ak.
Nee tootennek," ti hiia tea.
Puetam veha etaatevok.
Hunama veha woi gentineelam hapne,
kaave yeu katne. Am etak.
Ho, kia ili aa mansotek
intuchi veintetaka yeu saka'ane. Saka'ane.

Luisa: Ili aa hoiwatuak.

M.H.: Heewi, saka'ane.
Ta saa, saa suan uka sentineelata.[11]
Barda wanna'avotana katek.
Hunaman ika peronta kokkocheu
woika huni yeu tennine.
"Inen teakapo te itot tenne."
Vatwepo, woi ta'apo huni aman emo voovitne,
ama voovitne.
Mala veha lonchita am . . . watem . . .
a'apo aa hihi'ibwatuan uu maala, ume yoeme.
Malatau yaahine.
"Imcha ta'apo lonchita nee ya'ariane maala.
Te saka'avae.[12] Hante maala,
kat im tatawa," ti au hiune ume yoeme malatau.
"Hante, wam saka'ane'ete," ti au hiune.
Papa intok kulupti pos hakun eskolta vittuana
Ciudad Juarez o imin Ciudad Madero.
Aman veha weamne.
Pos kaa am hahamne, bwan.
"Ho, wiko'ita ama su'utohaka
aman hak kurvapo kom chepte," ti au hiune papatawi.
"Haisaakai?" ti hiune.
"Bwihwaka intok nee me'ena," ti hiune.
Hunak intok katin yee susuawan.

---

11. *Saa* here is a contraction of *si* (really) and *aa* (him).
12. Maria Hesus whispers this in the recording.

that I am here like this," he said.
"Ah, and now they did this to me.
They ran away from me," they say he said.
Then he had the doors locked.
Then two guards would be posted there,
no one would escape. They were locked up.
See, just when they became a little more tame,
again another twenty would run away, run away.

Luisa: They let them get careless.

M.H.: Yes, they would leave.
But the guard was watching intently.
He was on the other side of the fence.
When this bald one was falling asleep over there,
at least two would run out.
"We will meet each other at this named place."
They would even wait for each other for two days at the river,
wait there.
Mom would make them lunch . . . some . . .
my mom used to feed the men.
They used to come to Mom.
"On this day, make lunch for me, mother.
We are going to leave. Let's go, mother,
don't stay here," the men would say to Mom.
"Let's go, we'll go over there," they would say to her.
And Father, well, sometimes he would be sent out as an escort
to Ciudad Juárez or here in Ciudad Madero.
Then he would be over there.
Well, he would not catch up with them, well.
"See, leave the rifle over there
and step down over at the curve," they would say to Father.
"Why?" he would say.
"If I am captured, I will be killed," he would say.
And in those days, remember, they would kill us.

Luisa: Hunak susuawan tennekame.

M.H.: Kaa hunuen eene bwan. Haksa weeka, veha
pos tua, tua bwan naikiamtaka
ama taawak ume Hiakim.
Sahak, si'ime sahak hoawau vicha.
Sahak, sahak.
Pues papa veha, papa hiva hoara . . .
i'an veha kia apela ama taawak.
A'apo papa intuchi Miki Vuitimea,
intuchi kompae Florentino intuchi,
intuchi hunaa Luis.
Hunaa veha hunuen am ya'ak.
Aman, am, am, papa pos
hiva kaa, kaa casota am ya'ariak.
I'an, I'an hunuka Kukata empo ta'a? Waa Kuka teeve.

Luisa: Hmm, hmm.

M.H.: Hunum yeu siika Casa Grandepo hunu'u senyoa Kuuka.

Luisa: [*Laughs.*]

M.H.: Ili asoaka, hunama. Lencho tea uu chea ili yo'owe.
Huname ama yeu tennekame.
Hose Huan tea uu yoeme aemak yehsukame.
Hunaimak yeu vuitek, hunum Kasa Grandepo.
Hunuen am ya'awak intok imin intok
Chihuahuau vicha intok wate vittuawak une peronim, Hiakim.
Hunaman veha ospitalta ya'asaewa.
Hunaman veha waate im,
im veha haivu kaita ume yoeme, haivu yeu saka'asuk.
Wamintok aman yeu tennek
ume wate Hiakim Chihuahuau.
Hoarau vicha yeu sahak.
Asta ke kaave ama taawak. Papa hiva.

Luisa: Then, they used to kill the deserters.

M.H.: He would not want to, well. Then one day,
well, really, really, well, they were counted,[13]
the Hiakis who remained.
They left, all of them left to their homes.
Left, left.
Well, Father, then, Father [was the] only [one who had not gone] home . . .
Now then, he just stayed there by himself.
He, Father, again, Mike Buitimea,
again, compadre Florentino again,
again, that one, Luis.
So then this is what he did to them.
Over there, them, them, Father, well,
he just did not, not pay heed and do as they asked.
Now, now, that Cuca, you know her? That tall Cuca.

Luisa: Hmm, hmm.

M.H.: She escaped from Casa Grande, that Mexican woman Cuca.

Luisa: [*Laughs.*]

M.H.: She had little children there. The oldest was named Lencho.
They escaped from there.
José Juan is the name of the man who lived with her.
She escaped with him, there at Casa Grande.
And when they did this here
they sent some of the bald ones and Hiakis to Chihuahua.
Then they were told to construct a hospital there.
Then some, here, over there,
here, then, there were already no Hiakis, they had already left.
And over there, they ran out,
some of the Hiakis escaped from Chihuahua.
They left for home.
Until no one was left there. Only Father.

---

13. That is, there were only a handful of Hiakis left; this use of the Hiaki verb *naikiamtaka* to mean "few" is like the similar use of *contados* in Spanish.

Intok hunume'e, Luis intok papa intok Florentino intok Miki.
Naikika ama taawak.
Huname hiva nau etehone ama Hiakim, ho.
Hunaa veha inien au hiune.
Ini Luis ke haivu muksuk, si'ime kokosuk.
Papa huni muksuk. Kaave. Inien au hiune.
"Oye Huan, te saka'ane itom bwiarau vicha."
"Heewi, nooliama. Empo chea si emo oule.
Saka'aneete," ti au hiune,
uu yoi. Ta como Im Vahkompo hoome.
Hunum katek aa akowa Vahkompo.
Au Hiaki ti hiune.
Au Hiaki ti hiune. Hunum veha te, hunum veha te yeu . . .
Papa veha pos ama taawak, ama taawak.
Vahi wasuktiam yumak veha rengancheta ya'ane.
Ho, hachin huni kaa yeu weemachine.
Asta ultimopo veha nee hunuen au hiak.
"Papa, saka'ane'ete," ti nee au hiune.
"Hitasa te im hoone?
Eme'e chea kaa . . . itepo chea kaa im bwiarak.
Te kaa im bwiarak. Aa pos te saka'ane papa,"
ti nee au hiia.
"Si kaa voletom hippuetek huni'i,
wokimmea te katne, papa.
Nee chon chuktane, pantaroonim nee hinuriane,
ili wicholek intok nee nu'uriane, saka'ane'ete," ti nee au hiune.
Asta ke hunuen aa ya'ak. Vahata nee aa a'autuak.
Aman siika uu papa. Solisitudta ya'ak.
Eskeelam nu'uka veha aman am tohak.
Hoarau vicha te katvae.
Kaa hunuen ea uu yoi ya'ut. Kaa hunuen ea.
"E'e," ti au hiia. "Yu Huan," tiia uu kapitan Taachi.
Uu primera parte. "Yu Huan," ti au hiia.
"Diez y nueve wasuktiapo inim ee nah siika.
Inim ehersitopo ee kumpliaroak.
Ah, juname diez y nueve wasuktiam
premiaruava'awa'e Huan," ti au hiia.

And those, Luis and Father and Florentino and Mike.
Four stayed there.
Only those spoke to each other, the Hiakis, see.
That one, then, would say this to him.
This Luis also died already, everyone has died.
Even Father has also passed away. No one would say this to him.
"Listen, Juan, let's return to our land."
"Yes, come on, then. You are a very brave person.
We will leave," he would say to him,
the Mexican. Since he was from here in Vahkom,
his older sister is still there in Vahkom.
He would say he was Hiaki.
He would say he was Hiaki. Then, there we, then, there we . . .
Then Father stayed there, he stayed there.
After three years he would have to reenlist.
See, there was just no way that he could leave the military.
Then finally I said to him,
"Father, we will leave," I would say to him.
"What will we do here?
You all do not . . . These are not our lands.
We do not own these lands. Ah, well, we will leave, Father,"
I would say to him.
"Even if you do not have the [train] tickets,
we will start walking, Father.
Cut my hair, buy me some pants,
get me a little vest, and we will leave," I would say to him.
Until finally this is what he did. I made him ask for a discharge.
My father went over there. He made a request.
He picked up his notes and took them over.
We were going to go home.
But the Mexican official did not approve it. He did not approve it.
"No," he said to him. "Look, Juan," said Captain Tachi.
The first part. "Look, Juan," he said to him.
"Nineteen years you have been here.
You have done your service in the military.
Ah, those nineteen years
will be rewarded, Juan," he said to him.

"I'an huma wasukte," tiia.
"Ume kartam a'avo yaaha," tiia.
"A'avo yaaha ume kartam," tiia.
"Si'ime, si'ime ume, ume inim sontao o'olam," tiia,
"yeu, yeu saka'avaeme," tiia.
"Ta kaa hunuen kia suutoiva'awa,
si no ke pensionta em makva'awa.
Chuvala ee voovicha Huan," ti au hiia.
"Kaa kia em tomita im toosimne. Hiva empo aa makna.
Pensionaruana'e," ti au hiia.
Ah, pos hunum veha aman itou yeu weye uu papa,
vusanimpo kupteo.
Nee intok haivu allea, bwan te saka'avae.
Kia nee ili vahi chuu'um te hippuen kokome'elam.
"Te saka'ane'ete chuu'um,"
ti kia nee ameu hiune yoi nokpo.
"Imin Sonorau te yeu noitine." Si nee allene.
Bwan, kia chuvalatuk saka'ane'e ti nee eene,
Papa hunen hiiau. Chukula hunuen hiia pos.
"Hesusta si simpeau, intok
kia kaa nee vaahata makwak," tiia.
"Ay, haisaakai?"
"Pos kaa hunuen ea uu primer taasio.
Chuvala nee vooviicha porque como
itepo hakwo naatekai inim
ite yoimmak kaate tiia,
Pensionaruava'awane," ti hiia.
"Hunu'u intok hitasa, papa?"
"Bwe, tomita nee makna," tiia.
"No sé si Ermosiopo o Obregonpo," tiia.

Luisa: Ah ha.

M.H.: Pos hunama veha naatek ume hiosiam.
Veha vat i'an uka fe de bautismota au a'awa.
Pos uu papa intok haksa yeu tomtek intok hakunsa . . .
Si'imeta hunuka. Imin veha aa hiimak. Haisa teak imi'i?
Vem yo'otukaawi.

"Now, it has probably been a year," he said.
"The letters have been coming here," he said.
"Those letters have been arriving here," he said.
"All, all those, those old soldiers who are here," he said,
"they want to go out, out," he said.
"They are not just going to let them go like that.
Instead, they are going to give you a pension.
Wait a little while, Juan," he said to him.
"Do not just leave your money here. You will still receive it.
You will receive a pension," he said to him.
Ah, well, then this is when Father came to us
at six in the evening.
And I was already happy; well, since we were going to leave.
We just had three dogs that were short-legged.
"We are going to leave, dogs,"
I said to them in Spanish.
"We will go over here, out to Sonora." I was very happy.
Well, in just a little while, I felt that we would leave,
when Father would say. Later, he said this, well:
"Jesusita really felt like leaving, and
they just did not give me the discharge," he said.
"But why?"
"Well, the first soldier refused.
Wait for me a little while because since
we have been here for a long time,
with the Mexicans,
I will receive a pension," he said.
"And what is that, Father?"
"Well, I will be given some money," he said.
"I don't know if in Hermosillo or in Obregón," he said.

Luisa: Ah ha.

M.H.: Well, that is when the paperwork started.
Then, now, first they asked for the certificate of baptism.
Well, my father, where he was born and where . . .
All of that, he left it here. What is the name of this place?
Where they grew up.

Luisa: Santa Emilia, San, San . . . ?

M.H.: Im, imi'i. Empalme, Empalmepo wam heela . . .
Haisa teak, katin hita vatwe aa nuksiika hunuka ili
pueplota. [*Pause.*] Maytorena, o hitasa humak . . .
ta, bueno hunum karta vittuawak. Hunumun.
"No," ti au hiia uu huez.
"Huname hiosiam hakwo yeu sika," tiia.
"Haisa kaa au waate uu govierno?" tiia.
"Katin uka, uka kusoau si'ime ume hiosiam
nuksiika uu vatwe.
Haksa aa teune?" tiia.
"I'ani nim aukame vemela hiosiam," tiia.
"De ese señor no hay," tiia.
Ah pos hunume'e vempo veha aa ya'ak uka fe de bautismota,
rehistro civilta. Hunuka ya'ak.
Hunak veha kattaitek ume hiosiam Mehikou vicha.
Kaate. Intuchi hunaka yopnak.
Intuchi aa, aa intuchi aman aa vittuak.
Uu, kia vatte chikti he'ela hiosiam au yaaa,
hasta el último.
Mil nueve sientos kuarentai sinkopo veha yepsak
chikti voletommake.
"Ho. I'an ala te saka'ane, saka'ane'e te."
Ho, pos te sahak. Tua Octuvreta docepo te
aman yeu sahak Chihuahuapo.
Kaa im ta'akai. Ho.
Hunum veha te yahak, Obregonpo.
Papa veha haivu kaa sontao. Kaa sontaotaka weye.
Hunumpo veha te yahak, Obregonpo.
Ta ini papa aa hiula'apo,
"Hmm, Dios kaa nee waata.
Porque si nee waataateko, uu,
hakwo nee hakun muksu'ea'n.
Si mientras. Kaa kia, i'an veha, kaa kia haksa vempo . . ."

Luisa: Santa Emilia, San, San . . . ?

M.H.: Here, right here. Empalme, close to Empalme . . .
What is the name? Remember, some river washed it away,
that little town. [*Pause.*] Maytorena, or whatever it was . . .
but, good, that is where they sent the letter. Over there.
"No," the judge said to him.
"Those papers came out a long time ago," he said.
"Doesn't the government remember that?" he said.
"Remember, the, the *kusoau*,[14] everything, all the papers,
the river washed them away.
Where shall we find them?" he said.
"Now the ones here are new papers," he said.
"There are none here for that man," he said.
Ah, well, those, they, they made the baptismal papers,
the civil registry. They did that.
Then they started to send the papers to Mexico City.
They were sent. Then there was a reply to that.
Again, ah, ah, again they were sent over there.
The papers were always being sent to him,
until the last one.
In 1945 they finally arrived
along with the tickets.
"See. Now we will leave, we will leave."
See, well, we left. Exactly on October 12 we
left from Chihuahua.
Not knowing this place. See.
There, then, we arrived, in Obregón.
Father was no longer a soldier. He was not traveling as a soldier.
We arrived there in Obregón.
But, this, my father, as he said,
"Hmm, God does not want me.
Because if he wanted me, um,
I would have died somewhere, a long time ago."
If in the meantime, not just, now then, just where they . . .

---

14. Here Maria Hesus uses an unfamiliar word, perhaps referring to the river current.

A'apo bwan kia uka familiata aman nu'usaewaka siika, ho.
Hunaman taawak. Haksa intok nottek?
Kia traisionpo aman am suutohak ume am nuksahakame.
Chukula intok haisa yeu tennine?
Hunak chea oviachi, hak teuwak huni me'ena, me'ena.
Kaa kia i'anpo venasi.
"Te siika."
"Heewi, pos tu'isi hunum pasialoane."
Bwihwak huni me'ena.
Bwihwak huni me'ena.
Kaa . . . I'an intok pos, por eso hunen nee au hiune papatawi,
"Uuu, empo . . ." ti nee au hiia,
"uuu, hakwo naateka sontaotusuk papa,"
ti nee au hiune. "Wame vatnaataka hiosiam,
haksa empo am hippue, papa?"
"Uu," tiia.
"Hunak chea nee Mehikopo vetana yepsaka,
Ermosiopo nee am suutohak," tiia.
"Hunak primer ehersito,
mil nueve sientos diezpo, Tampikopo."
. . . Ho. Mekka, ho.
Hunaman yeu sikaa veha au kavotukan, tiia.
Tampikopo. Hunum vicha veha yeu yahak, Hermosiowi.
Ho, pos huname hiosiam au a'awan, uu ya'ut.
Para si kiara sarhentopo huni aa pensionaruavaen.
Haksa am teune? Haksa am teune?
Ho, pos uu wosa sontao.
Por eso nee hunen au hiune.
"Pos empo chea, yoi, yoi peronpo weamsuk.
Hiva, hiva ee pensionaroana,
con otro dinero más alto," ti nee au hiiune.
Pos kaa aawe bwan, kaa ito venasi bwan,
con este papel "lo voy a alzar."
Nunca. Intok, kaita . . .

Luisa: Kaita interesta amet hippun sontao hiosiammechi.
Semetian ni . . .
I'an vu'uka katin hunuen auk hunavo yahakame.

He, well, was just told to go and fetch his wife, so he left, see.
He stayed over there. When did he return?
The one who took them just betrayed them and left them there.
And later, how were they going to escape?
It was difficult then. If they found you, they would kill you, kill you.
It was not like it is today.
"We are leaving."
"Yes, well, go and have a pleasant visit over there."
If you were caught, they would kill you.
If you were caught, they would kill you.
Not . . . And now, well, that is why I would say to Father,
"Umm, you . . ." I would say to him,
"um, since when have you been a soldier, Father?"
I would say to him. "Those papers from a long time ago,
where do you have them, Father?"
"Uu," he would say.
"Then, when I returned from Mexico,
I left them in Hermosillo," he said.
"Then, the first battalion,
in 1910, in Tampico."
. . . See. Far away. See.
When he left from there he was a private, he said.
In Tampico. They went out that way, to Hermosillo.
See, well, so the authority was asking for those papers.
At least he wanted to give Father a pension for a sergeant.
Where could he find them? Where could he find them?
See, well, since he had reenlisted as a soldier.
That's why I would say to him,
"Well, you were going around as a Mexican, a Mexican soldier.
Still, still, you will get a pension,
with other monies, much higher," I would say to him.
But he could not, not like us, well.
"I will store it with this paper."
Never. And so, nothing . . .

Luisa: He had no interest in the soldier documents.
They went in . . .
Remember, many of them did that, those who came from there.

M.H.: Kaita, kaita interesta hippu'usuk.
A'apo kaa haksa. "Ay, pos heewi, ika nee ya'ak."
E'e, ya veh kee a'apo chea
hunuka seguro de vidata huni kaa vehe'etuak.
Kaita vehe'etuak.
Aun hunum vicha siika. Kaita.
Papa humak haisa humak machiakan. Poloove.
I'an kaa ya ves que hunuka Nehtota hunam kaa vo'oka?
Sewuropo aa yecha'akan.
Haksa aa teune?
Hakwo muukuk.
Treintai sinkotuk muukuk tea.
Mayo hunuen au hiia papatawi.

FIGURE 28 Hiaki soldiers on a transport train, ca. 1920. Arizona Historical Society, PC 078, Mathews Photograph Collection, box 3, BG327.

M.H.: Nothing, nothing, he never had any interest.
He did not. "Ay. Well, yes, I did this."
No, you see that he just did not
even pay for the life insurance.
He did not pay for anything.
Still, he left for there. Nothing.
Father, maybe, was like, like, I don't know how he was. Poor thing.
Today, not, you see that, that Nestor who is buried there?
He put him on his insurance.
Where are you going to find him?
He died a long time ago.
They say he died in 1935.
A Mayo said this to Father.

PART III

CONSEQUENCES

This part of the book presents accounts excerpted from the interviews discussing subsequent events, including the ongoing conflict over water rights, the internal divisions over "gray Mexicans" (those Hiakis who served in the Mexican military), everyday life in the community, dealing with Mexican bureaucracy, and the sense that modern Hiaki youth may forget the struggles of their elders and the great sacrifices that were made.

The stories in this part are organized into three chapters: "Mexicans, Deportees, and Divisions Among Hiakis," "The Contemporary Situation," and "People of Hiak Vatwe." As before, each story is summarized in a prose paragraph at the beginning and then presented in Hiaki with an English translation, exactly as recounted to the author.

CHAPTER 8

MEXICANS, DEPORTEES, AND DIVISIONS AMONG HIAKIS

Mexicans Moving into Hiaki Territory (Maria Hesus)

Maria Hesus reflects on how, despite the terrible history the Hiaki people have lived through, the Mexicans are moving into Hiaki land and she feels surrounded by them. She moved houses because there were too many Mexicans moving in close to her. She feels Mexicans still treat Hiakis badly. Luisa remarks that Mexican bankers are making money off of the Hiakis who still remain. Maria Hesus says that the Mexicans would be happy to see the Hiakis fighting among themselves and killing each other, some wishing to collaborate with the Mexicans and others resisting Mexican control. However, she trusts that Creator will not let that happen, as long as Hiakis continue to turn toward Creator and Holy Mother.

M.H.: Hunuen, hunuen itom ya'aka bwan.
Por eso hunuen hiune maala.
Nehpo. "I'an intok itepo ume yoim si tu'ule.
Aa karay! Kaachin itom ya'ak.
Itom yo'owam, kaa itom haksa haisa ya'ak.
Si te am waataka amenaapo ho'asasakane."
Nee reeve si nee ameu kuhte'ea.

Luisa: Hmm.

M.H.: Si nee ameu kuhtene. Aman in ho'apo . . .
hitavetchi'ivosu nee ho'araata ama toosiika.
Porque yoim neu ho'ate,
neu ho'ate. I'an haisa maachi?

Luisa: Hmm.

M.H.: Hiakim nasuk nee yehne.
Kaa hakun noitine. Im nee ho'atene.
Porque nee hiva nee malata etehoriau nee wauwa'ate.
Intok chuvala nee hunum nee nah siika.
Au nee wauwate, ho.
Hiva kuhtiachisi itom ya'ak itom hooa uu yoi.

Luisa: Hmm.

M.H.: Kuhtiachisi itom hooa.
Ta ket hiva ameu heela te ameu nokne o
"Vente pa'cá o no . . ." Kaa tu'i.

Luisa: Kialikun nee inen hiune,
ume yoim vankeom, si'ime.
Vem suave'etekeume veha

MEXICANS, DEPORTEES, AND DIVISIONS AMONG HIAKIS

M.H.: That is what, that is what they did to us, well.
That is why Mom would speak in that way.
Me: "And now we really like the Mexicans.
Ah, damn! They did nothing to us.
Our elders, they did nothing to us.
We care for them [Mexicans] so much that we live near them."
Half the time, I really hate them [the Mexicans].

Luisa: Hmm.

M.H.: I really feel hatred toward them. There at my home . . .
I do not know why I left my home there.
Because the Mexicans are moving closer to me,
closer to me. Now, how is it?

Luisa: Hmm.

M.H.: I sit among the Hiakis.
I do not go anywhere. I will live here.
Because I always remember what my mom used to say.
And I was there for a while.
I always remember it, see.
The Mexicans treated us hatefully and still do.

Luisa: Hmm.

M.H.: They treat us hatefully.
But also, still we stand close and talk to them or,
"Come here or no . . ." It is not good.

Luisa: That is why I will say,
those Mexican[1] bankers, all of them.
The ones [Hiakis] that they did not kill

---

1. After the revolution ended, farming societies were formed in Hiaki territory. Hiakis begin to plant wheat, soybeans, etc. They were given loans by the bankers who had established offices in Vikam to plant their fields, pay for the water, hire tractor drivers during the harvest, and have the produce processed. The banks would subtract their expenses and the farm expenses from the price paid for the final product. Sometimes what they skimmed off the top was more than what the Hiaki farmer

ian hi'ibwa,
kaa am suasukau, ti nee hiune.

M.H.: Aa, hunuka im hooa.

Luisa: Heewi, hunuen nee hihiia.

M.H.: I'an tahti hunen hiune.
"Si el indio no se arregla,
entre dos, tres años . . .
hunume bwiam itepo am nu'une, ho."
No Señor. Si Dios no quiere, tanto no pueden.
Ho, haisa am nu'une?

Luisa: Hmm.

M.H.: I'an hunum hita Ripaldom emo suau,
haisa hiia tea hunuu Michel, Carlos Michel?
"No le hace que estos, ume yoim,
ume Hiakim, itepo ume bwiam te am nu'une.
Ela'aposu si'ime emo suasune." ¿Por qué?

Reyno: [*Chuckles.*]

they are now eating.²
They did not kill all of us, I will say.

M.H.: Ah, that is what they are doing.

Luisa: Yes, that is what I say.

M.H.: Even now they say,
"If the Indians do not work things out,
in two, three years . . .
we will take those lands, see."
No, sir. If God does not want this, they cannot do so much.
See. How will they take them?

Luisa: Hmm.

M.H.: Now, there, the things,³ Ripaldos were killing themselves,
what is it he said, that Michel, Carlos Michel?
"It does not matter about those Mexicans,
the Hiakis, we are going to take those lands.
It does not matter if they all kill themselves." Why?

Reyno: [*Chuckles.*]

---

earned after all expenses were paid. Sometimes the Hiaki society members would receive as little as $300.00 in one year.

2. That is, Luisa is saying that the bankers are exploiting the remaining Hiakis to support themselves.

3. "Things" is how the Sonora Hiakis referred to the groups of Hiakis who were followers of a Hiaki man by the name of Ricardo Ripaldo, or Antonio Ripaldo Molina. Ripaldo was born in Guadalupe, Arizona, and had gone south to the Hiaki village of Vikam Pueblo. His intention was to help the Sonora Hiakis find a way to oust the Mexicans who were trying to coax the Hiakis into turning over their farmland to them. Many Hiakis felt that Ripaldo had their best interests at heart, so they elected him to the position of secretary, an integral part of the governing body of Vikam Pueblo. But there were two men (father and son), both of them *maehtom* (prayer leaders) in Vikam Pueblo, who were not in agreement with the villagers at large. There was a great deal of corruption, and those who stood to make money catering to the Mexicans beat up Ripaldo and his followers and dissolved his faction. Ripaldo is now a very old man, still living in Vikam Swiichi at the time of writing.

M.H.:	Si Dios no quiere, no.
	Solamente que waa vato'i kaa Diostat . . . kaa . . .
Luisa:	Kaa Diostau remremte.
M.H.:	. . . remremteka, kaa itom Aetat rerem . . .
	hunak ala. Haisa humak te aune.
	Pero menos no . . .
Reyno:	Hiva tu'ine, tiempommake.
M.H.:	Hiva, hiva te . . .
Reyno:	Dios ibwan. Dios . . .
M.H.:	Dios huna'a. Kaa hunuen e'ateko,
	es porque kaa hunuen eene.

On Renting Hiaki Land to Mexicans (Luisa)

Luisa and Maria discuss the seeming change in the attitude of modern Hiakis toward the ancestral land. Those who fought and died to defend

Luisa:	Hiva emo defendiaroa.
	Hasta que inim weeka veha hunule venasi weye, ho.
Maria:	Aa heewi.
Luisa:	Heewi. Hasta que inim weeka
	inien itom tosaa kovak veha
	hunuen weye, ho.
Maria:	Es que huname'e, tua huname'e aa pasaroakame,
	uka Hiak bwiata nahsuariakame,
	huname pos im haivu kaave.
Luisa:	Hmm.

M.H.: If God does not want it, then no.
Only if the baptized ones do not . . . toward God . . . do not . . .

Luisa: They do not look toward God.

M.H.: . . . look, [but] not toward Our Holy Mother . . .
then yes. I do not know what we will do.
But only then, see . . .

Reyno: It will get better with time.

M.H.: Still, still we . . .

Reyno: God is, well, God . . .

M.H.: God is the one. If He is not willing,
it is because He does not feel like it.

---

the land are growing old and dying, and the younger people who did not experience those battles find it easy to sell or rent the land to Mexicans. Luisa sees this change among those in the pueblos when she comes down to visit.

Luisa: They always defended themselves.
Until now, at this time, then, it is going like this, see.

Maria: Ah, yes.

Luisa: Yes. Until now, at this time,
when we have white hair like this,
things are going like this, see.

Maria: It is because those, truly those who experienced it,
who fought to defend the Hiaki land,
they, well, are already gone.

Luisa: Hmm.

Maria: Ime intok pos komo kaa aa pasaroak . . .

Luisa: Heewi.

Maria: Pos, kaa . . .

Luisa: I'an kaita bwan.

Maria: O si te aa atteane o si te kaa aa atteane ti
kaa pensaroa.
Kia veha pos yoimmeu aa bwise.

Luisa: Heewi.

Maria: Haz de cuenta.

Luisa: Heewi. Intok aa nenka vu'uka, bwiam.
Intok kaa vempo am tekipanoakai,
yoimmeu am rentaroa.

Maria: Vempo kaa ohvota ama wootak;
hunue vetchi'ivo veha facilsi veha . . .

Luisa: Hm, hmm.

Maria: . . . yoimmeu am entregaroa.

Luisa: Hunuen weye i'ani.
I'an nee hunuen im aa vicha.
I'an inim, i'an inim yeu yepsaka
naateka veha hunuen nee im aa vicha, bwan.
Kaa, kaa hakwo venasia.

Maria: And these, well, since they did not undergo it . . .

Luisa: Yes.

Maria: Well, not . . .

Luisa: Now, nothing.

Maria: Whether it will be ours, or not be ours,
they do not think of that.
Then just hand it [the land] to the Mexicans.

Luisa: Yes.

Maria: It seems like that.

Luisa: Yes. And many of them are selling it, the land.
And it is not they who are working it,
they are renting it to them [the Mexicans].

Maria: They did not spill their blood;
it is for that reason, then, [that] it is easy, then . . .

Luisa: Hm, hmm.

Maria: . . . handing it to the Mexicans.

Luisa: That is the way it is going on now.
Now I see it here that way.
Now here, now here, arriving out here,
beginning then, that is the way I see it here, well.
Not, not like a long time ago.

The Legacy of Madero and Mori (Luisa)

Luisa describes how Madero spoke for the Hiakis following the deportations of the Porfiriato, gathered the deported Hiakis together into a battalion, and later released them and enabled them to return home. The Hiaki leader Mori was also instrumental in making this happen, traveling south to participate in peace talks in Mexico every time negotiations

---

Luisa: Bwan, ta hunak aman toiwakame, Maderota...
Katin hakwo
hunuen tua, tua am tohiwau,
katin Madero, katin amevetchi'ivo...

Maria: Hunaa veha am nokriak...

Luisa: ...kikteka am nokriak, ho.
Hiakita nokriak, pooverata,
ho, yoitakai, ho.
I'an nee hunen hihia kechia.
I'an huni ket hunuen haksa have poove, yoem,
yoitaka, kia hitatakai huni
am nokriane, hikkaina.
Dios chea Dios ti nee hiune.
Pos hunak... ma hunuen,
katin si am suawau,
Hiakita barkaruawau veha
hunuu yoi veha am nokriaka,
hunuen veha humak kiktek
kaa intok nuksaka'a hapteak.

Maria: Heewi.

[...]

Luisa: Hunak veha am vichaa sahak tea, ti hiia.
Ta hunak veha huname yoemem veha,
hunaa Madero veha si'imem nau tohak tea.

were under way, despite not being literate and not speaking Spanish. Luisa describes how the eight pueblos turned against Mori afterward, however, dispossessing him of his house and livestock in Vikam and whipping him. He was resigned to die in exile, then, not wanting to return to the place where he had been treated in this way, although it was his homeland. Nonetheless, Luisa remarks, his signature is still everywhere, reflecting his role in the repatriation of the Hiakis.

Luisa: Well, but then, the ones taken there, Madero . . .
Remember, a long time ago
when they were really, really being deported,
remember Madero, remember, for them . . .

Maria: Then, that one spoke for them . . .

Luisa: . . . stood up and spoke for them, see.
Spoke for the Hiaki, for the poor people,
see, being a Mexican, see.
Now I say this, also.
Even now, and also in that way, where some poor man,
being a Mexican, just being whatever, even,
he would speak for them, he would be heard.
God is more God, I will say.
Well, then . . . like then,
remember, when they were really being killed,
when the Hiakis were being deported, then
that Mexican then spoke up for them,
then maybe that is why it stopped
and they stopped taking them away.

Maria: Yes.

[. . .]

Luisa: Then they went over there, they said, she said.
But then, then, those men, then,
Madero then gathered all of them, they say.

Si'imem nau tohaka veha imin Mehikou,
vatayoonimmeu veha yeu am tohak, tea, ti neu e'etehon
a'apo uu Mikaila.

Maria: Hm, hmm.

Luisa: Hunaman veha si'ime sontaopo,
vatayonpo kimuk tea, ti hiia.
Ta te kiala hu'uneiyak, hunuen.
Porque hunaa veha
ika Hiakita nokria, Hiakira,
aa tohiwau.
Hunuen, hunum, hunumun kima'awakame,
si'imem yeu tohak uchi. Intok inii Heneral,
Moritukao huni ket hiva aman noitek
hunuu Maderotavewichi, hunumun Yukataanewi,
Meridau chukti noitek.
Hunuu chea au oulen, Moritukao.

Maria: Hmm.

Luisa: Chikti pastu'u veleki hiva Mehikou yeepsan.
Intok kaa yoi nokan, kaa hiosia ta'a,
intok hiva aman yeepsan.

Maria: Hmm.

Luisa: Hmm. Asta kee i'an veha
hunuen kaa intok nottivavaek, hewi?
Porque ime yoeme, komo i'an vem nau kateevenasi,
aamak kaate.
Hunumun, hunum kaata hootevou veha
ili hitasa muuram, wakasim aa hippueum veha
aa etbwala ti hiiaka veha
ime si'ime ocho pueplom veha
nau emo tohaka,
aman si'imeta aa u'urak.
Intok hunuen intok yeu aa tohaka intok aa vemmuchak.

He gathered all of them, then here to Mexico,
he took them to a battalion, they say, she used to tell me,
she, that Micaela.

Maria: Hm, hmm.

Luisa: Over there, then all of them became soldiers,
went into a battalion, they say, she said.
But we just learned about it, that way.
Because that one, then
he spoke for the Hiaki, the Hiaki people,
when they were being deported.
That way, there, over there, those that were inducted,
he released all of them again. And this general,
the late Mori, he also visited there
at the same time as Madero, there to Yucatán, [and]
he also went to Mérida.
He was very brave, the late Mori.

Maria: Hmm.

Luisa: Every time peace was made he would go to Mexico City.
And he did not speak Spanish, was not literate,
[but] he always went over there.

Maria: Hmm.

Luisa: Hmm. Until now then,
he did not want to return that way again, yes?
Because these Hiakis, the way they are behaving now,
they behaved that way with him.
Over there, there he was having a house made, then,
he had a few things, mules, the cattle he had,
then, they said he had stolen them, then
all the eight villages, then,
gathered together;
over there they took everything from him.
And that way they took him out[4] and whipped him.

---

4. "Took him out" is a phrase used when a villager from any of the Hiaki villages commits some kind of unacceptable act such as stealing, unruly behavior, or domestic

Maria: Malagradecidos, hewi?

Luisa: Heewi. Iiyim Vikampo yeu aa tohaka,
aa vemmuchak, ho. Hunaka kuhteiyaka veha,
ii, ii Moritukao veha kaa intok a'avo weeroka.
"Elaaposu nee aman mukne," ti hiia.
Kaa intok a'avo weeroka.
"Elaaposu nee inim hak mukne," ti hiia.
"Tu'i, kaachin huni maachi.
Imi'i hente nee nonokak,
hu'ubwasu aman yahine o'oven," ti hiia.
"Ta hunuka nee sentiaroa neu ya'awakamta," ti hiia.

Maria: Pues sí, heewi.

Luisa: Bweituk i'an aa mukiatuk huni'i,
waa firma si'imekut to'oka ketunia, i'an tahtia, ho.

Maria: Ungrateful, yes?

Luisa: Yes. Here in Vikam they took him [out]
and whipped him, see. Hating that, then,
this, this, the late Mori did not want to come here again.
"It does not matter if I die over there," he said.
He said he did not want to return here.
"It matters not if I die here somewhere," he said.
"Good, it does not matter anyway.
Here, the people are talking about me,
although they will get there soon," he said.
"But that makes me feel bad about what they did to me," he said.

Maria: Well, yes.

Luisa: Because even though he is dead,
his signature is everywhere still, until now, see.

---

violence. It is a form of punishment for all the villagers to witness. The offender is forced out of his or her home and taken to the guardhouse, where they stand in front of all. They are questioned and judged for their distasteful behavior. The villagers have an opportunity to voice their opinions and to offer suggestions as to the form of punishment to be meted out. Public whippings are usually harsh.

Those Who Stayed in the South (Luisa)

Luisa describes places in the south where Hiakis who were deported settled and stayed: Oaxaca, Mexico City, Perote, Villa Cardel. Some of them, who had been in the Mexican military, received a pension. Some

---

Maria: I'an intok ume wate yoeme aman toiwakame,
wate aman taawak?

Luisa: Heewi. Huevenaka aman taawak.
Wahaakao vichaa wate saka'ala, aman hooka.
Hunaman vittuawakan,
ta kaa saka'avae tea.

Maria: Kia si'imekut aane . . .

Luisa: Mehikopo huni vu'uka tawala,
Perootepo huni tawala, kia haamuchimtaka huni'i.
Intok Mehikopo chea kia suavisi ho'ak.

Maria: Tua?

Luisa: Heewi, ume chea vatnaataka i'an itom eteho'u
ume Yukataaneu toiwakame
intok vatnaataka hakwo Maderota aman tohak,
nau tohaka'um yeu toiwakame,
waate yo'otu'im hewi.
Mehikopo hokaa pensionaruawakame.
Kia tohsasalaim karek, katchan yoemem vevena.

Maria: Hm.

Luisa: Tua. Si'imekut hunait hooka.
Intuchi hunum Viya Kardelpo huni'i ket im . . .
Viya Kardelpo kom cheptek wokimmea simne.

live in sizable houses and have assimilated to Mexican culture. Around Villa Cardel they grow wheat and garbanzo beans. Luisa says that many felt that returning to Hiak Vatwe would be futile; they would be captured and deported again.

Maria: And now some of the men who were taken there,
did some of them stay there?

Luisa: Yes. Many stayed there.
Some have gone to Oaxaca, they are there.
They were sent over there,
but they do not want to leave there, they say.

Maria: They are just everywhere ...

Luisa: Even in Mexico [City], many have stayed there.
They even stayed in Perote,[5] even the women also.
And in Mexico [City] they just live very nicely.

Maria: Really?

Luisa: Yes, the very first ones that we now were talking about,
the ones that were taken to the Yucatán,
and at first, a long time ago, those that Madero took over there,
those he gathered that were taken there,
some are very old, yes.
They were in Mexico and received a pension.
They just have white houses and they do not even look like Hiakis.

Maria: Hm.

Luisa: Really. They are there all over.
Also there, even in Villa Cardel[6] they also ...
When you get down at Villa Cardel you go on foot.

---

5. Perote is in the state of Veracruz in Mexico.
6. It is possible that "Villa Cardel" here refers to the city of José Cardel, in the municipality of La Antigua, in the Mexican state of Veracruz.

Aamman hakun veha kamionta bwihne am vichaa.
Hunaman te ket hookan. Ket depreeso si bwe'uka ama katek.
Hunaman ket yoeme ho'ak.
Ket si tiiko e'echa, kaavansam e'echa.
Huname yoeme hunen hiia.
"Ite aman vichaa sahak huni
uchi a'avo tohina," ti hiia.
"Hitaa te aman nu'une?" ti hiia.

Maria: Hmm.

Luisa: Kia bwe'u ho'aka bwan, tu'ulisia.

Maria: Haivu aman hoiwala.

Luisa: Heewi. Si'imekut hunuat in nah sika'apo yoemem vichaa.

> Over there somewhere then you catch a bus that way.
> We were over there also. There is also a very big dam there.
> The Hiakis also live over there.
> They also plant a lot of wheat there, they plant garbanzo beans.
> Those Hiakis say this.
> "Even if we go over there [to Hiaki land],
> they will bring us back here again," they say.
> "What will we gain from going there?" they say.

Maria: Hmm.

Luisa: They just have big houses, very nicely.

Maria: They are already used to it over there.

Luisa: Yes. Everywhere there that I went I saw Hiakis.

The Loss of History, the Loss of Land, and Divisions Among Hiakis (Luisa)

Luisa tells more about Peo Maachil, the elder prayer leader who lived in Vikam. His family were called the Machilim, which means "Scorpions." Luisa was related to them, and she describes several of them. Chiika (Francisca) Maachil, who used to travel to Tucson but who has passed away, was a great-niece of Peo Maachil; her maternal grandmother, Luz Maachil, was his older sister. Peo Maachil's son, Guillermo Maachil, was still living in Vikam at the time of the recording, but all the elders had passed away. Maria wonders whether the children of the family ask to hear about the history, but Luisa thinks not. She thinks that this may explain why things are going the way that they are, because the children do not know their history. She mentions how the Hiakis, even with no money for supplies or ammunition, never surrendered to the Mexicans, who went into tremendous debt to the American government to buy ammunition

---

Luisa: Kia te hepela hoarimtaka
itou etehona, ho. Hiva tua aa hihikka.
Katin Peo Machil tea.
Vikampo ho'akan. Temahti Moll yo'otukan,
hunama'a Vikampo. Machilim tea.
Huna'a Komae Chiika Machil,
katin aman yeepsan, kechia Tusoonewi.

Maria: Heewi.

Luisa: Hunaa muukuk.
Hunai, Hunaim asu
aa waikan hunuka havi Peo Machilta.
Ite am wawaik kechia.
Hunum veha, hunaa veha chea yo'otukan.
Ne'esa Lus Maachil. Ta ket muksuk.
Si'ime yo'owe, si'ime kokosuk.

and military gear. The Hiakis, who were very poor, never surrendered. And now they are still very poor, and things are going badly. Maria mentions that although the Hiakis were undefeated militarily, the Mexicans are now dividing the people with politics. There are even factions among the Hiakis now, and this may signal the Mexicans' final success at getting the Hiaki land for themselves: they cause turmoil and infighting among the Hiakis, and they take over the land and plant it. Luisa comments that the Mexicans are building very big houses and living well, while the Hiakis are still very poor. Even society members, who receive a lot of money, live in small houses, although they could afford to build big ones. Maria suggests that perhaps some prefer the traditional life and are not interested in big houses or electricity. Luisa, though, is concerned about how to provide for her grandchildren after she passes on. She would like them to enter societies, so they could perhaps receive some land to live on and support themselves with. That is partly why she comes to visit, to try to help them find a means of support. She and Andres live very far away.

Luisa: They would just have us sit side by side, attentively,
and speak to us, see. Perhaps you heard about him.
Remember, his name was Peter Scorpion, they said.
He used to live in Vikam. He was the prayer leader,
there in Vikam. They were the Machilim.[7]
That one, comadre Francisca Scorpion,
remember, she used to go over there, also, to Tucson.

Maria: Yes.

Luisa: That one died.
With that, with those, their maternal grandmother
was the older sister of minor uncle Peter Scorpion.
We are related to them, also.
There then, that one, then, was older.
Aunt [mother's older sister] Luz Scorpion. But she also died.
All the elders, all have died.

---

7. Hiaki family name, which translates to "Scorpions."

Más de que i'an ume uusim hiva ama tawala.
Intok hunu'u kompae Giyermo Maachil.
Hunaa veha Peo Machilta u'usi. Ama tawala.
Ta ket ime'e, ket im watem vehe'e.
Wam am . . . ket ama tawala.
Maehto usiataka, yo'orapo . . .
yoemiataka intok hunule venak hooa, ti nee hiune kechia.
Hunum veha ama tawala ume ili usi vasiulam hiva ama
tawala, ta ume yo'owe si'ime kokosuk.

Maria: Vem usiwam intok haisa kaa, ori hunume istoriam . . .
gravaroa, o kaa ameu am a'awa . . . ha'ani?

Luisa: Kaita humaku'u. Kialikun,
i'an veha hunulevenasi kaate hunume uusim.

Maria: Porque i'an ume yo'owem lu'utek
istoria ket lu'utine.

Luisa: Heewi.

Maria: Kaitatune.

Luisa: Kaitatune, a'a. Lu'utine.
Así como . . . hunuen katin ii Hiaki hiva kaa au nenenkaka,
veha katin, katin si'ime
aa nokria tea i'i yoira, por . . .
bweituk hakwo huni kaa haksa yoita venasi
goviernota parketa, wikiria tea.
I'i intok govierno intok si aa wikiria tea, ika'a . . .

Maria: Demaspo . . .

Luisa: . . . parketa ringota si yu'in wikiria teaka etehowa.
I'i intok Hiaki, chea poovetaka
kaita aa wikiriaka
kaa haksa hunuen parketa nu'eka
huni kaa, kaa aa wikiriaka tea,
kaita hitasa hak nu'eka huni
hiva aa au ania teaka hikkaiwa . . .
i'ani, ti hiia, ume yoimtaka huni'i,
bweituk kaa au nenkila tea.

More than that, only the children have remained there.
And that one, compadre Guillermo Scorpion.
That one, then, is the son of Peter Scorpion. He stayed there.
But these also, are also against the people.
There, those . . . have also remained there.
Being the child of a prayer leader, with the elders . . .
being their child and he is doing that, I also will say.
There, then they have stayed, the little offspring, only
they have stayed there, but the elders have all died.

Maria: And their children, do they not, the, those stories . . .
recordings, or ask for them . . . maybe?

Luisa: Perhaps not. That is why
they are carrying out those things, those children.

Maria: Because now that the elders are gone,
their history will also disappear.

Luisa: Yes.

Maria: It will disappear.

Luisa: It will disappear, it will vanish.
Like this . . . that way, remember how this Hiaki never surrendered,
then remember, remember everyone
spoke for them, they say, these Mexicans . . .
because [the Hiaki] never, even like the Mexicans owed
the [American] government for ammunition, they say.
But this, the Mexican government owes a lot, this one . . .

Maria: A lot . . .

Luisa: . . . ammunition, they owed a lot to the gringos, they say.
And this one, the Hiaki, who is very poor,
does not owe them anything,
owes nothing to anyone,
does not get anything like ammunition, they say,
does not, not take anything from anywhere [but]
has always sustained himself, it has been said and heard . . .
today, they say, even the Mexicans say this,
because they [the Hiaki] never surrendered, they say.

Maria: Hmm.

Luisa: . . . ti hiia.

Maria: I'ansu kia kaa, kaa tu'isi maachi.

Luisa: Heewi. I'an intok hunulevena bwan. Kaa tu'i.

Maria: Intok mismo uu yoi, ori politika,
politikatamake hunuen am hippue, ume yoemem.

Luisa: Heewi.

Maria: Kia . . . entre ellos mismos, pos emo omta.
I'an chea divisionim chikti im aayuk.

Luisa: Heewi.

Maria: Ta hunuu yoi hunuka weetua.
Kaa geerapo intok pos hunuen armammak
kaachin am kova'amachi.
Kaachin am ya'ak. Ta politikapo veha . . .

Luisa: Heewi. I'an veha inien hiia . . . hunuen hiuwa.

Maria: Hunuen veha am konkistaroane
intok hunumun vicha weeye.

Luisa: Kia, kia lau lauti, tu'uwampo,
veha hunuen am weiya.

Maria: Heewi. De otra manera no se puede hacer.
A ver si . . .

Luisa: Hm, hmm.
Kia hiva ameu aa haiwa.

Maria: Hm, hmm. "Para que, vempo mismo nau omteka,
nau nahsuaka, itepo veha aman
kiimuka veha te vensiaroane."

Luisa: Vempo veha bwiamak tawane.

Maria: Ah, pos haivu . . .

Maria: Hmm.

Luisa: ... they say.

Maria: Now it is just not, not looking good.

Luisa: Yes. And now it is like that, well. Not good.

Maria: And it is the same Mexican, the politics, with the politics they are like this, the Hiakis.

Luisa: Yes.

Maria: Just ... even among themselves, well, they do not get along. Now there is even division among them.

Luisa: Yes.

Maria: But those Mexicans are doing that.
Not in war and, well, with arms
they were not able to defeat them.
They did nothing to them. But then with politics ...

Luisa: Yes. Now they say this ... they are saying this.

Maria: That is how they are going to defeat them
and this is the way it is headed.

Luisa: Just, just slow, slowly, in good faith,
then, this is how they are leading them.

Maria: Yes. They were not able to [conquer] them any other way.
We will see ...

Luisa: Hmm, hmm.
They [Mexicans] just keep looking for it.

Maria: Hm, hmm. "So that they will be fighting among themselves,
they will fight among themselves, then we [Mexicans]
will go in and conquer them."

Luisa: They will then keep the [Hiaki's] land.

Maria: Ah, well, already ...

Luisa: Hunuen . . .

Maria: . . . haivu hunuen weye.

Luisa: Heewi, hunuen weye.

Maria: Kia vemposu bwiam nu'eka
ama eecha.

Luisa: Bwebwekam, solarim chikti bwebwekam nu'e.

Maria: Kia uhyoisi ho'ak.

Luisa: Heewi.

Maria: Uu Hiaki intok kia hiva venasi . . .

Luisa: Kaita. Hiaki intok kia hiva venasi poloove.
Ya ves que im sosiom, yu'in tomita mavveta, likidaroawa intok
kaita karim haksa tutu'im hooa huni'i, ho.
Lo que es la vida, heewi?

Maria: Hmm. Ta pos humak wate hunuen allea, hewi?
Kaa uka . . . kaa hunuka kostumraroakai kechia.

Luisa: Um, um.

Maria: Bweere karim asi . . .

Luisa: Kaa aa waata.

Maria: . . . elektrisidad, o.

Luisa: Hm.

Maria: Kaa aa waata.

Luisa: Hmm . . . Pos ite kaita . . . ite tua poovem.
Pa qué me voy a decir que nee tomine.
Kaita. Kia hunum ili ranchopo tekipanoa
intok hunum hiva ili pensionaroari.
Hunaka hiva cada dia primeropo nee aa nu'e.
Ta kaa sosiom si'ime hunume ili uusim.
I'an hunamesan nee sosio kima'a'ii'aakai,

MEXICANS, DEPORTEES, AND DIVISIONS AMONG HIAKIS

Luisa: That way . . .

Maria: It is already going that way.

Luisa: Yes, it is going that way.

Maria: [Instead,] it is they [the Mexicans] who are taking over the lands and planting them.

Luisa: Wide plots of land, and they are buying them.

Maria: They live in very nice houses.

Luisa: Yes.

Maria: And the Hiaki is just the same way . . .

Luisa: Nothing. And the Hiaki is still just as poor as ever.
You see how the society members, they receive a lot of money, their liquidation of funds, and
they do not even build good houses, see.
It is how life is, yes?

Maria: Hmm. But maybe some are happy that way, yes?
They are not . . . are not accustomed to it also.

Luisa: Um, um.

Maria: That way, the big houses . . .

Luisa: They do not want them.

Maria: . . . or electricity.

Luisa: Hm.

Maria: They do not want it.

Luisa: Hmm . . . Well, nothing . . . we are really poor.
Why should I say that we have money.
Nothing. We just work on that ranch
and receive a small pension.
That is all on the first [of the month].
They are not society members, those little children.
Now I would like to have them enter the societies,

hunuavetchi'ivo chukti nee inim nah weene, ho.
Kaa haksa yoko hakwo kia haksa
wikichim venasi cha'asasakame to'omukvaekai.
"Haksa bwiam lelevelaim huni makwak
hunama ho'aka hunama emo aniane,"
ti in hiavetchi'ivo veha.
Nee hunum nah weye o'oven, kechia.

Maria: Pues sí.

Luisa: Hunumevetchi'ivo huni'i.

Maria: Haveesa intok am nokriane?

Luisa: Heewi. Hunuen chukti nee im nah weye.
Intok hunaa ili uusi hunumun katekamtavetchi'ivo.
Si mekka te ho'ak.
Im te kaita solaarta hippue hoarapo.

The Charcoal Contract (Jose Juan Buitimea)

Jose Juan Buitimea recounts how, after some leadership changes, a governor whom he had favored was finally appointed. However, things did not work out as he had imagined. A Mexican charcoal maker named Castillo and the prayer leader Locario Wahu tried to push forward a deal wherein all the mesquite would be cut down to make charcoal for ten thousand pesos. They went to the governor with this offer, and the governor said he couldn't sign the contract without speaking to all those who lived in the area and getting their permission. The news of the plan thus came out, and Castillo and Locario were stymied, since the people did not want the work to go forward. However, they remained in positions of influence

J.J.: . . . veha Chiika Machil veha ta'abwik a'awak.
Hunak veha uka aa moonewata ama kovanao ya'atevok,
Wero Leon teame.
Hunama naatek intuchi naasontuk.

MEXICANS, DEPORTEES, AND DIVISIONS AMONG HIAKIS 481

> that is why I come here, see.
> So that tomorrow or later, they will not be aimlessly
> flying around like birds, after I die.
> "If they were given even half a hectare of land
> they could live there and support themselves,"
> is what I say, then.
> I am walking around here nonetheless, also.

Maria: Well, yes.

Luisa: Even for them.

Maria: And who else is going to speak for them?

Luisa: Yes. It is for that reason that I am walking around here.
And for that little child who is over there.
We live very far.
We do not have a home here.

---

and power, and the work looked like it would proceed, until Jose Juan's son, who had been to school and worked in agriculture in Mexico City, came back. Although Jose Juan did not understand everything that was said in the subsequent meeting, since it was in Spanish, the end result was that the general of the Vikam Swiichi barracks was ousted and another colonel appointed. However, the new colonel was also in accord with Locario, and so then Jose Juan's son demanded that a commission be sent from Mexico City. The commission arrived, and the eight villages were united once more, after having been divided. Jose Juan places the blame on Castillo and the governor, who had an agreement with the Mexicans, the commissioner, and the general.

J.J.: . . . Then Chiika Maachil asked for a different one.
Then she had her son-in-law appointed governor,
whose name was Güero León.
From then on it again began to go bad.

> Hunaa kovanaopo aa mavetaka veha
> uka intuchi uka itom yeu himaatevokamta intuchi
> hunaka intok pueblo yoo ya'ak.
> Pues te kaachin ama anmachi.
> Ahta i'an veha wai wasuktiachi, wai wasuktiat veha
> uu yoeme veha vempo mismo ket hiva hiva, veha ori
> Principalta hiovekavenasi,
> vempo mismo hioveka tanto itotana wemta veha
> kovanao ya'ak.

Chema Tosaria: Ahh...

J.J.: Hunama, veha uu, uu tomi,
ori uka hu'upata veha
uu yoi carboneo, heewi...

Chema: Heewi...

J.J.: Uka hu'upata hetochivela me'evaeka veha
uu, uu i'an uu, Castillo intok Locario maehto,
wahu veha uka, uka contratota aa firmaroaii'aa
dieh milta au nanateho uu yori intok
vempo uu i'an uu Locario intok uu secretario
aman nau sahaka veha,
"Dieh milta ee makva'awa aa firmaroa inika contratota."
"Inika nee kaa aa firmaroane.[8]
Necesito de que nee
woh naiki pueblota, uka pueblota yumaisi,
uka im ho'akamta amak etehok.
Si hunaka nee lisensia makak
hunak hu'ubwa nee enchim aa firmaroriane achaim."
Iiyilen am yoopnak.
Iiyilen au aa, au aa yoopnak, tia.
Huntuan, hunum veha yeu machiak
veha uu, uu veha uu gente veha aa kecha'ii'aa,
wa'a uka wa'a uka hunaka...

Chema: Tekilta.

---

8. This was the response from the governor as reported by Mr. Jose Juan.

He accepted the governorship and then
he again appointed the one that we had removed from office
as the mayor of the pueblo.
Well, we did not know what to do.
Finally, last year, last year,
the men, they made a mistake just like, just, um,
Lead Prayer Leader had made a mistake,
they, the person whom we favored,
they made him governor.

Chema Tosaria: Ahh . . .

J.J.: There, then the money,
um, then, the mesquite,
the Mexican charcoal burner, yes . . .

Chema: Yes.

J.J.: He wanted to chop down all the mesquite,
he, now, Castillo and Locario Wahu, the prayer leader,
they wanted him [the governor] to sign
the contract for ten thousand pesos that the Mexican offered to them,
they, Locario and the secretary,
went together [to see the governor] and said,
"You will receive the ten thousand if you sign this contract."
"I will not sign this," [said the governor].
"It is necessary for me [to speak]
to all eight pueblos, to the whole people,
to speak to all of those who live here.
If they give me permission,
then I will sign it, fathers."
This is how he answered them [Locario and the secretary].
This is how he, how he answered, they said.
Therefore, that is how it came out
the people wanted it stopped,
that, that . . .

Chema: The work.

J.J.: Tekilta.

Chema: Carbonerata ...

J.J.: Heewi.
Hunumsam veha uu veha uka si'imeta vem,
vem au teuwaka'u pueblota vichapo veha,
ya'ura, tropata vichapo
aa teuwak.
Uu tropa intok pues aa ivaktak uka kovanaota,
vempoim vetana kovanaota.
Entonces ume atala yu'utevok.
Pues hiva, hiva huni kaachin am ya'amachi,
pos im naawak uu pueblo yoowe.
Ahta haksa weeka veha uu ian uu in uusi
ori, ori hunen estudiaroaka veha yepsaka veha
uka generalta ama yeu veeptevok.
Vat uka generalta yeu veevak
um swiitchipo estakamento hippuemta.

Chema: Heewi. Oh oh oh.

J.J.: Intuchi senu coronel intuchi yepsak.
Hiva hunaka lutu'uriata au toosiikan uu general.
Entonces uu itotana weeme
uka leyta huni kaa hikhaka,
uka Huan Kastiota lutu'uria weiya kechia.

Chema: Ketchia?

J.J.: Hunaka huni mekka veptevok.
Pues uu veha como aman Mehikou tekipanoan, heewi, in uusi,
ori ket hiva hunuka ian in emou etehokau
agradismopo hunaman hakun tekipanoan.
Pues uka yoi generalta hunama juntapo si aa vuisuk.[9]
Pues haisa humak, pos vempo yoi noka heewi,
waa escuelala.

---

9. *Si aa vuisuk*: get mad, bark at.

J.J.: The work.

Chema: The charcoal making . . .

J.J.: Yes.
That is when everything was said to them,
in front of all the villagers,
in front of the tribal authorities and the custom authority,[10]
it was said.
The custom authority then embraced [accepted] the governor,
from their side, the governor.
That is how the others [Locario and the secretary] were rejected.
Well, they still were not able to do anything to them,
since the home of the mayor of the village is here.
Until one day, my son,
having studied, arrived
and then he ousted the general.
First he had the general kicked out,
the one in charge of the Vikam Swiichi barracks.

Chema: Yes. Oh, oh, oh.

J.J.: Then another colonel arrived.
He still carried the same truths of the general.
Then the one who we thought was on our side
did not listen to the governor,
he still had the same truths as Juan Castillo.

Chema: Also?

J.J.: He even had him chased away.
Since he had worked in Mexico City, yes, my son,
the one I spoke with you about,
he worked there in agriculture.
Well, there at a meeting, he chewed out the Mexican general.
I really do not know, since he spoke in Spanish,
since he had gone to school.

---

10. This refers to the leaders (*ya'ura*) of the *kohtumbre*, the ceremonial society that serves and organizes the processions during Lent.

Chema: Heewi.

J.J.: Uu waa hitaa palabram aa teuwa'u,
pos ite kaa amet hu'unea,
hitasa au tewa'u uka usita.
Hunak kee huuven.
Hoo, pues hunuka utteata am u'uraka
veha plebesito intok a'awak Mehikowi.
Uu plebesito veha yepsak.
Pues te am koovak.
I'an veha kia yanti yehtelatavena.

Chema: Ah, ah ili pasiwaroala.

J.J.: Ili pasiwaroala.
I'an veha uu woh naiki pueblo
uka Pota pueblota chikti atala yu'ulatukan.[11]
I'an uu Huan Kastillo intok uka Rahuta.
Uu Veene intok Wiivis
ume hikattana pueblommak lutu'uriakan.
Ite intok Pota intok Rahutamake.
I'an veha uu woh naiki pueblo veha nau yaaha.

Chema: I'an veha nau eteho.

J.J.: Nau eteho haptek.

Chema: I'an veha wepul lutu'uriapo aa yechak uka . . .

J.J.: Heewi.

Chema: . . . woh naiki pueplo.

J.J.: Heewi, I'an uu kovanao.

Chema: I'an uu Vikampo kovanao?

J.J.: Uu Vikampo kovanao.
I'an ume yoimmak luturiakan iibwan uu gobierno, uu Kastio, generaltamake intok comisaariommake.
Hunume veha yoimak iibwan itou torokoyoimtuk.

---

11. *Yulataka*: push something or someone back, leave out.

Chema: Yes.

J.J.: Those words that he spoke,
well, we did not understand them,
what the boy said to him.
At that time he was not yet married.
See, he took away their authority
and sent word to Mexico City asking for a commission.
The commission then arrived.
So we won them over.
Now it seems that things have quieted down.

Chema: Uh huh, things have quieted down a little.

J.J.: Quieted down a little.
The eight pueblos had
pushed the pueblo of Potam aside.
And Juan Castillo the village of Rahum.
The pueblos of Veene and Wiivis
had made agreements with the pueblos to the north.
And we were united with Potam and Rahum.
And now the eight pueblos are meeting once again.

Chema: And now they are speaking to each other once again.

J.J.: They are speaking to one another again.

Chema: And now they share one truth . . .

J.J.: Yes.

Chema: . . . the eight pueblos.

J.J.: The one who is governor now.

Chema: The one who is now governor in Vikam?

J.J.: The governor of Vikam.
The governor and Castillo had an agreement with the Mexicans,
with the general and with the commissioner.
They were the traitors against us.

The Flies That Came Out of Boxes Thrown from Planes (Jose Juan Buitimea and Chema Tosaria)

Maria asked Chema Tosaria and Jose Juan Buitimea to describe an event where boxes of flies were dropped from a plane. She had heard that the flies had apparently bitten people and animals and caused sickness and death. Chema and Jose Juan initially describe an event in which the Hiakis' livestock were killed by some poisoned corn that had been spread along the banks of the canals. Luckily the people did not eat the corn, because they were not hungry at that time. They also remembered

Chema: ... para matar a los animales. Vacas o caballos.

J.J.: Hunuu ala ama yeu siika ori.
Chiivam, wakasim, kavaim, chikti kokok.

Maria: Uu gentesu?

J.J.: Ume yoeme kaa, kaa kokok porque
pos kaa tua tevaurek. Ta tevauretek humak . . . [*inaudible*]
Ori, vachita, tiikommak kuraikai
hunu'u, hunu'u hita pahtituawaka
canalimmak bwikola bwan wootawak.
Chiivam, chu'um, wakasim, intok
ume wakasim, ili vachita posoi ya'aritaka veha
pos kaa tua posoi ya'ari heewi, kia nau kuuti,
pos im aa bwa'aka.

Chema: Kia napovakta ya'arita . . . [*inaudible*].

Maria: Heewi.
Ta katin ili kahampo
aeroplan ha'ani, aman ori, weaman tea.
Hunak intok ili kaham intok ama kom wootan tea.
Hunama intok ili seevo'im, hita ama yeu sahak.

J.J.: Ah heewi, bweere seevoi'm ama kom wootawak.
Huname ha'ani ume, ume i'an Sonorapo seevo'im vea suua tea,

boxes of flies being distributed by plane; these were large-bodied flies but not the more commonly known large green flies. The flies were apparently supposed to be a measure to control some other kind of fly that had always lived in the area and that damaged crops. There were serious problems when people and animals were bitten by the new flies. People would develop significant sores from scratching; Jose Juan himself was affected. Many animals, including hundreds of goats, as well as pigs and horses, were killed. It was said that the Mexicans were responsible, and Jose Juan suggests that someone should collect one of the boxes and have it tested in Mexico City.

Chema: To kill the animals, cows or horses.

J.J.: That did take place there.
The goats, cows, horses died.

Maria: How about the people?

J.J.: The people did not die because
they did not go too hungry. Had they gone hungry . . . [*inaudible*]
They mixed the corn with wheat
and it was poisoned
and spilled along the banks of the canals.
The goats, dogs, cows, and
the cows, the little corn that was made into a soup,
well, maybe not really a soup, yes, but a mixture,
well, they ate it.

Chema: They had made it into a soup . . . [*inaudible*]

Maria: Yes.
But remember, small boxes
were tossed out of a single-engine plane flying around there.
And these small boxes were being tossed out of the small plane.
And from those boxes, some flies or something came out of them.

J.J.: Ah yes, some big flies were dropped there.
Those Sonoran flies [dropped from the plane], then, kill, they say,

am bwabwa'e tea, ti hiuwa.
Bweere ume sevo'im ama kom wootawame.
Ta bweere.

Chema: Hunue hissoa.

Maria: Huname veha uka gente ama ... [*inaudible*]

J.J.: E'e, uka, uka sevo'ita ama yu hoakamta,
hunaka ti im susua tea.
Hunuen hiupo ama wootawak.

Chema: Hunuen hiupo ama wootawak.

J.J.: Nee ama am teula wahpo.
Haksa ama kopanla.
Kia kuuti ama yeu sahak ume seevo'im.
Ta bweere ume siari seevo'imvena ta kaa sisiari.

Maria: Hitasa intok ori hunuen uka genteta, am orek,
am huhako, hunaa, o esa persona veha ori,
si elesikia veha aet vootene tea,
hunuen ume sa'awam chikti aet yeu katne.
Hunume chikti te hikkaha.

Chema: Am ... [*inaudible*]

Maria: Heewi.

Chema: ... Dañota ya'avaevetchi'ivo ... personata, gente [*inaudible*] ...

Maria: Intok ume animalim chikti,
huname intok kia haisa bwibwichiane tea [*inaudible*]
... ume sevo'im.

J.J.: Pues, ama huni kia hunama luula weye uu i'an,
uu enchim aa hu'uneiya'apo amani.
Pues si'ime he'ela ume yoeme, ori, kia ori,
uu takaachi bwan emo woksasakane,
bwan, ori, kia, ori woo'o haisa katin yoemta bwa'ane?
Hunama au woktaitek sa'awitune bwan.

they eat them, it is said.
They are big, the flies that were tossed out.
But they are big.

Chema: They kill with that.

Maria: Those, the people there . . . [*inaudible*]

J.J.: No, the flies that have always existed there,
those are the ones they [the large flies] kill, it is said.
It was for that reason that those large flies were thrown there.

Chema: It is said that for that reason those large flies were thrown there.

J.J.: I have found them in my fields.
They were resting there.
When they flew out, the flies made a loud buzzing sound.
They are big like the green flies, but they are not green.

Maria: And what, um, what did they do to the people,
when they stung them, that, or that person, then, um,
would feel very itchy all over the body,
in that way later they would have open sores all over their body.
We heard about that also.

Chema: Them . . . [*inaudible*]

Maria: Yes.

Chema: . . . To create injuries for the people . . . a person, people [*inaudible*] . . .

Maria: And the animals that were bitten,
and those just had maggots on their bodies, they say . . . [*inaudible*]
. . . the flies.

J.J.: Well, perhaps it is even true what you say, now,
what you know about it there.
Since most of the people, um, just, um,
all over their bodies they were scratching themselves,
well, um, just, um, you know when a mosquito bites a person?
When one starts to scratch there, you get sores, well.

Chema: Heewi.

J.J.: Si'ime, kaave ve'ekai.
Ahta nee huni hunain, hunain tawala.
I'ansan nee im veha uu ori,
in mara veha hittoam nee nu'uriak.

Maria: Ta empo kaa medicotau noitek?

J.J.: E'e. Kaa nee medikotau noitek.

Chema: Hunuka hippue hunume sevo'im.

J.J.: Si elesikine bwan, kia hiva huni wokmachine.

Chema: Heewi. Hivatua, pos . . .

J.J.: Si'ime he'ela hunuen aulam pocho'oku ho'akame.

Chema: Tukaapo hak rehteme.

J.J.: Heewi.

Chema: Tukaapo hak rehteme hunuen am sisse ume animalim.

J.J.: Hunama ni'ine . . . sisse.

Chema: Mmm-hmm. Mmm, mmm . . .
. . . [*lengthy inaudible comment*] . . .

J.J.: Hunama kavaim, chiivam. Si'imem suak.
Kia sesenu partidam lu'utek ume chiivam.

Chema: Chiivam.

J.J.: Heewi, sisientomtaka kokok.
Koowim, vu'u animalrata suak hunume'e.

Chema: Hmmm.

Maria: Ta uu yoi hunuka ya'ak?

J.J.: Yoi iibwan hunuka ya'ak.

Chema: Tua huevena ama aayuk.

Maria: Hunuka si'imek hiohte'ea'n ume ian sakame.

Chema: Yes.

J.J.: Everybody, no one was left out.
Even I was that way, affected that way.
Now then, I here, then, the, um,
my daughter, then, bought some medicines for me.

Maria: You did not go to a doctor?

J.J.: I did not go to a doctor.

Chema: That is what those flies do to one.

J.J.: It was very itchy, well, one just always felt like scratching.

Chema: Yes. I am sure, well . . .

J.J.: Most everybody who lives in the woods has been affected that way.

Chema: Those who walk around at night.

J.J.: Yes.

Chema: Those who walk around at night, the bugs pee on them.

J.J.: There they fly . . . pee.

Chema: Mmm hmmm. Mmm, mmm . . .
. . . [*lengthy inaudible comment*] . . .

J.J.: There they killed the horses, goats. They killed everything.
They killed groups of goats.

Chema: Goats.

J.J.: Yes, hundreds of them died.
Pigs, they killed a lot of other animals.

Chema: Hmmm.

Maria: But it was the Mexicans who did that?

J.J.: Yes, it was the Mexicans who did that . . .

Chema: There is so much there.

Maria: Those who are leaving should document all that.

Heewi. Si'imek.

J.J.: Hunuka ... como para comprobante ori una ...
[cajita] partida aunque sea ...

Maria: Heewi, una cajita.

J.J.: Principal ... hunuka wootita ...
Iani ... pudiera pasar ...

Maria: Heewi ... eso es lo que nos están haciendo.

J.J.: ... [*inaudible*] ... aa tovoktane, aa eriane, examinaroatevone, Mehikowi.

Yes. Everything.

J.J.: That ... as proof of the ... um, a [box], even a group at least ...

Maria: Yes, a box.

J.J.: From the beginning ... that which was thrown there ... Now ... it could come to pass ...

Maria: Yes ... that is what they are doing to us.

J.J.: ... [*inaudible*] ... they should pick it[12] up and have it examined, in Mexico [City].

---

12. One of the boxes full of flies that was thrown out of the plane.

CHAPTER 9

THE CONTEMPORARY SITUATION

Peo Maachil and the Big Black Snake (Luisa)

Luisa and Maria discuss the way the elders used to pass on knowledge to children, giving them predictions of how the future would unfold. Luisa mentions an older prayer leader, Peo Maachil, as an example. He would speak to the gathered children about the road that would be laid down along the railway, calling it "the big black snake," and tell them how the road would be deadly for many people. And sure enough, many Hiakis and even many Mexicans have since died on that road.

Luisa: Intok hakwo
inime yo'owe hunuen itom hoarika
itommak e'etehon.
Havi Peo Maachil, maehto, temahti moll,
hunuen hiune, mamai Remeetrio.
"Eme'e," ti hiia. "Eme'e aa vitne," ti hiia.
"Eme'esu ketuni uusim," ti hiia.
"Intok wame'e enchim uusim,
huname si'ime aa vitne," ti hiia.
"Itepo te kaita emomak vitne," ti hiia.
"Intok kia iiyika kareterata vo'otemta.
Bwe'u chukui vaakot inim wam vo'otene, tea.
Hunaa veha huevena henteta bwa'ane tea."
Ilen chukti itou aa teuwak.
Pos amma'ali hiia.
I'an veha huevena hente ama koko . . . hunum kareteerapo.

Maria: Heewi.

Luisa: . . . huevena hente.

Maria: Heewi.

Luisa: I'an veha nee hunuau si'imekuu waate, hunuen aa hiiau.
"Hunu'u veha si'ime, hunu'u bwe'u vaakot chukuika veha
kia lautipo inim wam vo'otene," ti hiia.
"Kia senu repiktiapo," ti hiia.
"Hunak veha si'ime veha vato'orata bwa'ane, kaa ilikik," ti hiia.
Pos i'an veha haivu huevenak bwa'e hunu'u kareteera.
Huevenaka aet koko,
kia yoimtaka huni'i. Yoeme.

Maria: Hunuka si'imek haivu aa hu'uneiyan, hewi?

Luisa: Heewi. Si'imeta im hu'uneiyak,
kia kee, kee aa vo'oteneu.
Ta si'imeta haivu itou e'etehon.

Luisa: And a long time ago,
 these elders would make us sit down
 and would talk with us.
 Older maternal uncle Pete Scorpion, prayer leader, church elder,
 would say to Mom's younger brother Demetrio,
 "You-all," he said. "You-all will see it," he said.
 "You-all are still children," he said.
 "And those, your children,
 all of them will see it," he said.
 "We shall not see anything with you," he said.
 "And just this road that will be laid here.
 A big, black snake will lie through here, it is said.
 That one will eat many people."
 This way, also, it was told to us.
 Well, they spoke the truth.
 Now many people have died there . . . on that road.

Maria: Yes.

Luisa: . . . many people.

Maria: Yes.

Luisa: Now, then, I remember all that, when he said that.
 "That, then, that big snake, a black one, then
 just will quickly lay down through here," he said.
 "In just one wink of an eye," he said.
 "Then it will eat all the baptized ones, not a few," he said.
 Well, now it is eating a lot, that road.
 Many have died on it,
 even Mexicans. Hiakis.

Maria: All that, everyone already knew it, yes?

Luisa: Yes. They knew everything,
 just before, before it was laid down.
 But everything had already been told to us.

The Highway, the Railroad, and Broken Promises (Andres)

Andres describes how his battalion was made to repair the highway, and how they were told that houses would also be built for the Hiakis who served, but only seven houses were ever built. The highway had been

---

Andres: Pues hunuen, hunuen te aayuk itepo.
    Hunuen veha te a'avo sahak.
    Im yahaka te veha im, im hiva hooka.
    Ika intok im kareteerata vo'okamta,
    hunuka intok te si'imeta tu'utetuawak.
    Veha karim ama ya'ariava'awa tea.
    Ta hita huni kaita te ya'ariawak.
    Aman hakun hiva siete karim,
    hunum lu'utek, lu'utek.

Maria: Ume, uu viiya intok hiva ama vo'oka?

Andres: Ii hiva ama vo'oka, hakwo naateka.

Maria: Hakwo naatekai.

Andres: Heewi, vinwatuk naatekai.
    Ume treenim intok i'an rehteme
    kaitaikan hunak, ala.

Maria: Oo.

Andres: I'an itom im hoksu veha yeu machiak hunume treenim.
    Vaporea rehteme hiva.

Maria: Heewi.

Andres: Hunuen ori, orea rehtekan katinia, tatapootea rehten.
    Chea vatnaatakai intok
    ume treenim bwee'ek soto'ekan, hewi?
    Ta huname intok kutammea rehten.

Maria: Kutammea, heewi?

built more recently, but the railroad had always been there, all the way back to the time of the fighting, although the modern diesel trains that run on it are new. Before those newer trains came, Andres remembers the coal-burning trains, and, before that, wood-burning trains with a large funnel on top.

Andres: Well that's, that's what we did, us.
    That, then, is how we came over here.
    Arriving here, we, then, here, we have always been.
    And this here highway lying there,
    and, that one, we were made to repair all of it.
    Then we would have some houses made, they said.
    But even so, nothing was ever made for us.
    Over there somewhere only seven houses were made,
    and that is where it ended, ended.

Maria: And those, the railroad was always there?

Andres: This was always there, starting a long time ago.

Maria: For a long time.

Andres: Yes, starting a very long time ago.
    And the trains traveling now,
    they did not exist then, for sure.

Maria: Oh.

Andres: Now that we are here, then, those trains showed up.
    Only the steam trains ran.

Maria: Yes.

Andres: That way, with, remember, with coal they ran.
    And a very long time ago
    the trains had a big pot on top of them, yes?
    But those used wood for fuel.

Maria: With wood, yes?

Andres: Heewi.

Luisa: Siari kutam.

Andres: Siari kutammea rerehten chea vatnaatakai.

Luisa: Porque kuta karboonim hunume'e.

Maria: Hm, hmm. Enchi kaa yo'owe naateka entonces ama, ama vo'okan hunu'u?

Andres: Ii haivu vo'okan uu riel voo'o.

Luisa: Haivu.

Andres: Ii haivu aukan iibwan.

Luisa: Pos si nahsua hapteak haivu im vo'okan.

Andres: Haivu vo'oka uu'u.

Luisa: Nahsuawau.

FIGURE 29 Track-laying camp, Santa Cruz Canyon. Arizona Historical Society, PC 180, Norman Wallace Photographs, box 42, album #1, page 49, B.

Andres: Yes.

Luisa: Green wood.

Andres: They were operated with green wood a very long time ago.

Luisa: Because they were charcoal, those.

Maria: Hm, hmm. Beginning when you were not old, then there, that one was lying there?

Andres: This was already lying there, the railroad.

Luisa: Already.

Andres: This was already there, well.

Luisa: Well, when the fighting started, it was already lying there.

Andres: It was already lying there, that one.

Luisa: During the fighting.

Andres Gets a Pension (Andres)

Maria has been asking Andres about his birthdate, so he and Luisa find his military ID card. This leads to a discussion of how pensions are distributed to veteran soldiers. This particular card was made when he re-

---

Maria: Inii veha yoi sontaommak weamatek veha ika makna?

Andres: Heewi. Ika tarheetata makna.
　　　　　Bwe im te kia ori retiraroarika,
　　　　　aa ya'ariawak ime'e.

Luisa: Pension.

Andres: Pensionariari inepo.
　　　　　Kaita ama hiia imi'i. Kia kaita . . .

Luisa: Apoko uka rehistrota empo kaa hippue?

Andres: Hunaa chea aman tawala.
　　　　　Haivu im katek ime'e.

[. . .]

Luisa: Ime si'ime machime veha tommi'u.

Andres: Bwe ii kaa ama . . .
　　　　　ii chea nee ae revistavae matchuko.

Luisa: Bweta hiva aa vitne.

Maria: Hitaa intok revista?

Andres: Bwe revistane itepo retiraroarim, sontaom.

Voice in background: Hunume seyaaroariana.

Andres: Hunum kaa seyaaroari, ho.
　　　　　Ii, ii huni ket seyaaroana imi'i amapo.

Voice in background: Ime ili kuadrompo veha seyom hoana ineni.

tired, and it, together with another card, must be presented for review in Ciudad Obregón every four months in order for him to continue receiving his pension. If a card is not presented for review on time, it expires, and no pension is issued until a new card is made. Andres and Luisa will be taking Andres's card to Ciudad Obregón soon.

Maria: This, then, is given when you are a Mexican soldier?

Andres: Yes. This card is given to you.
Well, here, we just, just were photographed,
it was made for us, these.

Luisa: Pension.

Andres: I am retired.
There is nothing heard here. Just nothing . . .

Luisa: Perhaps you do not have the registry?

Andres: That one stayed over there.
These are already here.

[. . .]

Luisa: All those like these, then, receive some money.

Andres: Well, there, this one does not . . .
I am going for review with this [the card], day after tomorrow.

Luisa: But they will still see it.

Maria: And what is the review?

Andres: Well, we go for review, we retired ones, soldiers.

Voice in background: Those [cards] will be stamped.

Andres: It is stamped there, see.
This, this will also be stamped on the back.

Voice in background: These little squares will then be stamped like this.

Andres: Heewi.

Maria: Hunuen veha kia revistata ya'awak veha
ori komo, eme aman ori sentavom mamakwa o . . .

Andres: Kada kinse diapo.

Luisa: Kada vusam metpo, hewi?
Cada seis meses pasan revista como que
si ketuni sontaom . . .

Andres: Naiki metpo te revista.

Luisa: . . . filapo rehtemevenasi.
Porque . . . hunuen veha im veha,
kaa, kaa revistak,
hunuat veeki ta'apo kaa revistak,
revistapo faltaroak
intuchi vemelasi aa ya'atevone.
Hunak veha kaa tomiune.

Andres: Haivu kaa tomiune.

Luisa: Haivu kaa tomiune.

Andres: Asta uchi aa ya'ariawateko.

Luisa: Haivu kaa tomi yo'one
kaa revistako.

Maria: Oo. Hunuen veha tiene kee aman kumpliaroane.

Luisa: Heewi.

Andres: Heewi.

Maria: Pensionaroana.

Luisa: Hmm. Hunuen weye.

Andres: Hunum woika ve'e bwan, ketunia.
Kialikun nee aa weiya.

Andres: Yes.

Maria: That way, then, when the review is done, then the, like, you all will be given money over there or . . .

Andres: Every fifteen days.

Luisa: Every six months, yes?
Every six months they are reviewed as if they were still soldiers . . .

Andres: Every four months we are reviewed.

Luisa: . . . as if they were still in the ranks.
Because . . . that way then, here then,
[if they are] not, not reviewed,
for those many days that they are not reviewed,
when the review is needed,
they will have to have it [the card] renewed again.
[Until] then, they will not receive any money.

Andres: Already they will not receive any money.

Luisa: Already they will not receive any money.

Andres: Until it is made again.

Luisa: Already they will not receive any money if they are not reviewed.

Maria: Oh. That way, then, they have to go there and accomplish it.

Luisa: Yes.

Andres: Yes.

Maria: They will receive the pension.

Luisa: Hmm. That is how it goes.

Andres: There, two are needed, well, still.
That is why I take it.

>   Aa weiya'ane empo hunuka'a,
>   bwe'uk moraalek empo.

Maria: Ovregonneu eme . . . ?

Luisa: Ovregonnewi.

Tata Va'am (Hot Water) and Papalote (Luisa and Andres)

Andres and Luisa talk about the landmark village called Hot Water close to their ranch. They explain that there is a warm spring there that you can still bathe in even when it's cold. The water always has steam and is very clear. It's a little way off from their place and wouldn't take long to get to if the road was good, but unfortunately the road is quite bad, eroded into gullies. They live eleven kilometers farther on, at a ranch called Papalote de Arriba (Windmill Above). It's challenging to get to their place, and

---

Luisa: . . . hiva hunuen ama.
    Kialikun Tata Va'am tea.
    Huname veha hiva suka va'am.
    Yoi hitam huni ama u'uva.
    Seveak huni hiva amea u'uvane bwan.
    Kaa sesevea bwan, suka.

Maria: Kaa sesevea?

Luisa: Heewi, kia haawa hiva.
    Intok si kalahko, kia nah mamachine.

Maria: Hittoam tea, huname'e?

Luisa: Heewi. Hunum Tataa Va'ampo,
    ama kimuwa'apo, puetapo hunum.

Maria: Im enchimmeu kaa mekka?

You will take it, that one,
you have a big bag.[1]

Maria: To Obregón you-all . . . ?

Luisa: To Obregón.

---

best to go with someone who knows the way. Luisa and Andres disagree about whether Reyno knows the way there; Luisa describes a time when they hosted Reyno, Chema, and Hilario, during the time when Reyno was governor and a large group of governors came in three buses. They made tortillas for everyone, which were eaten with gusto. Some of Andres's children also live in the area, one at Papalote and others at Hot Water. When something is going on at Hot Water, they are picked up to go to the meeting there. But when the children are home, things get noisy.

Luisa: . . . always that way there.
That is why they call it Hot Water, they say.
Those waters, then, are always warm.
Even the Mexican things bathe there.
Even when it is cold, you still bathe with it, well.
It does not get cold, well, it is warm.

Maria: It does not get cold?

Luisa: Yes, it is just steam, always.
And it is very clear, you can see through it.

Maria: It is medicine, they say, those [waters]?

Luisa: Yes. There at Hot Water,
at the entrance, at the door, there.

Maria: Here, it is not far from you?

---

1. Here Andres gives the card to Luisa.

Luisa: Ili mekka.

Andres: Ili mekka.

Maria: Ili mekka. Oo.

Andres: Bwe hoapo kaa tua mekka hewi,
ta vo'ota tu'iriako.
I'an intok vo'o kaa tu'i, hakiam.

Luisa: Hunum, hunum am vichaa katwa'apo,
wam vicha itom hoau vichaa katwa'apo.

Maria: Im chea aman?

Andres: Im, heewi. Tun ori,
kasi humak onse kiloometro tua itom hoawi.

Luisa: Tataa Va'ampo wam vicha itom hoau tahti.

Maria: Oo, entonces eme'e chea mekka ho'ak?

Andres & Luisa: Heewi.

Andres: Chea mekka, omot ranchowi.

Luisa: Nattemaitek huni'i, inien veha
"Papaloote de Arriba" hausa taawa.
Pos inen hiuna hunama hoarapo.

Andres: Karo omola vo'oka pos kaivu aman yevihne.

Luisa: Heewi. Aman ta'amtau vicha.
Bweta kompae chea aman ta'a.

Andres: Have?

Luisa: Hunak aman am sahakan, Reyno.

Andres: Hoarau kaa noitila.

Luisa: Bwe, hunu'u chea aman noitila.
Katin aman to'e.
Hunak kovanautakai.

Andres: Nee chea kaa . . . Ta Tataa Va'ampo!

Luisa: A little far.

Andres: A little far.

Maria: A little far. Oh.

Andres: Well, from the house it is not too far, yes,
but when the road is good.
And now the road is not good, the gullies.

Luisa: There, there going that way,
that way, going toward our home.

Maria: Here, farther on?

Andres: Here, yes. So then,
almost, maybe eleven kilometers exactly to our home.

Luisa: From Hot Water that way, close to our home.

Maria: Oh, so then, you-all live farther away?

Andres & Luisa: Yes.

Andres: It is farther away, on another ranch.

Luisa: If you do ask, then this way,
"Windmill Above," where is it?
Well, this is what they call it, our home.

Andres: If the car goes on another road, you will never get there.

Luisa: Yes. You need someone who knows which way it is.
Well, but Compadre knows where it is.

Andres: Who?

Luisa: They went over there then, Reyno.

Andres: He has not visited our home.

Luisa: Well, that one has been there.
Remember, they slept there.
He was the governor then.

Andres: I do not . . . But at Hot Water!

Luisa: E'e, aman hoawi!

Andres: Heitu, nee kaavetukan.
In wain humak nee . . .

Luisa: Kompae Ilaario huni aman aanen.
Katin te si ousi am tahkairiak.
Chema, huni, Chematamak si'ime nau rehten,
uu komandantetamake.

Maria: Hee. Hunuu aman au ta'a ti hiia.

Andres: Hunu'u ala hoau ta'a.

Luisa: Heewi, hunuu aman noitila.

Maria: Heewi, hunuusan
itom aman noitarokan uchi a'avo itom sahako.

Luisa: Heewi. Aman aa weiya'ane.

Andres: Hunuu ala aman ta'a.

Luisa: Aman ta'a. Si'ime aman aanen,
Kompae Ilaario intok kompae, ini
Reyno hunak kovanautakai.
Katin aman to'e,
kompae Hose Hoan.
Hunak ketun nau tu'ika,
si'ime aman aanen.
Katin kia wako'opo ume tahkaim
bwaseme im kia nunu'en.
"Nee ime nu'uvae," ti hiia.
Pos si kia ume yeu weyeme
im kia kaitapo hoan, ume tahkaim.
Tokti te vahi saktiriam am tahkairiak.
Pos si si'ime pueplo
aman aanen, kovanaom.
Vahi kamionimtaka aman rehten hunako.

Maria: Huname intok wate yoeme,
yoemem ili huevena o eme'e
hiva ama ho'ak?

Luisa: No, there at home!

Andres: I do not know, I was not there.
   I was probably here . . .

Luisa: Even compadre Hilario was there.
   Remember, we made a lot of tortillas for them.
   Even Chema. All of them were with Chema,
   with the commandant.

Maria: Oh. That one knows where it is, he says.

Andres: That one does know where our home is.

Luisa: Yes. That one has gone there.

Maria: Yes, that one
   says he is going to take us there when we come here again.

Luisa: Yes. Take him over there.

Andres: That one does know where it is.

Luisa: He knows where it is. They were all there,
   compadre Hilario and compadre, this
   Reyno was governor then.
   Remember, they slept there,
   compadre Jose Juan.
   Then they were still on good terms,
   they were all there.
   Remember the tortillas
   that were cooking on the hot plate, they were just grabbing them.
   "I am going to get this one," they were saying.
   Well, they were so delicious, the ones that were coming out
   here, they just finished them off, the tortillas.
   Totally, we made tortillas from three sacks of flour.
   Well, all the villagers
   were there, governors.
   Three buses were there, perhaps.

Maria: And those other people,
   the people, are there many there or are you-all
   the only ones that live there?

Andres: E'e, kia inen, ili te wepul ranchompo,
wewepulaika hooka. Yu'in useka,
bwan usim hiva ama hipu'une.

Luisa: Yu'in usek. Ma itepo.

Andres: Ma nehpo, ho.
Huevenam ori, in usi veha am uusek.
Huname veha ama hooka.
Amani nemak intok in uusi, wepulaika.
Senu intok hu'ubwa um
weaman ta siika im vicha,
waitana vichaa siika.

Maria: Oo.

Luisa: Hunum hooka, ta Tataa Va'ampo
veha chea ili vu'uka hooka.

Andres: Heewi, chea ili vu'u.

Luisa: Porque hunum oficina katek, Tataa Va'ampo.
Ime veha hitasa weevau
ama watiawatek veha
aet nau totoiwaka.
Hunum nau huhuntate, Tataa Va'ammewi.

Andres: Heewi. Kada ranchompo chea
wepul vakeo hiva katek.
Ta usek veha
yu'in ama am hippu'une, i'anvenasia.

Luisa: Uu, usim ama hok kia sooti hiune.

Andres: Heewi.

Andres: No, just like this, on one ranch,
   one or two are there. With many children,
   well, you will always have the children there.

Luisa: Many children. Like us.

Andres: Like me, see.
   Many, um, my child, my son, he has many children.
   Those, then, are there.
   And over there, with me is my one child.
   And another one was there
   a while ago, but he left to go this way,
   he left to go to the other side [of the tracks].

Maria: Oh.

Luisa: They are there, but at Hot Water
   then, there are a little bit more there.

Andres: Yes, there are a little bit more.

Luisa: Because there is an office there, at Hot Water.
   These, then, when something is going to take place,
   when they are needed there,
   then they are gathered around together there.
   There they have a meeting at Hot Water.

Andres: Yes. At each ranch perhaps
   only one cowboy was there.
   But when one has many children,
   they will have many of them there, like now.

Luisa: The children, when they are there, they will make a lot of noise.

Andres: Yes.

Luisa and Andres's Life at Papalote (Luisa)

Luisa describes how she and Andres came to live in Papalote and what their lives are like now. When Andres was discharged in Vakateeve (Tall Bamboo), he received a pension, which continued when he took a job at Tetaviekti (Rolling Stone) on Gómez's ranch. He worked there for three years, but then the work dried up and they went to Vauwo, near Wasimas (generally written "Las Guásimas" on Mexican maps). Then the people of Pitaya gave him work as a cowboy in the mountains, and they moved to their current home in Papalote, where they have been since the cattle company was created. However, his employers did not pay him bonuses as he expected, even when the cattle were finally sold. He received only a salary of 1,300 pesos, which was paid every fifteen days. He continues to ask the societies for payment for the missed bonuses. Luisa estimates that they have been in Papalote since 1922 but doesn't remember exactly. Andres also receives a pension, 1,400 pesos a month. Living on so little, sometimes they run out of food and have nothing to eat. And sometimes even if they have money, up where they live there is nothing to buy. They have to find a way to go to Ciudad Obregón and purchase food from a cooperative there. However, the quantities that can be bought are limited and often not enough to last them fifteen days. Sometimes they

---

Luisa: Im te kaita solaarta hippue hoarapo.
Hunaman vittuawaka naatekai . . . ho.
Im, imin Vakateeveu katekan.
Hunumun estakamento katekan.
Hunum estakamento kateka
hunum retiro au yepsak.
Intuchi hunum Tetaviektipo mismopo.
Um Gomeztau ranchopo tekipanoataitek.
Hunum veha te vinwa teki . . . a'apo tekipanoa.
Vahi wasuktiapo ama tekipanoa.
Tun hunuen vahi wasuktiapo ama aa tekipanoau
intok veha pos, kaa intok,
kaita intok tekil ti hiiaka veha aa su'utohak.

can have someone buy larger quantities for them—a large sack of flour, ten or fifteen kilos of beans—which can last, but not if one has a lot of children. They ask for a ride in one of the two bank trucks that regularly make the trip into town, and then ride back with their purchased food. Their home is east of Tata Va'am (Hot Water). The last ranch is called Martimiano, opposite from Aguilita (Little Eagle), toward Se'epo Va'am (Water in the Sand). Their boys all live together in Tata Va'am and work as fence menders. In Papalote there's just the one house, and also only one house at Martimiano, where Elogio Tortola, Aurelia's son, lives. He never goes out except to come in to Swiichi on the thirtieth, thirty-first, or first of the month to receive his money, and he stays with Luisa and Andres at comadre Geralda's house. He usually gets drunk and then goes home. Comadre Geralda would urge him to invite Luisa and Andres to come visit. But in the past they lived by themselves, two people with no one around. When Luisa would visit Vikam, Andres would be home alone. Once Andres went camping, leaving the house unoccupied, and they were robbed by other Hiakis. They lost all their food and two brand-new nylon ropes that were the property of the ranch owners. Now that Luisa's children are all grown and working, sometimes she is completely alone there. Two of her children are currently working in Torim cutting sesame plants.

Luisa: Here we do not have property, a home,
  since we were sent over there . . . see.
  Here, here he was at Tall Bamboo.
  He was stationed out there.
  While he was stationed out there,
  he received his pension.
  Again, there at Tetaviekti [Rolling Stone] the very same.
  There, at Gómez's ranch, he started to work.
  There we . . . he was working for a long time.
  He was working there for three years.
  So that way, after he had worked there for three years,
  and, well, well, and no more,
  and saying that there was no more work, he left.

>   Hunak intok hunum te yeu sahak
>   intok te Vauwou aman Waasimam vewit,
>   inen katin moitiwasuk, hunaman te hookan.

Maria: Hmm.

Luisa: Intuchi hunaman te hokaa intok
ime pueplom intok Pitayau hokame veha
a'apo'ik nomvraroak hunum vicha vakeopo, ho.
I'an, intok hunum, hunum te
yeu sahaka veha te hunum vicha sahak, ho.

Maria: Haivu aman vinwatu.

Luisa: Heewi.

Maria: Haiki wasuktiapo . . .

Luisa: Hunuka ganaderata mavetwak
naatekai te aman hooka, ho.

Maria: Hunuka kargota veha hippue.

Luisa: Heewi. Kialikun yeu veepva'awa, tea.
"Hunume si'ime wasuktiam veha
si'imem nee vehe'etuane," ti hiia.

Maria: Pues sí. Haisa i'an kia gratispo . . . tekilta hoone.

Luisa: Hmm. Hunuen hiiak a'apo veha.
"Kaa . . . nee kaa in e'apo ama yeu simne," ti hiia.
"Ela'apo im nee vehe'etuane
si'ime hunuka tekilta," ti hiia.
Intok kia wakasim nenkiwak
huni kaita ama mimikwa.

Maria: Bwe!

Luisa: Kaita!

And then we left from there
and at Vauwo, over there, near Wasimas,
remember, after the land was plowed, that is where we settled.

Maria: Hmm.

Luisa: Again, we were over there, and
these people and those who were in Pitaya then
named him as the cowboy over there, see.
And now, there, there we
left from there, then we went over there, see.[2]

Maria: You have already been there for a long time.

Luisa: Yes.

Maria: For many years . . .

Luisa: When they received that cattle company
we started to live there, see.

Maria: Now then, he has that responsibility.

Luisa: Yes. That is why they are going to remove him, they say.
"All those years then,
all of them they will pay me," he says.

Maria: Well, yes. Now, how can he just . . . do the work for free.

Luisa: Hmm. This is what he said then.
"I am not leaving here because I want to," he says.
"It does not matter. Here they will have to pay me
for all that work," he says.
And just when the cattle were sold,
even then he received nothing.

Maria: Well!

Luisa: Nothing!

---

2. She means that Pitaya Pueblo hired Andres to work on the cattle ranch at Papalote as the cowboy in charge. With that job, they went to Papalote, where they lived at the time of the recording.

Maria: Hmm! Siendo que . . .

Luisa: Más de que uu sueldo aa kova'u;
ili aa tekipanoaka aa kova'u hiva makna.
Mikwa cada quince diapo.
Ili senu mil ama vahi cientota.

Maria: Sosiadam am atteak ume wakasim?

Luisa: Heewi. Hunum aa kargaroawa uka . . .
si'imeta aa wikiriawamta.

Maria: Intok kaita vehe'etuawa?

Luisa: Intok kaita.

Maria: Haiki wasuktiapo eme'e ama hooka?

Luisa: Oh, vinwatuko, humaku'u.
Humaku'u, veinti dospo haku'u, hunum haku'u.
A'apo au waate . . .
inika ganaderata mavetwak naatekai, kaita.
Kaita mimikwa,
bwan ume vato'im.
Kia veha tua ama tekipanoa.

Maria: Kaa, kaa empo sueldota aa nu'e ti hiia,
cada quince días?

Luisa: Ana'aka.

Maria: Ta hunu'u intok hitaavetchi'ivo?

Luisa: Abwe kia tomi. Hunuka kova'atuawa.
Quince diapo vehe'etuawa.
Imin intok aa pensionaruari vetana intok ket
ili senu mil ama naiki cientota ili tommi'u senu metpo.

Maria: Kia kaita.

Luisa: Heewi. Kia kaita.
Intok kaita, [*coughs*] kaita,

Maria: Hmm. Inasmuch as . . .

Luisa: Only his salary that he was earning;
the little bit of work and his earnings were all he was paid.
He is paid every fifteen days.
One thousand and three hundred pesos.

Maria: Are the societies the owners of the cattle?

Luisa: Yes. That's where he is asking for payment . . .
for all that they owe him.

Maria: And he was not being paid?

Luisa: And nothing.

Maria: For how long have you been there?

Luisa: Oh, a long time, maybe.
Maybe since 1922, around then, there sometime.
He remembers it . . .
Beginning when they received this cattle company, nothing.
They do not give him anything,[3]
well, those baptized ones.
Then, he is just working there.

Maria: Did you not, not say he was receiving a salary
every fifteen days?

Luisa: Of course.

Maria: But what is that for?

Luisa: Well, it is just money. That is what they are paying him.
On the fifteenth day he is paid.
And here from his pension he also receives
a few pesos [1,400 pesos, or $140.00 USD] each month.

Maria: Just nothing.

Luisa: Yes. Just nothing.
And nothing, [*coughs*] nothing,

---

3. She is referring to not receiving any bonuses.

>
> kaita bwa'amtuk intok te si suffrifriaroa.
> Kaita, ainam, hita munim huni kaita.

Maria: Hmm.

Luisa: Pos intok kia ili cien pesota
tomeka huni kak aa hinune.
Kaave ama hita nenka
hunaman itom hoapo ... kawiwi.

Maria: Hakun tahti veha yaaha?

Luisa: Bwe, kaa ...

Maria: Provisiontavetchi'ivo.

Luisa: Abwe umu'u.

Maria: Ovregonneu?

Luisa: Ovregonneu aa nunu'e.
Koperativa ama ya'ari.
Ta pos limitaupo aa nunu'e.
Kaa itou yuyuma.

Maria: Hmm.

Luisa: Necesita que senu ili tomek
im waim veha aa hinutevok ...

Maria: Huevenak nu'une.

Luisa: Heewi. Hunak veha ili aina bwe'u sakom nu'uk
hunak veha ili wantaroane.
Muunim, diez kilo, quince kilo.
Hunu'u veha ili au yuma'ane quince diammeu, ho.
Pos si yu'in usek veha hitaa? Kaita.

Maria: Haisa eme'e kom yaaha? Trookek, o ...

Luisa: Trookepo. Vanko trookem woi hiva.

Maria: Hunaka veha eme reuwari?

and when we have no food, we suffer a lot.
Nothing, flour, anything, even no beans.

Maria: Hmm.

Luisa: Well, and with just a little hundred pesos[4]
there is nowhere we can buy anything.
No one sells anything
there where we live . . . in the mountains.

Maria: How far do you have to go?

Luisa: Well, not . . .

Maria: For food.

Luisa: Well, over there.

Maria: In Obregón?

Luisa: We buy it in Obregón.
They made a cooperative there.
But, well, we are limited in what we buy.
It is not enough for us.

Maria: Hmm.

Luisa: It is necessary when one has a little money,
over here, then have someone make purchases here . . .

Maria: Purchase a lot.

Luisa: Yes. Then, then one can get a big sack of flour,
then it will last.
Beans, ten or fifteen kilos.
That will last the fifteen days, see.
But with many children, then what? Nothing.

Maria: How do you come down? A truck or . . .

Luisa: In a truck. Bank trucks; there are only two.

Maria: Then they have loaned it to you?

---

4. At the time this was equivalent to about ten U.S. dollars.

Luisa: Rereuwawa.
Intok a'avo am sakau
ameu nokak veha amemak simne.
Si sep aa nottivau
intok sep aemak nottine
bwa'amta a'avo nu'uko.
Hunuen hiva.

Maria: Intok eme'e huevenaka aman hooka?

Luisa: Ili vu'uka aman hooka.
Intok kia hunuen memekka nau te hooka.
Ite maa si mekka hooka.
Hunum Tataa Va'ampo,
huchi inim ta'ata yeu weyeo luula weene,
hunum yeu sik intok hunaman ito wanna'avo,
veha ultimo rancho, Martimiano tea huna'a.
Hunai wanna'avo intok inen Agili'ita tea.

Maria: Hmm.

Luisa: Ket hiva mismo huna'a.
Ori . . . huna'asan Se'epo Va'am vetana taawa,
Martimiano teame.

Maria: Hm, hmm.

Luisa: Intuchi hunu'u, Agilita teame huni'i.
Hunum pa'ariau vichaa taawa.

Maria: Em asoam, ume o'owim
ket si'ime aman hooka?

Luisa: Si'ime.

Maria: Ta kaa enchimmak?

Luisa: E'e. Tataa Va'ampo hooka.
Hunume ume tuusam. Koram tu'uteme.
Hunume veha si'ime ama mochala nau ho'ak,
hunumu'u, Tataa Va'ampo.

Luisa: Loaned it to us.
   And when they are coming here,
   [we] speak to them and leave with them.
   If they are returning right away,
   right away [we] will return with them
   after buying food here.
   That is the only way.

Maria: And are there many of you living over there?

Luisa: There are quite a few over there.
   And just that way we are far from each other.
   As for us, we are very far away.
   There at Hot Water,
   then again, here, toward where the sun rises [east],
   leaving from there and on the other side of us,
   then, the last ranch is known as Martimiano.
   And on the other side of that it is named Aguilita [Little Eagle].

Maria: Hmm.

Luisa: Also, that one is still the same.
   That . . . that one then is toward Sand Waters,
   the place known as Martimiano.

Maria: Hmm.

Luisa: Again, that one, known as Aguilita, also.
   That is toward the wilderness.

Maria: Your children, the boys,
   are they all also over there?

Luisa: All of them.

Maria: But not [living] with you?

Luisa: No. They are in Hot Water.
   Those are fence menders. They fix fences.
   Those, then, all of them live together,
   over there, at Hot Water.

Maria: Empo intok aman Papalootepo, hewi?

Luisa: Heewi, itepo aman hooka.
We . . . wepul hoara hiva.
Intok hunaman Martimianou huni wepul hoara hiva.

Maria: Hunaman intok havee katek, Martimianopo?

Luisa: Ori, Loohio.
Ori, komae Aureliata asoa . . . hmm.

Maria: Ketun hiia.

Luisa: Ite . . . nee intok kia chukteka ama yeu weene.

Maria: Kaachin maachi.
Al kabo que huevena ume sintam.

Luisa: Heewi. Nee veha . . . hunaman te veha hookan.
I'an hunumu'u bwan. Kaita.
A'apo uu yoeme tua kaa . . . ket kaakun yeepsa.
Más de que dia ultimopo hiva a'avo yeepsa,
dia primeropo o amak treintaunotuk,
o veha tua treintaunopo tomi'une.
Kaa treintaiunotuko intok kia treintapo tomine'u.

Maria: Im yeepsa?

Luisa: Heewi.

Maria: Swiichipo?

Luisa: Heewi. Hunum komae Heraldatou yaaha.
Hunum mismo bwan tuka in weeka'apo.

Maria: Heewi.

Luisa: Huntuen hunum veha yeepsa.
Hunum yepsak veha tomi'uk veha simne a'apo.
Naamuksuko.

Maria: And you are at Windmill, yes?

Luisa: Yes, we are over there.
   One . . . one house only.
   And even over at Martimiano, there's only one house.

Maria: And over there, who is there at Martimiano?

Luisa: That, Loohio.[5]
   That, comadre Aurelia's child . . . hmm.

Maria: It is still on.

Luisa: We . . . I will just come out in a choppy recording.

Maria: Not a problem.
   Anyway, there are a lot of cassettes.

Luisa: Yes. Then I . . . that is where we were.
   Now there, well, nothing. Nothing.
   He, the man [her husband] really not . . . also doesn't go anywhere.
   Except that only on the last day he comes here,
   on the first or sometimes on the thirty-first,
   or then right on the thirty-first, he will get his money.
   And if not on the thirty-first, then just on the thirtieth.

Maria: He comes here?

Luisa: Yes.

Maria: To Swiichi?

Luisa: Yes. We go to comadre Geralda's [house].
   There, in the same place, well, where I was standing yesterday.

Maria: Yes.

Luisa: So that is where he goes.
   He gets there, then gets his money, then he leaves.
   After he gets drunk.

---

5. Loohio is the Hiaki version of the Spanish name Elogio. This man's last name was Tortola, which means "Inca Dove."

Maria: Oo.

Luisa: [*Laughs.*] Naamuksuko veha simne.
Ta pos uu komaeta tehwak, tu'isi aa tehwa'ane bwan.
Kaa senuk vena. "Kia amemak etehone."
Si imin hakun huni yeepsan.
"Kamiinotuk humak yahivae ti hiuwau,
am tehwa'ane," ti au au hiuvae ti hiia.
"Aman itou noitine," ti
ameu au hiuvae, ti hiia.

Maria: Eme aman yaaha kechia . . .
Vahkommewi, Kamiinotuko?

Luisa: Uh, uh. Kaa aman nee yeepsa.

Maria: Aa.

Luisa: Porque te vatnaatakai
tua itepola ama hookan,
woika hiva. Kaave ama tatawa.
Hunak te inen auka im wain i'anvenasi katekan, hewi.
A'apo intok aapola aman tawalatukan.
A'apo intok kampiaroane, hewi, pocho'okun weamne.
Hoara intok apela ama tawane.
Hunuen te bwa'amta si'imeta ama taaruk.

Maria: Bwe!

Luisa: Heewi.

Maria: Wate ama kiimuk?

Luisa: Heewi. Um humak hu'ubwa haksa humak aa nu'uka bwan, ho.
Wikiam makritukan, nylam, veemelam, woim.
Ori, asienda atteatukan huname'e.
Kee sauwaka aman am chaya'ikan kaapo waiwa.
Pos hunaka si'imeta ama taaruk.

Maria: Bwe!

Luisa: Heewi.

Maria: Oh.

Luisa: [*Laughs.*] After he gets drunk, he leaves.
But if he tells Comadre, it will be all right if he tells her, well.
She is not like anyone else. "She will just speak to him."
Very often he even used to go somewhere out here.
When they say, "Perhaps they will arrive for the Camino fiesta, you will tell them," she said she would say to, to him.
"Come over there to visit us," she said
she is going to say to them, she said.

Maria: Do you also go over there . . .
to Vahkom, during the Camino fiesta?

Luisa: Uh, uh. I do not go there.

Maria: Ah.

Luisa: Because a long time ago,
we were truly there by ourselves,
only two [of us]. No one stayed there.
When we did this, over here, like now, I was here, yes.
And he stayed over there by himself.
And he was out there walking around near the wilderness.
And the house was left there by itself.
That is how all our food was lost there.

Maria: Well!

Luisa: Yes.

Maria: Well! Some people went in there?

Luisa: Yes. There, perhaps recently he got it somewhere, well, see.
[They had] given him some rope, nylon, new, two of them.
Well, they were the property of the ranch owners.
They were not used, they were just hanging inside the house.
Well, so we lost everything there.

Maria: Well!

Luisa: Yes.

Maria: Mismo yoeme?

Luisa: Heewi. Hunuen auka bwan.

Maria: Kaita na . . . bwe, kaita kia vicha.

Luisa: Hunak, hunak naateka veha te kaa . . .
nee kaa, nee veha ama tatawa, amak inepola.
Tua ime ili usita, wepulaik kaita ama hippuetek,
veha nee inepola ama tawane,
porque ume ili yo'owe tekipannoa
huat hakun ili emo a'ania.
Ma i'an woika Torimmeu hooka.
Hunaman ili honholin chukte.
Aman intok im kaa tekilta am mamaka.
Kia ume ili ama plantam, hunama hiva ili tekipanoatuane.

Maria: Hmm.

Luisa: Heewi. Hunuen veha huet hak
ili emo a'ania. Wepulaka hiva hunaman . . .
hunume vahika hiva tua aman hooka.

Maria: Hmm.

Luisa: Kaave intoko.

Maria: The same Hiakis?

Luisa: Yes. That is what they did.

Maria: Nothing . . . Well, they do not just see things.[6]

Luisa: Then, then, beginning then we do not . . .
I do not, I, then, stay there, sometimes by myself.
Really, this little child, one, if I have no one,
then I will stay by myself,
because the slightly older ones are working
out there somewhere to support themselves a little.
Look now, two are staying in Torim.
Over there, they are cutting sesame plants.
And over there [in the mountains], they do not give them work.
Only the ones assigned there, only they will be given a little work.

Maria: Hmm.

Luisa: Yes. Then, that is how, somewhere, out there,
they support themselves. Only one over there . . .
those three are the only ones who always stay there.

Maria: Hmm.

Luisa: No one else.

---

6. By this she means that the temptation to steal is ever present.

FIGURE 30 The Hiaki River. Arizona Historical Society, PC 180, Norman Wallace Photographs, box 42, album #1, page 32, A.

Maria: Hunak uu vatwe hiva va'akan?

Andres: Hiva va'akan hunako.
    I'ansu itom im yahak veha pattawak um Oviachipo.
    Hunak pattawak haivu im itom hooko.
    Hunak pattawak.
    Hunum ket ume ringom si yaaha,
    Oviachipo, kovi'ikuni. Hewi?

Luisa: Hm.

Andres: Nee chea kaa aman am yaaha tean [ti e'an].

The Dam at Oviachi and Hiak Vatwe Nowadays (Andres)

Andres mentions that the river always had water in it back during the war. Since then, it was dammed at Oviachi, and many Americans go there. They also go to Huatabampo, in Mayo land, where there is a beach and some big restaurants. He visited there with three friends, Alfonso, Ramon Velasquez, and Miki Ruiz, who lived at Little Mesquite in Tucson for a long time. Ruiz's family came to live in Tucson during the war.

Maria: At that time the river had water?

Andres: It always had water then.
Now when we arrived here, then it was dammed up at Oviachi.[7]
It was dammed up when we were already here.
It was dammed up, then.
There, also, the gringos frequently go there,
to Oviachi, in the corner. Yes?

Luisa: Hm.

Andres: I did not think they went there.

---

7. Oviachi (a Hiaki word meaning "difficult, hard") is the name of the dam placed on the Hiak Vatwe (Hiaki River) north of the small town of Esperanza, in Sonora, Mexico. All of the water flowing in the Hiak Vatwe has been diverted south for use by the Mexican farmers who have taken possession of the Hiaki lands and are now rich and powerful, while the Hiaki farmers do not have the resources to farm their lands.

Maria: Si hunaman Watavampo huni yaaha tea.

Andres: Hee?

Maria: Mayo ori, bwiawi.

Luisa: Hunaman iibwan ket yaaha.

Maria: Plaaya ama katek tea.

Luisa: Bweere estauraanim ama hooka.

Andres: Tua kovi'iku, hikachi, lomat hikau ha'amune.

Maria: Oo. Si uhyoi humaku'u?

Andres: Heewi.

Luisa: Va'a kia patti.

Andres: Heewi. Senu ama yepsak
im luula va'ata kia haisa vitne.
Ili kanoam, ume ili orim ama nah tenne.

Luisa: Ili lancham . . . ume'e . . .

Andres: Lancham, motoorim.

Luisa: . . . ama kuchu sussua ume yoim.

Andres: Nee si kaa . . . nee kee aman noiten hunaman kovi'iku.
I'ansu veha ket aman noitek u'e Alfonsotamake,
Ramon Velaskes, Miki Ruiz.
Hunuka empo kaa teuwa hikkaila Miki Ruizta hewi?

Maria: He'e.

Andres: Hunumun, hunumun
vinwa katekan, Tusoonewi.

THE CONTEMPORARY SITUATION

Maria: They even go to Huatabampo,[8] they say.

Andres: Oh?

Maria: To Mayo, um, land.

Luisa: There, well, they also go.

Maria: There is a beach there, they say.

Luisa: There are some big restaurants there.

Andres: Right in the corner, on top, you climb up on the hill.

Maria: Oh. It must be very beautiful, perhaps?

Andres: Yes.

Luisa: The water is just turned off.

Andres: Yes. When one arrives there
this way you will see a lot of water.
Some little canoes, the little things run around there.

Luisa: Little canoes... the...

Andres: Canoes, motors.

Luisa: ... the Mexicans fish there.

Andres: I just do not... I had not been there to the corner.
But now I also did go there with Alfonso,
Ramon Velasquez, Miki Ruiz.
That one, you have not heard his name, Miki Ruiz, yes?

Maria: No.

Andres: Over there, over there,
he was there for a long time, in Tucson.

---

8. Huatabampo is a city in Sonora, in northwestern Mexico. *Huata* is "willow tree." *Bampo* is "water." Both of those spellings are in the Mayo language, while in the Hiaki language the sound and spelling are slightly different: *wata* is the Hiaki spelling for "willow tree" and *va'ampo* means "in the water."

Maria: Empo aa teuwaakan, hewi?
Kaa, kaa empo aa teuwakan?
E'e, hewi, um sintampo.

Andres: Vinwa aman katekan.
Hunume'e Ili Hu'upapo hok, hiva ho'akan.
Si tutuli sami kaapo . . .
inime Miki Ruiztaim. Vinwa aman ho'akan.
Ume wilom yee hahhaseu
aman wattekan.

FIGURE 31 The dam at Oviachi in 2006. Photograph by Javier Martínez Rosas.

Maria: You had mentioned him, yes?
Did you not, not mention him?
No, yes, on the tape.

Andres: He was there for a long time.
They were at Little Mesquite, always lived there.
In a very pretty adobe house . . .
these Miki Ruizes. They lived there for a long time.
When the skinny ones were chasing us,
they went over there.

CHAPTER 10

PEOPLE OF HIAK VATWE

Kala (Maria Hesus and Luisa)

Maria Hesus and Luisa reminisce about relatives. Luisa remembers how Chema Tosaria's mother Kala Nestor was taken care of by her second son, Xavier, one of Chema's older brothers. (Antonio Tosaria was the other of Chema's brothers and the eldest of Kala's three sons.)[1] Xavier would lead her down to the cemetery on All Souls' Day. She would always want to go, even in extreme old age. Toward the end of her life, she would call out to someone named Beto to show her the way home.

---

1. The reader may remember from the biographical note at the beginning that Chema and Antonio were separated from their parents in the mountains as young children when the *peronim* attacked. The two children, who thought their parents were dead, were taken in by two Hiaki mountain men and raised by one of them. As a young man, Chema eventually arrived in Tucson, Arizona. While there, Chema took a wife, Maria Theresa. They had six children: five boys (one who died as an infant) and one girl. During the time that Chema lived in Tucson, he lost track of his brothers Antonio and Xavier. Chema spoke of his brother Antonio, but never mentioned his other brother, Xavier.

M.H.: Ii Tio Chemata papa haisa teakan,
tio Chema, heewi? Mariata suegrosuka'u?
Kaa aa ta'ak?

Luisa: E'e.

M.H.: Ahhh. Por eso nee Mariata . . .

Luisa: Vem papawata nee kaa ta'ak.
Vempoim hiva. A'apoik uka'a . . .

M.H.: Papata?

Luisa: E'e, uka Kala Nestorata, intok uka'a tata
Huanta hiva, intok uka chi'ila Ramonata,
pos hunaka haivu aa huuvek intok
Maria hiva ilitcheakan, wepulaika.
Kaaveta intok asoak. Hunuka hiva.
Hunume intok uusim, woi hiva,
uu Chema intok Haviel. Woi hiva. Haviel.
Huntuan uu, uu Haviel veha
aa tekiakan uka Kalata.
Panteoneu vicha haivu aa wiksimne.
Animam mikwau huni,
hunaman panteoneu
haivu aman aemak anne.
Hunu'u hiva aa teakiakan.

M.H.: Ah, ta hunuu Papa hunuen ibwan . . .
hunume uusim,
nee huni ameu waatine
ta kaivu am etehone.
Au sissioka tiia.

Luisa: Pos, haisa i'an e'e.
Tua si'ime lu'utisuk.
Ite hiva aman ameu yaahan.
Mala hiva aman ameu yeepsan.
Si hakia inen bwe'uka waitana vo'oka.

M.H.: This uncle, Chema's father, what was his name,
Uncle Chema, yes? Maria's late father-in-law?
Did you know him?

Luisa: No.

M.H.: Ah. That is why I, Maria's . . .

Luisa: I did not know their father.
Only them. That one, that . . .

M.H.: Father?

Luisa: No, that Kala Nestor, and that grandfather,
Juan, only, and that mother's younger sister Ramona,
well, when that one [Juan] was already married,
and since Maria was still little, only that one [child].
She had no other children. Only that one.
And those children, two only,
that Chema and Xavier. Only two. Xavier.
Then that, that Xavier
had the job of taking care of Kala.
He would take her to the cemetery.
On All Souls' Day also,
there at the cemetery
he would already be there with her.
Only he had this job.

M.H.: Ah, but he, Father, that way, well . . .
those children,
I also remember them,
but he never will speak about them.
He feels very sad, he says.

Luisa: Well, how could he not feel that way?
All of them are truly gone.
Only we always used to go visit them there.
Mom always used to go visit them there.
A creek, this big, was on the other side.[2]

---

2. She indicates the width of the creek with her arms.

| | Hunaman ho'akan vempo.
Itepo intok ivotana. |
|---|---|
| **M.H.**: | San Haviel tea. Heewi. San Haviel.
I'an, I'an lu'utivaeka hunen hiune,
"In, in hoarau vicha nee weevae.
Noolia Veeto," ti au hiune Hose Huantawi.
"Nepat weye," ti au hiune.
"Nee, nee tehwa haksaluula tu'i voo'o," ti au hiune.
"Hante pale."
Tukaapo chaene bwan.
"Nolia Veeto, hante. Nee weiya," ti au hiune.
Hiokot ansuk a'apo bwan.
Hiva, hiva weene bwan.
Hiva weeva'ane bwan.
Hunuen au hiune tiotawi,
"Hunum taawa Chema," ti au hiune.
"Yo'otusuk. Haivu nee kaa
enchi puanama," ti au hiune.
Aa ilitchiakavenasi bwan. |
| **Luisa**: | Heewi. |
| **M.H.**: | "Hunum taawa Chema," ti au hiune.
"Ika ala nee weiyavae. Ketun ilitchi," ti hiune
Hose Huanta.
"I'an nee kaa enchi puananama," ti au hiune,
tio Chematawi, aa vichamtavenasi.
Nee intok kia au kateka aa hikkaine. |
| **Luisa**: | Hunuen iibwan. Hunume hivatukan.
Hunume hiva. Kaavem intok nee ta'a. |

They lived over there.
And we were on this side.

M.H.: San Xavier was the name. Yes. San Xavier.
Now, now, when she was going to die, she would say,
"I want to go to my, my home.
Come on, Beto," she would say to Jose Juan.[3]
"Go ahead of me," she would say to him.
"Tell me, me, which way is the good road," she would say.
"Come on, young boy."
At night she would call out.
"Come on, Beto, let's go. Take me," she would say to him.
She suffered very much, well.
Always, always she would walk, well.
She would always want to go, well.
She would say to my uncle,
"Stay there, Chema," she would say to him.
"[You are] grown up. Already I cannot
carry you anymore," she would say to him.
As if he was still little, well.

Luisa: Yes.

M.H.: "Stay there, Chema," she would say to him.
"I am going to take this one. He is still little,"
she would say [about] Jose Juan.
"Now I do not carry you anymore," she would say to him,
to Uncle Chema, as if she was really looking at him.
And I would just sit next to her listening to her.

Luisa: Well, that is how it was, well. Those were the only ones.
Only those. I didn't know anyone else.

---

3. We speculate that "Beto" was Kala's deceased husband, whose name we do not know.

Antonio Tosaria's Wives and Children (Maria Hesus and Luisa)

Following on the previous conversation, Maria Hesus and Luisa remember Tio Antonio Tosaria, "Uncle Antonio White Skin," the oldest of Kala's sons. He was sold to a Mexican in Yucatán and grew up down there. When he returned with others who were repatriated from Yucatán, he took a wife, Nacha, and had a child, Soori. However, before Soori could sit up, Antonio had abandoned them. Another man, Lazaro Bule, then took Nacha as a wife, and both she and Soori had the Bule name after that. However, Lazaro abused Nacha, on one occasion pistol-whipping her and cutting her scalp. She ran to the house of comadre Ramona, who put a cardboard box on her head. Soori became a soldier, and when he was

Luisa: Antonio intok haivu im katekan.

M.H.: Ta hunu'u katin i'an hunume,
uka yo'orata katin Yucataneu toiwak,
katin Antonio nenkiwak tea, yoitawi.

Luisa: Heewi.

M.H.: Tio Antonio Tosaria.

Luisa: Hunuen ibwan aa ya'ak tea.

M.H.: Nenkiwak tea. Katin?
Kaa, kaa tua amemak yo'otuk tea bwan.
Yoimmak yo'otuk.

Luisa: Uu, hmm.
Hunu'u intok wepulaik hiva uusek, Antonio.
Katin uka Sorita.

M.H.: E'e. Hunaksu uu Loloes?

Luisa: Havee Loloes?

M.H.: Bwe, aa usiwa.

discharged Lazaro was hoping he would move in on land he had bought for him, but Soori refused, saying that Lazaro had killed his mother and he would not take anything from him. Antonio Tosaria also had another wife, Inez, with whom he had another son whom Luisa remembers as Willie and Maria Hesus calls Dolores. Luisa describes how Willie was in the hospital with worms as a child, and also had an operation to remove a swelling; he died young. Maria Hesus mentions that Dolores had two children, Lolo and Kira, with a woman named Juana. She also tells a story of Dolores traveling in the mountains with her father Juan and uncle Chema, each man carrying some supplies: Juan, beans; Chema, wheat; and Dolores, salt. It began to rain, and Juan told Dolores not to let the salt get wet. Dolores said he wouldn't, and that he was sitting on it to protect it. They pretended to worry: "Oh no! You'll pee on it!"

Luisa: And Antonio was already here.

M.H.: But that one, remember, now those,
the elders, remember, were taken to Yucatán.
Remember, Antonio was sold, they say, to a Mexican.

Luisa: Yes.

M.H.: Uncle Antonio White Skin.

Luisa: That is, well, what they did, they say.

M.H.: He was sold, they say. Remember?
[He did] not, not really grow up with them, they say.
He grew up with the Mexicans.

Luisa: Uu, hmm.
And Antonio has only one child.
Remember that Soori.

M.H.: No. Then what about Dolores?

Luisa: Which Dolores?

M.H.: Well, his child.

Luisa: Ah pos, hunuka ala nee kaa ta'a.

M.H.: Kaa aa ta'a? Hunu'u chea papa . . .
itommak katekan hoapo.

Luisa: Hee?

M.H.: Hitasa?

Luisa: Huna'a bwan Sorita ket uusek.
Uka Komae Nacha Buleta nu'ukan,
inim yeu yaiwako.
Hu'ubwa im yeu yaiwak, vemetuk aa nu'ukan.
Huntuan hunuka Sorita yeyesau aa hiimak.

M.H.: Hunuka Komae Nacha Buleta?

Luisa: Heewi.

M.H.: Apoko?

Luisa: . . . Hunumemak kateka hunuka uusek.
Ta i'an Bulempo katek, heewi?
Ta kaa aa achaik.
Hunu'u Antonio aa uusek.
Kialikun si aa omtan
uka Kompae Lasarota Buleta porque ii:
Kompae Lasaro Bule; ika Komai Nachata,
i'an im katekamta nu'uka;
hunua vetchi'ivo veha si aa vevaka
aa me'ak.

M.H.: Hmm.

Luisa: Kialikun inii uusi,
Soori, pos a'apo au sontao ya'atevok.
Chukula aa vahtawau, aa simvau intoko,
a'apo a'avo aa tohirokan,
bwiata aa makrokaka, karim chukti aa ya'ariatevorokan tea.
"Nee kaita em mampo waata," ti au hiia, tea.
"Empo in mala kia veha nee me'eriak," ti au hiia, tea.
"Kaita nee eu waata," ti au hiia tea.

Luisa: Oh, well, I do not know that one.

M.H.: Do not know him? That one, Father . . .
he was with us at home.

Luisa: Oh?

M.H.: What is it?

Luisa: That one, well, Soori was also his child.
He [Antonio] took comadre Nacha Bule [as a wife]
when they arrived here.
When they had recently arrived, she was very young.
When Soori started to sit up, he left her [Nacha].

M.H.: That comadre Nacha Bule?

Luisa: Yes.

M.H.: Really?

Luisa: . . . When he [Antonio] was with them, he had that child.
But now he [Soori] has the Bule name, yes?
But he is not his father.
That Antonio had that child.
That is why he [Soori] really hates him,
compadre Lazaro Bule, because of this:
compadre Lazaro Bule, this comadre Nacha,
now, the one buried here, he took her [as a wife],
for that reason, then: he used to beat her so much
that he killed her.

M.H.: Hmm.

Luisa: That is why this child,
Soori, well, he became a soldier.
Later when he was discharged, [and] going to leave,
he [Lazaro] wanted to bring him here,
saying he would give him land and have a house built for him.
"I want nothing from your hands," he said to him, they say.
"You, then, just killed my mother," he said to him, they say.
"I want nothing from you," he said to him, they say.

"Empo im mala kaa hiokoleka
aa me'ak," ti au hiia tea.
Kia hunua komae Nachata bwan,
hunuka nu'uka, hunuamak weamaka si aa vevan.
Tua pistolai, im kia kova pehti aa veevak.
Hunak veha itom, itom hoarau yeu wechekan,
komae Ramonatukautawi.
Huna'a intok kia uka ori kahata aet movektaikan.
Kompae intok kia nah wanteka aa haiwan.
Hunuen aa hooan.
Ta hunu'u aa uusek, Antoniotukau, poloove.
Ta im Swiichipo,
hu'ubwa yeu yahiwau aa nu'uka.
Kia hu'ubwa ili aa yeyesau aa hiimak.
Ta chukula veha hunuemak weamtaitek.
Hiva veha au yo'otuk hunuu uusi.
I'an veha pos Bulim uhteak.
Ta kaa aa achaik . . . Hunaka nee kaa ta'a . . .

M.H.: Haveeta, Loloesta?

Luisa: Heewi. [*Chuckles.*]

M.H.: Ah, hu'ubwa yo'otuka muukuk kechia.

Luisa: Ahh, muukuk?

M.H.: Muukuk.

Luisa: Ahh . . .

M.H.: Inez, Ineza teame aa asoakan hunaka'a.

Luisa: Ahh! [*Laughter.*] Hunaka ala nee ta'a.

M.H.: Pos Loloes ibwan.

Luisa: Wilita.

M.H.: Wiili.

Luisa: Wilita, poloove.

"You had no pity on my mother so
you killed her," he said to him, they say.
He [Bule] just took her, comadre Nacha [as a wife],
he was going with her, yet he used to beat her terribly.
He pistol-whipped her on the head and tore open her scalp.
Then she came stumbling and falling to our, our house,
to the late comadre Ramona's house.
And that one just took a cardboard box and put it on her head.
And compadre [Lazaro] was just running around looking for her.
That is what he used to do to her.
But that [Soori] is the late Antonio's child, poor thing.
But here in Swiichi
when they had recently arrived, he took her [as a wife].
Just recently, as he [Soori] was starting to sit, he abandoned her.
But later then, she [Nacha] began to go around with him [Lazaro].
Still, then, that child [Soori] grew up with him.
Now, then, well, Bule is his last name.
But he is not his father . . . That one, I do not know . . .

M.H.: Who, Dolores?

Luisa: Yes. [*Chuckles.*]

M.H.: Ah, he was a young man when he died, also.

Luisa: Ah, he died?

M.H.: He died.

Luisa: Ahh . . .

M.H.: Inez. Ineza was the name of his mother.

Luisa: Ahh! [*Laughter.*] That one I do know.

M.H.: Well, Dolores, well.

Luisa: Willie.

M.H.: Willie.

Luisa: Willie, poor thing.

M.H.: Hoapo katin vo'okan.
I'an hunu, hunuka ili hamutta kaa yo'otuk,
huyum katekame
katin ospitaleu au yeepsan aman aa vo'oko.
Katin bwiachiak.

Luisa: Hunuen aukan bwan, poloove.

M.H.: Bwichiak.

Luisa: Hunau nee waate.

Voice in background: Havee bwichiakan?

M.H.: Heh?

Voice in background: Havee bwichiakan?

M.H.: Tio, tio Antoniota uusi.

Luisa: Wilii tea. Inez aa asoakan hunaka'a.

Voice in background: Haisa aukan?

M.H.: Pues quién sabe, la gente,
haz de cuenta que tenía un . . .
arriba tenía un . . .
haz de cuenta que . . .

Luisa: Si ousi vahiatukan, heewi?

M.H.: Lo cortaron. Lo quisieron cortar.
Le quitaron eso . . .

Voice in background: Ahh.

M.H.: Se murió.

Luisa: Wilitukau. Au nee waate, au waate.
Huna'a Inezata asoa . . .

M.H.: Hunu'u bwan.
Hunuavetchi'ivo nee kee lutu kokte.
Im aa koktevae.

M.H.: Remember, he was lying down at our home.
Now, when that, that one little girl was not grown up,
the one sitting there,
remember, she used to visit him when he was in the hospital.
Remember, he had worms.

Luisa: That is what happened to him, well, poor thing.

M.H.: [He had] worms.

Luisa: I remember that.

Voice in background: Who had worms?

M.H.: Heh?

Voice in background: Who had worms?

M.H.: Uncle, Uncle Antonio's child.

Luisa: Willie, they say. He was Inez's son.

Voice in background: What happened to him?

M.H.: Well, who knows, the people . . .
It seems like he had . . .
on top he had a . . .
it seems like . . .

Luisa: He was really swollen, yes?

M.H.: They cut him. They decided to operate.
They cut off his . . .

Voice in background: Ahh.

M.H.: He died.

Luisa: The late Willie. I remember him, I remember.
He was Inez's child . . .

M.H.: Well, that one.
It is for that reason that I have not taken off mourning.
I am going to remove it here.

Luisa: Ahh.

M.H.: Papa, intok ini'i anima intok tio Chema.
Kee am lututeria.

Luisa: A'apo intok wepulaik uusek, hewi?

M.H.: Havee?

Luisa: Hunu'u, Loloes.

M.H.: [*Holds up two fingers.*]

Luisa: Woi? Hee?

M.H.: Lola intok . . .

Luisa: Abwe heewi.

M.H.: . . . Kiira.

Luisa: Hamut intoko, Huana am asoakan.

M.H.: Huana. Hunu'u katin?
Papatamak kaupo weamsuk tea,
hunu'u Loloes, intok tio Cheema.

Voice in background: Cota??

M.H.: Hmm? E'e. Antonio . . .

Voice in background: Oh.

Luisa: Si ilitchiaka tampareotukan.

M.H.: Tampareo?

Luisa: Sontao tampareo.

M.H.: Hunu'u Loloes hunuen au hiune.
"Nee, ini'i kumui inim kaupo itom rehteu,
tua kaa a'avo weeva'ane. Si mahaine," tiia.
Ta hak weekai, "Haksa ta'apo?" ti hiia.
"Te aa yu'uk uka kumuita," tiia.
"A'avo te aa tohak."
"Itom aniaka huni tiikom weiyane kumui.

Luisa: Ahh.

M.H.: Father, this deceased one, and Uncle Chema.
I have not taken off mourning for them.

Luisa: And he has one child, yes?

M.H.: Who?

Luisa: That one, Dolores.

M.H.: [*Holds up two fingers.*]

Luisa: Two? Oh?

M.H.: Lola and . . .

Luisa: Well, yes.

M.H.: . . . Kiira.

Luisa: And a woman. They were Juana's children.

M.H.: Juana. That one, remember?
He went to the mountains with Father, they say,
that Dolores and Uncle Chema.

Voice in background: Cota??

M.H.: Hmm. No, Antonio . . .

Voice in background: Oh.

Luisa: He was very young when he became a ceremonial drummer.

M.H.: Drummer?

Luisa: A soldier drummer.

M.H.: That Dolores would say to him,
"I, this one, my great-uncle, when we were in the mountains,
he really did not want to come here. He was very afraid," he said.
But one day, "What day?" he said.
"We finally convinced my great-uncle," he said.
"We brought him here."
"At least help us to carry the wheat, Great-Uncle!

Noolia hante." Ta a'apo intok Loloes a'avo
emo aa tohak ti hiune, vatwewi.
Papa veha ili munim weiya tea.
Tio Chema intok ili tiikom.
A'apo intok ili onta au puate tiia uu Loloes.
Hunum haksa kaupo ha'amuwa'apo kaa
yuku am bwisek, tea. Vempoim, haivu am sakau,
inen au hiune tea anima papa.
"Omme, onta katee kommonia."
"E'e, nee chea aet katek," ti hiia uu Loloes.
"Ay, kat aet yeehte! Hiovek huni ee aa sisne!"
"Haisa inepo ilitchi?" ti au hiune uu Loloes.
Hiva aa atbwane papata.
"Hunak hiva te kumuita a'avo tohak," ti hiia.
"Itommak im aa pasaroak," ti hiia.
"Yukuta," ti hiia. "Hunum kaupo. Si'ime ha'ani."
"Noolia kumui, hante amani vatwewi.
Hita te teune."
"Haisakai. Ama huni ko'okosi ya'ana," ti hiune uu papa.
Tio Chema intok amemak weene, tea.
Amemak nah siika uu tio Chema,
im kaupo.

Luisa: Si haivu yo'otukan.

M.H.: Heewi, yo'otukan.

Luisa: Hunume si'ime itowit kawiu wattekan.

M.H.: Heewi, hunuen ibwan.
Vempo bwan inim aanen humaku'u.
Papa pos humak a'avo visitan ta
hunum vicha veeviak . . . kawiu vicha.

Come on, let's go." But he and Dolores
brought him [Father] here to the river, he said.
Father would carry a little bit of beans, he said.
And Uncle Chema would carry a little bit of wheat.
And he carried a little bit of salt, Dolores said.
There, somewhere while climbing the mountains,
the rain caught them, he said. When they were already leaving,
my late father said this to him [Dolores]:
"Man, don't let the salt get wet."
"No, I am sitting on it," Dolores said to him.
"Ay, do not sit on it! You might pee on it!"
"Am I a little child?" Dolores said to him.
He always laughed at Father.
"That was the only time we took Great-Uncle over here," he said.
"He experienced it here with us," he said.
"The rain," he said. "There in the mountains. Everything, maybe."
"Come on, Great-Uncle. Let's go over there to the river.
We will find something."
"Why? They might hurt us," my father would say.
And my uncle Chema would go with them, they said.
He traveled around with them, Uncle Chema,
here in the mountains.

Luisa: He was already grown up.

M.H.: Yes, he was grown up.

Luisa: All of them went to the mountains with us.

M.H.: Yes, well, so it is.
They, well, were probably here.
Father, well, was probably visiting here, but
they were forcefully sent over there . . . to the mountains.

Dolores Maehto and Bartolo Pa'amea
(Maria Hesus, Reyno, and Luisa)

Maria Hesus, Reynaldo, and Luisa recall Maria Hesus's relative Ramona and her husband Dolores Maehto (Rorores Maehto), a prayer leader

M.H.: Ah pos, in wawai ket hunaman hakun noitek.
Isidro... Alvarez... o...

Reynaldo: Cota.

M.H.: Ah, Isidro, kaa Sevisa?

Reyno: Luis Molino, huna'a aa ase'ebwakan. [*inaudible*]
... Potampo, bueno, itepo amea weriakan,
malatatuka'uta vetana. [*Inaudible, kids hollering in background.*]
Roroes Maehtukau, Potampo
weweamame maehtotukau,
huna'a aa familiakan, hamut yo'owe.
Ramona tea.

Luisa: Hmm, hmm.

Reyno: Mala veha, Ramona, hunaa veha malatamak weri.
Roroes maehtotuka'u, veha aa...
[*inaudible*]. Nee chavalotuka'u aa ta'an.
Por eso, mala hunuen e'etehon.
Hunama tiempopo sosiadata hiapsau,
ite Potammeu ho'akan, imi'i, ori,
Potammeu ho'aka huni'i, uu senu pueplota [*inaudible*].
Heewi porque maa uu mala veha
Potammeu yoemiataka
veha imin Torimmeu toiri.

Luisa: Hmm. Huna'a veha...
uu mala veha im toitaka [*inaudible*]...
Pa'amea tea.
Vattom Pa'amea tea.

from Potam. Ramona's mother was born in Potam, but they moved to Torim when she was still a child. This leads to a discussion of a man named Bartolo Pa'amea (Vattom Pa'amea), who was a corporal in the military. As a soldier he was sometimes called one of the *toroko yoim* (gray Mexicans)—that is, a traitor. His father also was called Bartolo.

M.H.: Ah, well, my cousin also visited there, somewhere.
Isidro... Alvarez... or...

Reyno: Cota.

M.H.: Ah, Isidro, not Sevisa?

Reyno: Luis Molina, that one was his father-in-law. [*inaudible*]
... in Potam, well, we were related to them
on my late mother's side. [*Inaudible, kids hollering in background.*]
The late Dolores, the prayer leader, in Potam.
He used to travel around there, he used to be a prayer leader.
An older woman who was with him was his wife.
Her name was Ramona.

Luisa: Hmm, hmm.

Reyno: Then, Mom, Ramona, then, that one was related to Mom.
The late Dolores, the prayer leader, then his
[*inaudible*]. When I was a child, I knew him.
That is why my mother used to speak in that way.
At that time, when the society was still active,
we used to live in Potam, here, that,
even when we lived in Potam, the other village [*inaudible*].
Yes, because, so, even though Mom, then,
having been born in Potam,
then she was taken here to Torim.

Luisa: Hmm. Then that one...
then Mom, when she was taken here [*inaudible*]...
Pa'amea was his [sur]name.
His name was Vattom [Bartolo] Pa'amea.

> Ta bwe, eme'e aa Vattom Pa'amea ti hiia.
> Hmm, hmm.

Reyno: Vinwatuko, senu ket Vattom Pa'amea tea,
ta kaavo, sontao kaavo.
I'an uu, kompae Hesus . . . Hesus ii
Vattome inika Hesusta . . .
Toroko yoim ti hiiune, ume waate intoko . . .

Luisa: Kaa . . . kaa kavotukan?

Reyno: Kavotukan . . .

Luisa: Ta i'an katin a'apo intok Vattome tea.
Ta aa achaiwa Vattome.

Reyno: Aa achaiwa Vattome . . .
ta hunaa uhteam . . .
am uhteaka bwan.

Birthplaces and Baptismal Locations (Luisa, Reyno, and Maria Hesus)

Luisa is describing where she and others were when a measles outbreak began, when Maria Hesus remembers that her father said he was born in Ortiz. Luisa mentions that don Andres was born in Maytorena, and Reyno says he was born at Tetakusim (Stone Crosses), but he was bap-

Luisa: . . . hunaman itou hookan . . .

Reyno: Hee.

Luisa: . . . San Bartolo, San Emiliou, te hokaa tomtek itepo.
Hunak tomtiam si yee suau.

Reyno: Hee.

But, well, you-all say he is Vattom Pa'amea.
Hm, hmm.

Reyno: A long time ago, there was one also named Vattom Pa'amea,
but he was a corporal, a corporal in the military.
Now, that compadre Hesus . . . this Hesus
Vattom, this Hesus . . .
A gray Mexican [a traitor], they would say, and others . . .

Luisa: Was he not . . . not a corporal?

Reyno: He was a private.

Luisa: But, now, remember that he is named Vattome.
But his father was also Vattome.

Reyno: His father was Vattome . . .
but his surname . . .
it was his surname, well.

---

tized in Hermosillo. Maria Hesus mentions that her brother was born in Hermosillo. Reyno says the ones who baptized him, very old now, had been taken to the Yucatán. He mentions that his godfather, when visiting for the Camino festival, told him to pick up his baptismal certificate in Hermosillo, which he was grateful for, although it did not result in him being able to claim any official allowance from the government, as can be done today.

Luisa: . . . they were over there with us.

Reyno: Oh?

Luisa: . . . San Bartolo, San Emilio, while there, we got the measles.
At that time the measles were killing many people.

Reyno: Oh?

Luisa: Hunak te kia aman hookan.

Reyno: Hee, hee. Malataim ket hunum emo aa pasaroak ti hiia, Hermosiopo . . . hasiendapo.

M.H.: Aa, imin Ortispo yeu tomtek ti hiia uu Papa . . .

Luisa: Hee?

M.H.: Ortispo.

Luisa: Aa?

Reyno: Hmm.

M.H.: Vehak nee tua kaa . . . kia hechukti au waatek. Ortis.

Luisa: Aa.

Reyno: Ortis.

M.H.: Hoara kaita.
Vatwe aa nuksika tea hakun hunuka hoarata.

Luisa: Aa.

Reyno: Ortis teapo, katin si bwe'u ori.
I'an tahti ama katek uu si bwe'u, ori . . .

Luisa: Heewi. Ta i'an chea si bwe'u hoara tea kompae.

Reyno: Heewi.

M.H.: Bwe'u hoara i'ani.

Reyno: Bwe'u hoara.

Luisa: Bwe'u hoara tea.

Reyno: Maarenau sahak te aa vivicha.

Luisa: Heewi. Si bwe'u hoara.

Reyno: Hunu'u kwarteltukan ti hihia ume yoeme . . .

Luisa: Heewi.

Reyno: . . . hunum Ortispo.

Luisa: At that time, we were just there.

Reyno: Oh, oh? Mom said they were also there, they say,
In Hermosillo . . . on the hacienda.

M.H.: Ah, my father said he was born here in Ortiz . . .

Luisa: Yes?

M.H.: In Ortiz.

Luisa: Ah?

Reyno: Hmm.

M.H.: A while ago I could not . . . just now I remembered it. Ortiz.

Luisa: Ah.

Reyno: Ortiz.

M.H.: The house is not there.
The river took it somewhere, they say, that house.

Luisa: Ah.

Reyno: At the place known as Ortiz, remember, it is a big city.
Even now it is still here, that is very big, well . . .

Luisa: Yes. But now it is a bigger city, they say, compadre.

Reyno: Yes.

M.H.: It is a bigger city now.

Reyno: Big city.

Luisa: It is a big city, they say.

Reyno: On our way to Magdalena, we see it.

Luisa: Yes. It is a very big city.

Reyno: That used to be a big military garrison, the men say . . .

Luisa: Yes.

Reyno: . . . there in Ortiz.

Luisa: Hm.

Reyno: Pos hunuen veha, hunuen veha te aa pasaaroak.

Luisa: Pos si kia ... hmm.

Reyno: Hunum veha ...

Luisa: Hunak ... kia hunuet hoasasakan, hewi?
Uu yoeme i'an nemak ho'akame
ket hunumum Maitorenou yeu tomtila.

Reyno: Oo ... heewi.

Luisa: Ket hunumum yeu aa hima'ariawak uka rehistrota
i'an pensionaroava'awakai.

Reyno: Hmm, bwe.

Luisa: Hmm.

Reyno: Nee intok katin ket im yeu tomtek tea, kechia, inepo, imi'i ...

M.H.: Tetakuusimpo.[4]

Reyno: Tetakuusimpo. Heewi.
Saetaim intok inim Hermosillopo.

Luisa: Hmm.

Reyno: Ta nee, nee, nee hunumun vato'owa'awak tea, ori, Hermosillopo.

Luisa: Hmm.

Reyno: I'an, i'an he'ela ketuni hiapsan,
hunume nee vato'owak teame ...

Luisa: Hmm.

Reyno: Ta hunumum toirimtukan tea ...

M.H.: Yukataanewi.

---

4. Tetakusim means "Stone Crosses." It is also a small town between Empalme and the Hiaki fishing village of Wasimas. The Hiakis moved away due to continued encroachment by the Mexican people. A stone cross buried in the ground marks the original northeasternmost boundary of Hiaki territory.

Luisa: Hm.

Reyno: Well, that, then, that then, is how we experienced it.

Luisa: Well, so just . . . hmm.

Reyno: There, then . . .

Luisa: Then . . . they just lived anywhere here, yes?
The man who now lives with me[5]
was also born there in Maytorena.

Reyno: Oh . . . yes.

Luisa: There, also, they took out his birth certificate
now that he was going to receive his pension.

Reyno: Hmm, well.

Luisa: Hmm.

Reyno: And I, I, remember, I was also born here, they say, I, here . . .

M.H.: At Stone Crosses.

Reyno: At Stone Crosses. Yes.
And my older brother there at Hermosillo.

Luisa: Hmm.

Reyno: But I, I, I was baptized there, they say, well, in Hermosillo.

Luisa: Hmm.

Reyno: Now, now, lately they were still alive,
those who, they say, baptized me . . .

Luisa: Hmm.

Reyno: But they were taken over there, they say . . .

M.H.: To Yucatán.

---

5. Don Andres.

Reyno: Yukataanewi. Si yo'otulim hunume'e.

M.H.: Yo'otulim.

Reyno: Nim, nim kamiinotuko aman yaaha.

Luisa: Hm, hmm.

M.H.: Ermosio vetana.

Luisa: Hee?

Reyno: Ermosio vetana ama yaaha.
Intok hunuen neu hiian, si tu'isi neu hiian iibwan huna'a in vato'o achai.

Luisa: Hmm?

Reyno: Hunaman uka orita
Fe de Bautismota nee nu'usaen...

Luisa: Hmm.

Reyno: Ermosiowi.

M.H.: Oo ta hunak chea...

Reyno: Kaita.

M.H.: ...kaita.

Reyno: Kaita. Kaa i'anpovenasia.

M.H.: Siquiera i'an ili mimikwa.
Ta hunak chea kaita.

Reyno: Kaita. Kia tekilpo veha te ito ania.

Luisa: Hmm.

Reyno: To Yucatán. Very old, those.

M.H.: Very old.

Reyno: Here, here during the Camino fiesta,[6] they go there.

Luisa: Hm, hmm.

M.H.: From Hermosillo.

Luisa: Oh?

Reyno: They go there from Hermosillo.
And he said that to me, well, he said a very good thing to me, well, he, my godfather.

Luisa: Hmm?

Reyno: Over there, the, well,
[he] told me to get the baptismal certificate.

Luisa: Hmm.

Reyno: In Hermosillo.

M.H.: Oh, but then more . . .

Reyno: Nothing.

M.H.: . . . nothing.

Reyno: Nothing. It is not like now.

M.H.: At least now they receive a little something.
But then there was nothing.

Reyno: Nothing. We just supported ourselves, then, with just our work.

Luisa: Hmm.

---

6. Annual ceremony held in Loma Vahkom (Loma de Bácum) in Sonora. This commemorates the travel of St. Mary as she made her way to visit Santa Rosa, who was great with child. They met on the road; thus, the Spanish term *camino*, which means "road" or "travel." The ceremony is very colorful, and all the eight Hiaki villages, as well as the Arizona Hiakis, gather at Loma Vahkom to celebrate this occasion on July 1 and 2. Vahkom means "lagoons" or "puddles of water."

Reynaldo's Family and Their Tucson Connections (Reyno)

Reynaldo discusses the different places his family lived. His mother came with him to Potam from Torim when he was small, so his younger siblings were all from Potam even though he was from Torim. His father, Manuel Romero, was from Vahkom. His father was related to Romeros in the United States, including one named Nacho Romero, a Fariseo in Ba-

---

Reyno: Entonces nee, entonces in mala veha, veha,
   imin toiwak.
   Por eso que imi, imin, imin veha
   Potata lisensiak.
   Entonces ime, ime'e aa asoawam
   pos huname imin Potatau pertenesiaroa.
   Nee intok Tori. Vaa.
   Vat aa usi hunak . . .
   I'an intok chukula intok achaituka'u,
   Manwe Romeo teame
   hunaa veha Vahko.

Luisa: Hmm, hmm.

Reyno: Romeo. Ta Romeommak te weri.
   I'an aman katek
   senu Nacho Romeo teame,
   waitana, Tusonpo.
   Naa hunaman chapayekatukan
   ta hunum Varrio Libre tean,
   hakwo hunuen teteuwawan, ti hiia maala.
   Chea vatnaataka intok Varrio Lokoopo veha ta'ewan.
   Hunak nee aman katekan.

Luisa: Hmm, hmm.

Reyno: Nee kaa yo'owetukan.
   Ta malatam hunuen aa e'etehon.
   Varrio, Varrio Looko ti aa teteuwan.

rrio Libre. Reyno had also heard Barrio Libre referred to as Barrio Loco, and he also mentions Little Mesquite and Big Mesquite, two other Hiaki communities in Tucson. He also remembers his mother mentioning a ceremonial singer named Sewam who lived there. He was very young when they were in Tucson, but he remembers his parents conversing about the relatives and others they knew there.

Reyno: Then I, then my mother, then, then,
 were brought here.
 That is why, here, right here, here, here, then,
 they asked for permission from Potam.
 Then these, these her children,
 they were from Potam.
 And I am from Torim. Yes.
 Her first child . . .
 And later my late father,
 named Manuel Romero,
 he then [was from] Vahkom.

Luisa: Hmm, hmm.

Reyno: Romero. We are related to the Romeros.
 Now, one lives over there,
 one named Nacho Romero,
 on the other side, in Tucson.
 He was a Fariseo over there,
 but there in a place named Barrio Libre [South Tucson],
 a long time ago, that was the name, my mother said.
 And earlier, it was known as Crazy Barrio.
 That is when I was there.

Luisa: Hmm, hmm.

Reyno: I was not very old.
 But Mom used to talk about it.
 Barrio, Crazy Barrio, she used to call it.

>   Haisavetchi'ivo humaku'u.
>   Ta kovanao pa'aria tean intoko.
>   Aman chea wam he'ela intok ori Ili Hu'upa, tea.
>   I'ivo intok Bwe'u Hu'upa tea.
>   Hunuu hunak hunuen teuwawan.

Luisa: Hmm, hmm.

Reyno: Hunama intok senu havesa kantoora,
> Sewam teame,
> huname ama hoho'an tea.

Luisa: Hmm, hmm.

Reyno: Ti neu e'etehonwan.
> Nee kia veha etehowata hihikkan.
> Ilitchiaka ama yeu siika.
> Bueno, entonces ini, ini'i malataim,
> hiva inim ho'aka huni'i hunuen neu aa e'etehon.

        I do not know why.
        But they said it was named Greasewood Forest also.
        And a little farther on, it was named Little Mesquite, they say.
        And on this side it was named Big Mesquite.
        Maybe it was called that.

Luisa: Hmm, hmm.

Reyno: And over there, someone, a ceremonial singer,
        [sur]named Sewam [Flowers],
        used to live there, it is said.

Luisa: Hmm, hmm.

Reyno: It is what they used to tell me.
        Then, I just used to listen to the conversations.
        I was very young when we left there.
        Well then, this, this one, Mom,
        always, even when they lived here, she used to tell me about it.

FIGURE 32 Jose Maria "Chema" Cupis. Leyva family photo.

AFTERWORD

IIYIKA TE LUTU'URIATA HIPPUE
We Have These Truths

Jose Maria Cupis (Chema Tosaria) speaks to future generations, on the importance of respect for the words of the elders, on the responsibility of elders to guide the younger generations, on all Hiakis' responsibility to care for one another, on the impermanence of life here on earth, on punishment and consequences for evil deeds, on the unity and brotherhood of the Hiaki people, and on the responsibility of the Hiaki people to retain sovereignty over their own lands, which their ancestors fought and died for.

Chema: Pos hunuleni, in achalim, intok in maalam,
  nemak weri, wa Diosta yoremia,
  i'ani orapo inim hiapsame.
  Inilen weye'epo, nehpo iyilevenak,
  waka'a woi, vahi lutu'uriata nooka.
  Waka yo'orata lutu'uria, vatnaatakariapo, waka yo'orata inim
  bwan bwiapo nahkwaktisukame.
  Vem lutu'uriawa inim toosahak, vempo lu'utek,
  bwiataka to'oka, bwiata vetuk to'oka,
  intuchi hunaman vem yeu hu'unakteipo,
  intuchi aman kom yahak.
  Wa bwia toloochia vem ama yeu yahak intuchi
  huna'atuk bwiapo kuutek. Intuchi, bwiatuk, hivapovenasi,
  bweituk wa espiritu lu'utek, aa nu'uka Itom Achai.
  Hunulentuko veha waa itou chupukame, i'an orapo weye,
  komo in aa teuwapo amani. Inilen
  waka yoremiata itom aa naknevetchi'ivo,
  itom aa uhu'unevetchi'ivo
  aa suawata bwisepo tahti,
  kovapo suawata aa hippuepo tahtia
  aa uhu'une, au nokaka aa uhu'une.
  Aa tetehwane, waka kaa tu'ik intok waka tu'ik,
  ta vatnaataka waka tu'ik itepo am lutu'uria maksakane
  waka tu'ik amemak etehone.
  Kaa hitasavenak, waka kaa tu'ik vo'ota vem bwibwihnevetchi'ivo
  bweituk wa naiki vo'om aayuk inim bwan bwiapo.
  Wa tukaa ania, Santa Tinievla ayukame,
  hunaa tua kaa tu'i,
  wa'a anhelito kee hee yo'otu chupamtavetchi'ivo.
  Kaa tu'ik, kulupti weemtavetchi'ivo,
  wa ko'okoa aayuk,
  hunuu tukaa ania aa hippue. Kaita newosiok,
  kaa hak weampo cha'aka o'oven wa'a itom yoremia,
  kee hee waka yo'orata mavetame.
  Tea vesa nokne o'oven i'an lautipo, itepo etehone

Chema: Well, in that way, my fathers, and my mothers,
    my relatives, those who are God's children,
    at this hour, those who live here.
    The way it is going now, of something like this,
    of the two, three truths, I speak.
    The truths of the elders, in the beginning, the elders,
    who walked on this crying earth.
    They left their truths here, they are gone,
    they lie in the earth, they lie under the earth,
    again from where they were born,
    again they have returned down there.
    The dust of the earth from which they came, again
    that has been mixed with the dirt, forevermore,
    because their spirit is gone, Our Father has taken it.
    That is why, then, that which was created for us, now the hour moves,
    as I have stated it in this way. This way
    the children whom we will love,
    so that we will care for them,
    until they gain knowledge,
    until they have knowledge in their heads,
    care for them, counsel them and care for them.
    You will tell them about the bad things and the good,
    but before that, we will tell them these truths, the good things,
    we will speak of the good things with them.
    Not just anything, the bad road that they should not take,
    because there are four roads in this crying earth.
    The night world, the Holy Tenebrae[1] that exists,
    that one is really very bad
    for the little angel who has not yet reached adulthood.
    The bad things, sometimes, when one is traveling,
    there may be illness,
    that night world has it. It has no other business there,
    our children should not be out there [in the night world],
    those who have not yet become adults.
    But then, although we will speak at this time, we will speak

---

1. Darkness, night.

itom yoremiamake, tea vesa ite kaa aet nok hikaiwak,
kia te hiokot amemak, hiaka huni kaa aet nok hikoiwatek
pos te kaachin am ya'ane. Porque i'an ania,
ania kuaktila,
wa ania mundo hunuen kuaktila.
Chikti si'imeku wa vato'ora, kaa solamente Hiaki,
chikti mundopo[2] aneme, si'ime hunulen kuaktila. Heewi.
Kaa, kaa lanwa'apo aman kaate intok
kaa lanwa'apo aman nooka.
Kaa tu'ik nooka intok vichau, vicha wa vem yo'owa,
kaa nappat wanaheelavenasi am yo'ore.
Kaa kiala am hikka, o si ama wam katnekai
o si tu'isi annekai.
Kaa, kaa kiala am hikka intok kaa aa ya'aneka,
aa nok vehe'e, aa nok konta.
Itom nok konkonta hume itom yoremia, heewi.
Chea susuavae intok chea hita ta'avae,
ta kaa, kaa lutu'uria wa vem nokiwa.
Wa yoemiawai kia hainmaisi hita ta'aka huni
kaa waka aa yo'owawa nok vehe'epo cha'aka.
Kaa waka aewa nok vehe'epo cha'aka.
Chea waka saiwa, chea yo'ota nokau,
au nokwau kaa tu'ik aa hoau,
au aa nokau, kaa aa nok vehe'epo cha'aka.
Iyii lutu'uria aayuk o'oven, tea vesa kaa, kaa
hunen emo am uhu'u pos si kaachin am ya'ane.
Kia yoemiari, itepo achaiwaim, yoemiakame ameu nokaka
huni kaachin am ya'ane. Bweituk vempo, komo i'an orapo,
inime wasuktiampo, vichau, vicha waka eskuelata hippue,
edukasionta emo maka. Heewi.
Kia kaa yuyuma'isi huni im edukaroala waate, ta vesa hunai veha,
chea wa vem achai vepa o chea vem mala vepa,

---

2. Here Mr. Cupis uses a Spanish term, *mundo*, for "world," when we would have expected him to use *ania*, the Hiaki word for that concept.

to our children, but then if we are not obeyed,
even if we plead with them, even if our words are not heeded,
well, we cannot do anything to them. Because in today's world,
the world has changed,
the world, the earth world has changed that way.
Everywhere the baptized ones, not just the Hiakis,
all those in the world, everyone has changed. Yes.
They are not, not going in the right direction,
nor speaking the right way over there.
They say bad things, and tomorrow, in the future, those, their elders,
no longer do they respect them as in the past.
They just do not listen to them, if they should go by there,
or if they should do good things.
They just do not, not listen to them, and if they are not going to do it,
they argue with them and talk back.
They talk back, those, our children, yes.
They want to be smarter, they want to know more,
but their words are not the truth.
The children, even if they have learned much,
they should not argue with their parents.
They should not argue with their mother.
Be it an older brother,[3] be it an elder speaking,
when they are speaking to them when they are doing a bad thing,
if they are being counseled, they should not talk back.
Although there are these truths, if they do not, not
behave in this way, well, there is nothing that can be done to them.
Just the children, we, their fathers, their parents, will counsel them,
but there is nothing we can do to them. Because they, like it is now
in these years, in the future, they have schooling,
they are obtaining an education. Yes.
Even if they cannot afford a complete education, but with that, then,
more than their fathers or more than their mothers, they will have

---

3. Here, Mr. Cupis uses the word *sai*, which can be used by people of either gender to refer to their older brother. For example, the statement "In sai yo'owe Heripe tea" (My older brother is named Felipe) might be uttered by a younger male.

chea ili woi, vahi leetata ta'ak.
Hunai veha amae am yuu'a.
Taupo amet mamteka amae am yuu'a, ume vem yo'owam.
Iyika hooa i'ani wa vemelasi kateme,
i'an wa yoremiawai, inilen aane.
Ama hoori, kaa si'ime. Waate kechia am yo'ore vem aewam
kia hainmaisia kaa tua tu'isi emo uhu'uka huni'i,
wa yo'owatau kaita nooka. Wait pa'ariat haksa
hitasa vem noka'u nooka, ta vesa vem hoapo, vem solarpo,
vem ae vichapo, kaita hitasavenak,
waka kaa tu'ik, malapalabrata kaa aa nooka. Wai pariat
hachin machik hiapsa, ta vesa waka vem hoara...
bweituk huname veha hume ili pensaroame,
ili susuakame inika weiya, inien aa pensaroaka veha
vem yo'owam vichapo, vem hoa solarpo vichapo,
wa'a heka cha'akame, hunaka yo'ore intok hunuka yo'orisaewa,
waka hekata vem aetuk nahkuakteka'u intok
vem aetuk yeu yoemtuka'u,
hunaka naksaewa, intok hunaka yo'orisaewa
bweituk huna'a wa hekka, am yo'oturiakame,
wame vem yo'owam hunaka hekkata am makak
vempoim ama nah kuaktinevetchi'ivo intok
vempoim ama yo'otunevetchi'ivo, hunaka hekkaata am makak.
Hunama vempo yo'otuk, hunulenpo aman aa nakii'aawa,
aa naksaewa, aa yo'ori'ii'aawa, komo haisa
waka vem achai intok waka vem maala aa yo'ore
o chea akowa
wame ae vepa yo'owe, chea ume ili yo'owe si'ime
natcha'aka kateme,
hunulen emo hikkaipo cha'aka intok
inilen emo nakpo cha'aka, to'oven.
Ta vesa kaa hunenia.
Hunenia intok kia kaa hunenia huni'i, ta wame ama hoori,
hachin yoemiawa ama aane vem yo'orawa yo'ore.
Kia polooveta aekai, hachin polooveta achaika huni'i,
akim aa nake intok kia im aa yo'ore,
kaa hitasavenak au nokaka hiapsa.

learned more than two, three letters.
With that, then, they push them back.
They put their hands on their parents' chests and push them back.
This is what they do now, these new arrivals.
Now the children are doing this.
There are some, not all. Some also respect their mothers,
just anyway, even if they didn't treat each other very well,
they did not say anything to their elders. Out there somewhere
what they say, they say, but at home, in their house,
in front of their mother, nothing whatsoever,
the bad things, bad words, they do not say those words. Out there
something strange lives, but then, that, their home . . .
because those, then, those who give things a little more thought,
who are a little smarter, they have this, they think this way, then
in front of their parents, in front of their house,
where their shelter is, they respect it and were told to respect it,
the shelter under which they moved [i.e., lived],
and where they were born,
they were told to care for it, and are to respect it,
because that, the shelter, which raised them,
that, their elder gave them this shelter
so that they could move about [i.e., live] there and
grow up there, that shelter was given to them.
That is where they grew up, that is why they are told to care for it,
and told to care for it, respect it, just as
they respect their father and their mother,
and perhaps an older sister,
those who are older than them [and] all those who are a little older,
and follow each other in sequence.
This is how they should heed each other, and
in this way they should also care for each other.
But then, not that way.
That way and not even really that way, but they are placed there,
strange children are there who respect their elders.
Just a poor mother, strangely, even a poor father,
they care for him and they respect him,
they do not live speaking disrespectfully to him.

Kia vempo haksamaisi hiapsaka, ta wa vem hoara
aa nake intok vem achaiwa nake, vem aye nake.
Hunulenpo veha vo'o hooa waate. Inilen veha aayuk
uu vemelasi yoeme, itom yoremia, vichau vicha, intok
itom yoremia, yoremiam. Hununen veha kaate.
Ta vesa tu'i. Kaachin maachi wa'a kaa tu'ik,
tu'ik nokamtavetchi'ivo.
Tu'i. Ta wa'a kaa tu'ik nokame intok
pos kaa au nokwapo cha'aka, itepo yo'owa intok
kaa aamak peleitapo cha'aka. Su'utohine,
Diosta mampo aa su'utohine, ta Diostau aa bwaniane, intok
itom Aeveo aa bwaniasakane,
Diosta tu'i orata aa maknevetchi'ivo intok kaita hitasa venak
waka ko'okosimaachik au aa . . . au cha'atune'epovetana
intok kaita haksa pasaroane'epo aman, veha si'ime . . .
A'apo aa hiapsi aa bwaniane intok aa netanriane
waka tu'i tiempota, tu'i lugarta, bweituk a'apo aa yoemiane,
aa yoemiakame, itepo am yoemiak, kaa have . . .
aewai, malawai nakwa, aa yo'ore, inileni.
Hunulenpo vea pos hunulen nehpo aa teuwa intok hunulen
nehpo aa . . . intok hunulen aa hu'uneiya, wa yo'orata, nehpo.
Iyilen nehpo aa pasaroa
i'an orapo, inim bwan bwiapo nee ketuni Diosta e'apo, intok,
Diosta tu'i graciampo ketuni nee nah kuakte.
Waka ayukamta nee aa vehe'e.
Huevenak nee vehe'ela.
Ko'okosi machik nee vehe'ela.
Nukmaisi aa vehe'ela,
ko'okosi, hiapsita me'eri. Ko'okoata pasaaroasuk,
huevena tiempopo nee nah kuaktisuk. Kaa tu'ik,
hiapsita wiutawa'apo, hiapsita ta'aruwa'apo nah kuaktek,
ta vea Diosta e'apo, Diosta utteampo, Itom Aye utteampo
tua kaita hitasavenak neu pasaaroak,
kaita wa ko'okosi maachi, bueno,
wa Diosta kahtiwo ana aa pasaaroak,
kane kaita tua pasaaroak, ta nee aa vehe'ek,
aa ko'oko ta'ak. Ta vesa wa'a in espiritu kaa yeu siika intok

Even if they live anywhere, but that [place], their home,
they care for it, they care for their father, for their mother.
In this way, then, some of them travel. This is what they have done,
this generation, our children, and in the future,
our children's children. This is how they are traveling.
But then it is all right. Nothing is wrong with that, the bad,
for the one who is speaking well.
Good. But the one who speaks badly,
well, we should not say anything to them and
we should not fight with them. Leave them alone.
Leave them in God's hands, but [ask] God to bless them and
ask Our Holy Mother to bless them,
so that God will give them the good hour and nothing
that is painful to them . . . will stick to them,
and nothing whatsoever will happen to them, over there, then all . . .
They will ask for a blessing for their heart, and will ask for
the good times, a good place, because they will be his child,
his father, we are their parents, not anyone . . .
their mother, their mom is cared for, they respect her, like this.
In that way, then, well, that way, I say this and that way . . .
I, it . . . and that way I know it, the elders, I.
In this way I have experienced it,
at this hour, here in this crying world, I still, if God is willing, and
with the good graces of God I am still moving about.
That which is going on, I have experienced it.
Many things, I have experienced.
Painful things, I have experienced.
I have experienced things that cannot be spoken about,
painfully, the heart was killed. I experienced sickness,
for many years I wandered about. Nothing good,
where many lives were taken, where lives were lost, I was there,
but in God's will, God's strength, Our Holy Mother's strength,
really nothing whatsoever happened to me, good,
nothing that was very painful, well,
that, God's punishment, I did go through it,
I did not experience very bad things, but I did experience it,
I felt the pain. But then, that, my spirit did not leave me,

kaa . . . bweituk kaa hunuen chupia.
Kaa hunen neu chupia. Nehpo aa hippue
waka tiempota, orata in ae vo'otene'u.
Ta vesa nehpo aa pasaaroalataka hunen hiia.
Huevena weyemta, ko'okoata,
Dios kahtiwo ko'okoata huni
nee pasaaroala kechia, hee. Ta vesa A'apoik e'apo intoksan
nee Au bwaanan asta i'an tahti, ketuni naavuhti vicha
nee aa netane waka tu'i taiwaeta, tu'i orata. Woi, vahi Lionooki,
Diosta nooki, ili woi, vahi in ta'a'u,
hunaimak nee au bwaana. Hunaimak nee aa netane, naavuhtia.
Waka tu'i orata, in ae hiapsane'u.
Ta vesa waka taewaita yumak kaachin nee anne.
Kia have hittoa hoame, have tuu aneme
o chea loktortaka huni, kaachin nee nottane.
Intok kaaveta nottane kuando waka Diosta aa wawa'ataka,
Diosta waka orata yuma'u, Diosta hunaktei,
waka itom destino tea'u. Hunaka yumak,
kaita hittoa, kaita loktor,
kaita wa tu'i hittoata hoawame;
kaave, kaave aa tu'utene. Bweituk A'apo aa weiya,
Itom Achai, Itom Ae,
asoalakame aa waata.
Aa yoemiakame aa a'awa. Hunama tahti hiva.
Hunu'u huna'a, wa Diosta yee hiokoe'u,
hunulen aa hiokoene. Dios inilen yee hiokoe.
Hunu'u huna'a. I'an itepo hunen hiune,
"Nee hiokoene Achai o nee hiokoene komae."
Itepo inien nau aa lutu'uria hooa, ho.
O chea komaale o nemak weri, nee hiokoe.
Itepo ika nooka. Ta posi itepo kaa aa hippue uka poderta,
uka itom ito ae hiokoene'u.
Kaa, katta hippue.
A'apo Dios aa hippue uka poderta.
Hunaa yee hiokoe, ho. Iyilen aayuk iyi'i, itom lutu'uria,

and not . . . because I was not destined for that.
It was not destined for me. I do have it,
the time, the hour in which I shall lie down.
But because I have gone through it, I say this.
Many things that are going on, sickness,
God's punishment, even illness,
I have also experienced it, yes. But then, due to His will, and so,
I have cried to Him, until now, still on through the future,
I have requested the good day, the good hour. Two, three prayers,
God's talk, a few, two, three [prayers] that I know,
with that I cry to Him. I ask with that, on through.
The good hour in which I can live.
But then, when that day arrives, there is nothing I can do.
Just anyone who makes medicine,[4] someone who does good,
or, perhaps, even a doctor cannot revive me.
And no one will return when God wants them,
when the hour arrives that God has intended,
that which is said to be our destiny, when that arrives,
no medicine, no doctor,
there is no one who will make good medicine;
no one, no one will heal them. Because He will take them.
Our Father, Our Mother,
their Mother wants them.
Their Father is asking for them. It is only up to there.
That is it. That which God will forgive,
forgive them. This is how God forgives us.
That is it. Now we will say this,
"Forgive me, Father, or forgive me, Comadre."
We will say these truths to each other, see.
Comadre or my relative, forgive me.
This is what we say. But we do not have that power,
that with which we will forgive each other.
Nothing, we do not have it.
He, he, God has that power.
He forgives us, see. This is how it is, this, our truths,

---

4. A healer.

poloove lutu'uria. Im bwiapo itepo kaachin ito hiokoene
intok te kaachin ito salvaroane. Kia te hain hita hoaka
huni'i kaa ito salvaroane. Heewi. Hita kaa tu'ik ya'ak
huni te kaachin ito salvaroane,
bweituk kaa hunen itou chupia. Kaa hunen itot aa hu'unaktela wa
Itom Achai, Itom Ae. A'apo itot aa hu'unaktei
waka ayukamta.
Huntusan wa Diosta vepat aneme
hunaa kaa tu'ik hooa. Diosta vepat aane.
Hunaa a'apo aa hippue. Hunaa vato'i o maala
waka Diosta vepat aa hooa'u,
huevenaka yee ko'okosi hooa, takawapo ko'okoata yee maka.
Huname Diosta vepat aane.
Huname kaita, kaita hiokoewamta hippue.
Vem . . . ala aa hippue waka kahtiwota.
Ta kaa kokoarimtaka kahtikaroana huname'e.
Inim bwan bwiapo kahtikaroana.
Inim bwiapo vem nah kate'epo,
ketuni waka espirituta, espirituta aa hippue . . .
hiapsipo hippueteko. Bweituk A'apo, Itom Achaiwa, wa espiritu,
wa aet hu'unaktela intok hunaka kaa yeu aa wikne
asta ke kaa aa . . . uka kahtiwota yumau.
Hunaka yumaariak kahtiwopo si'imekut aa kahtikaroaka
aa vepsuk, hunak vea aa a'aune.
Hunak veha aa u'ane waka espirituta o hunaksan vea mukne,
tia itepo, mukne. Ta e'e, kaa mukne wa espiritu.
Wa takawa tawane, espiritu intok kaa mukne.
Yeu simne, bweituk A'apo aa nu'une, uchi vichaa, waka espirituta.
Iiyilen katek waa itom takawa. Ha.
Hunaa itot aayuk. Aa mammattene,
aa mammattene inika'a lutu'uriata bweituk hunulen katek.
Iyim hiapsipo itot katek, itom sare'echiam[5] tiapo.
Hunaa wa pulmon, hunaa, huna'a.
Komo hitasa wa yoi heofragata hippue. Hunalen weye.

---

5. *Sare'echiam* is the pancreas in the human body. Mr. Cupis incorrectly identifies the lungs as *sare'echiam*. He does, however, identify the lungs as *pulmón*, which is the correct Spanish term.

poor truths. On this earth we cannot forgive ourselves
and we cannot save ourselves. Even if we do just anything,
even so, we cannot save ourselves. Yes. If we do something bad,
even then we will not save ourselves,
because we are not made that way. It was not intended for us
by Our Father, Our Mother. He intended it for us,
that which exists.
That is why those who are trying to surpass God,[6]
those are doing bad things. They are trying to surpass God.
They are the ones who have it. That baptized one or Mom,
when they are doing things to surpass God,
many of them are hurting us, they cause sickness in our bodies.
Those are the ones who are trying to surpass God.
Those have nothing, nothing, no sympathy.
Their . . . do have it, the punishment.
But they will not be punished when they are dead.
On this crying earth, they will be punished.
Here on this earth where they walk around,
while they still have their spirit, their spirit
is still within them. Because He, Our Father, their spirit,
that which was intended for him, and that will not be taken out
until it is not . . . the punishment is given all over.
When that is given, the punishment is given all over,
when they are beaten, then they will be asked for.
That is when it is taken, their spirit, or that is when they will die,
we say, they will die. But no, the spirit will not die.
Their body will stay, and his spirit will not die.
It will go out, because He will get it back again, the spirit.
This is how it is, our body. Ha.
That is on us, you will understand it.
Understand it, this truth, because that is how it is.
It is here in our heart, in what we call our liver, as they say it.
That is our lungs, that, that.
A *heofragata*[7] such as the Mexicans say we have. That is how it is.

---

6. Witches.

7. Possibly referring to the esophagus here.

Hunaa waka ohvota, si'ime takawapo chivehta.
Kia kocheka huni tekipanoa, hunaa, wame pulmoonim,
huname tekipanoa. Kialikun vea, kia kocheka huni
chuyu, chuyukti anne porque hunama katek uu espiritu.
Hunaa weye. Hunaa vea hiva weye,
aa kocheu huni'i, itom kokocheu huni
posi hunaa, hunaa itom hiapsitua.
Ta vea espiritu huna'a aa atteak,
hunaa aa weetua. Heewi. Iiyilen, iiyinen katek wa itom takawa
intok iiyilen te hiapsa. A'apoik e'apo te hiapsa.
Heewi. Katte itom utteapo hiapsa;
A'apoik utteampo te hiapsa. Huntuksan te Au bwanii'aawa.
Au bwanii'aawaka te vevia. Heewi.
Ko'okosi te vevia, kuluptia.
Wame kaa Aa yo'oreme,
kaa Aa hatteiya intok kaa Aa sualeme,
pos humane ko'okosi vevia. Hunaa, huna'a uu kahtiwo. Heewi.
Hunulen vea kati'ikun hunen hiia.
Kaa, kaa hunum tenne itou wek, chikoteta machu'u cha'aka
itom witawitahti veva. E'e. Hunu kaita, ta itom veva.
Hunu huna'a wa takawapo itot yeu kikteme,
takawapo itom ine'a'u, Hunaa vea hunen aayuk.
Hunulen weye wa itom espiritu.
Hunulen yeu sika'apo vea itepo aa nake,
inilen itepo ito nakne,
inilen aa hu'uneiyakai. Heewi.
Hunaimak itepo nahkuakte bweituk hunulen itou chupa'i.
Poloove chupa'im te. Katte tomi chupiam mas de kee,
kee itom tekillea te ito ania.
Hunuen te itom yoemiam yo'oturia
intok A'apo'ik e'apo. Itom Achai O'olata e'apo,
Itom Aye Mariata Santissimata e'apo. Hunain te yo'otuk.
Hunain am uhu'u Huna'a.
Hunaasam uhu'u.
Itepo intok pos kia vea te am yo'oturia, am ania, heewi.
Lutula weepo te am hi'ibwatua.
Aa haiwa, waka chikti ta'apo waka

That one spreads the blood all throughout the body.
Even during sleep they are working, those, the lungs,
they are working. That's why, even when sleeping,
they are pulsating, pulsating because that's where our spirit is.
That one is moving. That then is always moving,
even when one is sleeping, even when we are sleeping,
Well, that one, that one kept us alive.
But the spirit, that one owns it,
that one makes it go. Yes. This is the way, the way our body is,
and this is how we live. Through His will, we live.
Yes. Not through our strength do we live;
through His will, we live. That is why we are told to cry to Him.
We are punished so that we may cry to Him. Yes.
We are punished severely, sometimes.
Those who do not respect Him,
who do not fear Him, who do not believe in Him,
well, they are punished severely. That, that is the punishment. Yes.
That way, remember, that is how it was said.
He does not stand over us with a whip in his hand,
whipping us. No. That is not what happened, but he does punish us.
That, that which appears on our body,
what we feel on our bodies, that is what He did.
That is how our spirit goes.
It came about that way, in that way we care for Him,
in this way we care for each other,
knowing this as we do. Yes.
We walk about with Him because that is how it was intended for us.
We are poor beings. We were not meant to be rich, only that,
that with our labor we support ourselves.
That is how we raise our children,
and through His will. Our Old Father's will,
through Our Most Holy Mother's will. That is how we grew up.
That is how He cares for us. That One.
He is the one who cares for them.
And we, well, we just raise them, we support them, yes.
In the straight truth, we feed them.
We look for it, that which each day

vem ae hiapsine'u. Hunaka te haiwa amevetchi'ivo
bweituk te kaa am sioktuapea,
kaa am tevaurituapea wame itom yoremiam.
Kia ili pan levelaim huni wam
hak am kova'ariane, ayuko.
Itom awepo, hita yeu nu'upak
vea ameu yeu aa toisakane.
Inileni, inilen weye wa vemelasi yeu yoemtume.
Inilen yo'otu.
Inilen kia itepo huni ket hunainsu hiva yo'otulamtakai.
Ta te vesa i'an Diosta te aet vaesaune. Inilen itom takawa weye,
intok inilen vea itom wasuktiam vea weye.
Ume wasuktiam kaa notteka weye.
Huntuksan nehpo iyilevenak eteho intok inilevenak nee nooka
bweituk inilen itou aayuk wa itom poloove kohtumvre, heewi.
Itom chupa'apo amani. Hunalen te hiva aa vehe'etuane,
intok hunalen te aa vo'o hooriasaka i'an orapo.
Huntuksan te ito ae nakpo cha'aka,
ito aet yo'oripo cha'aka, waka'a tu'uwa Santa devosionta,
vato'i, senu Diosta yoremia, tu'uwata ya'avaane.
Uhbwanne, i'ivo tetekiakamevetchi'ivo,
chikti maalam, malestom,
o chea matachinim,
o chea wa pahkoalente ti aewame.
Uhbwanne. Hunaa tua kaa, kaita ae vepa nokpo
cha'aka wa tekiakame, ofisiota hippueme.
Kaa huevena nokta waatane; woi, vahi palavra tua sopaaroa.
Aa mavetne. Aa mavetaka aa Lios bwaniasaewa. Ho.
Hunaka taewata au hunakteta, hunaka kaa ta'aruka, hunai taewata,
hunaka orata hahaseka aman au yeu yevihsaewa wa hoa solarpo
aa kateka'apo, aa wetuapo, waka orasionta, novenata,
hitasa weyemta o chea Santa alavansa, hitasa we'u
o miisa o vihpa, hitasa weye, teopopo.
Hunaa, pos inilen nau mochala cha'akai,

they will eat. We look for that for them
because we do not want them to feel sad,
we do not want them to feel hunger, our children.
We will earn even a small morsel of bread for them,
somewhere out there we will earn it, if available.
If we are able, then, we will bring something out,
then we will bring it to them.
In this way, this way it goes with the new generation.
This is how they are growing up.
In this way because even we will become old, in that way.
But now, we will be grateful to God. This is how our body is,
and in this way, then, our years, then, our years are going by.
The years do not return.
That's why I speak like this, and like this I speak,
because in this way we have our poor customs. Yes.
To our end, therefore. In this way, we still have to pay,
and that is how we shall walk this path, at this hour.
That's why we should care for each other,
we should respect each other, the holy devotion,
the baptized, one of God's children will want to do good.
You will make a request over here of those holding a ceremonial office,
each mother [female cantor], the prayer leaders,
or maybe the matachin dancers,
or the sponsors of the ceremony, as they are known.
You will request of them. That one really cannot say anything,
to those who are ceremonial persons, who hold an office.
They do not need many words; two, three words are truly sufficient.
Accept it. Accept and thank them. See.
That day intended for you, do not lose it, on that day, follow,
that day, that hour, [you are] to go out there to him, to the home,
the place where he is, where it is going on, the prayers, novenas,[8]
whatever is going on, be it holy prayers of praise, whatever is going on,
be it a Mass or Vespers, whatever is going on, in the church.
Those, well, in this way gathered together in a group

---

8. A recitation of prayers for nine consecutive days.

nau weweripovenasi, intok nau weweri.
Chikti wa pa'ala vato'ora nau weri
Hiakira intok uu kaa Hiaki. Bweituk te ito sailak,
ito te waik,
bweituk te wepul, wepul Diosta te nau aa achaik
intok wepul Itom Ae, te nau Aek, hiva kaave intoko.
Hunaka te Aek.
Huntuksan inilen itepo nau weri, nau te weri.
Ito te sailak, ito te ou sailak,
ito te maalak, o te hamut waik.
Iyilen aayuk wa itom poloove lutu'uria,
wa woh naiki pueplota lutu'uriapo, iiyilen aayuk.
Inilen ito yo'orisaewa. Hunulentuk vea,
hunaman bwiapo huni'i iyii wa woi, vahi lutu'uria,
konseho weyeme.
Iyilen aa konseho hooa wa, wa pueplo kovanao,
wa pueplo yo'owe o chea malesto achaitakai
o chea wa temahti mol achaita hoapo
konsehota weiyane.
Inilen aa entregaroa intok o chea wikoo ya'urataka huni'i
waka woh naiki pueplota nau yumaka'apo,
iyi, iyilen aa lutu'uria hooa.
O chea Santo Lominko misapo chikti vem pueplopo,
vem misa vitchuka'apo iyika lutu'uriata nau yecha.
Emo aet Lios bwania, sailapo, kompalepo, komaalepo.
Ika nau uhu'u, palavrata. Ini'i tu'i.
Hunalevenasi, vichau, vicha, kai . . . au waatisaewa,
wame woo vusan taewaim yuma'apo.
Aman yeu rukruktisaewa, kompanyaruasaewa uka Santa misata
o Santa vihpata. Amemak aa vo'o hooriasaewa.
Dios, A'apo waka taewa grasiata enchim mikne,
Itom Aye A'apo taewata enchim mikne,
emou aa hu'unaktene, emou kom aa vittuane,
chikti wame enchim yoremiampo yeu tahti.
Tua kaita hitasavenasi, wa Diosta kahtiwo ya'ari,
kaita emou aune bweituk inim bwan bwiapo, ti hiia,
inim bwan bwiapo wa Diosta hunaktei ya'ari kahtiwo,

as if they were related, and they are related.
All the people are related,
the Hiakis and the non-Hiakis. Because we are the younger brothers,
we are younger sisters,
because we have one, one God, Our Father
and one, one Mother, we have the same Mother only, no one else.
She is Our Mother.
That is why, in this way we are related, related together,
we are younger brothers, we are male brothers,
we are mothers, we are younger sisters.
This is how they are, our poor truths,
In the truths of our eight villages, this is where they are.
This is how we are to respect each other. That is why, then,
even over there, in that land, these two, three truths,
right here, the counsel is also going on.
This is the counsel of the village governor,
the village elder or maybe the prayer leader,
or maybe at the home of the sacristan father
whose counsel is followed.
This is how it is offered, or maybe the coyote society authorities,
where the eight village boundaries meet,
this, in this way, these truths are made.
Or maybe at the holy Sunday Mass, in each of their villages,
where they attended Mass, these truths are settled upon in unison.
They thank each other, older brother, compadre, comadre.
Together, they care for this, their word. This is good.
Like that, to the future . . . you are to remember it,
when those seven days are reached.
You are to go there, to accompany the holy Mass
or the holy Vespers. You are to join them on this trip.
God, He will give you the day's grace,
Our Holy Mother, she will give you the day,
She will make it available to you, She will send it down to you,
for each and every one of your children.
That nothing whatsoever, really, the punishment that God created,
none of that will affect you because on this crying earth, they say,
on this crying earth, God's intent, the punishment he created,

penitensia huevenaka aayuk.
Senu ili wichataka huni o senu ili kutatakai
o senu ili animaltakai o ime bwiapo ho'ak, yee huhaka aane.
Waka itom yoremia huhane o chea yo'ota huhane o aa ki'ine
o sosone o hitasa au cha'atune.
Hunuka kaa aunepo vetana vea ameu nokna.
Aa netanria waka taewata, grasiata wame
woo vusan ta'apo, huname yoremiampo yeu tahti.
Alla'eaka au yuma'ane. Kia Dios, A'apo enchim aa makne,
chikti enchim yoremiapo yeu tahtia.
Hunulen A'apo enchim waka indulhensiata makne.
Inilen eme'e aa kova'ane waka indulhensiata,
waka tu'ik, enchim asoalamvetchi'ivo,
enchim yoremiamvetchi'ivo intok wame emomak werimvetchi'ivo,
enchim ae, enchim yo'owa.
Si'imemvetchi'ivo aa mavet makna hunaka'a.
Emou kom aa vittuane,
hunulen enchim aet hiapseka,
enchim aet tekipanoau. Ika noka hume yoeme.
Iyii huna'a wa itom poloove lutu'uria. Iniemak emo uhu'une.
Inilen te aa uhu'u. Inilen te aa yo'ore.
Intoksan inilen nehpo emou aa lutu'uria hooa bweituk
"Dios, A'apo inilen net kom aa hu'unaktek i'an,"
ti hiia uu kovanao o uu temahti mol.
Nehpo iyilevenak emomak aa teuwasaewa
in yo'otaka weeka'apo amani o chea in malestotuka'apo
amani o in kovanao achaiwaituka'apo amani wa pueplota,
chikti wa yoremia hiapsame, i'an inim orapo
itepo wa nau pueplo inim aane.
Inika nehpo lutu'uriata emou hooa
bweituk nee wa Dios A'apo nee aet hiokoene iniachi kechia
intok Dios A'apo nee aniane,
intok waka taewai grasiata neu kom vittuane,
in yoremiamvetchi'ivo, intok in familiavetchi'ivo
o chea in aemvetchi'ivo. Iyiavetchi'ivo nehpo inika emou nooka
bweituk yooko, matchuk, Diosta, Diosta hustisia

there is much penance.
Even one little thorn or one little stick
or one little animal or those that live in the earth, they sting us.
They will sting our children or perhaps sting or bite an adult,
or a thorn will get stuck in them, or something will happen to them.
So that this will not happen, we talk to them.
[We] request for them the day, the grace of God, those
seven days, for all your children, all the way through.
Happily, you all will earn it. Only God, He will give it to you all,
to each of your children.
That way, He will give you His grace.
This way, you will earn it, His grace,
the good, for your infants,
for your children and for those who are related to you,
your mother, your elders.
For everyone you will be given it, receive it, that [grace].
It will be sent down to you, all that,
if you really have it set in your heart,
if you work for it. This is what the men say.
This is it, our poor truths. With these, you will care for each other.
This is how we care for it. This is how we respect it.
And so, this way, I give you these truths because
"God, He gave this to me today,"
says the governor or the sacristan.
I was told to say this to you all
because I stand an elder, therefore, or because I am the prayer leader,
therefore, or I am the governor, therefore, to the villagers,
all the people who are alive, now, at this hour
the villagers are here, together.
I give these truths to you
because God, He will forgive me for this also,
and God, He will help me,
and He will send down to me the grace of God,
for my children and for my wife
or perhaps for my mother. It is for this that I speak to you,
because tomorrow, day after tomorrow, when God's, God's justice

inim bwan bwiapo neu kom yumak, pos nehpo vo'otene.
Hunak nehpo inim yo'otaka weyeka i'an orapo
nehpo waka lutu'uriata aa hippue.
Nehpo kaita inilevenak wa in yoremia, pueplomak nokaka'atek,
nehpo humak ket aet kahtikaroana komo hunenia.
Nehpo humak aet penaruane wa in ora muerte,
huisiota yuma'apo nehpo aet penaruane.
Kaa aa mukne. Ho.
Mumukeka huni vea hihiavihtene,
bweituk iniavetchi'ivo waka lutu'uriata in kaa in yoremiam
makakavetchi'ivo, waka pueplo leita, pueplo malata,
pueplo achaita, pueplo yoremiata, si'imeta nehpo,
kaa, kaaveta etehoriak, ho.
Huna'atukao veha hunaman nee penaruatuane.
Hunaatukao, kaa in ya'aka'u hunait nehpo penaruatuana.
Huntuksan inika kaa neu aunevetchi'ivo
waka tu'i ora muerte huisiota in atteanevetchi'ivo
pos inika enchim lutu'uria maka. Inilen nehpo emou aa teuwa.
Chikti weye'epo, Lominkopo misa ta'apo, misata chupuko,
nehpo inilen enchim aa etehoria. Inilen nehpo enchim aa maka
Hunuutuksan inilen Dios A'apo nee hiokoene, intok
Itom Aye Maria Santissima A'apo nee hiokoe,
nee aet hiokoene iniechi. Hunulen nehpo emou aa teuwak,
inilen nehpo enchim aa lutu'uria makak,
maalam, pueplo, chikti, sokchikti pa'ala vato'ora,
Diosta yoremia, Santora, inia veekik Santora
inim nau yumakame.
Inilen nehpo enchim mampo aa bwisek, intok inilen
nehpo emou aa teuwak. Nechem vaesae, nechem aet vaesae,
intok nehpo nee enchim aet vaesae.
Ket hunalensu, iyika in teuwaka'u,
amma'ali o kaa amma'ali ta vesa nee emou aa bwisek.
Ta vesa pos nee kaita, kaa tu'ik nookak.
Chikti wa hunamavetchi'ivo tu'i intok neevetchi'ivo tu'i.
Ana aa teuwak; emou nee aa teuwak. Iiyilenpo
amani nehpo emou aa teuwak intoksan inilen vea nehpo Dios
A'apo nee aet hiokoene, Itom Achai, itom Aye Maria intok

comes down to this crying earth to me, then I shall lie down.
Then I, since I stand here an elder, at this hour
I have the truths.
If I do not speak to my people, the villagers, this way,
then perhaps I will be punished like that.
Maybe I will suffer the penance at the hour of my death
when justice is given, I will suffer the penance.
I will not be able to die. See.
Even if I am dying, I will continue to breathe,
because I did not offer the truths to my children,
to the village officials, the village mothers,
the village fathers, the village children, all of them,
if I do not speak of it, see.
That, then I will suffer.
That way, that which I did not do, for that, I will be made to suffer.
So that this does not happen to me
at the good hour of my death, so that justice will be mine,
well, I give you all these truths. In this way, I say this to you all.
In every way, on the day of Sunday Mass, when Mass is over,
I speak to you all in this way. In this way, I give it to you all.
In that way, then, He, God will forgive me and
Our Holy Mother Mary, She will forgive me,
forgive me for this. In this way, I have said this to you all,
in this way I have given you all the truth,
mothers, villagers, each, every one of the baptized ones,
God's children, the Saints, these many Saints,
those who have gathered here.
This way I have left it in your hands, and in this way,
I have said this to you all. You can thank me, thank me for it,
and I will also thank you all for it.
Also, this that I have said to you all,
truthfully or not truthfully, but then I have handed it to you all.
But then I, nothing, nothing bad have I said.
For each of them it is good, and it is good for me.
I have said it; to all of you I have said it. In this way,
I have said it to you all and this way then I, God,
He will forgive me for it, Our Father, and Our Holy Mother Mary,

nee aet hiokoene. Iiyilen vea nehpo emou hiiak.
Ama naavuhti vicha kechia, aayuk, wa ayukame,
aayuk intok wa weyeme, weye, vichau, vicha
itou weyeme. Inii'i itom poloove bwia inim vo'oka.
Wa Hiak vatwe, "Hiak bwia" ti aewame. Haksa tiempopo, Diosta,
Diostuka'apo naatekai, wa Dios hunen aa hu'unaktek,
Dios itou aa hu'unaktek. Hunaatuka'u,
i'an inim itepo aet cha'asasaka,
aet te tekipanoa, tukaariat naavuhtia. Yeteta te aet ta'aru,
tevaata te aet pasaaroa. Si'imeta te aet pasaaroa.
Aet te va'ai koko intok hiapsita te aet ta'aru.
Iyii ili kawi sanwitala vo'okame, hunu'u huna'a wa itom attea
intok iyii bwia inim vo'okame, itepo te aa atteak.
Itou hu'unaktei.
A'apo Senor, desde kee inim kom aa yumaka'apo
naateka hunulen itou aa hu'unaktek. Iiyilen katek wa lutu'uria.
Wame vatnaatakariapo, inim wa lei hiapsisukame
intok inim wa vato'ora hiapsisukame,
iiyilen aa etehok intok iiyilen itou aa tookokok.
I'ansu tolochiaka to'oka, bwiataka to'oka.
Tolochia heka'apo, to'ochia heka'apo to'oka.
Ta wa vem lutu'uriawa inim tawala.
I'an wa in teuwa'u, inii hunaa wa vem lutu'uria.
Hunuutukau hunulen nehpo emou aa teuwa,
bweituk hunulen itou aayuk
intok hunulen itepo au hapsasakane.
Polovemtaka huni'i te au hapsakane tua te kaa haivu ta'apo
wa yoita mampo aa su'utoisaewa. Kaa haivu ta'apo
yoita ama su'utoisaewa inim poloove bwiapo, itom Hiak bwiapo.
Kaa im aa watasaewa waka yoita. Iyika te lutu'uriata hippue.

and you all will forgive me for it. In this way then I have said it to you.
Going forward, also, those are things, those things
are there and that which is going on, is going on, [it is] going forward,
that which will happen to us. This, our poor land, lies here.
The Hiaki River, "the Hiaki land," as it is known. At some time, God,
in the beginning, because he is God, that God intended it that way,
God gave it to us. He is the one,
now we are still holding on to it,
we work on it, throughout the night. We lose sleep over it,
we experience hunger over it. For it, we are enduring everything.
For it we are dying of thirst and we lose our lives.
This little mountain lying there at length, that one is ours,
and this land that lies here, we own that.
It was intended for us.
He, God, from the time that he came down here [to earth],
beginning then, He intended it for us. This is how the truth is.
Those from the beginning, the authorities who lived here
and also those baptized ones who lived here,
this is how they spoke about it, they died, and left it to us.
Now they have become dust, they lie there as dirt.
In the dusty wind, they lie in the dusty wind.
But their truths remain here.
Now what I said, this is their truth.
That, then, that way I have said it to you,
because that is how it is with us
and that way we will continue to defend it.
Even being poor, we shall defend it so that at no time
shall we leave it in the Mexican's hands. We are never
to leave this poor land to the Mexicans, our Hiaki land.
We shall never accept the Mexican here. We have these truths.

TIMELINE

Hiaki Military and Political Events in Mexico and Sonora, 1875–1952

This summary of the historical record throughout the time period covered by the narratives is based on the textual documentation presented in Hu-DeHart's 1984 history *Yaqui Resistance and Survival*.[1]

1875–1885: Autonomous Hiaki state created and governed by Jose Maria Leyva of Hermosillo, aka Cajeme.

March 1883: Porfirista Luis Torres appointed governor of Sonora.

December 1884: Porfirio Díaz returns to the presidency of Mexico and begins the Porfiriato dictatorship. Governor Torres of Sonora and General Ángel Martínez begin a military offensive to crush the Hiaki state. Overwhelming military forces and an epidemic of yellow fever force the Hiakis to surrender in May 1886. Cajeme becomes a fugitive.

April 12, 1887: Cajeme is captured near Guaymas by Martínez. He is executed by a Mexican firing squad on April 26, 1887. His band of guerrillas (*"broncos"*), operating from the Bacatete (Vakateeve) Mountains, continues the resistance, with material support from hacienda Hiakis (*"pacíficos"*). The next military commander of Sonora, General Marcos Carrillo, continues the campaign against them.

December 1891: Rebellion continues. The hacienda Hiakis continue to provide support to the few hundred rebel Hiakis in the Bacatete Mountains, now led by Juan Maldonado, called Tetabiate. The So-

---

1. Evelyn Hu-DeHart, *Yaqui Resistance and Survival: The Struggle for Land and Autonomy, 1821–1910* (Madison: University of Wisconsin Press, 1984).

noran governor Izábal and the military leadership beg the ranchers and farmers to detain rebels and turn in those of their Hiaki workers who support them, to no avail: the Hiaki workers are indispensable to the productivity of the ranches and farms, and their employers cannot operate without them.

1894: Former governor Luis Torres becomes commander general of the Sonoran military. The Hiaki River valley is now nearly empty of Hiakis, as most of the population has left to work or fight rather than participate in the government's program to subdivide their land and assign private ownership to individual Hiakis and colonizing Mexicans. They also object to the continued presence of military garrisons in their communities.

1895: Deportation of captured rebels to southern Mexico begins on a small scale. Most deported Hiaki fighters are conscripted into the Mexican army. Some women and children are also deported and sold into slavery.

1896: Guerrilla warfare is continued by rebel bands with Tetabiate in the Bacatete Mountains. They continue to be supported by the Hiaki workforce in mines, on railroads, and on haciendas.

May 15, 1897: "Peace of Ortiz." Tetabiate and his captains sign an agreement to lay down arms and return to the Hiaki communities, having been led to believe that the Mexicans and the military garrisons will be withdrawn from Hiaki land; however, the treaty document contains no language to that effect. The rebels as well as the dispersed workforce return to Hiaki land. Many individual Hiakis are assigned ownership of lots in their own territory and given tools and seeds to become farmers on their own behalf.

July 23, 1899: The pueblos of Bácum (Vahkom) and Vícam (Vikam) send a notice to General Torres demanding that the military, still garrisoned in Hiaki communities, be withdrawn, and that the Mexican settlers leave. Torres responds with threats. The rebels and most of the repatriated workers take up arms and return to the mountains.

January 18, 1900: A pitched battle at Mazocoba between three thousand Hiakis (including women and children) and one-thousand-plus Mexican troops under General Torres leaves four hundred or more Hiakis dead. More than a thousand, mostly women, children, and wounded men, are taken prisoner. More than a hundred also die on the forced march to Las Guásimas (Wasimas); only 834 prisoners survive it. Tetabiate resumes leadership of about half the remaining warriors, again returning to guerrilla warfare in the Bacatete Mountains; the other half disperse back to hacienda and mining work outside the Hiaki territory. Torres begins large-scale deportations.

1901: Tetabiate is killed in a skirmish at Mazocoba. On August 31, the Mexican secretary of war declares the Hiaki campaign over.

1902: Governor Izábal issues orders to control the *pacíficos*, noncombatant Hiakis working on haciendas and elsewhere. They are to be confined to undefended, easily surveilled camps and prevented from leaving the worksite. Hiakis living in towns and cities are to be moved into Hiaki-only barrios. In urban areas like Guaymas and Hermosillo all Hiaki men are required to report for investigation once a week. All Hiaki men older than fifteen years are to be registered and issued a passport or identification card; any Hiaki without such a card will be arrested and investigated. The system is easily subverted by Hiakis, who exchange papers among themselves as needed.

April 1904: The "Nine Captains," representing working Hiakis in Hermosillo, Horcasitas, Ures, and Magdalena, again attempt to negotiate peace with Izábal, demanding withdrawal of all government troops from the Hiaki River. These terms are again rejected, and warfare from the Bacatete Mountains continues.

June 1904: The American Richardson brothers buy the remaining interests of the bankrupt Sonora and Sinaloa Irrigation Company, acquiring a huge portion of the Hiaki River valley land. They form the Yaqui Land and Water Company to develop and exploit it.

1904–1905: Izábal expands the deportation campaigns to include both working and rebel Hiakis. All Hiakis in a region that has been hit by a rebel raid will be rounded up and deported, women and children included.

1906: The United States and Arizona cooperate with Mexico's campaign against the Hiakis, implementing new immigration laws prohibiting Hiakis from entering the United States, prohibiting the sale of arms and ammunition to any Indian, and stepping up immigration enforcement specifically against Hiakis in the United States. In response, Hiakis conceal their identities from American officials, often claiming to be Opata or Pima instead.

1907: All Hiaki laborers by now have been removed from mines and railroads and rendered for deportation. No further employment of Hiakis is allowed. By this time at least two thousand Hiakis have been deported to slave labor, some in Valle Nacional, and many others on henequen plantations in Yucatán.

June 1908: Luis Bule, who has been leading one of the rebel groups in the Bacatete Mountains, negotiates for peace with the Díaz government, again stipulating the withdrawal of all troops and the return of the seized land in the Hiaki River area, and in addition requesting that all deported Hiakis be returned to Sonora. Negotiations fail in June, and deportations resume and intensify. It becomes official government policy to deport every single Hiaki, man, woman, or child, away from Sonora. A five-hundred-peso reward is offered for the capture of any Hiaki in the northern districts of Sonora. U.S. efforts also intensify. American troops commanded by Captain Henry C. Wheeler capture and turn back any Hiakis entering the United States. The U.S. Department of Commerce and Labor specifically orders the detention and extradition of all Hiakis who have entered the United States illegally. In all, between eight and fifteen thousand Hiakis are deported from Sonora between 1902 and 1908, between a quarter and a half of the total population.

September 1908: Bule accepts the government's terms for peace on behalf of the eight pueblos, and his own group of four hundred rebels descends from the Bacatete Mountains. Other rebel groups do not follow suit.

January 5, 1909: The peace treaty is signed by Bule and several of his captains (including Ignacio Mori, photo p. 396) in the military camp at Pitahaya. Bule and sixty of his men are enlisted and paid as a special auxiliary unit to pursue rebels who have not surrendered and persuade or force them to do so. The remaining rebels, now led by Luis Espinoza, refuse.

1910–1915: The Mexican Revolution breaks out. Díaz is deposed. Hiaki troops are conscripted into revolutionary armies. General Salvador Alvarado, serving Álvaro Obregón, has a force of two thousand Hiaki soldiers, led by Luis Bule, Lino Morales (who later becomes a battalion commander), and Francisco Urbalejo (who rises to the rank of general). Another contingent of nine hundred Hiakis are recruited by Colonel Fructuoso Méndez and fight in the cavalry. Bule is killed in battle. The Espinoza rebels remain in the Bacatete Mountains, continuing to raid haciendas and demanding the withdrawal of Mexicans from Hiaki territory.

1915: Obregón emerges victorious and initiates a military campaign against Espinoza's rebels. The Hiaki troops commanded by Morales are sent to fight their fellow Hiakis. Espinoza's rebels are reinforced by Hiaki revolutionary troops returning to the Bacatete Mountains after the defeat of Pancho Villa. They fight the government troops to a stalemate after a year.

1917: The Sonoran government, led by provisional governor Adolfo de la Huerta, offers the Hiakis some of their primary desiderata: withdrawal of troops from the Hiaki River and evacuation of Mexican settlers from the land, which is to be returned to the Hiaki people. Luis Espinoza descends from the mountains and signs a peace treaty.

1918: The government reneges on the treaty. General Fausto Topete leads troops into Hiaki territory, provoking a hostile response; Topete then orders his troops to fire into a crowd of Hiakis attending a pascola dance at Lencho station, killing sixty, including women and children. War resumes, as does the wholesale deportation of Hiaki families.

1919: Adolfo de la Huerta becomes governor and initiates a new round of negotiations. President Carranza continues to insist on deportation of Hiakis, and deposes de la Huerta. Obregón and de la Huerta form a coalition and go into battle against Carranza; the Hiakis support this effort with 2,500 soldiers.

1920: De la Huerta becomes interim president. He repatriates deported Hiakis to their homeland and assists with the rebuilding of the pueblos, even evacuating Mexican colonists from Cócorit and Bácum (though not from the agricultural land that has been ceded and developed). A period of relative calm follows. In 1923 Obregón becomes president in a struggle with de la Huerta that the Hiakis are not much involved in, but which sees the rise of General José Gonzalo Escobar. Obregón steps down again in 1924 and buys land in the Hiaki River valley. Obregón and president Plutarco Elías Calles together force the nationalization of the Richardson Company, a major landholder in Hiaki territory. Water from the Hiaki River is diverted by canal to farms thirty miles north of Cócorit and sent to supply Mexican farms, including those owned by Obregón and Calles. In 1926, the town of Cajeme is incorporated and developed, to be renamed Ciudad Obregón in 1928.

September 1926: Hiaki leader Luis Matus meets Obregón's train at Vikam and presses him to honor the 1920 agreement. Obregón wires for troops, who conduct a bloody massacre of Hiakis in Vikam. The Hiakis take up arms again. Twenty thousand federal troops commanded by General Román Yocupicio, a Mayo, are sent to defeat them once more. Several airplanes bomb the Hiaki pueblos. After a year, most rebels have descended from the Bacatete Mountains, and many are conscripted into the army and sent far away from Sonora.

1929: Obregón is assassinated and Calles's term as president ends. General José Gonzalo Escobar launches a coup, rebelling with thirty thousand soldiers, including a large contingent of Hiakis. Escobar sends General Jesús M. Aguirre to attack Veracruz (unsuccessfully).

1934: Lázaro Cárdenas becomes president of Mexico.

1937: Cárdenas creates the Zona Indígena Yaqui, comprising the eight pueblos, land on the north bank of the Hiaki River, and the Bacatete Mountains. This is the first *zona indígena* in all of Mexico. The large private landholdings south of the river are broken up and distributed to landless Mexicans.

1942: La Angostura Dam is completed on the Bavispe River.

1952: The Álvaro Obregón dam, also known as the Oviáchic dam (photo p. 536), is constructed on the Hiaki River, giving the government total control over all water in the Hiaki River valley, ending seasonal flooding, and ending Hiaki subsistence agriculture. Hiaki collectives are extended credit to buy water from the Hiaki River, on the condition that they cultivate cash crops only, since only cash crops are valuable enough to enable them to repay the debt to the Banco Ejidal. The cultivation of cash crops after the Green Revolution requires the Hiakis to contract cultivation out to trained Mexican tractor operators and others, and after all loans and contracts are paid, the Hiaki portion of the profits is not enough to support a family. Hiakis turn to other means to supplement their income, including charcoal-making, which over time destroys the mesquite forests of the river valley (already threatened because of the lack of water). To make ends meet, private Hiaki landholders have to hire themselves out to the contracted Mexican cultivators to work as laborers on their own land.

INDEX

Names of smaller towns and regions parenthetically include the name of the state, where noted. Other clarifications also follow terms parenthetically. Hiaki names are typically followed by a common English or Spanish term used by interviewees.

Agua Caliente. *See* Tata Va'am
Alvarez de Tapia, Maria Carlota, 5
Alvarez, Paula Buitimea, 273
Alvarez, Ramon, 5
Álvaro Obregón dam. *See* dams, Oviáchi
Amarillas, Antonio, 277
Amarillas, Jose, 277
Amarillas, Luz, 343
Andres, don, 9, 11, 14, 558, 563
Angostura Dam, 602
Ania, Antonio. *See* World, Antonio
Antonio Soto'oleo (Antonio Potmaker), 379
Apaches, Chiricahua, 6

Bacatete Mountains. *See* Vakateeve (Bacatete—Tall Bamboo) Mountains
Bácum, 565, 598, 602
Badillo, Miguel, 399, 407, 411, 415, 432, 435
Barrio Libre (Tucson), 4, 21, 567
Bavispe River, 602
Big Mesquite (Tucson). *See* Bwe'u Hu'upa
birds, 140, 143, 481
Black Rat Mountain, 131
Buitimea, Casillas, 13

Buitimea, doña Luisa (Chata), 8–11; brother Dolores, 128; nursing baby, 290. *See also* Sol, Don Andres
Buitimea, Jose Juan, 19, 480, 488–89
Buitimea, Mike, 433, 439
Bule, Lazaro, 218, 225, 378, 379, 381, 391, 397, 544, 547
Bule, Luis, 600, 601
Burnt Grass. *See* Vah Veetia (Burnt Grass)
Bwe'u Hu'upa (Big Mesquite) settlement, 5, 116, 119, 154, 155, 567, 569

Cajeme (person). *See* Leyva, Jose Maria
Cajeme (town), 602
Calles, Plutarco Elías, 389, 602; deportations by, 110, 113
Camino fiesta, 529, 565
Cárdenas, Lázaro, 200, 213, 602
Carrillo, Marcos, 597
Carranza, Venustiano, 601
Charcoal, 480, 483, 485, 503, 603. *See also* Buitimea, Jose Juan
Chavez, Ezekiel, 277
Chayo Loco (Crazy Rosario, Crazy Chayo), 378, 385
Chooki, Hoana (Jenny Star), 343

Choparau, Rita (Rita Raccoon), 343
Ciudad Juárez, 399, 411, 413, 433, 437
Ciudad Madero, 437
Ciudad Obregón, 9, 180, 215, 389, 505, 516, 602. *See also* Cajeme (town)
Comalcalco (Tabasco), 291, 301
Cócorit, 602
Coyote Waters. *See* Wo'i Va'am (Coyote Waters)
Creator, xvii, 12, 23, 81, 453
Cupis, Jose Maria (Chema Tosaria). *See* Tosaria, Chema

dams, La Angostora, 602; Oviáchi, 471, 533, *536*, 603
dance. *See* music and dance
de Cota, Herarda Romero (Heera), 9, 12, 17, 18
de la Huerta, Adolfo, 601, 602
deaths, 4, 11, 12, 19, 128, 145, 149, 252–53, 271, 277, 423, 593; at sea, 10, 282–85; from disease, 271, 356–57, 488; from plants, 302–3, 305
deportation, 3, 4, 5, 7, 9,12, 14, 16, 20, 24, 85, 110, 111, 113, 191, 241, 273, 598; and conscription, 598; and settling afterwards, 468; of men, 255; of mothers, 250–51; of women and children, 266, 273, 275, 331, 366, 598; release from and repatriation, 462, 602; large-scale deportation of, 274, 462, 465, 599, 600
Desert Spiny Lizard Waters (Vehoori Va'ampo), 125, 135
Díaz, Porfirio, regime of, xiv, 3–4, 6, 14, 274, 597, 600, 601
disease and sickness, 271, 356–57, 363; measles, 16, 558, 559. *See also* poisonous substances
doña Luisa. *See* Buitimea, Doña Luisa (Chata)
Dreadlocks (Veetam), 168
Durango, 252, 255

El Papalote (The Windmill), 8; de Arriba (Windmill Above), 11, 508; de Abajo (Windmill Below), 11
Escobar, José Gonzalo, 602
Escobar Rebellion, 200, 271, 398, 401

Flores, Paula (Paava), 279, 326, 327, 329, 417, 427
Flores, Vicente, 5
Frog Mountain, 55, 131, 135, 139

Gray Waters. *See* To'okopo Va'amme (Gray Waters)
Guadalajara, 253, 257, 263, 309, 311
Las Guásimas (Wasimas). *See* Wasimas (Las Guásimas)
Guaymas, 9, 10, 72, 89, *230*, 231, 233, 243, 245, *272*, 273, 275, *283*, 287, *288*, 289, *340*, 599; deportation from, 16, 241, 255, 267, 273, 281
Gulf of California, 3
guns and ammunition, 31, 154, 203, 407

Haros, Chiko, 143
hefeim (large knives), 173
henequen plantations, 271, 311, 313, 319, 321, 323; deportation to, 4, 5, 271, 274, 309, 313, 333; labor on, 318, *319*, 321, 330; specific plantations deportees sent to, 274
Hermosillo, 23, 43, 110, 111, 113, 169, 181, 185, 193, 215, 243, 275, 447, 559, 563, 565, 599
Hesus, Maria. *See* Rivera de Romera, Maria Hesus
Hesus, Raahu, 169, 175, 177
Hiak Vatwe (the Hiaki River and territory), 6, 15, 19, 23, 116, 134, 186, 271, 469, 533
Hiaki, 86th Regiment, 398, 399, 401; capture of, 4, 6, 9–11, 13, 20, 27, 100, 103, 134, *155*, 164–65, 168, 173, 199, 200, 208, 218, 228, *230*, 231–69;

diaspora, 3; diet, 291, 293, 297, 299, 419, 431; executed, 128, 129; given Spanish surnames when captured, 20; hostages, 266–67, 269; inter-Hiaki violence, 194–95; language, 16; promises of restoration of, xiv; settlements (*see specific settlement names*); slavery of, 309, 311, 313; soldiers and strategy, 24–39, 213, 396, 398; strategies used against Mexican soldiers, 24–25; travels of, 21–22, 497, 500–501; war injured and dead, 146–50, 157, 417, 419, 421, 423, 428; weapons, 22, 37, 49, 159, 161, 416

Highway 15 (Fifteen), 9, 17, 500, 501

Hoan Sivame'a (Hoan Killed on a Cliff), 379

Hot Water. *See* Tata Va'am (Hot Water)

Hu'upa Rohi Kahon (Twisted Mesquite Canyon), 125

Huatabampo (Sonora), 533, 535

hunting, 35, 63, 153

Ili Hu'upa (Little Mesquite), 21

Ili Wok Kottim (Little Broken Leg), 141, 145

Itom Toosa (Our Nest). *See* Vakateeve (Tall Bamboo) Mountains

Jagged Rocks, 125, 127

Juan Maria. *See* Ili Wok Kottim (Little Broken Leg)

Juárez, Benito, 3

Kapo Va'ampo (Water Lily Waters), 116, 165

Kavayito, 356, 359

Kontia Kawi (Procession Mountain), 129

Ko'okoim, 187, 200, 201, 205, 429

labor, 134, 186, 309, 600; farming, 189, 191; threshing, *187*; henequen harvesting, 318, 319, 321; selling food, *340*;

soap factory, 271, 339, 342–43, 351, 355, 356, 357; tortilla-making, 251, 299, 301, 336, 337, 513. *See also* wages and income

Lencho (settlement), 14, 601

Leyva, Jose Maria (Cajeme), 597

Little Mesquite (Tucson), 21, 116, 119, 533, 537, 567, 569. *See also* Bwe'u Hu'upa

Lizard Waters. *See* Vehoori Va'am (Lizard Waters)

Loma Vahkom (Loma de Bácum) (pueblo), 565

Loohio (Elogio), 527

Looria Kahon (Gloria Canyon), 125, 127, 129, 267, 269

Maachil, Chiika (Francisca), 472, 481

Maachil, Guillermo, 472

Maachil, Luz, 472

Maachil, Peo, 472, 481, 497

Machilim ("Scorpions"), 472, 473

Madero, Francisco, 18, 274, 330, 333, 367, 369, 462–63, 465, 469

Maehto, Dolores, 556

Magdalena (Sonora), 5, 25, 33, 561, 599

Maldonado, Juan. *See* Tetabiate

mamyam (American nightshade), 61, 71, 145

Manzanillo (port), 245, 255, 267, 273, 281

Maria, Juan, 141

Martimiano (Sand Waters) (ranch), 517, 525, 527

Martínez, Ángel, 597

Masa'im (Queen's Wreath), 125

Matus, Luis, 602

Maytorena (Sonora), 12, 445, 558, 563

Maytorena, José María, 37

Mazatlán, 245, 252, 255, 267

Mazocoba (battle site), 598–99

Méndez, Fructuoso, 601

mental health, 322, 323

Mexican soldiers and military service 154, 373; Aguilenyom ("Eagles"), 128, 133; Calvary Troop E, 155; conscripts, 160, 218, 219, 223, 226, 227, 228, 275, 315, 330, 331 333, 378, 392, 432–33; Papagos (Tohono O'odham), 164; *pelones* or *peronim* ("the bald ones"), 4, 89, 145, 159, 179, 211, 227, 229, 233, 235, 245, 263, 311, 341, 349, 361, 383, 385, 387, 401, 405, 409, 421, 439; *toroko yoim* ("gray Mexicans"), 16, 128, 223, 393; *wilom* (Labwes, "skinny ones"), 160, 161, 163
Michoacán, 398, 399, 401, 405, 411, 417, 425, 427
Mikaela, 135, 139, 291, 366–67, 369, 371, 465
monaha (monarch), 19, 171
Morales, Lino, 601
Mori, Ignacio, 218–19, 225, 357, 363, 378, 379, 381, 389, 393, *396*, 462, 463, 465, 467
Moso Canyon. *See* Tehapo Va'ampo
mosquitos, 290, 293, 491
mountains, 265. *See also* Kontia Kawi (Procession Mountain); Samawaka; Vakateeve (Tall Bamboo) Mountains; To'okopo Va'amme (Gray Waters)
music and dance, 171, 367; deer dance singers, 365, 367; drummers, 367, 553; *matachin* dancers, 171; *pahko'ola* dancers, 17, 19, 137, 365; violins, 19, 365, 367

Nacha Bule, 547
Navo (Prickly Pear), 125
Navohoa, 432, 435
Nayarit, 252, 259
Nestor, Kala, 20, 449, 539, 541. *See also* Tosaria, Antonio
nightshade. *See mamyam* (American nightshade)
Nogales (Sonora), 5–6, 110, 113, *155*, 157

Oaxaca, 274, 468, 469
Obregón, Álvaro, 379, 389, 601, 601
Orizaba, 303
Ortiz, 558, 561
Oviáchi. *See* dams
Oviáchic dam, 603

Pa'amea, Bartolo (Vattom Pa'amea), 556, 557, 559
palacio (burial site), 205
Papalote. *See* El Papalote (windmill)
Paraíso (Tabasco), 290, 291
peace conference, 372
Peace of Ortiz, 598
Pérez, José, 379, 391
Perote (Veracruz), 218, 221, 357, 363, 378, 385, 468, 469
pets, 240–41, 243, 245
Pitahaya (military camp), 600
Pitaya Pueblo, 135, 141, 209, 377, 379, 387, 516, 519
Plan de Tuxtepec, 3
Plano del Valle del Yaqui (survey map), *180*
plants, 65, 301, 302, 307, 321, 517, 531. *See also* henequen plantations; poisonous substances
poisonous substances, 145, 302–3, 305, 307
Porfiriato. *See* Díaz, Porfirio, regime of
Pori Soso'oki (Pockmarked Paul), 378
Potam (pueblo), 133, 371, 487, 557, 566, 567
Progresa (transport ship), 287; deaths aboard, 282; sinking of, 289

queen's wreath, 76
Querétaro, 378, 385

Rat Waters. *See* To'i Va'am (Rat Waters)
ration cards, 336–37, 339
religion and spirituality, 102–3, 105, 107, 351, 353; Lent (Waehma), 350, 353, 355, 385, 587; *maehtom* (prayer

leaders), 457; prayer in battle, 409; references to God, 91, 93, 277, 401, 409, 445, 457, 459, 463, 573, 579, 581, 583, 585, 587, 589, 591, 593, 595. *See also* Creator
Revolt of Escobar. *See* Escobar Rebellion
Richardson Construction Company, 58, 186, 192, 229, 230, 288, 599, 602
Rivera de Romero, Maria Hesus, 9, 15–19, 252; and dog, 240–41; and story of cookies, 236–37, 239; and story of shawl, 231, 233, 235; as a child in mountains, 84–85, 87, 89; as interviewee, 8–9; jailed, 273, 275; on transport ship *Progresa*, 282–83, 285, 287, 289; relations via kinship system, other family ties, 9, 22, 556; searching for wounded father, 417, 419, 421, 423. *See also* Romero, Reynaldo
rock house (prison), 27, 265, 273, 275
Romero de Cota, Herarda (Heera), 9
Romero, Reynaldo ("Reyno" or "Chikul"), 15, 16, 17, 18, 19, 60–61, 251, 302, 509, 513; difficulties with alcohol, 15, 19; family, 18, 251, 566, 567; nicknames for, 16; size, 17. *See also* Buitimea, doña Luisa (Chata)

Samawaka (mountain), 163, 231, 233, 247, 249, 266, 269, 273
Sartucho (General), 134, 137
Silvame'a, Juan, 387
Sisto, 134, 135, 137, 139. *See also* Mikaela
Sol, don Andres, 9, 11, 12–14, 558, 563. *See also* Buitimea, doña Luisa (Chata)
Sonora and Sinaloa Irrigation Company, 599
Southern Pacific Railroad, 22, 372, 448, 500–501, 503

Tabasco, 290, 291, 295, 299, 301, 379, 391
Tata Va'am (Agua Caliente), 241, 247, 508, 509, 515, 517, 525
Tehapo Va'ampo (Moso Canyon), 141
Tetabiate (Maldonado, Juan), 597, 598, 599
Tetakusim (Stone Crosses), 558, 562
Teta Chusaraim (Jagged Rocks), 125
Teta Hiponim (Rock Drums), 125
Tetaviekti (Rolling Stone), 117, 173, 516, 517
To'i Va'am (Rat Waters), 128
To'okopo Va'amme (Gray Waters), 49, 181, 199
Tomase Woho'okuni, 14
Torim (settlement), 14, 15, 17, 517, 531, 557, 566, 567
torim (rats), 61, *72*
Torreón, 128, 131
Torres, Luis, 37, 597, 598, 599
Tosaria, Antonio ("Uncle Antonio White Skin"), 20, 21, 23, 253, 539; family, 544, 545
Tosaria, Chema, 8, 20–25, 169, 179, 543, 545, 555, *570*, 571; family, 8, 20, 539, 541
Tubac, 6
Tumacacori, 6
Twisted Mesquite Canyon. *See* Hu'upa Rohi Kahon (Twisted Mesquite Canyon)

Urbalejo, Francisco (military supervisor), 273, 275, 277, 279, 601

Vah Veetia (Burnt Grass), 125, 128
Vakateeve (Bakateeve—Tall Bamboo) Mountains, 4, 41, 180, 597, 598, 599, 600, 601, 602
Valencia, Anselmo, xviii, 7, 9, 19
Valenzuela, Eusebia, 5
Vasolihti, Guillermo, 140, 141, 143
Vehoori Va'am (Lizard Waters), 125, 135
Veracruz, 221, 274, 287, 301, 378, 379, 385, 391, 469, 602
Vikam Pueblo, 10, 19, 20, 457

Vikam Swiichi (Vícam Switch), 17, 18, 19, 135, 139, 457, 481, 485, 517, 527, 549
Villa Cardel, 468–69
Villa, Pancho, 601
Villahermosa. *See* Tabasco

wages and income, 8, 12, 21, 186, 191, 200, 218, 223, 336–37, 339, 343, 347, 392–93, 479, 516, 521
Wasimas (Las Guásimas), 516, 519, 562, 599
Water in the Cave, 145
water, 97, 121, 129, 135, 137, 145, 147, 149, 151, 293, 295, 508–9, 533–34; acquiring, 51, 53, 55, 61; irrigation, 191, 533, 602–3; lack of, 43, 45, 85, 87, 125, 127, 129; political promises regarding, 213, 214, 215, 451, 455
Water Lily Waters. *See* Kapo Va'ampo (Water Lily Waters)

Wheeler, Henry C., 600
White Mountain, 201, 217
wilom (Labwes, "skinny ones"). *See* Mexican soldiers
Wo'i Va'am (Coyote Waters), 181
World, Antonio, 7, 209, 375, 379

Xochimilco, 209, 221, 356–57, 361, 362, 363, 365, 373, 375, 378, 379

Yaqui. *See* Hiaki
Yocupicio, Román, 602
Yucatán, 10, 27, 233, 252, 253, 255, 263, 274, 282, 287, 309, 311, 313, 314, 322, 323, 327, 329, 333, 366–67, 465, 469, 559, 563

Zona Indígena Yaqui, 602
Zócalo, 356, 359

ABOUT THE AUTHORS

Maria Fernanda Florez Leyva is a Hiaki woman from Tucson, Arizona, and the former director of the Pascua Yaqui tribe's language program. In 2001 she began working with Heidi Harley on a detailed study of the grammar of the Hiaki language. Together they co-authored *An Introduction to Hiaki Grammar: Hiaki Grammar for Learners and Teachers, Volume 1* (CreateSpace Independent Publishing Platform, 2017), the first of a three-volume series. Leyva is currently compiling a Spanish-, English-, and Hiaki-language dictionary intended for anyone interested in teaching or learning about the Hiaki language.

Heidi B. Harley received her PhD in linguistics from Massachusetts Institute of Technology in 1995, and she is currently a professor of linguistics at the University of Arizona. Harley's research focuses on the syntax, morphology, and lexical semantics of language. She is the author of *English Words: A Linguistic Introduction* (Wiley-Blackwell, 2006), and her work has been published in numerous edited volumes and other publications such as *Language*, *Linguistic Inquiry*, and *Journal of Linguistics*. Harley has taught at various linguistics summer schools in the United States, Germany, Mexico, and Brazil, and she served on the executive committee of the Linguistic Society of America.